Polyphony in Medieval Paris

Polyphony associated with the Parisian Cathedral of Notre Dame marks a historical turning point in medieval music. Yet a lack of analytical or theoretical systems has discouraged close study of twelfth- and thirteenth-century musical objects, despite the fact that such creations represent the beginnings of musical composition as we know it. *Is musical analysis possible for such medieval repertoires?* Catherine A. Bradley demonstrates that it is, presenting new methodologies to illuminate processes of musical and poetic creation, from monophonic plainchant and vernacular French songs, to polyphonic organa, clausulae, and motets in both Latin and French. This book engages with questions of text–music relationships, liturgy, and the development of notational technologies, exploring concepts of authorship and originality as well as practices of quotation and musical reworking.

CATHERINE A. BRADLEY is Associate Professor at the University of Oslo. She has published widely on the earliest motets, in journals including *Speculum*, *Journal of Musicology*, *Music Analysis*, and *Early Music History*.

MUSIC IN CONTEXT

Series editors

The aim of Music in Context is to illuminate specific musical works, repertoires, or practices in historical, critical, socio-economic, or other contexts; or to illuminate particular cultural and critical contexts in which music operates through the study of specific musical works, repertoires, or practices. A specific musical focus is essential, while avoiding the decontextualisation of traditional aesthetics and music analysis. The series title invites engagement with both its main terms; the aim is to challenge notions of what contexts are appropriate or necessary in studies of music, and to extend the conceptual framework of musicology into other disciplines or into new theoretical directions.

Books in the series

Simon P. Keefe, *Mozart's Requiem: Reception, Work, Completion*
J. P. E. Harper-Scott, *The Quilting Points of Musical Modernism: Revolution, Reaction, and William Walton*
Nancy November, *Beethoven's Theatrical Quartets: Opp. 59, 74, and 95*
Rufus Hallmark, *'Frauenliebe und Leben': Chamisso's Poems and Schumann's Songs*
Anna Zayaruznaya, *The Monstrous New Art: Divided Forms in the Late Medieval Motet*
Helen Deeming and Elizabeth Eva Leach, *Manuscripts and Medieval Song: Inscription, Performance, Context*
Emily Kilpatrick, *The Operas of Maurice Ravel*
Roderick Chadwick and Peter Hill, *Olivier Messiaen's 'Catalogue d'oiseaux': From Conception to Performance*
Catherine A. Bradley, *Polyphony in Medieval Paris: The Art of Composing with Plainchant*

Polyphony in Medieval Paris

The Art of Composing with Plainchant

CATHERINE A. BRADLEY
University of Oslo

CAMBRIDGE
UNIVERSITY PRESS

University Printing House, Cambridge CB2 8BS, United Kingdom

One Liberty Plaza, 20th Floor, New York, NY 10006, USA

477 Williamstown Road, Port Melbourne, VIC 3207, Australia

314-321, 3rd Floor, Plot 3, Splendor Forum, Jasola District Centre, New Delhi - 110025, India

79 Anson Road, #06-04/06, Singapore 079906

Cambridge University Press is part of the University of Cambridge.

It furthers the University's mission by disseminating knowledge in the pursuit of education, learning and research at the highest international levels of excellence.

www.cambridge.org
Information on this title: www.cambridge.org/9781108407571
DOI: 10.1017/9781108290456

First published 2018
First paperback edition 2020

A catalogue record for this publication is available from the British Library

Library of Congress Cataloging in Publication data
Names: Bradley, Catherine A. author.
Title: Polyphony in Medieval Paris: The Art of Composing with Plainchant / Catherine A. Bradley.
Description: Cambridge, United Kingdom; New York, NY: Cambridge University Press, 2018. | Series: Music in context | Includes bibliographical references and index.
Identifiers: LCCN 2018013738 | ISBN 9781108418584 (hardback)
Subjects: LCSH: Music – 500–1400 – History and criticism. | Motets – 500–1400 – History and criticism. | Clausulas (Part songs) – History and criticism.
Classification: LCC ML172.B83 2018 | DDC 782.2/2–dc23
LC record available at https:// lccn.loc.gov/2018013738

ISBN 978-1-108-41858-4 Hardback
ISBN 978-1-108-40757-1 Paperback

Contents

Figures

Musical Examples

Tables

Acknowledgements

First and foremost, I wish to thank Rebecca Maloy – who reviewed this book with care, generosity, and insight, and improved it immeasurably – and Mark Everist, whose reading of the complete manuscript was invaluable.

I am deeply indebted to Susan Rankin, under whose supervision ideas for this project began, and to Elizabeth Eva Leach: both have offered me unstinting kindness, guidance, and encouragement. I am also grateful to Emma Dillon for her very thoughtful and constructive response to the material in its early stages.

I wish to thank, in particular, those who so generously read drafts of individual chapters, offering detailed and extensive feedback that proved transformative: Edward H. Roesner, Rebecca A. Baltzer, Sarah Fuller, Lawrence Earp, David Maw, Dolores Pesce, Elizabeth Eva Leach and her Graduate and Postdoc Reading Group, Susan Rankin and her Covent Garden Seminar.

I have benefited immensely from conversations resulting from presentations of this material at the *Ars Antiqua* conference in Southampton in 2013; the Medieval Renaissance Music Conference in 2013, 2014, 2016, and 2017; the Yale Song Lab in 2014; the Annual Meeting of the American Musicological Society in 2014 and 2016; the Annual Meeting of the Medieval Academy of America in 2015; and the Novacella International Symposium on Late Medieval Music in 2017.

The completion of this book has been made possible by the following grants and fellowships: a Junior Research Fellowship at The Queen's College, Oxford; Grants from the Faculty of the Arts, Humanities, and Social Sciences, and the Arts, Humanities, and Lettered Social Sciences Faculty Research Programme at the State University of New York at Stony Brook; a Visiting Fellowship at St Catherine's College, Oxford; and a EURIAS Fellowship (co-funded by Marie Skłodowska-Curie Actions under the 7th Framework Programme) at the Institut d'Etudes Avancées de Paris.

I warmly thank all those who have contributed to this project, offering valuable insights and assistance, especially Wulf Arlt, Sam Barrett, Nicolas Bell, Margaret Bent, Katherine Butler, Ardis Butterfield, David Catalunya, Sean Curran, Karen Desmond, Eleanor Giraud, Huw Grange, Andrew Hicks, Henry Hope, Sylvia Huot, Sara Lipton, Henry Parkes, Thomas Payne,

Owen Rees, Gaël Saint-Cricq, Jennifer Saltzstein, Matthew Thomson, and Anna Zayaruznaya.

I am grateful to Kate Brett, Paul Harper-Scott, and Julian Rushton for their help and solicitude throughout the publication process. I acknowledge the Biblioteca Medicea Laurenziana, which provided the book's images, and the American Musicological Society for their generous offer of a subvention from the Kenneth Levy Endowment, funded in part by the National Endowment for the Humanities and the Andrew W. Mellon Foundation.

My profound thanks go to all of the colleagues, friends, and family – particularly my parents – who have unfailingly supported me throughout.

Note on the Text

Transcriptions

Original text spellings are retained. Capitalisation, punctuation, and text-line numbers are editorial.

Square brackets indicate editorial insertions.

Round brackets indicate erasures.

In transcriptions of plainchant, slurs indicate ligatures, dashed slurs indicate conjuncturae, and liquescents are shown by joined pitches. An asterisk indicates the juncture between a solo and a choral section of the plainchant.

In transcriptions of polyphony, ligatures are indicated by square brackets, conjuncturae by dashed slurs. Plicae are shown by a line through the stem, and in unmeasured polyphonic transcriptions plicae are indicated by slurs. Repetitions of the tenor plainchant melody (cursus) are numbered beneath the stave in roman numerals.

The medieval note value of the long (*longa*) corresponds to a crotchet in modern notation, a ternary long (*longa trium temporum*) to a dotted crotchet. The breve (*brevis*) is equivalent to a quaver in transcription.

The term 'perfection' refers to the length of a dotted crotchet in transcription. In the early thirteenth century this is described as a ternary long (*longa trium temporum*). For the sake of concision, the later-thirteenth-century term of perfect long (*longa perfectum*) or perfection is adopted throughout as the unit by which musical time is measured.

Numbering Systems

Motet numbers – from Friedrich Gennrich, *Bibliographie der ältesten französischen und lateinischen Motetten*, SMMA 2 (Frankfurt, 1957) – are prefaced by Mt.

Clausula folio numbers are followed by an arabic numeral that indicates their position in the sequence of clausulae on this folio.

For the shorter so-called mini clausulae (**F**, fols. 178r–183v), the folio number is followed by a roman numeral that identifies the stave on which the mini clausula is copied, and then by an arabic numeral that indicates its position in the sequence of mini clausulae on this stave.

Clausula numbers in **F** follow those in the edition by Rebecca A. Baltzer, *Le 'Magnus liber organi' de Notre-Dame de Paris V: Les clausules à deux voix du manuscrit de Florence, Biblioteca Medicea-Laurenziana, Pluteus 29.1, fascicule V* (Monaco, 1995).

Manuscript Sigla

ArsA	Paris, Bibliothèque de l'Arsenal, 135
ArsB	Paris, Bibliothèque de l'Arsenal, 3517–18
ArsC	Paris, Bibliothèque de l'Arsenal, 8521
Ba	Bamberg, Staatsbibliothek, Lit. 115 (formerly Ed.IV.6)
Basel	Basel, Universitäts Bibliothek, Fragmentensammlung F X 37
Ber	Berlin, Staatsbibliothek der Stiftung Preussischer Kulturbesitz, lat. 4° 523
Bes	Besançon, Bibliothèque municipale, I, 716
Ca	Cambrai, Médiathèque d'aglommération (formerly Bibliothèque municipale), A 410
Ch	Châlons-en-Champagne, Archives départementales de la Marne, 3.J.250
Cl	Paris, Bibliothèque nationale de France, nouv. acq. fr. 13521, 'La Clayette'
CTr	Cambridge, Trinity College, O.2.1
Da	Darmstadt, Hessische Landesbibliothek, 3471
Douce 308	Oxford, Bodleian Library, Douce 308
Erf	Erfurt, Wissenschaftliche Bibliothek, fol. 169
F	Florence, Biblioteca Medicea Laurenziana, Plut. 29.1
Fauvel	Paris, Bibliothèque nationale de France, fr. 146, 'Roman de Fauvel'
Her	Louvain, Bibliothèque universitaire, no shelf mark (now destroyed: photographs in Göttingen, Universitätsbibliothek, Ludwig Nachlass, IX, 14)
Hu	Burgos, Monasterio de Las Huelgas, 11 (formerly IX)
LoA	London, British Library, Egerton 2615
LoB	London, British Library, Egerton 274
LoC	London, British Library, Add. 30091
LoD	London, British Library, Add. 27630
LoHa	London, British Library, Harley 978
Lyell	Oxford, Bodleian Library, Lyell 72
Ma	Madrid, Biblioteca nacional, 20486 (formerly Hh 167)
Mo	Montpellier, Bibliothèque interuniversitaire, Section de médecine, H. 196
MüA	Munich, Bayerische Staatsbibliothek, Mus.ms. 4775 (gallo-rom. 42) and fragments in Berlin, Staatsbibliothek zu

	Berlin, Musikabteilung 55 MS 14 (formerly in the private library of Johannes Wolf, Berlin)
MüB	Munich, Bayerische Staatsbibliothek, lat. 16444 (Musikfragmente E III 230–1)
N	Paris, Bibliothèque nationale de France, fr. 12615, 'Noailles chansonnier'
PsAr	Paris, Bibliothèque nationale de France, lat. 11266
R	Paris, Bibliothèque nationale de France, fr. 844, 'Manuscrit du Roi'
Reg	Rome, Biblioteca Apostolica Vaticana, Regina 1543 (fragments)
Silos	Santo Domingo de Silos, Bibloteca de monasteria, MS s.n.
StS1	Stary Sącz, Konvent Swaty Kingy, D.2
StV	Paris, Bibliothèque nationale de France, lat. 15139, 'St Victor'
Trouv. C	Bern, Stadtbibliothek, 389
Trouv. U	Paris, Bibliothèque nationale de France, fr. 20050
Vat	Rome, Biblioteca Apostolica Vaticana, Regina 1490
W1	Wolfenbüttel, Herzog August Bibliothek, Cod. Guelf. 628 Helmst. (Heinemann no. 677)
W2	Wolfenbüttel, Herzog August Bibliothek, Cod. Guelf. 1099 Helmst. (Heinemann no. 1206)
Worc	Worcester, Cathedral Library, Add. 68; Oxford, Bodleian Library, Lat. lit. d. 20; and London, British Library, Add. 25031

Abbreviations

BVM	Blessed Virgin Mary
CSM	Corpus scriptorum de musica
M	Mass Chant number as assigned in Friedrich Ludwig, *Repertorium organorum recentioris et motetorum vetustissimi stili*, ed. Luther A. Dittmer, 2 vols. in 3 (New York, 1964–78 [1910])
Mt	Motet number in Friedrich Gennrich, *Bibliographie der ältesten französischen und lateinischen Motetten*, SMMA 2 (Frankfurt, 1957)
NOHM	New Oxford History of Music
O	Office Chant number as assigned in Friedrich Ludwig, *Repertorium organorum recentioris et motetorum vetustissimi stili*, ed. Luther A. Dittmer, 2 vols. in 3 (New York, 1964–78 [1910])
PMMM	Publications of Mediaeval Musical Manuscripts
RRMMA	Recent Researches in the Music of the Middle Ages and Early Renaissance
SMMA	Summa musicae medii aevi
vdB	Refrain number in Nico van den Boogaard, *Rondeaux et refrains du XIIIe siècle au début du XIVe*, Bibliothèque française et romane, Série D: Initiation, textes et documents 3 (Paris, 1969)
WMB	Wiener musikwissenschaftliche Beiträge

Introduction

The polyphonic music associated with the Parisian Cathedral of Notre Dame in the late twelfth and early thirteenth centuries marks a paradigm shift in music history. Linked to the authorial identities of Léonin and Pérotin, and intimately connected with significant advances in written musical transmission and systems of rhythmic notation, this music has long been understood to represent a historiographical beginning, a paradigm shift of lasting consequences in the scale, organisation, and ambition of polyphonic composition.[1] Unsurprisingly, organa, clausulae, conducti, and especially the innovative new thirteenth-century genre of the motet, have received considerable attention since the mid-nineteenth century. Much early scholarship was philological, involving the transcription of contemporaneous theoretical treatises, extensive cataloguing of musical concordances and variants, production of manuscript facsimiles, and publication of musical editions in modern notation.[2] As a means of rationalising a huge amount of dense material, these resources – especially Friedrich Ludwig's breathtakingly comprehensive 1910 catalogue of almost the entire thirteenth-century polyphonic repertoire[3] – established and reinforced large-scale evolutionary narratives of musical development that have proved powerfully indelible.[4] In the last several decades, research has taken a hermeneutic

[1] This accepted historiographical premise is acknowledged also by Edward H. Roesner and Anna Maria Busse Berger. See, respectively, 'Who "Made" the *Magnus liber?*', *Early Music History*, 20 (2001), 227–66; and *Medieval Music and the Art of Memory* (Berkeley, 2005), p. 1.

[2] The most monumental achievements include Friedrich Ludwig's catalogue – *Repertorium organorum recentioris et motetorum vetustissimi stili*, ed. Luther A. Dittmer, 2 vols. in 3 (New York, 1964–78 [1910]) – and Hans Tischler's edition, showing every musical variant for each piece: *The Earliest Motets (to circa 1270): A Complete Comparative Edition*, 3 vols. (New Haven, 1982). The seven-volume edition *Le 'Magnus liber organi' de Notre-Dame de Paris* (Monaco, 1993–2009) was recently completed under the general editorship of Edward H. Roesner.

[3] The conductus is the only thirteenth-century polyphonic genre that is not explicitly included in Ludwig's *Repertorium*. As a type of composition that is not directly related to earlier plainchant traditions, neither is the conductus a focus of this book.

[4] Ludwig's *Repertorium* was reformulated in 1957 as a motet catalogue by Friedrich Gennrich: his *Bibliographie der ältesten französischen und lateinischen Motetten*, SMMA 2 (Frankfurt, 1957) (motet numbers in this catalogue hereafter indicated by Mt). In 1989, Hendrik van der Werf published his *Integrated Directory of Organa, Clausulae, and Motets of the Thirteenth*

turn away from the details of manuscript sources, to focus instead on the interpretation of motet texts and on the sonic and semantic consequences of polytextuality.[5] Yet in spite of the status of organa, clausulae, and motets as paradigmatic chiefly in a compositional sense – as the first 'notated' and 'complex' polyphony – these medieval repertoires remain firmly outside the analytical mainstream.[6]

This book gives serious consideration to the primarily musical and compositional concerns that have previously been overshadowed by interests in the philological, poetic, and polytextual characteristics of thirteenth-century polyphony and obscured by general evolutionary narratives. In contrast to, and in order to redress the emphases of, previous studies, polytextual motets feature less prominently here than their two-voice counterparts, which constitute an almost equally significant proportion of the surviving repertoire, and predominate in early- and mid-thirteenth-century sources.[7] Crucially, the book's musical objects of study have been selected for their potential to unsettle scholarly preconceptions about the repertoire at large, and to lead outwards towards an array of broader issues and topics extending well beyond the purely analytical and purely musical. The aim is to pose fresh and different compositional and chronological questions that challenge still persistent developmental and historical presumptions, thereby opening up new approaches to organa, clausulae, and motets. The study is not delineated by genre, function, or language, but is instead focused on a practice already well established in the thirteenth century and of continued relevance to current-day musical cultures. This practice is the act of borrowing, quoting, and reworking pre-existing musical and textual materials, in particular the use of plainchant melodies as the basis of new polyphonic compositions. The quotation of an older

Century (Rochester, 1989), essentially a new version of the *Repertorium* in English. Although Ludwig's original lacks some more recent source and concordance discoveries, the *Repertorium* remains the most reliable catalogue, and its extensive commentaries on the contents and characteristics of individual manuscripts have yet to be supplanted.

[5] Key examples include Sylvia Huot, *Allegorical Play in the Old French Motet: The Sacred and the Profane in Thirteenth-Century Polyphony* (Stanford, 1997); and Emma Dillon, *The Sense of Sound: Musical Meaning in France 1260–1330*, New Cultural History of Music Series (New York, 2012).

[6] Notable exceptions include the essay by Norman E. Smith, 'An Early Thirteenth-Century Motet', in Mark Everist (ed.), *Models of Musical Analysis: Music before 1600* (Oxford, 1992), pp. 20–40; and work by Dolores Pesce, such as her 'A Case for Coherent Pitch Organization in the Thirteenth-Century Double Motet', *Music Analysis*, 9 (1980), 287–31.

[7] See the discussion of the relative proportion of two-voice and polytextual motets in Catherine A. Bradley, 'Seeking the Sense of Sound', *Journal of the Royal Musical Association*, 139 (2014), 405–20 (pp. 407–8).

plainchant melody, 'held' in the lowest voice or tenor, was a defining characteristic of the thirteenth-century genres explored here: liturgical organa and clausulae, and Latin motets, as well as French-texted ones. As a conceptual focus, the borrowing of plainchant in organa, clausulae, and motets serves to dissolve binary oppositions, not only of monophony and polyphony, but also of sacred and secular, and of Latin and vernacular genres.

Seven contrasting case studies are offered in the following chapters with the aim of underlining the richness and variety of thirteenth-century polyphony, and the necessity of corresponding variety in its historical and analytical treatment. These diverse case studies are proposed as new methodological blueprints, proffering possible 'ways in' to the vast repertoire of thirteenth-century polyphony, with its intimidating arsenal of esoteric catalogues and comparative editions. Exploring ways in which thirteenth-century music 'works', this book seeks to redefine the idea of musical analysis in a context where analytical approaches that focus on compositional processes might be thought inappropriate or impossible. At the forefront of such concerns are the strongly oral and performative dimensions of medieval musical culture, which might seem to militate against the definition of a musical 'text' for close reading.[8] If so, this would strike also at the heart of the paradigmatic status of thirteenth-century polyphony, suggesting that its perceived compositional importance might reflect our own aesthetic preoccupations more than those of the past.

The relationship between orality and any 'text' is complex. As part of the collision of existing oral practices with the highly literate environment of the Parisian university in the late twelfth century, polyphony was not simply an orally created repertoire that was later written down, nor was it a repertoire conceived exclusively in writing that was subsequently memorised. The nature of its musical objects could be shaped in and by performance as well as by compositional attitudes and techniques facilitated by writing. This notwithstanding, Edward H. Roesner has demonstrated that the categories of a composed musical 'text' (whether physically recorded in writing or worked out mentally) and of a carefully crafted 'original conception' of a piece remain appropriate.[9] For although surface variation in this repertoire is occasionally considerable (particularly in the genre of organum), it cannot disguise a stability of written transmission that is remarkable. This

[8] Oral and mnemonic practices in this repertoire have been the focus of studies by Busse Berger, *Medieval Music and the Art of Memory*; and Steven C. Immel, 'The Vatican Organum Treatise Reexamined', *Early Music History*, 20 (2001), 121–72.

[9] Roesner, 'Who "Made" the *Magnus liber*?', pp. 256–8.

evident medieval desire to preserve and respect the integrity of a musical composition facilitates and encourages its analysis. That such compositions must inevitably be accessed through the medium of manuscript sources is not to deny their orality, of which traces can be uncovered within written documents.

From a theoretical point of view, undertaking close analysis of thirteenth-century polyphony may be daunting, not least because it requires sensitivity to elusive oral and performative aspects, as well as the vagaries of manuscript transmission and preservation. This (pre-tonal) repertoire lacks the kind of well-developed analytical systems and conventions that exist for later musics, and there is a paucity of relevant contemporaneous theoretical or circumstantial evidence that might help to establish such tools. Although we know the names of Léonin and Pérotin and of a handful of Pérotin's compositions, any direct indication about how works such as theirs were created, according to what rules or priorities, is distinctly absent. The surviving testimonies of medieval theorists are typically abstract codifications of rhythmic notation, genres, or harmonic intervals, with almost nothing akin to practical compositional advice. What is more, extant theoretical documents are relatively late chronologically: they date chiefly from the second half of the thirteenth century, at a time when the repertoires and practices to which they pertain could have been almost 100 years old. A similar gap in time complicates the interpretation of musical manuscript sources themselves. A decree by the Parisian Bishop Odo of Sully in 1198 proves that four-voice organa were already an established part of the Christmas celebrations at Notre Dame in the late twelfth century, but the earliest surviving manuscript to record such pieces is dated to the 1230s.[10] Examinations of compositional process must therefore accommodate questions to which there may be no definitive answers: how do these comparatively late written records relate to any initial conception (written or oral) of the pieces they contain; what sorts of scribal intervention may have occurred; and what kinds of earlier more contemporary musical sources may have been lost?

Difficulties inherent in the state of surviving thirteenth-century theoretical and musical sources are compounded by the large scope and complex nature of the musical repertoire itself. Interrelationships between multiple versions and different generic incarnations of the same musical material are such that listing and describing them can be an onerous task.

10 On Odo of Sully's decree, and for a translation of the text, see Craig Wright, *Music and Ceremony at Notre Dame of Paris 500–1550* (Cambridge, 1989), p. 239.

Scholars are both helped and hindered by a profusion of specialist terminology to describe generic types. On the one hand, the definition of multiple sub-genres may seem problematic and artificial: conductus motets, *Kurzmotette*, cento motets, motets entés, and *rondeau* motets, are just several of the debated categories.[11] On the other, taxonomy was a genuine concern of thirteenth-century theorists, and most manuscripts of this music are scrupulously, almost obsessively, ordered, displaying intricate conventions for groupings on both the large and the small scale. A neat segregation of thirteenth-century genres is reflected in current scholarship. Studies and editions of organa and clausulae, for instance, are typically set apart from those of motets. And work on motets, in turn, often considers Latin-texted pieces separately from their vernacular counterparts. In consequence, investigations of thirteenth-century polyphony have remained preoccupied by and dependent upon general evolutionary narratives to explain inescapable relationships between genres. Linear advances from sacred compositions to secular ones, from Latin-texted clausulae and motets to those in the vernacular, continue – implicitly and explicitly – to form the basis of understandings of this music.[12]

Such narratives already underwrote Ludwig's still indispensable catalogue of thirteenth-century polyphony. They are enshrined within his numbering systems – all in current use – and in his terminology: *Quelle* (source) is employed in place of the generic designation 'clausula' when listing the versions of a motet. These narratives have arguably discouraged close and critical readings of the musical evidence, whose sheer volume intimidates. Developmental models permit ready-made chronologies to be accepted instead of investigated in individual cases, thereby obscuring (perhaps even deterring) serious consideration of any instances of deviation. Furthermore, such models have encouraged reductive conceptualisations of chronologies in this repertoire. The genealogies of motet families, for instance, have frequently been plotted in stemma diagrams that unquestioningly follow a pre-planned chronological sequence, placing a clausula source at the top of the tree, followed by an obligatory series of sub-genres.[13]

[11] In particular, Mark Everist has queried the validity of motet sub-genres, notably the motet enté the *rondeau* motet, and the cento motet. See his *French Motets in the Thirteenth Century: Music, Poetry and Genre* (Cambridge, 1994), pp. 75–125.

[12] For a recent example, see Thomas B. Payne (ed.), *Philip the Chancellor: Motets and Prosulas*, RRMMA 41 (Middleton, 2011), esp. p. xxv.

[13] Gordon A. Anderson's 'A Small Collection of Notre Dame Motets *ca.* 1215–1235', *Journal of the American Musicological Society*, 22 (1969), 157–96, proceeds on exactly this kind of chronological basis. For more recent examples of stemmata, see Rebecca A. Baltzer, 'The Polyphonic Progeny of an *Et Gaudebit*: Assessing Family Relations in the Thirteenth-Century

Even Wolf Frobenius's controversial denial of the well-established clausula-before-motet hypothesis was primarily a simple reversal of the accepted generic progression.[14] Although more recent scholarship has acknowledged the possibility of less straightforward genealogical lines, this is often as a means of avoiding, rather than addressing, chronological issues.[15]

This study tackles chronological issues head-on, tracing sequences of compositional events, and proposing local reversals and qualifications to presumed genetic relationships between thirteenth-century genres that challenge conventional scholarly accounts and origin theories. Nevertheless, chronology does not inevitably dictate the analytical agenda, neither is it privileged to the narrow exclusion of other matters of compositional and cultural interest. Individual analyses participate in wider musical debates about the relationship between monophonic and polyphonic performance (Chapter 1), between theory and practice (Chapter 3), and about the impact of notational technologies and scribal activities (Chapters 4 and 7). Chapter 7, which extends into the fourteenth century, additionally offers a concluding reflection on ideologies of old and new in the age of the self-proclaimed *Ars nova*. Beyond the musical realm, liturgical concerns are central to Chapters 1 and 2. The former charts the unexpected fate of an Assumption Gradual in its various polyphonic forms, while the latter engages with a curious unique collection of very short two-voice settings of snippets of Mass and Office plainchants, for which it is difficult to imagine a clear function. This raises codicological questions about the intended purpose and/or practicality of medieval written documents that are revisited in Chapter 4, which probes motivations for the textless transcriptions of vernacular motets that were apparently placed among liturgical clausulae. Chapter 5 contributes to an on-going discussion in both musicology and French studies about the status of quotation as a defining characteristic of the vernacular refrain, comparing motets in which quoted refrain melodies and those that have the *appearance* of quotations, but were apparently created afresh, play analogous formal roles. Chapter 6 reflects on ideas of

Motet', in Dolores Pesce (ed.), *Hearing the Motet: Essays on the Motets of the Middle Ages and Renaissance* (New York, 1997), pp. 17–27; and Alejandro Enrique Planchart, 'The Flower's Children', *Journal of Musicological Research*, 22 (2003), 303–48. I have queried the assumed priority of clausulae in both cases. See Catherine A. Bradley, 'Contrafacta and Transcribed Motets: Vernacular Influences on Latin Motets and Clausulae in the Florence Manuscript', *Early Music History*, 32 (2013), 1–70 (pp. 16–17 and 40–57, respectively).

[14] Wolf Frobenius, 'Zum genetischen Verhältnis zwischen Notre-Dame-Klauseln und ihren Motetten', *Archiv für Musikwissenschaft*, 44 (1987), 1–39.

[15] See, for instance, David J. Rothenberg, *The Flower of Paradise: Marian Devotion and Secular Song in Medieval and Renaissance Music* (New York, 2011), esp. pp. 39–40.

femininity and female sainthood in the Middle Ages in the context of a newly identified network of musical compositions that evoke and venerate St Elizabeth of Hungary. That this music opens up and is open to such a range of interdisciplinary perspectives invites closer engagement.

In foregrounding the idea of reuse and quotation – the adoption and elaboration of pre-existing plainchant melodies in polyphony – this study sets aside concepts of authorship and originality that are often central to studies of compositional sketches and processes in later repertoires. Thirteenth-century polyphony offers an alternative and non-authorial forum for such analytical investigation: not only do musical and textual reworkings and additions proliferate, but this repertoire is persistently anonymous, especially in comparison to its monophonic counterpart, the vernacular songs of the trouvères, where the individual personalities of poet-composers take centre stage. Ideas of compositional process here, therefore, are necessarily formed independently of any attendant complications surrounding the identity or personality of a specific composer. This study thinks about composition in the literal sense of the word, the 'putting together' (*componere*) of different musical and textual materials.

Intertextual practices of borrowing themselves offer fertile and varied compositional possibilities inviting correspondingly diverse analytical perspectives. The quotation of plainchant in polyphony may have a strongly hermeneutic dimension, alluding to and situating the polyphonic instantiation within the broader sacred contexts of an existing liturgical tradition (as demonstrated in Chapter 6). But reuse has more practical, musical ramifications, too, for the construction of a new piece (addressed particularly in Chapters 3, 5, and 7): how are new melodies shaped around and adapted to old foundations, or how might texts be added to pre-existing musical structures? Perhaps most importantly, an examination of borrowing helpfully keeps open the subject of chronology that has dominated previous discussions of this repertoire, but without requiring that chronological conclusions be reached in every instance, or subscribing to overarching developmental models. It is possible and productive to posit small-scale linear chronologies in certain cases, and these may operate in various directions. The subsequent chapters are able to demonstrate, for example, that a particular melody is an established quotation accommodated in a new polyphonic context (Chapters 4, 5, and 6); that a text was conceived for a pre-existent musical material (Chapter 3); and conversely that musical material was conceived in conjunction with a text that was later removed (Chapters 4 and 5). In other instances, there is insufficient evidence to reach absolute conclusions (Chapter 7), and it is therefore more productive to ask different kinds of questions, to map and observe interactions without the imperative of establishing any definitive chronology.

Reflecting the complexity and diversity of medieval musical practices, this book does not seek to propound any totalising analytical methodology. The heuristic analyses proceed 'from first principles': analytical questions and tools are tailored to the nature of the material at hand, responding to features of a particular work or group of works that emerge as unusually pronounced or unconventional in the repertoire at large. In Chapter 3, for instance, a pair of highly repetitive motets on the intricate REGNAT tenor prompts a study of melodic repetition as a compositional strategy and its harmonic consequences in practice and in theory. Chapter 5 explores the parallel motivic and constructional procedures involved in vernacular motets that are self-consciously 'framed' by opening and closing refrains, developing a wider concern raised in Chapter 4 about the combination of multiple melodic quotations to sound simultaneously in polyphony. Chapter 6 investigates the far-reaching hermeneutic implications of building a motet on an obscure plainchant melody, in this case a plainchant quotation that evokes a female singing voice.

While Chapters 3, 5, and 6 use the details of individual works as a platform for wider compositional and interpretative issues, the remaining case studies show ways in which larger groups of pieces within the vast thirteenth-century repertoire can productively be defined and scrutinised. Chapter 1 takes a new holistic approach that is centred on a single chant melody, tracing the treatment of segments of this melody as the basis of organa, clausulae, and motets across a wide variety of manuscript sources to reveal musical behaviours and generic interrelationships that force a rethinking of current models. By contrast, Chapter 2 engages with a little-studied set of compositions – a collection of so-called 'abbreviation' or 'mini' clausulae – that already have the status of a group in the manuscript source in which they are uniquely preserved. It demonstrates how salient liturgical and musical characteristics may be identified and brought to bear on questions of function, performance contexts, and transmission, querying and recasting understandings of these apparently marginal mini clausula vis-à-vis the mainstream polyphonic tradition represented by the 'Great Book of Organum' (*Magnus liber organi*).

A new corpus is defined in Chapter 4, with the purpose of bringing to the fore a characteristic that has previously proved historiographically disruptive: namely the shared musical currency of liturgical and vernacular genres. Analysis of particular examples pinpoints musical and notational traits that reveal melodic material within sacred clausulae to be genuine quotations of secular French refrain melodies. This facilitates chronological conclusions about the relationship between clausulae and motets that invite a reversal – within the context of this corpus – of the current default presumption that motets derive from the addition of text to the clausula whose music they share. Only Chapter 7 employs an organising principle with an established pedigree. This is the idea of a motet family, in which a single musical composition takes multiple forms (with various added voices and accompanying texts) as Latin and French motets and a clausula. A textbook example of a conventional concept is invoked here in order to query the developmental narrative it usually typifies. I propose an alternative emphasis to the usual chronological one, asking instead *why* one melody should prove so memorable and long-lived, and how exactly its fame might depend on identifiable musical and poetic techniques.

The case-by-case approach advocated in this book is, I would argue, crucial to a proper appreciation of this music. A recommendation that thirteenth-century compositions should be studied individually was central also to Mark Everist's 1994 monograph, the first to be devoted to the music of thirteenth-century French motets.[16] Yet in charting the musical terrain, Everist's study inevitably continued to be shaped by still-pervasive global narratives within which specific motets were situated or reconciled. Heuristic analytical engagement with the compositional constitutions of certain works and groups of works is put to the opposite purpose here, serving to undermine existing archetypes and to promote an alternative, less totalising conceptualisation of this repertoire. This book's wide generic and chronological range additionally facilitates a new and deeper contextualisation of motets with relation to the genres of organum and clausula, inextricable connections that are difficult to ignore at the level of individual pieces but can only be reductively characterised in abstract terms. The interactions between these genres are fluid, with the result that Chapters 4 and 5 illustrate precisely the reverse genetic relationship between motet and clausula to that proposed in Chapter 3. Chapter 1, meanwhile, reveals a striking lack of any connection at all between clausulae and motets. These kinds of seemingly contradictory behaviours can be accommodated within a methodology that, instead of proceeding from the general to the particular, begins with the particular, as a means towards understanding and embracing the complexity of thirteenth-century musical culture and its multifaceted compositional practices.

[16] Everist, *French Motets in the Thirteenth Century*, p. 13.

1 Plainchant in Polyphony: The Gradual *Propter veritatem* in Organa, Clausulae, and Motets

Practices of polyphonic composition were, from their inception, heavily dependent on monophonic plainchant traditions: pre-existent and well-known liturgical melodies served as musical and textual underpinnings for the addition of newly created voices. The various stylistic conventions for selecting and adding to plainchant foundations in the thirteenth-century genres of organa, clausulae, and motets are well understood.[1] Yet procedures that occur during the interpretative moment at which a chant is transformed from a flexible linear melody into a formalised polyphonic tenor are rarely considered. Plainchant tenors are typically characterised as pre-determined material that is straightforwardly placed in the lowest voice of a polyphonic composition.[2] It cannot be assumed, however, that there was a single standardised version of a chant melody to which a composer of polyphony could automatically turn. And inevitably, subtle melodic inflections in the plainchant – the decorative 'folded notes' or *plicae* whose precise pitches are not specified in chant sources, or the vocal pulses in a *repercurssio* – had either to be omitted, or to become concretised components of rhythmicised strings of individual tenor notes.

The potential for minor differences between plainchant melodies and polyphonic tenors has been noted: Craig Wright, for instance, observed that certain twelfth- and thirteenth-century tenors contain slight musical variants that are nowhere to be found in contemporary chant manuscripts.[3] Wright suggested that these variant readings of the chant might

[1] See the overview of conventions for plainchant treatment in organa in Norman E. Smith, 'An Early Thirteenth-Century Motet', in Mark Everist (ed.), *Models of Musical Analysis: Music before 1600* (Oxford, 1992), pp. 20–40 (pp. 20–4); and in Mark Everist, 'The Thirteenth Century', in Mark Everist (ed.), *The Cambridge Companion to Medieval Music* (Cambridge, 2011), pp. 67–86 (pp. 73–7).

[2] In the context of motets, Dolores Pesce illustrated and challenged the conventional characterisation of tenor chants as an 'immutable guiding foundation'. See her 'Beyond Glossing: The Old Made New in *Mout me fu grief/Robin m'aime/PORTARE*', in Dolores Pesce (ed.), *Hearing the Motet: Essays on the Motet of the Middle Ages and Renaissance* (New York, 1997), pp. 28–51 (p. 28).

[3] Craig Wright, *Music and Ceremony at Notre Dame of Paris 500–1500* (Cambridge, 1989), p. 250.

sometimes represent errors, and at other times intentional alterations in polyphony. But the possibility for more drastic and deliberate manipulations of plainchant tenors in organa, clausulae, and motets, and the motivations for and consequences of such manipulations, have not been investigated. Previous admissions or discussions of significant adaptation in tenor chant quotations are typically confined to late-thirteenth-century motets, and linked to their association with vernacular songs and increasing 'secularisation'.[4]

This chapter questions the idea that polyphonic compositions in the twelfth and thirteenth centuries, be they liturgical organa or vernacular motets, invariably adopted a 'given' chant melody as their tenor foundation. It offers an investigation of three segments of the Gradual *Propter veritatem* – VERITATEM, FILIA, and AUREM TUAM – whose earliest polyphonic instantiations differ substantially from extant monophonic witnesses. Remarkably, thirteenth-century monophonic sources of this Gradual are highly consistent, while thirteenth-century polyphony presents versions of this plainchant that depart from those established in monophonic records, and that are themselves subject to variation and reworking across different polyphonic recensions and genres. The unusual version of the *Propter veritatem* chant employed as an organum tenor previously attracted the attention of Heinrich Husmann and Helmut Hucke, but neither scholar was in a position to compare organum tenor melodies against plainchant sources from a similar time and place.[5] In 2002, Danielle Pacha surveyed the transmission of the *Propter veritatem* Gradual in forty thirteenth-century (principally Parisian) chant books, in order to support her analysis of a particular group of motets based on a special form of the VERITATEM chant melody.[6] I draw here on

[4] Klaus Hofmann, for instance, considered the manipulation of tenor chants characteristic only of late-thirteenth-century motets. See his 'Zur Entstehungs- und Frühgeschichte des Terminus Motette', *Acta musicologica*, 42 (1970), 138–50 (p. 140). Previous discussions of tenor manipulation have been confined principally to instances in which this manipulation is motivated either by vernacular refrain quotations or by song forms (such as the *rondeau*). See, respectively, Pesce, 'Beyond Glossing'; and Mark Everist, 'The Rondeau Motet: Paris and Artois in the Thirteenth Century', *Music and Letters*, 69 (1988), 1–22.

[5] See Heinrich Husmann, 'The Origin and Destination of the "Magnus liber organi"', trans. Gilbert Reaney, *Musical Quarterly*, 49 (1963), 311–30 (pp. 327–8); and Helmut Hucke, 'Zu einigen Cantus Firmi der Notre-Dame Organa', in Michel Huglo, Christian Meyer, and Marcel Pérès (eds.), *Aspects de la musique liturgique au moyen âge*, Actes des colloques de Royaumont de 1986, 1987, et 1988 (Paris, 1991), pp. 159–75, esp. pp. 166–75.

[6] See Danielle Pacha, 'The *VERITATEM* Family: Manipulation, Modeling and Meaning in the Thirteenth-Century Motet', Ph.D. diss. (Washington University, 2002), pp. 298–9. Pacha explores wider plainchant contexts as a backdrop to textual interpretation, and her dissertation is principally focused on a particular group of seven VERITATEM motets.

the monophonic data collated by Pacha in a new examination of *Propter veritatem* tenors, which encompasses, for the first time, the complete span of thirteenth-century polyphonic genres: organa, clausulae, and motets. Comprehensively tracing three individual tenor segments across genres in a geographically and chronologically wide spectrum of polyphonic sources, this chapter reveals and seeks to explain the nature and extent of its different incarnations.

The *Propter veritatem* Gradual proved one of the most popular sources of polyphonic tenors in the thirteenth century, and the flexibility with which it was handled is exceptional.[7] Nevertheless, detailed study of the ways in which this chant melody was transformed offers significant glimpses of the kind of compositional and performative possibilities for which we typically lack concrete evidence. Did creators of polyphony use versions of the plainchant for which no monophonic witnesses survive, or did they artificially lengthen and/or elaborate an established chant melody in order to expand the scope of their polyphonic settings? On the whole, the latter emerges as the more likely hypothesis, but modifications to the *Propter veritatem* Gradual in polyphony are nevertheless strongly in keeping with the character of the plainchant and with the conventions of monophonic practices. Significantly, however, sensitivity or faithfulness to the monophonic heritage of this melody does not necessarily go hand in hand with the function, liturgical or otherwise, of its polyphonic elaborations. This chapter uncovers instances in which liturgical organa are much freer and more compositionally stylised in their treatment of a certain plainchant tenor than later vernacular motets. It also challenges conventional presumptions about the relationship between polyphonic genres, demonstrating a complete lack of any connection between extant traditions of clausula and motet composition on the *Propter veritatem* plainchant – a circumstance from which different modes of compositional modelling emerge as significant. Although exceptional, therefore, the case of *Propter veritatem* promotes a more nuanced and complex understanding of polyphonic development and behaviours – especially of correlations between compositional freedom and liturgical function – in the thirteenth century.

[7] VERITATEM is the only tenor for which Friedrich Ludwig observed a divergence from established monophonic transmission. See his *Repertorium organorum recentioris et motetorum vetustissimi stili*, ed. Luther A. Dittmer, 2 vols. in 3 (New York, 1964–78 [1910]), Vol. II, p. 59. Husmann noted that the *Propter veritatem* Gradual constituted a 'particularly remarkable example'. See his 'Origin and Destination', p. 327.

The Gradual *Propter veritatem*

The text of the plainchant Gradual *Propter veritatem*, paraphrasing Vulgate Psalm 44, addresses a female subject as 'daughter': 'For truth, and mercy, and justice: and he shall lead you marvellously by your right hand. Hear daughter, and see, and incline your ear, for the king has desired your beauty.'[8] In its liturgical context, the daughter in question is typically the Virgin Mary. At Notre Dame Cathedral in the thirteenth century, this chant was sung at Masses during the week following the feast of the Assumption (15 August), prescribed for the second day of the Octave.[9] Notre Dame was not only dedicated to Our Lady, but was specifically associated with her Assumption into heaven, thereby elevating this feast to the same rank as Christmas, Easter, and Pentecost. In addition to its place in the Assumption celebrations, *Propter veritatem* was sung also on the feast of Mary's Nativity (8 September) in a number of French cathedrals, and the Gradual was included within the common liturgy for other female saints in Parisian chant books.[10]

Propter veritatem is widely transmitted in Graduals and noted Missals of thirteenth-century northern French and English provenance.[11] Example 1.1 presents the chant as recorded in Paris, Bibliothèque nationale de France, lat. 15615, a mid-thirteenth-century Parisian noted Missal for Notre Dame. The melody of this mode-five Gradual is relatively stable across its monophonic witnesses, and the chief source of variation concerns conventions for the pitch level at which the opening respond is notated: while the majority of notations of the chant begin and end on F (as in Example 1.1), some place the entire opening respond up a tone, on G; others up a fifth,

[8] The translation is adapted from those offered by Sylvia Huot, *Allegorical Play in the Old French Motet: The Sacred and the Profane in Thirteenth-Century Polyphony* (Stanford, 1997), p. 99; and Sean Curran, 'Feeling the Polemic of an Early Motet', in Almut Suerbaum, George Southcombe, and Benjamin Thompson (eds.), *Polemic: Language as Violence in Medieval and Early Modern Discourse* (Farnham, 2015), pp. 65–94 (p. 72). See also Curran's discussion of the relationship of this Gradual text to Psalm 44 (p. 72).

[9] On the place of *Propter veritatem* within the Assumption liturgy at Notre Dame, see Wright, *Music and Ceremony*, pp. 254, 261.

[10] See Husmann, 'Origin and Destination', pp. 324, 325 n. 24. The organum cycles in **W1** and **F** place *Propter veritatem* at the appropriate liturgical juncture for use either on the feast of the Assumption or for the Nativity of the Virgin: the Gradual M 37 follows the Assumption Alleluia *Ora pro nobis* (M 36) and precedes the *Alleluia Nativitas* (M 38) for Mary's nativity. In **W2**, however, the *Propter veritatem* organum appears among the common of saints, the usual position for this Alleluia in Parisian chant books.

[11] See the list and comparison of forty different monophonic sources of this melody in Pacha, 'The *VERITATEM* Family', pp. 298–9.

Example 1.1 *Propter veritatem V. Audi filia*, Paris, Bibliothèque nationale de France, lat. 15615, fol. 332v.

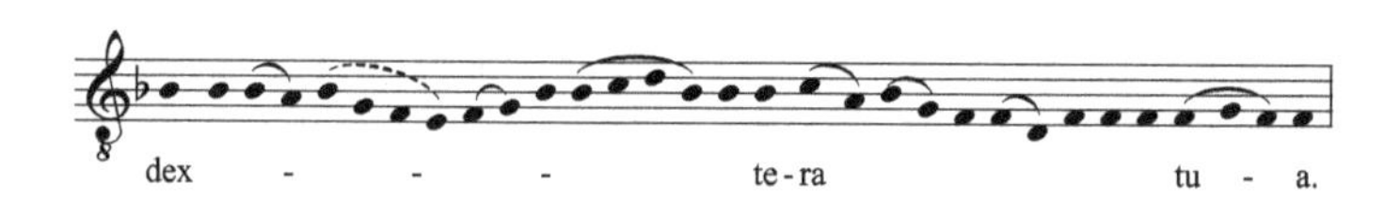

on C.[12] Associated with Notre Dame's dedication feast, featuring an elaborate melisma on the word 'filia', and with its exhortation to 'hear' and to 'incline your ear', this Gradual was understandably an inviting prospect for polyphonic reworking.

[12] A significant proportion of Parisian chant sources notate the *Propter veritatem* respond on G rather than F, including the early-thirteenth-century Notre Dame Missal, Paris, Bibliothèque nationale de France, lat. 1112.

Organa and Clausulae

The often-quoted late-thirteenth-century theorist now dubbed Anonymous IV referred to a *Magnus liber organi*, the work of masters Léonin and Pérotin. This 'Great Book of Organum' does not correspond exactly to any single manuscript source surviving today. Although Anonymous IV's 'Great Book' may be lost, his description can also be interpreted as a more general reference to a body of liturgical polyphony associated with the Cathedral of Notre Dame. Based on plainchant quotations in their lowest voice or tenor, organa in the *Magnus liber* furnished with polyphony only the sections of a chant melody sung by soloists. In the case of Graduals and Alleluias – the two types of plainchant for the Mass to receive polyphonic settings at Notre Dame – this constituted the opening solo intonation and the solo verse. Choral responds (following the solo intonation and preceding the verse, and at the end of the solo verse, indicated by an asterisk in Example 1.1) were excluded from polyphony, presumably supplied monophonically in performance.

Creating an organum for the solo sections of a plainchant required a choice between two alternative polyphonic styles. The chant could be treated either to a melismatic elaboration in *organum purum* – with extended flourishes in the upper voice(s) over long, held notes in the tenor – or to a setting in 'note-against-note' discant, where the tenor and the upper voice(s) progress at a similar rate in measured rhythm. The nature of the plainchant tenor itself usually, and practically, determined these polyphonic choices: syllabic parts of the chant melody were typically elaborated in the extended *organum purum* style, while lengthy melismas in the plainchant tenor were treated in faster-moving discant. The choice of discant or *organum purum* in polyphonic settings of *Propter veritatem* remained fairly consistent: Example 1.2 shows visually the choice of polyphonic style as typically applied to this monophonic Gradual in organa, omitting the choral sections of the chant that did not receive a polyphonic setting (compare Example 1.1).[13] X-shaped note heads indicate the predominantly syllabic portions that were treated to an *organum purum* setting, and round note heads represent the chant melismas set in note-against-note discant.

Organa for the *Propter veritatem* tenor are recorded in all three of the principal sources associated with the so-called *Magnus liber* repertoire: **W1**, **F**, and **W2** (see Table 1.1). These three manuscripts present related versions of a two-voice *Propter veritatem* organum. There are two

[13] Exceptionally, the organum in **W2** treats 'et inclina' in discant rather than *organum purum*.

Table 1.1 Organum settings of *Propter veritatem* (M 37)

Version number	Number of voices	Manuscripts	Folios
1	2	**W1**	41r–42r
		F	128r–129r
		W2	84r–v
2	2	**W1**	23v–24r
3	3	**Hu**	31r–v

Example 1.2 Typical polyphonic approach to the *Propter veritatem* chant, as recorded in Paris, Bibliothèque nationale de France, lat. 15615, fol. 332v. (X-shaped note heads indicate *organum purum*; round note heads indicate discant.)

further unique organa on this chant, both considered to represent non-Parisian compositions. **W1** preserves a second two-voice *Propter veritatem* organum that seems to be a later local Scottish creation.[14] And the Spanish source, **Hu**, copied in the fourteenth century, contains a partial three-voice

[14] Norman E. Smith made the case for the **W1** organum on fol. 23v as unusual and later; see his 'Tenor Repetition in the Notre Dame Organa', *Journal of the American Musicological Society*, 19 (1966), 329–51 (pp. 332–4). Edward H. Roesner identified it as a 'peripheral' composition; see his 'The Problem of Chronology in the Transmission of Organum Duplum', in Iain Fenlon (ed.), *Music in Medieval and Early Modern Europe: Patronage, Sources, and Texts* (Cambridge, 1981), pp. 365–99 (p. 372); and 'Who "Made" the *Magnus liber*?', *Early Music History*, 20 (2001), 227–66 (p. 251).

organum setting (concluding at the word 'inclina') unrelated to those in earlier *Magnus liber* manuscripts.[15]

Veritatem

The preponderance of the discant, rather than the *organum purum* style, in *Propter veritatem* organa is evident in the dominance of round note heads in Example 1.2. Although a polyphonic treatment predominantly in discant is due in part to the melismatic nature of the Gradual itself, it seems also to represent a compositional preference. Certain of the chant melismas set in discant are relatively brief – 'et vide', for instance – and could plausibly have been set in *organum purum*. An inclination to discant is further evident in the highly unusual treatment of the opening melisma on VERITATEM. Since the chant melisma on VERITATEM as recorded in monophonic sources is only eight notes in duration (see Examples 1.1 and 1.2), the Gradual's opening solo intonation could realistically have been expected to be in *organum purum* throughout.[16] In fact, the Parisian organa in **W1**, **F**, and **W2** feature a shared, different, and longer version of the VERITATEM chant melisma (see Example 1.3), which is set polyphonically in the note-against-note style.[17]

The different and longer VERITATEM tenor found in polyphonic organa constitutes the most common opening for Graduals in mode five, an especially formulaic body of chants that are often constructed, mosaic-like, of stock melodic gestures.[18] A well-known and stereotypical musical beginning, the use of this popular formula for the start of *Propter veritatem* is entirely conceivable within the conventional practices of fifth-mode Graduals. Nevertheless, this opening formula never features in extant contemporaneous monophonic transmissions of *Propter veritatem*.[19] Instead,

[15] For the most recent study of **Hu**, its date, and provenance, see David Catalunya, *Music, Space and Ritual in Medieval Castille, 1221–1350*, Ph.D. diss. (Universität Würzburg, 2016).

[16] Of the additional seventeen Graduals used as organum tenors in the *Magnus liber* sources, eight feature settings of the opening intonation exclusively in *organum purum*.

[17] The duplum of this portion of the organum is identical in **W1** (fol. 41r) and **W2**. **F** has a different passage of discant on VERITATEM, with a double statement of the tenor melody. In **F**, the repetition of the opening respond after the Gradual verse is unusually copied out in the manuscript. This second setting of the respond replicates the opening *organum purum* on PROPTER (in a slightly contracted version), followed by a new discant setting of VERITATEM, using the same tenor melody also in a double statement.

[18] See the discussion of fifth-mode Graduals and the table of their melodic formulae in Wili Apel, *Gregorian Chant* (Bloomington, 1958), pp. 345–50.

[19] Compare the summary of contemporary monophonic transmissions in Pacha, 'The *VERITATEM* Family', pp. 298–9.

Example 1.3 Melodies associated with *Veritatem* as a monophonic plainchant and a polyphonic tenor.

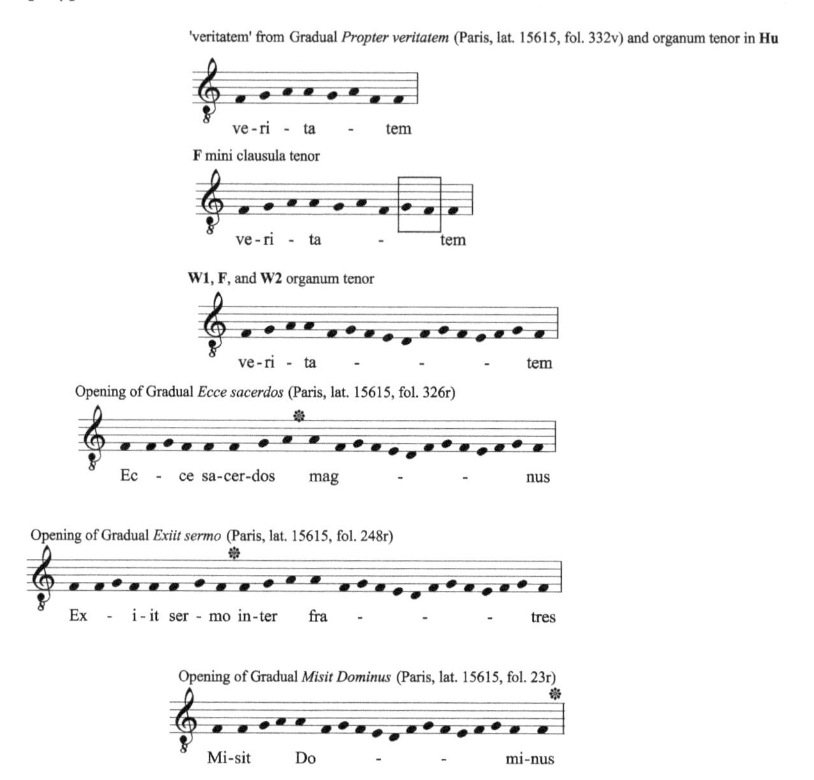

monophonic records of the chant conventionally begin with a melody that is unique among Graduals of its type.[20] Why, then, was this unique *Propter veritatem* chant opening not furnished with polyphony in the *Magnus liber*, and how can the setting of a more popular alternative chant incipit, but one not typically associated with *Propter veritatem*, be explained?

Husmann proposed that the opening melodic formula adopted as the VERITATEM tenor in polyphony was explained by a process that he described as *Tenortausch* (tenor exchange).[21] That is, the creators of the *Propter veritatem* organum simply borrowed from different organa in the *Magnus liber* whose tenors (correctly) employed this popular fifth-mode Gradual beginning. The melodic formula accompanying VERITATEM is

[20] See Apel, *Gregorian Chant*, pp. 346–9. The opening of the *Propter veritatem* respond (*L* 1602) is unique (and thus receives no standard designation in Apel's table), while the polyphonic VERITATEM tenor corresponds to formula Fb.

[21] On *Tenortausch*, see Heinrich Husmann, 'The Enlargement of the "Magnus liber organi" and the Paris Churches St Germain l'Auxerrois and Ste Geneviève-du-Mont', trans. Andres P. Briner, *Journal of the American Musicological Society*, 2 (1963), 176–203, esp. pp. 182–3.

used in two mode-five Graduals set as organa elsewhere in the *Magnus liber* (see Example 1.3). The stock phrase appears accompanying the words 'inter fratres' after a brief opening recitation in *Exiit sermo* (M 5), and in conjunction with 'sacerdos magnus' in *Ecce sacerdos magnus* (M 50).[22] Significantly, however, the melodic formula does not receive a complete polyphonic setting in either case. In *Exiit sermo*, 'inter fratres' corresponds to a choral portion of the Gradual that is omitted from organa. Likewise, in *Ecce sacerdos*, the solo intonation ends after 'sacerdos', excluding the remainder of the formula accompanying 'magnus'. This therefore argues against any cross-fertilisation of polyphonic settings as an explanation for the VERITATEM tenor, denying the possibility of Husmann's *Tenortausch*.[23]

In spite of the overwhelming stability of thirteenth-century chant books – which agree without exception on the unique opening melody for *Propter veritatem* – the polyphonic VERITATEM tenor adopted in the *Magnus liber* could represent the sole remaining trace of an unwritten performance practice for this chant. That is, singers of plainchant in thirteenth-century Paris might have been accustomed to performing *Propter veritatem* with the popular opening formula, rather than as consistently notated in manuscript sources.[24] Yet even if this is the case, evidence suggests that scribes and composers of polyphony were simultaneously aware that this practice was an alternative to another established beginning for the *Propter veritatem* Gradual. It is significant that, although the polyphonic VERITATEM tenor is never found in monophonic sources, the conventional plainchant opening is featured within a polyphonic setting in **F**. This is the single surviving clausula on VERITATEM, a short passage of discant excerpted from any organum context and presented alongside other similarly excerpted clausulae. The VERITATEM clausula is extant only in **F** (see Example 1.4), found within a unique collection of very brief discant settings, described by Alejandro Enrique Planchart as 'mini clausulae', whose origins and functions are explored in the following chapter.[25] The mini clausula

[22] Husmann explored briefly the connection between the M 37 and M 50 (but not M 5) Graduals. See his 'Origin and Destination', pp. 327–8.

[23] See also Hucke's rejection of Husmann's *Tenortausch* theory in 'Zu einigen Cantus Firmi', pp. 166–7, 174–5.

[24] Only Hucke was fully alert to the status of the polyphonic VERITATEM tenor as an established mode-five opening; see ibid., p. 169. Pacha, in 'The *VERITATEM* Family', was unaware of this. Roesner ('The Problem of Chronology', p. 327) referred to the polyphonic VERITATEM tenor as a 'somewhat synthetic version ... that was apparently fashioned specifically for the Parisian [organum] setting'.

[25] Alejandro Enrique Planchart, 'The Flower's Children', *Journal of Musicological Research*, 22 (2003), 303–48 (p. 310).

Example 1.4 Mini clausula on VERITATEM, **F**, fol. 183r–IV, 1.

states the conventional VERITATEM plainchant once, differing from the usual version of the melody in monophonic sources only in its insertion of two additional pitches (G–F, marked by a box in Example 1.3) before the concluding F.

The presence of this mini clausula in **F** confirms that the *Propter veritatem* incipit as recorded in monophonic sources was known and available to the compilers of the manuscript. There is additional proof that another later-thirteenth-century scribe was conscious that the polyphonic VERITATEM tenor formula was more conventionally associated with a different host Gradual. As discussed further below, a copy in the late-thirteenth-century Bamberg manuscript of the most popular VERITATEM motet contravenes established transmission to label its chant tenor MISIT DOMINUS. This fifth-mode Gradual does not feature anywhere in the *Magnus liber* or elsewhere in the motet repertoire, but its opening solo intonation typically employs exactly the same formula as the VERITATEM tenor (see Example 1.3).

Such awareness of different incarnations and contexts for the VERITATEM melody suggests that the common mode-five opening formula was knowingly selected for use in polyphony as an alternative to the unique *Propter veritatem* chant incipit. A musical justification for this selection is convincing. Tonally and melodically, the polyphonic VERITATEM tenor is more expansive – encompassing the typical fifth-mode gesture of a falling fourth from G down to D – than the *Propter veritatem* opening recorded in chant books. Crucially, it also contains twice as many pitches, offering a much more effective discant tenor, the style seemingly preferred to *organum purum* in *Propter veritatem* organa in the *Magnus liber*.

That the selection of the VERITATEM tenor was deliberately undertaken to facilitate a polyphonic treatment in discant in the *Magnus liber* is supported by a three-voice *Propter veritatem* organum preserved outside this context, and recorded uniquely in the later Spanish manuscript **Hu**. This is the single extant organum to use as its tenor the shorter VERITATEM melody conventional in plainchant sources (see Example 1.3), and the entirety of the opening respond is here treated in *organum purum*, as befits the brevity of the melisma.[26] Interestingly, the only other 'peripheral' organum setting of this chant – the aforementioned unique local Scottish composition in **W1** – also favoured an *organum purum* treatment of VERITATEM. As Edward H. Roesner argued, the creator of this Scottish organum was evidently adapting the Parisian setting recorded elsewhere in **W1**.[27] In contrast to the composer of the **Hu** organum, he also employed its longer VERITATEM tenor, but curiously without availing himself of its heightened potential for discant treatment, perhaps because he did not share this stylistic concern of the *Magnus liber* organa.

The unusual case of the VERITATEM tenor complicates conventional understandings of the relationship between plainchant and polyphony. It is possible that polyphonic compositions on *Propter veritatem* exclusively record an established monophonic performance practice, in which a popular opening formula was sung at the beginning of this plainchant, in place of the Gradual's unique incipit. This practice was presumably germane to early-thirteenth-century Parisian contexts, since it was unknown – as the organum in **Hu** attests – in later Spanish ones. More probably, however, the deliberate substitution of a popular opening chant formula was motivated by the creation of polyphony for *Propter veritatem*, to facilitate and enhance a setting in the discant style. Creators of organum, therefore, took advantage of the potential to manipulate their plainchant tenor in a manner that was entirely consonant with (if not actually exploited in) monophonic practices. In so doing, they firmly established as a polyphonic tenor a version of *Propter veritatem* that diverged from the formalised written identity of the chant melody. This reveals an important agency in the handling of chant tenors in organa – one seemingly driven by expressly musical concerns – that is often belied by a sense, on the one hand, of plainchant as 'an immutable guiding foundation',[28] and on the other, of the function of organa in the liturgy 'simply [to] replace those sections of plainsong that they set'.[29]

Aurem Tuam

Significantly, two further portions of the *Propter veritatem* Gradual exhibit a similar independence in polyphony from the monophonic transmissions

26 Pacha noted the use of the conventional monophonic opening in **Hu** ('The *VERITATEM* Family', pp. 86–7), suggesting also that the extended polyphonic tenor might represent a Parisian practice.

27 Roesner, 'The Problem of Chronology', p. 372.

28 As critiqued by Pesce in 'Beyond Glossing', p. 28.

29 Everist, 'The Thirteenth Century', p. 73.

of this melody. As Husmann noted in 1963, the *Magnus liber* tenor melodies for AUREM TUAM also present a more elaborate version of this melisma than is recorded in contemporary chant books.[30] Husmann's observation is corroborated by Pacha's broader survey of chant readings, demonstrating once again a stable written monophonic identity from which variants common to the polyphonic sources are entirely absent.[31] Example 1.5 compares the typical plainchant melody for *Aurem tuam* with extant polyphonic versions: as recorded in organum settings in **W1**, **F**, and **W2**, within a mini clausula in **F**, and as the ending of the *Et vide et inclina aurem tuam* clausula in the St Victor manuscript (dated to the 1270s).[32] Like all others in **StV**, this three-voice clausula is actually a transcription of a motet, the frequently copied *Dieus je fui/Dieus je n'i puis*, whose motetus incipit is cued in the margin.[33] Boxes highlight differences between the versions, while dashed boxes indicate variant or alternative tenor readings that correspond with the conventional form of the plainchant rather than with other polyphonic sources.

The AUREM TUAM tenor recorded in organa in **W1**, **F**, and **W2** exhibits several characteristics distinct from its typical monophonic transmission. The endings of the polyphonic tenors are extended by four additional notes, emphasising the final pitch, C. And the organum tenors elaborate an early portion of the chant melisma: additional pitches – dropping either a tone or a third – are inserted between the repeated iterations of C, mimicking the figuration at the opening of the melisma (on 'AU-'). As in the case of VERITATEM, these polyphonic tenors could record an otherwise unwritten plainchant practice, in which the chant melody was decorated by inserting passing tones and alternating between pitches a third apart. The polyphonic AUREM TUAM tenor is similarly in keeping with the performative contentions for its plainchant, and its pitch oscillations – between C and A, in particular – exploit a musical characteristic definitive of fifth-mode Graduals. Yet once again, the case that this particular decoration of the AUREM TUAM tenor was polyphonically motivated is strong: the oscillations lengthen the melisma, and furthermore, they divide neatly into

[30] Husmann, 'Origin and Destination', p. 328. See also Smith's corrections to Husmann's musical examples in 'Tenor Repetition', p. 332 n. 4.

[31] See Pacha, 'The *VERITATEM* Family', pp. 304–5.

[32] Hucke also offers a comparative transcription of these tenors in his 'Zu einigen Cantus Firmi', p. 172. Hucke reads the Notre Dame tenors against the 'Gregorian' melisma (based on Laon 239 and St Gallen 359) and does not include the **F** or **StV** clausulae.

[33] See Fred Büttner, *Das Klauselrepertoire der Handschrift Saint-Victor (Paris, BN, lat. 15139): Eine Studie zur mehrstimmigen Komposition im 13. Jahrhundert* (Lecce, 2011), pp. 265–8.

Example 1.5 Melodic comparison of AUREM TUAM.

trios of pitches, which complement the rhythmic profile of the tenor in the groups of three longs characteristic of the fifth rhythmic mode.[34]

The precise pitch content of the polyphonic AUREM TUAM tenor varies, and in ways that are best accounted for by a written transmission of this

[34] Hucke also intimated that the elaboration of the AUREM TUAM chant could have been undertaken with a view to three-note groupings in the polyphonic tenor; 'Zu einigen Cantus Firmi', p. 174.

tenor melody. The decorative pitches inserted in the AUREM TUAM tenor are variously either A or B, even when the tenor appears in conjunction with the same duplum material in all three Parisian organa. Such instabilities are unusual, given the shared polyphonic context, and plausibly arise because the middle notes of the oblique ligatures that join the trios of pitches (C–A–C or C–B–C) can be very difficult to distinguish. A difficulty in reading these ligatures would explain too why the same type of variation is also encountered at the very outset of the melisma, on the first syllable of AUREM. No extra pitches are inserted here, but the Parisian organa in **W1**, **F**, and **W2** begin C–B–C, deviating from the established C–A–C plainchant opening that is more conventional for a mode-five Gradual. The B (rather than A) in the tenor here is not a copying error, since it sounds an octave below the accompanying duplum, which was evidently conceived with the C–B–C tenor opening in mind. The absorption of this variant from the outset of the discant composition on AUREM TUAM suggests engagement with a written and fundamentally polyphonic form of the chant, as a tenor notated in the fifth rhythmic mode. Significantly, in the version of this discant found as the second tenor cursus of the Scottish organum preserved in **W1**, the scribe reinstated the chant's more conventional C–A–C opening, despite the resulting harmonic dissonance of a ninth.

The treatment of the AUREM TUAM tenor in the local **W1** organum raises important questions about the status and function of this polyphonic composition. In the Scottish organum, the most widely known AUREM TUAM discant – whose tenor was apparently 'corrected' here to the more conventional monophonic opening – is preceded by a new polyphonic setting. The new discant setting also employs and is evidently designed for the C–A–C chant opening.[35] But its AUREM TUAM tenor has two subsequent variant pitches vis-à-vis the version of the tenor that immediately follows it (see Example 1.5). In an unusual procedure discussed further below, two independent discant compositions with slightly different tenors were evidently placed side by side here: there is a noticeable gap in **W1** between the two statements of the melisma, and the text 'aurem tuam' is unconventionally copied twice.[36] It seems unlikely that this organum – juxtaposing different

[35] The duplum sounds an octave above the second tenor pitch, A.

[36] Edward H. Roesner noted that this passage 'is remarkable for its repetition of the text, a sign that it was added to an existing work'. See Edward H. Roesner (ed.), *Le 'Magnus liber organi' de Notre-Dame de Paris VII: Les organa et les clausules à deux voix du manuscrit de Wolfenbüttel, Herzog August Bibliothek, Cod. Guelf. 628 Helmst.* (Monaco, 2009), p. 359. The repetition of text in an organum occurs on only four occasions in the *Magnus liber* sources: twice in **W1**, twice (within the same organum) in **F**. See Smith, 'Tenor Repetition', pp. 332–6. For detailed

instantiations of the same tenor and, moreover, repeating its accompanying text – would have been suitable for use in performance in exactly the form documented here. This underlines the possible artificiality of *Magnus liber* sources: not necessarily functional liturgical books, but written repositories of musical compositions.

The AUREM TUAM melody employs many repeated pitches and figurations – features that by their very nature encourage elaboration and the development of divergent versions. It differs in this regard from VERITATEM, whose extended polyphonic incarnation adopts an established melodic formula and remains very stable. Yet as in the case of VERITATEM, there is evidence that creators of organa would have been aware that the form of AUREM TUAM used as a polyphonic tenor was a more extended version of the established plainchant melody. A mini clausula in **F** on AUREM TUAM retains decorated aspects of the chant melody common to other polyphonic versions of the tenor (and that complement its rhythmic grouping in threes). Yet unlike the Parisian organum tenors, the mini clausula opens with the more conventional C–A–C figuration, and it concludes at the same point as the chant melody, employing the plainchant's standard ending. As for VERITATEM, this is a further instance in which the tenor of a mini clausula in **F** is closer to the established monophonic transmission of a chant than that found in the organa of the *Magnus liber*. The existence of such a mini clausula once again confirms that the polyphonic AUREM TUAM tenor was recognisable as a different and elaborated version of the typical written recension of the melody in thirteenth-century chant books.

The position of the mini clausulae with respect to the organa and clausulae of the *Magnus liber* is explored further in Chapter 2, where I suggest that they may represent part of a different polyphonic tradition. That the practice of extending and decorating tenor chants was particular to the *Magnus liber* is corroborated by another version of the AUREM TUAM tenor employed in **StV**, a clausula transcription of the vernacular motet *Dieus je fui/Dieus je n'i puis/ET VIDE ET INCLINA AUREM TUAM*. This motet uses the version of the AUREM TUAM tenor that is closest to its notations in contemporary monophonic sources (see Example 1.5). This indicates a disjunction between the motet and earlier traditions of clausula and organum composition on the AUREM TUAM tenor, a disjunction at odds with a more general continuity in tenor melodies across thirteenth-century

discussion of the **F** organum (for O 16) containing text repetitions that apparently result from the insertion of two separate clausulae, see Planchart, 'The Flower's Children', pp. 309–12.

polyphonic repertoires. In *Dieus je fui/Dieus je n'i puis*, the less elaborate form of the AUREM TUAM tenor – and a form matching the version conventional in monophonic transmissions – suggests that this motet sits somewhat outside earlier practices of organum composition. Despite the perceived monumentality of the organa of the *Magnus liber*, therefore, certain of its tenor conventions seemingly constituted short-lived and self-contained Parisian phenomena, which did not persist in polyphonic repertoires at chronological and geographical remove.[37]

Filia

Extended versions of the VERITATEM and AUREAM TUAM melismas were apparently adopted in the tenors of polyphonic organa in order to facilitate their treatment in discant rather than in *organum purum*. The elaboration of their plainchant melodies notwithstanding, these melismas remained fairly brief and – outside the mini clausulae – they were not treated to any clausula reworkings in extant sources. The melisma on FILIA, however, presents a different case. Noticeably the longest in the Gradual and with an internally repetitive melodic structure, FILIA unsurprisingly proved the chant's most popular clausula tenor, circulating independently of its organum context in two clausulae each in both **W1** and **F**, and in an additional mini clausula in **F** (see Table 1.2).[38] Yet despite its natural suitability as a discant tenor, the FILIA melisma also survives in an alternative version exclusively recorded in the polyphonic *Magnus liber*, and that circulated concurrently with the conventional monophonic form of the melody.[39]

The two alternative versions of the FILIA tenor in the *Magnus liber* repertoire are shown in Example 1.6: version α corresponds to the melisma as notated in the vast majority of thirteenth-century chant books, while

[37] This is corroborated also by the Spanish organum in **Hu**, which uses the more conventional VERITATEM melody. Since this organum breaks off after 'et inclina', it unfortunately offers no comparand for the AUREM TUAM melisma.

[38] Motets transcribed as clausulae in **StV** on PROPTER VERITATEM and ET VIDE ET INCLINA AUREM TUAM are once again excluded here. The status of the **StV** pieces as motets accounts also for their unconventional tenor segments vis-à-vis the *Magnus liber* clausulae, discussed further below.

[39] The music of the FILIA melisma is found elsewhere in the *Magnus liber* repertoire, associated with the text LAQUEUS in the Gradual *Anima nostra V. Laqueus* (M 7). There are no direct concordances between the polyphonic settings of these shared melismas. Unlike FILIA, LAQUEUS did not feature in any independent clausulae, and only one motet (Mt95) employs the LAQUEUS melisma as part of a longer M 7 tenor.

Table 1.2 Clausulae on M 37 tenors

Clausula tenor	Clausulae and sources	Folios	Clausula numbers
VERITATEM	1 **F** mini clausula	183r–IV, 1	436
FILIA	2 **W1** clausulae	59v–1 and 2	79 and 80
	2 **F** clausulae	168r–2 and 3	177 and 178
	1 **F** mini clausula	183r–IV, 2	437
ET INCLINA	1 **F** clausula	168r–4	179
ET INCLINA AUREM TUAM	1 **F** mini clausula	183r–V, 1	438
CONCUPIVIT REX	1 **F** clausula	168r–5	180
	1 **F** mini clausula	183r–VI, 1	439

Two clausula settings of M 37 tenors – PROPTER VERITATEM and ET VIDE ET INCLINA AUREM TUAM – in the St Victor manuscript (**StV**) are excluded from discussion here in the context of organa or clausulae. As outlined below, these clausulae are in fact motet transcriptions, and are therefore considered in this generic context.

Example 1.6 Two versions of the FILIA melisma.

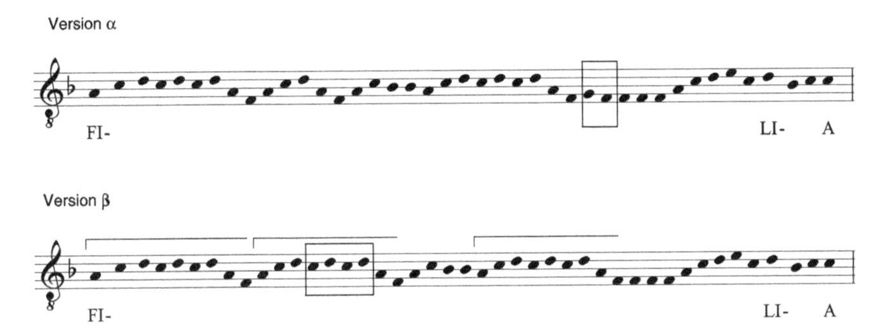

version β survives exclusively as a polyphonic tenor.[40] The two versions differ in two respects. Version α contains two pitches, G–F (marked by a box in Example 1.6) absent from version β. At an earlier point in the melody, the β melisma has four extra pitches, C–D–C–D (also marked by a box) that do not feature in version α. The extra pitches in version β create a more exact reiteration of a recurring melodic pattern with a threefold C–D oscillation, found earlier and later in the chant melisma (marked by square brackets), once again constituting the kind of elaboration typical in plainchant. Given the omission as well as addition of pitches, it seems the purpose of the β

[40] Monophonic sources for the FILIA melisma vary slightly, but twenty-three of the forty monophonic sources surveyed by Pacha (including almost all of the sources of Parisian provenance) match tenor version α exactly. See 'The *VERITATEM* Family', pp. 300–1. All versions of the LAQUEUS tenor in the related M 7 Gradual in the *Magnus liber* also correspond to version α.

Table 1.3 Organum and clausula settings of FILIA

Version number	Manuscript sources	Folio numbers	Context	Tenor version	Discant tenor starting pitch
1	**W1**	41v	Organum	α	C
	F	128r (cursus II)	Organum		
	W2[a]	84r–v	Organum		
	W1	59v–1	Clausula		
2	**F**	128r –v (cursus I)	Organum	β	D
3	**W1**	23v–24r	Organum	β	D
4	**Hu**	31r–v	Organum (3vv)	α	A
5[b]	**W1**	59v–2 (cursus I)	Clausula	β	A
	F	168r–2	Clausula		
6	**W1**	59v–2 (cursus II)	Clausula	β	A
	F	168r–3	Clausula		
7	**F**	183r–IV, 2	Mini clausula	α	A

[a] It seems that the **W2** organum was designed for FILIA discant beginning on the third pitch of the melisma, D, rather than the second pitch, C. The discant unnecessarily duplicates the melisma's second pitch, C, which has already been set in *organum purum*.

[b] The duplum of this clausula is in the second rhythmic mode in **F**, but appears, modally transmuted, in the first in **W1**.

version here was not necessarily to lengthen the FILIA melisma, but rather to highlight a particular musical symmetry. The apparent motivation for a FILIA tenor that differs from the usual chant form of the melisma, therefore, differentiates it further from the VERITATEM and AUREM TUAM tenors, as does the remarkable circumstance that organa and clausulae within the *Magnus liber* itself freely alternate and even combine the two distinct versions of the FILIA melisma.

Table 1.3 lists all extant passages of discant recorded within organa, independent clausula, and mini clausula settings of the FILIA melisma, and the tenor version they employ. The popularity of the two versions is evenly matched: while the conventional α form serves as the tenor of the most widely transmitted discant setting (Table 1.3, no. 1), the polyphonic β version features in a larger number of individual pieces. Tenors α and β appear side by side in the two FILIA clausulae on the same folio of **W1** (nos. 1 and 6 in Table 1.3). Remarkably, the FILIA discant within the *Propter veritatem* organum in **F** adopts version β in its first tenor cursus, and version α in its second (nos. 2 and 1 in Table 1.3). Since this second cursus normally circulated independently of the first as a stand-alone setting, the mismatch of FILIA tenors must result – as in the case of the AUREM TUAM setting in the locally composed **W1** organum – from the combination of two previously independent discant compositions. Differences between the two versions of the FILIA tenor combined in **F**, however, are more pronounced than the slightly variant readings of AUREM TUAM joined together in **W1** (a tenor whose transmission is, in any case, more unstable). Moreover, the two FILIA cursus also adopt different tenor starting pitches: the first (no. 2) begins on the third note of the melisma, D, while the second (no. 1) opens on the melisma's second pitch, C.

What might explain the cultivation and even combination of two different FILIA tenors within the *Magnus liber*? The practice of placing side by side within an organum setting what were essentially two independent discant compositions is rare in the repertoire as a whole.[41] Norman E. Smith, in his comprehensive investigation of tenor repetition, identified only twelve further instances (all occurring within organa in **F**) where independent discant passages had typically been combined with 'no real attempt to disguise the break between the two [tenor] statements or to relate the new statement to the existing one'.[42] In view of this, and as in the case of AUREM TUAM in the **W1** organum discussed above, it seems unlikely that cursus I in **F** – the unique setting of a FILIA tenor specific to the *Magnus liber* repertoire – was intended to be sung in conjunction with the following cursus II, a well-established discant elaboration of the different version of the plainchant melody conventional in chant books.[43] Yet even if they would not have been performed as a pair, the scribe or compilers of **F** evidently wished both of the discant settings to be preserved for posterity. Hucke, the only other scholar to comment on this disjunction of FILIA tenors here, considered a lack of concern for these differences as proof that the two passages of discant were 'works of art' (*Kunstwerke*) in their own right.[44] And the very fact that a musical flexibility in this chant tenor was maintained stems plausibly from a principally artistic or compositional interest, rather than a straightforwardly practical or liturgical one. Creators of polyphony evidently relished the opportunity to draw out and to embellish subtly different forms of their chant foundation, despite the resulting inconsistencies that presumably

41 See Smith, 'Tenor Repetition', p. 336.

42 Ibid., p. 338.

43 This is also Planchart's conclusion in the similar case of the IESSE and EIUS discant in the three-voice O 16 organum in **F**. See his 'The Flower's Children', p. 312.

44 Hucke, 'Zu einigen Cantus Firmi', p. 175. Hucke's understanding of the unusual combination of tenor versions in the FILIA discant in **F** is confused by a comparison with the NON DEFICIENT tenor in the M 40 Gradual *Timite. Inquirente*. Failing to recognise a scribal omission in **F**, Hucke erroneously concluded that the NON DEFICIENT tenor existed in a substantially different version in **W1** and **F** but in conjunction with the same duplum melody.

posed some challenges for the workable use in performance of particular organa and clausulae.

Motet Tenors

Given the preference for discant rather than *organum purum* style in polyphonic elaborations of *Propter veritatem*, it is unsurprising that this Gradual prevailed in later-thirteenth-century compositions in which the note-against-note style predominated. In fact, just one other host plainchant in the thirteenth century rivalled *Propter veritatem* to yield as many as four different motet tenors.[45] VERITATEM is by far the most popular tenor, with twelve different motet compositions (three Latin, nine French); FILIA is used in five extant motets (two Latin, three French); and ET VIDE ET INCLINA AUREM TUAM and QUIA CONCUPIVIT REX each feature in a single French motet.[46] Semantic relationships between certain motet texts and these tenor chants have already been illuminated.[47] The following discussion offers a new perspective, closely analysing the flexible handling of tenors in *Propter veritatem* motets, and their relationships to earlier plainchant and polyphonic traditions.

The AUREM TUAM melody, featured within a single motet, presents the most straightforward case. This melisma concludes the longer chant tenor of the three-voice *Dieus je fui/Dieus je n'i puis/ET VIDE ET INCLINA AUREM TUAM*, disseminated in four versions across six different manuscript sources.[48] The three-voice French motet recorded in **W2** and **Ba** is found with Latin contrafact texts in **Hu** and **Reg**, with a French quadruplum in **Mo**, and transcribed as a clausula in **StV**. As already noted, all of these motets employ the conventional and unelaborated form of the AUREM TUAM melody (see Example 1.5). Crucially, however, the use of the chant melody as conventionally recorded in monophonic sources here seems to indicate distance from, even ignorance of, its elaborated form in the *Magnus*

[45] Four different motet tenors also originate in *Alleluia. Letabitur iustus* (M 49).

[46] The QUIA CONCUPIVIT REX tenor as recorded in the organa of the *Magnus liber* matches exactly the monophonic version of this melody in lat. 15615. In the motet *C'est la jus par desous/QUIA CONCUPIVIT REX* (Mt428, unique to **N**, fol. 191r–v) the tenor is reworked in order to accommodate melodic repetitions in the motetus, but maintains aspects (such as the opening six pitches) of the chant melody.

[47] See especially Huot, *Allegorical Play in the Old French Motet*, pp. 99–106. See also Curran, 'Feeling the Polemic'.

[48] Mt479–81b. The ET VIDE ET INCLINA portion of the tenor in organa and in this motet matches exactly the version of the melody recorded in lat. 15615.

liber, rather than any sense of restoring a more established version. The motet sources demonstrate confusion as to the identity of their plainchant quotation: this unusual tenor was wrongly labelled ET SUPER in **W2** and ALLELUYA in **Ba**, and left untexted in **Hu**. The scribes of **Mo** and **Reg** were nearer the mark with ET VIDEBIT and ET VIDE, respectively, but only in the clausula transcription in **StV** was the plainchant accurately texted in full.

Interestingly, **StV** is also the only version of this musical material to present the chant at its conventional pitch level, beginning and ending on C. All motet sources transpose the tenor melody down a fifth to F, which allows their triplum (and, in **Mo**, quadruplum) to occupy a more typical range. As Fred Büttner demonstrated, the **StV** clausulae – despite, or perhaps because of, the fact that they are textless transcriptions of vernacular motets – are fastidious in their tenor identifications and alignment of text syllables.[49] The *Et vide et inclina aurem tuam* clausula opens the collection of forty motet transcriptions in **StV** and may be a symbolic statement: Büttner proposed that, in inviting users of the manuscript to 'see and to incline their ear', this clausula promoted the manuscript's aim to rehabilitate the liturgical genre of the clausula, which was under threat from the secular motet.[50] Even though the compilers of **StV** may have chosen to include this motet because of its tenor – probably reinstating the conventional tenor pitch level and text – their interest in and awareness of the chant source was atypical.[51] In spite of the use of the AUREM TUAM melody as formalised in contemporary chant books, therefore, practices of transposition and mis-texting in the *Dieus je fui*/*Dieus n'i puis* motets generally indicate a lack of concern for the monophonic, as well as polyphonic, heritage of their tenor foundation.

The VERITATEM tenor, by contrast, had the opposite fate in the motet repertoire (see the list of VERITATEM motets and details of their tenors in Appendix 1.1). The polyphonic organum tenor is the basis of all twelve extant VERITATEM motets, none of which uses the established monophonic chant incipit. Pacha has demonstrated a highly unusual feature common to seven of the VERITATEM motets:[52] these pieces share a distinct

[49] See Büttner, *Das Klauselrepertoire der Handschrift Saint-Victor*, pp. 254–5.

[50] Ibid., p. 33 n. 60.

[51] Thomas Walker demonstrated that the tenor of the motet *A Cambrai avint l'autrier* (Mt857, unique to **Mo**, fol. 84v) labelled SOIER closely resembled the *Et vide et aurem tuam* melody. See his 'Sui *Tenor* Francesi nei motetti del "200"', *Schede medievali: Rassegna dell' officina di studi medievali*, 3 (1982), 309–36 (p. 324). The chant here is also transposed down a fifth, suggesting that the SOIER tenor was known from the motet *Dieus je fui*/*Dieus je n'i puis*. See also the discussion of this motet in Chapter 6, pp. 207–8.

[52] See Pacha, 'The *VERITATEM* Family', pp. 91–2. Pacha, however, misleadingly identified four components to the extended VERITATEM tenor, mistakenly including within her large-scale

Example 1.7 The extended VERITATEM motet tenor.

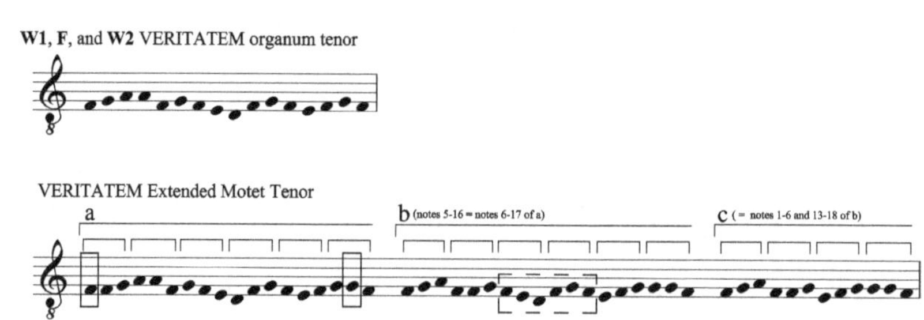

and consistent continuation of the usual polyphonic VERITATEM tenor, in which material from an initial statement of the tenor is freely repeated and reworked.[53] Example 1.7 shows this extended motet tenor, emphasising its tripartite form. Section a reproduces the standard VERITATEM tenor with the addition of two pitches (marked by boxes); this a material is effectively repeated in section b, but with slight alterations to its opening and conclusion. The third part of the motet tenor, section c, is a shortened version of the b material, excising its six internal pitches (marked by a dashed box).

This freely extended motet tenor – expanding what was already an expanded form of the VERITATEM plainchant – was, I propose, adapted and designed to facilitate the tripartite groupings of tenor pitches characteristic of the fifth rhythmic mode.[54] In section a, the two pitches added to the standard version of the tenor – an extra opening F, an extra penultimate G – permit the arrangement of its pitches in six three-note groups (shown by square brackets in Example 1.7) – groups that principally end either on F or G. Internal tripartite divisions are at work also within the freer reworkings of the VERITATEM tenor that follow in section b (which has the same number of pitches as section a) and the shorter section c. It is likely that extended motet tenor originated within the most widely transmitted VERITATEM motet, *O Maria, maris stella*, which appears in fourteen different manuscripts, is cited also as a musical example by seven

tenor structure the first section of what, in fact, constituted a wholesale repetition of this structure. See also Pacha's discussion of the seven motets on the extended VERITATEM tenor at pp. 105–38.

[53] Chapter 6 explores another unusual instance in which a plainchant tenor (here DECANTATUR) is subject to free continuation in a motet, and where this extended version of the motet tenor is adopted in further compositions.

[54] Five of the seven motets on this extended VERITATEM tenor are in the fifth rhythmic mode, consistently presenting the tenor pitches in regular groups of three ternary longs followed by a rest. The remaining two intersperse a fifth-mode pattern with faster movement, but continue to group their tenor pitches in threes or sixes.

different theorists, and is recorded in the earliest extant motet collection in **F**. In *O Maria, maris stella*, the VERITATEM motet tenor is stated once in the extended form shown in Example 1.7. Notably, the melodic relationship between sections b and c of the tenor corresponds exactly with that in the motetus. The motetus repeats, in section c, precisely the portions of the melody that accompanied the same tenor material in section b.[55] It appears, therefore, that this version of the VERITATEM motet tenor, the nature of its continuation and of the relationship between sections b and c, was inspired by the particular polyphonic circumstances of *O Maria, maris stella*. Possibly this version of the tenor was then taken up in the motet *In veritate comperi*, a much longer composition built on several iterations of the *O Maria, maris stella* tenor. *In veritate comperi* directly follows *O Maria, maris stella* in **F**, and its incipit 'In veritate' adopts the textual explicit of *O Maria, maris stella*. As a response to *O Maria, maris stella*, *In veritate comperi* was the only other VERITATEM motet to approach the popularity of its model: *In veritate comperi* survives in nine different manuscript sources, while no other of the VERITATEM motets appears in more than three. Remarkably, this pair of widely attested Latin compositions on a freely extended version of the polyphonic VERITATEM tenor seems to have sparked a subsequent motet-centred tradition of tenor transmission and modelling.

A kinship between VERITATEM motets is observable even beyond the group of seven pieces that shares the special extended motet version of the tenor. The two 'extra' pitches in the VERITATEM melisma absent from any earlier organum settings – the additional opening F, and the repetition of the penultimate pitch, G – are found across the entire motet corpus.[56] And the tripartite groupings of the tenor melody that these additional pitches

[55] Pacha also noted this characteristic, which she described as 'isomelism'. See 'The *VERITATEM* Family', pp. 107–8. She did not, however, propose that this could explain the design of the extended VERITATEM motet tenor, and she remained equivocal about identifying a progenitor for this motet tenor tradition. In the monotextual or conductus motet version of *O Maria, maris stella* the melodic design of the triplum matches that in the motetus in sections b and c. Double motet versions of this piece, however, have a different triplum design.

[56] The 'extra' repeated F is, however, technically excluded from motets that use the tenor PROPTER VERITATEM, and begin with the four pitches – F–F–G–F – that accompany the word PROPTER. Here the fourth note and final F of PROPTER is effectively co-opted as part of the VERITATEM tenor's F–F–G opening (and this preserves any three-note groupings). The copy of *Quant se siet belle/PROPTER VERITATEM* in **StV** presents an exceptional case. **StV** records the form of VERITATEM exactly as found in the tenors of the *Magnus liber* (without the extra opening F and closing G). The copy of this same motet in **N**, however, adopts the opening repeated F and gives the VERITATEM tenor in a different rhythm, grouping the

facilitate remain the overwhelming norm.[57] The importance of motet models for compositions on VERITATEM, and of cross-references and internal conventions established within this genre, is particularly plausible given the complete absence of any existing tradition of independent clausulae on this tenor, a highly unusual circumstance examined further below. It seems that the VERITATEM motets initiated a new and exclusively motet-based practice of compositional reworking of this tenor, which had not previously attracted the attention of clausula composers. Yet these motets simultaneously remained connected to their organum heritage, consistently employing the *Magnus liber* version of their tenor rather than the chant's established monophonic form. It is therefore possible that the liberties taken in further extending the VERITATEM melisma as a motet tenor were rooted in, perhaps sanctioned by, an awareness of flexibilities already inherent in the approach to this chant in organa.

Motet versions of the FILIA tenor invite a similar conclusion. Although the five extant motets (two Latin and three French) basically rely on the α version of the melisma that is most common in plainchant sources, it seems that both α and β forms of the melisma were known to motet creators (see Example 1.8 and details of these motets and tenors in Appendix 1.2). Interestingly, three motets share a slightly altered form of the α FILIA tenor (labelled α′ in Example 1.8) that is never found in organa and clausulae. This α′ version involves variation of the same kind as that found between the α and β versions: a C–D repetition late in the FILIA melisma is omitted (marked by a box in Example 1.8). The two Latin motets show some further and equally explicable variations from the α′ melisma. *Divinarum scripturarum* omits the initial two C–D repetitions to commence on the sixth note of the FILIA melisma, and it alters by a tone (marked by an X in Example 1.8) three of the chant's pitches. Significantly, *Audi filia egregia* combines features of both the α′ and β versions, omitting the two α pitches excised in the β version (marked by a dashed box in Example 1.8). It is noteworthy that an α′ version, which differs from all organa and clausulae versions of the tenor, is common to these three FILIA motets and does not match any contemporary

VERITATEM pitches in threes. Unfortunately, the tenor in **N** breaks off before the end of the VERITATEM melisma, thus it is unclear whether the extra G is included here or not. The variant tenor extant in **N** may be evidence that the version of the motet transcribed as a clausula in **StV** attempted to 'correct' or standardise the form of its tenor plainchant.

[57] Three exceptions are: *A la cheminee*, whose tenor is in duplex long groups of four or five notes; the **StV** – but not the **N** – version of *Quant se siet belle*; and *Tuit cil qui sont*, whose tenor pattern is irregular overall, but nonetheless retains certain of VERITATEM's established three-note groupings. Significantly, all three motets use the PROPTER VERITATEM tenor (rather than just VERITATEM).

Example 1.8 Variant motet versions of the FILIA melisma.

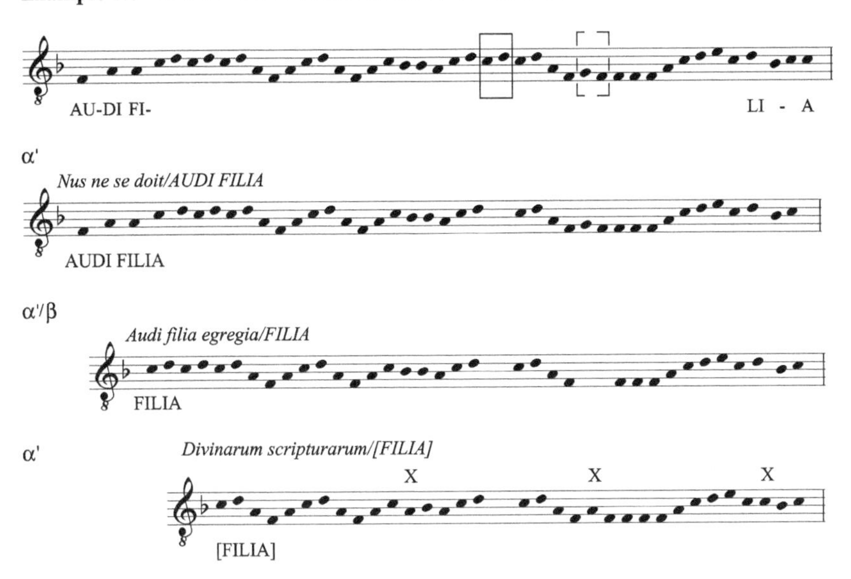

monophonic sources. This, in addition to shared compositional procedures in vernacular motetus voices that are examined in Chapter 5, indicates the development of an internal motet tradition for the FILIA tenor. Like the VERITATEM motets, those on FILIA seem to show awareness of earlier tenor practices in the *Magnus liber* and take advantage of similar opportunities for flexibility in their handling of the plainchant, while referring to and modelling themselves primarily on other motets, and notably lacking any concordances with extant FILIA clausulae.

New Beginnings and Tenor Labels: PROPTER VERITATEM and AUDI FILIA

A certain independence between motet traditions for *Propter veritatem* tenors and earlier polyphonic practices of organum and clausula composition is reflected also in the precise demarcation of chant segments as motet tenors. In organa, only VERITATEM and FILIA are treated in note-against-note discant, while the immediately preceding chant melodies – setting the words 'Propter' and 'Audi' respectively – are invariably in *organum purum*. Yet four VERITATEM and three FILIA motets take as their tenors the longer PROPTER VERITATEM and AUDI FILIA segments of chant, even though the initial portions of these melodies were (in line with the stylistic conventions of organum composition) previously excluded in any discant settings. These new and longer discant tenors are notably exclusive to vernacular motets, and the choice of the AUDI FILIA versus the FILIA tenor is consistently differentiated by language: all three French motets employ the AUDI FILIA melody, while both Latin motets are restricted to FILIA only. This could indicate a greater respect for (or at least lip service to) established organum practices in Latin motets, but does not invariably imply a chronological proximity to these practices. Although the Latin motets on VERITATEM and FILIA recorded in **F** may well be older than any French counterparts on PROPTER VERITATEM and AUDI FILIA, the FILIA motet in **Ma** and **Hu** is plausibly a later Spanish composition in an earlier vein.

It appears that the loosening of organum tenor conventions in motets was musically motivated. In particular, pitch repetition at the beginning of a tenor was apparently desirable to establish and prolong a clear tonal identity at the outset of a motet. This explains the unconventional demarcation of the French motet tenor QUIA CONCUPIVIT REX, which adds the two As accompanying QUIA to the beginning (also on A) of the traditional discant and clausula tenor CONCUPIVIT REX.[58] In the case of PROPTER VERITATEM, the addition of the four pitches accompanying PROPTER (F–F–G–F) firmly inaugurates the final pitch, F. And the preference for repeated pitches is evident in the VERITATEM motet tenor, as discussed above, which also begins F–F–G (mimicking the Gradual's PROPTER opening), even though the VERITATEM melisma as recorded in monophonic sources or in the organa of *Magnus liber* has just a single iteration of F. Significantly, other instantiations of the mode-five formula adopted as the polyphonic VERITATEM tenor begin with a repeated F, as in the Graduals *Misit Dominus* and *Ecce sacerdos* (see Example 1.3). In selecting and adapting their tenors, motet creators were, therefore, sensitive to the character, contexts, and possibilities of their plainchant material, simultaneously taking full advantage of melodic features that could have valuable polyphonic consequences.

Yet initial care and sensitivity in crafting the VERITATEM motet tenor seems quickly to have given way to a lack of awareness and precision concerning its identity as a plainchant quotation, as previously discussed in the case of ET VIDE ET INCLINA AUREM TUAM. This is indicated by the

[58] On Mt482, see n. 46 above. ET VIDE ET INCLINA AUREM TUAM is the only M 37 motet tenor never to breach organum protocol, since this section of the chant is also treated in discant throughout in the **W2** organum. The two extant clausulae set only portions of this tenor, however.

occasionally casual approach to the texting of motet tenors as PROPTER VERITATEM or VERITATEM, suggesting that at the very least the scribes who copied these pieces were not fully alert to the signification of their tenor labels. Although PROPTER VERITATEM tenors were correctly identified in **N**, **R**, and **StV**, the more usual VERITATEM designation was imprecisely employed in **Ba** and **Mo** (see Appendix 1.1). The incipit of the Latin motetus *In veritate comperi* also prompted a corruption of the text of the VERITATEM tenor, since it is given as IN VERITATE in **Ba** and **W2**.[59] And this corruption spread beyond the context of the *In veritate* motet: the tenor of the motet *O Maria, maris stella* is labelled IN VERITATE in **ArsA**, **Ch**, and **Cl** (and as IN VERITATO in **Lyell**), as is the tenor of *Benigna celi*/*Beata es* in **Ba**.[60] It seems appropriate that the newly coined tenor designation IN VERITATE should chiefly be associated with the two Latin motets in which a new motet tenor was apparently established, freely extending the already extended VERITATEM tenor of the *Magnus liber*.

Textual treatments of the VERITATEM tenor were, like the treatment of its melody, unusually liberal. Motet tenors are frequently misidentified, particularly those that feature in just one or two pieces, as for ET VIDE ET INCLINA AUREM TUAM. But it is unprecedented for a tenor to circulate with a variant form of its correct plainchant text, arising as the result of a motetus incipit. More remarkable still is the fact that, in the PROPTER VERITATEM motet *Mout sont*/*A la cheminee*, a new syllabic and vernacular text is fitted to the tenor melody throughout. Beginning with a direct translation of the Latin incipit – *Par verite* – the tenor in **W2** continues with a text exerting the superiority of Rhine wines over those from France. In **Mo** the conclusion of the *Par verite* tenor is, amusingly, the opposite, praising the qualities of French wines.[61] Roesner has proposed that this vernacular tenor text was a late addition to the motet, and it is

[59] This incipit may also have been encouraged by the ending 'in veritate' in the motetus *O Maria, maris stella*. The intrusive 'in' of the IN VERITATE tenor may in turn have prompted the erroneous IN SECULUM label in **LoB**.

[60] In **Cl**, it is noteworthy that the tenor of *In veritate comperi* is correctly labelled as VERITATEM, while the *O Maria, maris stella* tenor is designated IN VERITATE. Interestingly, the tenor of *Amoureusement me*/*He amours*/*OMNES* (Mt9–10) is erroneously labelled IN VERITATE in the copy of the motet in **Vat** (fol. 114r), presumably a confusion arising from the shared opening tenor pitches (F–G) of both OMNES and VERITATEM.

[61] For further discussion of these motet texts, see Mary E. Wolinski, 'Drinking Motets in Medieval Artois and Flanders', *Yearbook of the Alamire Foundation*, 6 (2008), 9–20 (pp. 12–14).

lacking in the third manuscript witness, **Ba**, which gives VERITATEM as the more conventional (if imprecise) tenor word.[62] Nevertheless, the provision of a vernacular text for a plainchant tenor, a text whose opening openly parodies its Latin liturgical tag, is almost unique in the motet repertoire.[63]

In every respect, therefore, VERITATEM enjoyed an outstanding degree of flexibility in its various motet incarnations. Employing an extended version of an already extended plainchant, or incorporating (as desired) the preceding music for PROPTER, the VERITATEM motets avail themselves of several alternative motet versions of this tenor. All are based upon, but none employs, exactly the version of the chant consistently recorded in the *Magnus liber organi*, and this relaxed approach to musical quotation is reflected also in accompanying tenor texts. One final and unique 'mis-texting' of the VERITATEM melisma is particularly revealing. In **Ba**, the tenor of the most popular VERITATEM motet, *O Maria, maris stella*, is labelled MISIT DOMINUS. Although erroneous – since the motetus, closing with 'in veritate', is clearly designed for a VERITATEM tenor – it is, musically and liturgically, the most 'correct' designation possible in terms of the identities of these plainchant melodies as formalised in monophonic sources. As noted above, the melodic formula used as the VERITATEM tenor is the same as that which begins the Gradual *Misit Dominus*. Moreover, this Gradual, like the motet tenor, opens with a repeated F, while the melisma on VERITATEM recorded in chant books or in the organa of *Magnus liber* does not. It is understandable, then, that the scribe of **Ba** proffered an alternative plainchant text, one that was more typically associated with both the popular fifth-mode opening formula, and an initial repeated F. The choice of the designation MISIT DOMINUS implies some distance from the *Magnus liber* tradition: this chant features nowhere else in the extant repertoire of thirteenth-century organa, clausulae, or indeed motets. Since this identification of the tenor also obscures textual relationships between the upper voice and the plainchant foundation in *O Maria, maris stella*, it is most likely that the composer or scribe who supplied MISIT DOMINUS was unaware of polyphonic traditions for the VERITATEM tenor, and – quite understandably – did not identify the popular fifth-mode opening formula with the *Propter veritatem* chant.

[62] See Edward H. Roesner, 'Review of *The Earliest Motets (to circa 1270): A Complete Comparative Edition* by Hans Tischler', *Early Music History*, 4 (1984), 362–75 (p. 371).

[63] The only other known example of a motet with a vernacular-texted tenor is uniquely recorded in **W2** (fols. 213r–214r), directly following the *Par verite* motet. This is *Domine ainz qe j'aie digne/Domine qi t'a ci amene/DOMINE* (Mt67–8), whose DOMINE tenor receives a syllabic vernacular text beginning *Domine tant ai ame*.

In comparison with PROPTER VERITATEM and VERITATEM, the motet tenor transmission of AUDI FILIA versus FILIA is straightforward: melodically, AUDI FILIA and FILIA are less easily confused, and scribes consistently label their tenors correctly.[64] Curiously, it is the organa and clausulae of the *Magnus liber* that in this instance exhibit greater and somewhat inexplicable variation in the musical demarcation of their tenors. In the *Magnus liber*, discant settings are confined exclusively to the FILIA melisma. The melisma consistently ends on C, but various starting pitches of the FILIA tenor are indicated in the final column of Table 1.3. Almost all of the independent clausulae (nos. 5–7) set the FILIA melisma in full, beginning on its opening pitch, A. Yet the most widely transmitted discant setting (no. 1) starts on the meilsma's second pitch, C, and two other discant settings (nos. 2 and 3) begin on the third, D. Discant couched within an organum need not be tonally self-contained; this need seems greater in a clausula. Ironically, it is a discant setting preserved within the context of an organum that exploits the tenor's potential both to begin and to end on C. All independent two-voice clausulae in **F**, by contrast, 'correctly' use the FILIA melisma in full, beginning on A–E sonorities but ending their duplum voices either in unison with the tenor C or on the F a fifth below.

Significantly, the two extant FILIA motets do not imitate the conventions of the FILIA clausulae. Instead, and understandably, the FILIA motets effect a tonal coherence lacking in clausulae, by omitting the melisma's initial A, and employing C – the opening and closing pitch of their tenor segments – as their motetus final.[65] The three motets on AUDI FILIA avail themselves of an alternative tonality: the added F–A opening accompanying AUDI, in addition to the insistence on F near the end of the melisma, makes F a natural motetus final, and one also compatible with the conclusion of the chant melisma on C.[66] AUDI FILIA motets, therefore, adopt the mode of their original host Gradual, which, owing to an initial lack of emphasis on F, was less easily achieved when only the FILIA melisma was treated in discant. This tendency to enlarge discant tenors, to include portions of the chant melody previously set in *organum purum*, surely represents a growing independence from the earlier liturgical polyphony and seems to be musically driven. Paradoxically, the relationship of these tenors to their original plainchant context is often more faithful as a result. Both PROPTER VERITATEM

[64] Both copies of the motet *Divinarum scripturarum* in **Ma** and **Hu** omit the FILIA tenor text.

[65] The tenor of *Divinarum scripturarum* begins on C, but slightly later in the melisma: on the sixth rather than the second pitch (see Example 1.8).

[66] *Biaus cuers* is the only AUDI FILIA motet to cadence on a unison C, despite its F-mode opening and melodic profile throughout.

and AUDI FILIA tenors incorporate structural beginnings in the chant: the very opening of the Gradual respond and the commencement of its verse. Accordingly, these chant segments better serve the ends of a self-contained motet which, independent of any broader organum setting and divorced from any host plainchant, has a greater need for tonal coherence in its own right.

Motets and Clausulae

Motets on tenors from the *Propter veritatem* chant are unique in terms of their relationship to the clausulae of the *Magnus liber*. Although this Gradual has an established, if relatively modest, tradition of clausula reworkings in **W1** and **F**, not one of the nineteen motets on M 37 tenors shares its musical material with a clausula.[67] This circumstance does not apply to any other plainchant tenors of even vaguely comparable popularity: the few tenors whose motets have no connections to previous clausula traditions otherwise feature in just one or two motets.[68] And the relative popularity of individual M 37 motet tenors also reflects this distance from clausula conventions. Based on their treatment in clausulae one would expect FILIA to become the principal motet tenor, perhaps followed by ET INCLINA or CONCUPIVIT REX. Instead, VERITATEM – even though it received only a mini clausula setting in **F** – is the pre-eminent motet tenor, with more than double the number of motets of any other.

Motets on tenors drawn from the *Propter veritatem* Gradual effectively skip a musical generation: they may share the particular form of their tenors with earlier organa but are highly unusual in their lack of any clausula concordances and in flouting clausula conventions. Given this lack of interest in clausulae – usually regarded as the bridge between organum and motets – it is perhaps surprising that tenors from the M 37 Gradual ever entered the motet repertoire at all. Why do these motets either avoid a typical link in their evolutionary chain (as in the case of FILIA) or (like VERITATEM) rehabilitate earlier organum tenors that never featured in clausulae? In the case of ET VIDE ET INCLINA AUREM TUAM and VERITATEM, the appeal may have been their tenor's textual label. As

[67] Hendrik van der Werf mistakenly identifies a concordance between the three-voice M 37 organum in **Hu** and the Latin motet *Divinarum scripturarum* in the same manuscript. See his *Integrated Directory of Organa, Clausulae, and Motets of the Thirteenth Century* (Rochester, 1989), pp. 67, 69.

[68] The exception is the very popular motet tenor SUSTINERE (M 22, also labelled PORTARE): the music of the single extant SUSTINERE clausula in **F** lacks any concordance in the motet repertoire.

Büttner proposed, the invective to 'see and incline your ear' – quoted in full in the motet *Dieus je n'i puis* but in no extant clausula in the *Magnus liber* – surely made this tenor an attractive one. Likewise, an emphasis on 'truth' is particularly apt for the polemical motet *In veritate comperi*, which belongs within a well-established category of Latin motets and songs that seek to expose the hypocrisy of the clergy.[69]

The hermeneutic potential of an associated tenor word is naturally of greater consequence in motets, with their added upper-voice texts, than in un-texted clausulae. This could explain why tenors that were never the intense focus of clausula composition belatedly shot to fame in motets. VERITATEM invites comparison, in this regard, with the similarly themed tenor APTATUR, 'it is fitting'. Also in mode five and featured in twelve different motets, APTATUR seemingly originated in an obscure responsory for St Winoc (Ludwig's O 45) and does not appear anywhere in the *Magnus liber*.[70] Its unprecedented introduction and popularity in the motet repertoire, where it can function as an 'ironic underpinning', remain mysterious, and must principally have been the result of its textual potential.[71] The semantic attraction of the VERITATEM melisma, along with its clear, F-centred tonal profile and its history of musical flexibility, seems best to account for the popularity of this unusual tenor in motets, which – in the absence of any clausula models – established their own internal tenor traditions. Despite considerable reworking of its chant melody, and even when any liturgical context or authority had faded, the VERITATEM tenor retained a special textual and musical status in the motet repertoire, defining and unifying groups of polyphonic pieces. This status and function seemingly extended also to the FILIA tenor, for which extant clausulae were eschewed in favour of new and interconnected motet models and practices.

[69] See Curran's interpretation of this motet in 'Feeling the Polemic', where he also proposes that the text plays on ideas of listening (esp. pp. 88–9). Pacha has commented on the strongly Marian character of several VERITATEM motets; see 'The *VERITATEM* Family', pp. 153–68. This seems highly appropriate given both the broader context and function of the M 37 chant and the immediate meaning of *veritatem*.

[70] On the source of the APTATUR tenor, see Jean François Goudsenne, 'L'office de S. Winoc de Bergues (Flandres, XIe siècle) est-il à l'origine d'une teneur dans les motets du XIIIe siècle?', in Bruno Bouckaert and Eugeen Schreurs (eds.), *The Di Martinelli Music Collection (KULeuven, University Archives): Musical Life in Collegiate Churches in the Low Countries and Europe; Chant and Polyphony*, Yearbook of the Alamire Foundation 4 (Leuven, 2000), pp. 283–96.

[71] Suzannah Clark, "'S'en dirai chançonette": Hearing Text and Music in a Medieval Mote', *Plainsong and Medieval Music*, 16 (2007), 31–59 (p. 37). Huot has emphasised the parodic and allegorical potential of M 37 tenors; see *Allegorical Play*, pp. 99–106.

Conclusions

Creators of polyphony for the *Propter veritatem* Gradual took advantage of a wide variety of different possibilities for musical manipulation presented by this plainchant. In constructing polyphonic tenors, they variously exploited flexibilities inherent in their monophonic material: exchanging melodic formulae, embellishing repeated pitches, and recasting internal melodic patterns. Remarkably, these polyphonic tenors exhibit a greater variety in their transmission of the Gradual than contemporary chant books, which largely agree on a notation of the melody that was evidently conventional. Polyphonic composers also knew and employed these more conventional forms of the *Propter veritatem* chant, and so they knew too when they were deviating from or manipulating them. This evident cultivation of alternative tenor melismas, sometimes circulating simultaneously, offered considerable scope in the creation of accompanying voices, and its motivation seems primarily to have been compositional and stylistic, rather than purely practical or liturgical. That liturgical organa in the *Magnus liber*, in particular, can be shown to have knowingly altered their chant foundations challenges current understandings of tenor treatment, in which any significant freedom in the handling of tenor chant quotations is more usually associated with vernacular motets of the later thirteenth century.

Propter veritatem tenors usefully synthesise a complex relationship between flexibility and fixity that seems to reflect a collision of oral and written musical cultures in the thirteenth century. The manipulation and variation of these chant melodies in polyphony may embody informal monophonic performative possibilities or alternatives that were not typically committed to writing. Yet at the same time, these particular instantiations of a chant become fixed across different polyphonic contexts. All motets on the tenor VERITATEM, for instance, use the same mode-five opening formula, and they do not alternate between different incipits for this chant.[72] Although some of these motets take the opportunity further to elaborate this formula, this elaboration itself becomes a standardised version. In the

[72] In a study that appeared too late for proper consideration here, Gaël Saint-Cricq proposes that the motet *A vous pens/PROPTER VERITATEM* was conceived for the conventional monophonic version of VERITATEM melisma, even though the established motet tenor form was (wrongly) copied in **N**, the only extant manuscript to record the tenor music. See Gaël Saint-Cricq, Eglal Doss-Quinby and Samuel N. Rosenberg (eds.), *Motets from the Chansonnier de Noailles* (Middleton, 2017), pp. xxix–xxx. Saint-Cricq's explanation, that this motet was a local Arregois composition, offers additional evidence that the extended version of the VERITATEM tenor was, in certain respects, a geographically contained phenomenon.

case of AUREM TUAM, variations in the way in which the repeated pitches of this melody are decorated seem, in fact, to have arisen from written transmission of the tenor. And the reworking of melodic patterns within the FILIA melisma became confined to specific moments in this melisma in specific generic contexts.

Flexibilities in chant transmissions in polyphony for the *Propter veritatem* Gradual vis-à-vis monophonic records are, as already acknowledged, highly unusual. Even within this Gradual itself, the final segment to be taken up as a discant and motet tenor, CONCUPIVIT REX, is much more typical of tenor behaviour in the wider repertoire, circulating with a melody that is almost identical across its different polyphonic and monophonic recensions. It may, however, be significant that this CONCUPIVIT REX section of the tenor – featured in just one unicum motet – is also the least popular of all of those drawn from *Propter veritatem*. This highlights an important feature of polyphony for *Propter veritatem* more generally, which surely enhances the visibility of its flexible tenor treatment – namely the number of extant *Propter veritatem* compositions, their generic breadth, and their dissemination. Organa on this chant are preserved in all three of the principal *Magnus liber* sources, clausulae feature in both **W1** and **F**, and four different *Propter veritatem* tenors enter the motet repertoire. What might in other cases be dismissed as one-offs, simply as mistranscriptions or misidentifications of a chant, are here corroborated by multiple concordances. More significantly, two 'peripheral' organa from Scotland and Spain are extant, and the Gradual is unusually well represented within the mini clausulae in **F**, as well as in later motets. This offers an atypically large body of comparable polyphonic witnesses of *Propter veritatem* that sit outside the central *Magnus liber organi* tradition and, as shown here, often operate differently as a result. Now that possibilities for plainchant manipulations of the kinds especially visible and pronounced in the case of *Propter veritatem* have been established, similar behaviours may be identifiable in previously unsuspected and less well-documented contexts. In consequence, musical and compositional liberties in the handling of plainchant tenors could emerge as more widespread and less exceptional than is currently apparent.

A further unusual feature of polyphonic reworkings for *Propter veritatem* usefully challenges existing conceptualisations of musical development in the thirteenth century. This is the complete lack of any direct relationship between discant or clausula settings in the *Magnus liber* and subsequent motet reworkings. VERITATEM and FILIA motets are connected to their organal heritage through shared forms of their tenor melismas, but the lack of any shared upper-voice material with these organa is remarkable, as is the marked separation between motets and clausulae on *Propter veritatem*. As such, *Propter veritatem* exemplifies an important instance in which clausula composition did not stimulate or even substantially influence the creation of motets. These circumstances are, once again, exceptional, and they cannot overturn the traditional developmental narrative (explored in Chapter 3) that clausulae served as models for motets. Furthermore, the VERITATEM motets, in particular, show an engagement with earlier tenor traditions in organa that continues to support current perceptions of musical modelling and exchange as important processes in polyphonic composition. Nevertheless, the foregoing analysis of generic relationships in polyphony on *Propter veritatem* tenors has underlined an important circumstance, hitherto eclipsed by conventional historiographies, which do not admit the possibility that motets – even those Latin pieces preserved in the earliest manuscript sources – could be wholly independent of traditions of clausula composition on their shared tenor chants.

The concept of tenor 'families', of a connection between compositions on the same plainchant foundation, is most commonly applied to clausulae, where multiple reworkings of the same tenor are invariably presented side by side in manuscript sources, and neighbouring pieces showcase the different possibilities of a common duplum motive.[73] Motets on VERITATEM and FILIA demonstrate conclusively that a sense of kinship inspired by a shared tenor may operate powerfully within this generic context also, even though the individual members of a motet tenor family are typically much more diffuse, in terms of their manuscript dissemination and chronology. VERITATEM and FILIA motets not only bear the musical influence of other motets based on the same plainchant foundation, but also build their own exclusive tenor versions on the basis of those inherited from organa. This understanding of musical reworking and sharing within motets as a complementary and probably multi-directional relationship, without the need for a linear chronological basis linked to a straightforward progression of genres, serves as a useful antidote to conventional understandings of clausula–motet interactions.

Motets on *Propter veritatem* tenors illustrate a broad spectrum of possible approaches to a plainchant foundation in terms of the degree of respect for

[73] See, for instance, the discussion in Chapter 3 of REGNAT clausulae that rework shared duplum motives. See also the discussion of this same procedure among LATUS clausulae in **F** (fol. 158r–v) in Catherine A. Bradley, 'Origins and Interactions: Clausula, Motet, Conductus', in Jared C. Hartt (ed.), *A Critical Companion to Medieval Motets* (Woodbridge, 2018), pp. 43–60.

or awareness of its liturgical heritage. If motets on *Propter veritatem* tenors availed themselves of a musical flexibility sanctioned by earlier organum and plainchant traditions, then they occasionally also reinstated more conventional melodies and texts as formalised in monophonic sources. On the one hand, a motet whose tenor is labelled with the motetus incipit IN VERITATE employs a freely extended version of a plainchant melody, already extended by the substitution of a longer opening formula. On the other, there is the motet that hyper-corrects its tenor designation to MISIT DOMINUS, naming a plainchant Gradual more usually associated with the musical formula appropriated by the VERITATEM organum tenor. Such alignment with the conventions of liturgical chant books does not typically seem to be an aim in itself.[74] Rather, it is apparently the unintentional result of a lack of knowledge of earlier and somewhat self-contained Parisian organum traditions. The demarcation of tenor melodies offers a parallel example. Stylistic criteria underpinning the careful division of plainchants for discant and *organum purum* sections in organa often dissolve in later motets, whose tenors incorporate portions of the host chant previously excluded from discant clausulae, but the inclusion of which results in a more logical and coherent section of the original plainchant. Principally musical or compositional concerns in *Propter veritatem* motets, therefore, can paradoxically result in a handling of chant quotations that is ultimately more sympathetic to the character of the original plainchant than was the sectional division of this chant in earlier organa. It is, therefore, stylised compositional choices in organa, rather than in vernacular motets, that in many cases present a greater compromise to the melodic identity of their plainchant foundations, and this thwarts a still pervasive tendency automatically to associate the manipulation or distortion of plainchant melodies with increasing distance from liturgical contexts and functions.

Thirteenth-century polyphonic elaborations of the *Propter veritatem* Gradual, early and late, are among the most liberal in their handling of plainchant. The opportunities for musical freedom presented by this fifth-mode Gradual – a genre of chant that was itself particularly flexible – seem key to the popularity of this tenor source throughout the century. Yet treatment of the Gradual in polyphony is often so free that one wonders, for instance, why motet composers clung to the idea of the VERITATEM tenor, when there was no independent clausula tradition to refer to, and the melody had assumed a different and extended form that bore only the faintest resemblance to monophonic witnesses of its proclaimed plainchant

[74] A possible exception is the unusual manuscript **StV**.

source. Motets quickly ceased to be ordered liturgically; no longer grouped by tenor as in clausula collections, their chant quotations may have been chosen for the semantic potential of their texts, or selected with a view to the tonal requirements of a self-contained motetus, rather than to older conventions governing the alternation of discant and *organum purum* style. In spite of all this, the idea of a musical foundation rooted in liturgical monophony, even if this was, strictly speaking, a pretence, remained central to the motet as a genre. These shared plainchant foundations fostered musical and compositional connections between different motets, linking pieces that currently appear dispersed across surviving manuscript sources and are divorced from any explicitly liturgical context. It is paradoxical, and historiographically provocative, that composers of secular vernacular motets could choose superficially to invoke plainchant as an authority when there was seemingly no necessity to do so, while chant melodies in organa – presumably intended to take the place of this plainchant in liturgical performance – were freely adapted to a chiefly musical purpose. Motivations behind tenor selection were undoubtedly varied and complex, but the ingenious and sensitive manipulation of pre-existent plainchant in different ways and to different ends consistently offered a productive focus for compositional creativity in liturgical, sacred, and secular genres throughout the thirteenth century.

Appendix 1.1 VERITATEM Motets: Sources and Tenor Designations

Typical motetus text	Gennrich motet nos.	Tenor	Sources and version	Variant or incorrect tenor designations
O Maria, maris stella	448–50	Extended VERITATEM	**ArsA**	**[I]n veritate**
			ArsB	
			Ba	**Misit Dominus**
			Bes	*no designation*
			Ca	*no designation*
			Ch	**In veritate**
			Cl	**In veritate**
			Da	*incomplete*
			Erf	*incomplete*
			F	**Verita**
			Hu (3vv)	**Tenor**
			Hu (4vv)	*no designation*
			Lyell	**In veritato**
			Mo	
			W2	
			W2 French	
In veritate comperi	451–2	Extended VERITATEM (three tenor cursus, third ends after section b)	**Ba**	**In veritate**
			Cl	
			Ch	*no designation*
			CTr	*no designation*
			F	*incomplete*
			Hu	*no designation*
			LoB	**In seculum**
			Mo	
			W2	**In veritate**
A la cheminee	453–6	PROPTER VERITATEM	**Ba**	**Veritatem**
			Mo	**Par verite** etc.
			W2	**Par verite** etc.
A vous pens	457	PROPTER VERITATEM	**N**	
			R	*tenor stave empty*
Quant se siet belle	458	PROPTER VERITATEM	**N**	
			StV[a]	
Navres sui pres	459–60	Extended VERITATEM (two tenor cursus, second ends on note 15 of section a)	**Ba**	
			Mo	
Amours me tienent	461–2	Extended VERITATEM (added six-note variant ending)	**Mo**	
Au cuer ai	463–4	VERITATEM	**Mo**	
He Dieus, je n'ai pas	465–6	Extended VERITATEM	**Mo**	

(continued)

Appendix 1.1 (*continued*)

Typical motetus text	Gennrich motet nos.	Tenor	Sources and version	Variant or incorrect tenor designations
Tuit cil qui sunt	467–70	PROPTER VERITATEM (omits first F)	**Mo** **Mo** Latin	**Veritatem** **Veritatem**
Biau cors qui a	471–2	Extended VERITATEM (ends early, on note 12 of section b)	**Mo**	
Beata es, Maria	473–4	Extended VERITATEM	**Ba** **Mo**	**In veritate** **Verita**

[a] In **StV** the tenor is correctly designated PROPTER VERITATEM, with the text VERITATEM punctiliously copied again under the second tenor statement, which omits the music of the PROPTER incipit. **N** simply gives the correct text, PROPTER VERITATEM, at the outset of the tenor.

Appendix 1.2 Motets on FILIA Tenors

Motet	Manuscript sources	Tenor melisma	No. of tenor cursus	Tenor version	Tenor starting pitch
Audi filia egregia/ FILIA	**F**, fols. 408v–409r	FILIA	II	α′/β	C
Divinarum scripturarum/ [FILIA]	**Ma**, fol. 135r **Hu**, fol. 111r	FILIA	I	α′ altered	C
Nus ne se doit/ AUDI FILIA	**Mo**, fol. 246v **N**, fol. 187v **R**, fol. 208r	AUDI FILIA	II	α′	F
M'ocirres voz dous/ AUDI FILIA	**Mo**, fol. 250r	AUDI FILIA	II	α (end cursus II altered)	F
Biaus cuers desirres et dous/ AUDI FILIA	**Mo**, fol. 255v **Douce 308**, fol. 257v (text only)	AUDI FILIA	II	α (end cursus II altered)	F

2 Mini Clausulae and the *Magnus liber organi*

Within the space of fewer than seven folios, the Florence manuscript records a collection of 154 individual pieces.[1] These are the so-called 'abbreviation' or 'mini' clausulae, whose chief characteristic is their brevity, both written and sounding.[2] Hardly any of the two-voice clausulae fill up a full system in the manuscript, and the upper voice of the shortest contains just five pitches.[3] Arranged in two separate liturgically ordered cycles for the Church year – 54 clausulae for the Office, followed by 100 for the Mass – these pieces are chiefly unique, found only within the context of this idiosyncratic collection. Dismissed as a group of compositions 'of little purely musical interest',[4] the mini clausulae remain, as Alejandro Enrique Planchart noted in 2003, 'a largely unexamined repertory'.[5]

This lack of scholarly interest is surely a symptom of the piecemeal nature of the mini clausulae, which makes them difficult to address on their own terms. Like all independent or substitute clausulae, these polyphonic elaborations of snippets of plainchant are presented as excerpts, divorced from the context of their complete host plainchants or of the polyphonic settings of these chants in two-voice organa. But for the mini clausulae, the sheer volume and concentration of these individual excerpts on each folio is visually disorientating, evidently also testing the painter of the red and blue initials on several occasions. The musical and textual brevity of their tenors, moreover – often comprising only part of a melisma on a single syllable – can render them nondescript, so that the identification of individual pieces

[1] The clausulae begin at the start of the penultimate system of **F**, fol. 178r and conclude in the first system of fol. 183v.

[2] The label abbreviation clausula derives from the article by William G. Waite, 'The Abbreviation of the "Magnus liber"', *Journal of the American Musicological Society*, 14 (1961), 147–58. Alejandro Enrique Planchart coined the term 'mini clausulae' in his 'The Flower's Children', *Journal of Musicological Research*, 22 (2003), 303–48 (p. 310).

[3] The clausula on QUI E[UM], **F**, no. 340, fol. 179v–VI, 5. See the complete edition of the **F** clausulae by Rebecca A. Baltzer (ed.), *Le 'Magnus liber organi' de Notre-Dame de Paris V: Les clausules à deux voix du manuscrit de Florence, Biblioteca Medicea-Laurenziana, Pluteus 29.1, fascicule V* (Monaco, 1995).

[4] Norman E. Smith, 'Tenor Repetition in the Notre Dame Organa', *Journal of the American Musicological Society*, 19 (1966), 329–51 (p. 334).

[5] Planchart, 'The Flower's Children', p. 310 n. 28.

requires an intimate knowledge of particular plainchants and their position in the liturgical year. The mini clausula cycles are preserved towards the end of **F**'s fifth fascicle, a section of the manuscript wholly devoted to clausulae and within which the mini clausulae contrast noticeably in appearance with the more extended clausulae typically associated with this generic label and that make up the bulk of the fascicle. This striking contrast raises questions about the status of the mini clausulae in **F**: why are they so short, and what are they for?

William Waite offered an answer to these questions in 1961, connecting the mini clausulae to an often-quoted passage in Anonymous IV's late-thirteenth-century treatise:

Et nota, quod magister Leoninus, secundum quod dicebatur, fuit optimus organista, qui fecit magnum librum organi de gradali et antifonario pro servitio divino multiplicando. Et fuit in usu usque ad tempus Perotini Magni, qui abbreviavit eundem et fecit clausulas sive puncta plurima meliora, quoniam optimus discantor erat, et melior quam Leoninus erat.

And note that Master Leoninus was an excellent organista, so it is said, who made the great book of organum on the Gradual and Antiphonary to enrich the Divine Service. It was in use up to the time of Perotinus Magnus, who *abbreviavit eundem* and made many better clausulae, that is, puncta, being an excellent discantor, and better [at discant] than Leoninus was.[6]

Developing an early intimation of Friedrich Ludwig's, Waite argued that the mini clausulae in **F** were unambiguous examples of an 'abbreviation' procedure described here by Anonymous IV. Mapping this theoretical evidence directly onto the surviving musical repertoire, Waite identified two 'distinct processes' in Anonymous IV's description of Pérotin's activities.[7] First, Pérotin 'shortened the *Magnus liber*' with the 'abbreviation' or mini clausulae, as preserved in the third and fourth liturgical cycles of clausulae in fascicle 5 of **F**. Second, he 'made many better clausulae' – that is, the more usual type of clausula: self-contained and intricately structured discant settings of a melismatic plainchant tenor, comparatively extended in length and often stylistically adventurous. Such pieces are exemplified by the collections of clausulae in **W1** (the fifth and sixth fascicles of the manuscript) and in the first, second, and supplementary cycles in fascicle 5 of **F**.

[6] The text and translation are adapted (emphasis mine) from Edward H. Roesner, 'Who "Made" the *Magnus liber*?', *Early Music History*, 20 (2001), 227–66 (pp. 227–8).

[7] Waite, 'The Abbreviation of the "Magnus liber"', p. 150.

Waite's very neat explanation for the mini clausulae remains accepted in current scholarship, and his seemingly perfect fit between theoretical evidence and the surviving repertoire may have discouraged further engagement with these curious pieces in **F**.[8] Yet Edward H. Roesner's more recent interpretation of Anonymous IV's famous statement suggests that the authority of this theorist in describing the mini clausulae as 'abbreviations' should be invoked with caution, if at all. Translating *abbreviare* in the more neutral sense simply of 'producing a redaction', Roesner cites an independent instance later in the treatise in which the theorist uses the term in a context that cannot imply shortening.[9]

This chapter seeks to challenge Waite's hypothesis that the mini clausulae are Pérotin's abbreviations of an older *Magnus liber*.[10] Building on and substantiating hitherto neglected intimations by Rudolf Flotzinger, it opens up new questions about the mini clausula collection, which lead to new hypotheses for its function, broader performance contexts, and compilation.[11] Close engagement with the mini clausulae reveals several curious features of this unique and neglected collection. I propose that these small pieces are excerpts from complete Office and Mass cycles of two-voice organa that differ – in their liturgical ordering and in the particular versions of their plainchant tenors – from the extant *organum duplum* cycles of the so-called *Magnus liber*. As possible evidence of otherwise lost organum cycles that are noticeably simpler and more functional than those preserved within the *Magnus liber* repertoire, the mini clausulae offer an alternative perspective on the monumental *Magnus liber organi* and its position in relation to wider liturgical polyphonic practices in Paris and beyond.

[8] Both Smith and Planchart accepted Waite's abbreviation hypothesis. See Smith, 'Tenor Repetition', p. 334; and Planchart, 'The Flower's Children', p. 310.

[9] Roesner, 'Who "Made" the *Magnus liber*?', p. 229 n. 2. Mark Everist remarks that '"abbreviavit" could have meant anything from "shortened", to "edited", or even just "written down"'. See his 'The Thirteenth Century', in Mark Everist (ed.), *The Cambridge Companion to Medieval Music* (Cambridge, 2011), pp. 67–86 (p. 72).

[10] See also Ernest H. Sanders's discussion of the mini clausulae in 'The Medieval Motet', in Wulf Arlt, Ernst Lichtenhahn, and Hans Oesch (eds.), *Gattungen der Musik in Einzeldarstellungen: Gedenkschrift Leo Schrade* (Bern, 1973), pp. 497–573 (pp. 501–4). Sanders continues to associate the mini clausulae directly with Pérotin and, although he accepts that the abbreviation theory is convincing in many cases, he also notes (p. 501) that several of the mini clausulae are replacements for passages already in discant and are almost double these passages in length. He views these mini clausulae replacements not as abbreviations, but as modernisations, initiating the birth of the genre of the independent clausula.

[11] Rudolf Flotzinger, *Der Discantussatz im 'Magnus liber' und seiner Nachfolge*, WMB 8 (Vienna, 1969), pp. 58–63.

Abbreviation Clausulae?

Waite's functional conception of the mini clausulae as abbreviatory did not depend exclusively on their unusual brevity or on the evidence of Anonymous IV, later problematised by Roesner. The abbreviation theory accounted also for what Waite deemed, with some cause, the 'most striking feature' of this repertoire: the use of syllabic rather than melismatic plainchant tenors that are not typically associated with the note-against-note discant style, but that instead usually receive extended *organum purum* settings in the *Magnus liber.*[12] Waite demonstrated an instance in which discant mini clausulae could be substituted for the syllabic portions of a plainchant, replacing what were once more lengthy *organum purum* passages, and thereby greatly curtailing the overall duration of a two-voice organum as a whole.[13] In their selection of syllabic tenors usually treated in *organum purum*, as well as in their brevity, the mini clausulae stand apart from other independent clausulae, whose tenors are largely confined to the melismatic portions of plainchant traditionally set in discant in the *Magnus liber*.

Waite's assertion that 'almost all' of the mini clausulae in **F** 'are settings of passages that in the original *Magnus liber* were written in organum style with a melismatic duplum over sustained tenor notes' is, however, more problematic.[14] This view has been reiterated in subsequent scholarship on the mini clausulae. Norman E. Smith states that they 'originated solely for the purpose of replacing corresponding organum purum sections', while Planchart likewise observes that the 'short sections of discant ... correspond not to sections of discant in the organa but to sections of organum purum'.[15] In fact, as many as 12 of the 54 mini clausulae for the Office, and 38 of the 100 mini clausulae for the Mass, employ tenor melismas that also receive discant settings within corresponding organa in **F**.[16] Almost one-third of the

[12] Waite, 'The Abbreviation of the "Magnus liber"', p. 151.

[13] Ibid., pp. 152–7. See also the example in Baltzer, *Les clausules à deux voix*, p. xl n. 4. Significantly, several mini clausulae provide discant settings of precisely the moments typically characterised by an extended *organum purum* flourish in organa: the very beginning of responsory verses, Gradual responds, or Alleluia verses. See, for example, nos. 304, on CORNELIUS (fol. 178v–IV, 2); 345, on DIES SANCTIFICATUS (fol. 180r–II, 1); and 361, on OMNES (fol. 180v–V, 1), respectively. I thank Rebecca A. Baltzer for drawing this to my attention.

[14] Waite, 'The Abbreviation of the "Magnus liber"', pp. 151–2.

[15] Smith, 'Tenor Repetition', p. 334; and Planchart, 'The Flower's Children', p. 310.

[16] I compiled this statistic with reference to the editorial commentary in Baltzer, *Les clausules à deux voix*, pp. 367–89. Without any numerical evidence, Flotzinger previously suggested that the phenomenon of non-discant tenors in the mini clausulae had been overstated; *Der Discantussatz*, p. 62.

mini clausulae, then, offer alternative discant, rather than *organum purum*, sections. Although this still constitutes a minority, it represents a far more significant proportion of the repertoire than is typically acknowledged. That these 50 mini clausulae are on established discant tenors further undermines Waite's neat alignment of this repertoire with the testimony of Anonymous IV. The mini clausulae employing tenor melismas conventionally set in discant could, in many cases, be declared 'abbreviations' of their corresponding passages of discant as found within organa in **W1**, **F**, and **W2**, but they cannot be read as straightforward evidence of 'new' discant created by Pérotin to replace sections of Léonin's 'older' *organum purum*.

Chronology, Characteristics, and Concordances

The relative age of the mini clausulae, in the context of **F** and in the wider repertoire of organa and clausulae, has preoccupied scholars. Yet the issue is greatly complicated by the fact that written manuscript sources and even individual pieces appear frequently to combine sections of music from different chronological layers. On the one hand, following Anonymous IV, the mini clausulae are apparently 'new' discant abbreviations of 'old' *organum purum* sections. On the other, their brevity is concomitant with a musical simplicity: they appear old-fashioned when compared with other outwardly more advanced clausulae and discant. In the two-voice organa of the *Magnus liber* as it currently survives, it looks as if much of what might once have been Léonin's 'old' *organum purum* stands already replaced by even 'newer' discant than the mini clausulae. Rebecca A. Baltzer observed that the arrangement of mini clausulae in separated series for the Office and Mass reflects a probably early mode of manuscript organisation, superseded by the amalgamated clausula cycles found elsewhere in **F** and in **W1**.[17] Certain compositional practices widely regarded as chronologically later and stylistically more 'advanced' are also notably absent. Advanced examples of the discant style often state their borrowed chant melismas more than once, and this melodic tenor repetition coexists with a regularly repeating rhythmic pattern. Multi-statement and rhythmically patterned tenors are also a hallmark of later-thirteenth-century motets, and they

[17] Baltzer, *Les clausules à deux voix*, p. xliv. Mass and Office chants are also separated in the *organa dupla* of the *Magnus liber* and in the second clausula series in **F** (for the Mass only), but the two are combined in a single cycle in the stylistically 'younger' *organa tripla*, the first and supplementary clausula series in **F**, and the two clausulae collections in **W1**.

characterise the majority of discant passages and clausulae with musical concordances in the motet repertoire. As Smith and Baltzer have helpfully emphasised, not one of the mini clausulae features a repetition of its tenor chant melody, and their single-statement tenors almost invariably proceed in irregular successions of long notes.[18] Furthermore, none of the mini clausulae shares its music with a motet.[19]

These striking organisational and musical features have led scholars to assume that the mini clausulae are earlier than most other extant examples in the clausula genre.[20] Yet mini clausulae could simply operate under different compositional and aesthetic norms, possibly eschewing more modern techniques for the cultivation of simplicity and brevity. The circumstances of their conception and intended function might have made the continued use or revival of an older musical idiom more appropriate than that of the latest experiments in discant composition. In any case, purely chronological factors cannot explain the complex relationship between the mini clausulae and the extant *Magnus liber* repertoire for which I argue below: while in some respects the mini clausulae have clear musical ties to other clausulae and to *organa dupla* in particular, in others they show signs of being an independent repertoire.

In the context of the extant clausula repertoire, the selection of mini clausula tenors stands out as anomalous. The majority of mini clausula tenors do not usually receive discant settings at all. But even those mini clausula tenors that *are* also treated in discant in extant organa do not typically appear in the independent clausula repertoire. The mini clausulae feature almost none of the conventional and recognisable extended chant melismas that were popular clausula tenors. This absence is both consistent and striking: tenors such as TANQUAM (O 2), DOMINUS (M 1), ET CONFITEBOR (M 12), CAPTIVITATEM (M 23), VIRGO (M 32), and REGNAT (M 34) – all of which receive seven or more independent clausula settings in **F** – do not appear among the mini clausulae, which provide

[18] Smith, 'Tenor Repetition', p. 334; and Baltzer, *Les clausules a deux voix*, p. xliv. Baltzer suggests that clausula tenors in 'ternary long simplices' represent a layer of composition that is pre-1200 (p. xlii).

[19] This was first emphasised by Friedrich Ludwig in his *Repertorium organorum recentioris et motetorum vetustissimi stili*, ed. Luther A. Dittmer, 2 vols. in 3 (New York, 1964–78 [1910]), Vol. I/1, p. 94.

[20] Only Flotzinger proposed that the mini clausulae might be later than other *organa dupla* in **F**, on the grounds that certain pieces borrow and elaborate older discant passages. See his *Der Discantussatz*, pp. 62, 113. This evidence alone is problematic, since there are many other instances (including the M 27 clausulae discussed below) when the mini clausulae are less elaborate than their discant counterparts.

instead (and uniquely) for other sections of these host plainchants.[21] And whereas the first clausula series in fascicle 5 of **F** records a group of eleven different clausulae on DOMINUS (M 1) and a cluster of thirteen on REGNAT (M 34), the mini clausula cycles never contain multiple alternative settings of a single chant melisma.[22] These differences are borne out by a remarkable lack of concordances between the mini clausulae and their counterparts elsewhere in the fifth fascicle of **F** and in the fifth and sixth fascicles of **W1**. There are only five clear correspondences between the mini clausulae and other clausulae in **F**, and none at all with clausulae in **W1**.[23]

In fact, nearly 80 per cent of the mini clausulae have no concordances whatsoever outside this corpus.[24] Where concordances exist they are often partial and they are principally with sections of *organa dupla* (most often as extant in **F**). Indeed, the mini clausulae more often resemble excerpts from complete organum settings than other independent clausulae. The multiple extended clausula reworkings of elaborate melismas such as DOMINUS and REGNAT seem to take on existences independent of any host plainchant or organum, as self-contained and musically coherent in their own right. Mini clausulae, by contrast, usually employ much shorter tenors, may begin and end tonally *in medias res*, and frequently lack any clear or autonomous phrase structure.[25] Some are not confined exclusively to the

[21] Only the M 23 mini clausula *Captivam du[xit]* (no. 387, **F**, fol. 181v–IV, 1) shares part of its tenor (and also its duplum) with another independent clausula, *Captivam* (no. 128, **F**, fol. 161v–3). Mini clausulae employ conventional clausulae tenors for just two plainchant melodies: M 16 and M 37, discussed below.

[22] A single exception is the ET FILIO section of the O 25 chant, and this seems to be erroneous. This portion of the chant is included in the *[Glori]a patri et filio* clausula (no. 324, **F**, fol. 179v–I, 2). Only the ET FILIO portion of this tenor is treated to a new polyphonic setting as no. 329 (**F**, fol. 179v–III, 2), incorrectly placed after the O 26 mini clausulae

[23] These are mini clausulae nos. 289, 308, 361, 389, and 434. See the lists of concordances in Flotzinger, *Der Discantussatz*, pp. 51–4. Baltzer also notes full and partial concordances for each mini clausula in the editorial commentary of *Les clausules à deux voix*, pp. 367–89.

[24] There are many partial concordances within the mini clausulae themselves, particularly within the Mass cycle. Occasionally the same music reappears with a different text: in the case of M 56 and M 30 – Graduals that share the same chant melodies – clausula no. 393a on CELI for M 56 (**F**, fol. 182r–I, 1) is almost identical to that for no. 396 on NATI for M 30 (**F**, fol. 182r–II, 1). The two clausulae dupla have the same basic melodic outline and cadence pattern, but there are two differences in pitch that subtly impact the duplum's local melodic character. This suggests that the clausulae were probably independent realisations of the same, recognised formula.

[25] Baltzer observes that several mini clausulae do not open with the expected perfect consonance between upper voice and tenor (no. 378 on CLAVOS, for instance, starts on the weaker interval of a third). See Baltzer, *Les clausules à deux voix*, p. 380.

discant style, including several internal linking and cadential passages of *organum purum*.[26]

Mini Clausulae in Context: The Pentecost Alleluia *Veni sancte spiritus* (M 27)

The three mini clausulae on plainchant tenors drawn from the Pentecost Alleluia *Veni sancte spiritus* (M 27) usefully illuminate continuities and discontinuities between this repertoire and organa and clausulae elsewhere in **F**. These mini clausulae are typical in their unconventional, somewhat inexplicable, tenor selections. And although they are mainly in discant style, they nonetheless give the impression of excerpts from longer organa, rather than genuine self-contained clausulae. Example 2.1 shows the version of the Alleluia chant employed as the tenor of the two-voice organum in **F** (fol. 119r–v).[27] This Alleluia – 'Come Holy Spirit, fill the hearts of thy faithful, and kindle in them the fire of thy love' – is for use during Pentecost week.[28] The M 27 tenor contains one particularly striking melisma, on the word 'amoris'. Extended in length, AMORIS also features an internal repetition (marked by brackets in Example 2.1). Unsurprisingly, it is this AMORIS melisma that constitutes the longest discant passage in the chant's two-voice organum setting.[29] This is the single prolonged moment of discant in the organum as a whole, and AMORIS is the only portion of the Pentecost Alleluia to feature prominently in independent clausula collections and as a motet tenor.[30]

The parts of the Pentecost Alleluia set in polyphony in the mini clausulae are marked by boxes in Example 2.1. The tenors of these three clausulae encompass a substantial portion of the chant melody but the

[26] For example, nos. 345, 347, 360, or 389. This feature is not, however, unique to the mini clausulae: several pieces in the first clausula series of **F** also include passages in the organal style (no. 114, for instance).

[27] An identical version of the opening of this organum is also recorded in **W1**, fol. 35v. Owing to a lacuna in the manuscript, the **W1** copy breaks off after 'tuo-'.

[28] As is conventional, the **F** organum sets only the solo sections of the melody in polyphony, omitting the choral continuation of the opening Alleluia and the conclusion of the verse ('ignem accende').

[29] In the **F** organum, the tenor melisma on '-MO-' is stated twice, lengthening the discant passage further still. This **F** discant is transmitted as an independent clausula in **W1**, fol. 58r–4, and has a motet concordance (*A cele ou j'ai/AMORIS*, Mt368).

[30] The AMORIS melisma received three independent clausulae settings in **F**, fascicle 5 (two in the first series – nos. 140 and 141 – and one in the second – no. 252), and it featured as a tenor for four different motets (Mt360–8).

Example 2.1 Alleluia *Veni sancte spiritus*, M 27 organum tenor, **F**, fol. 119r–v.

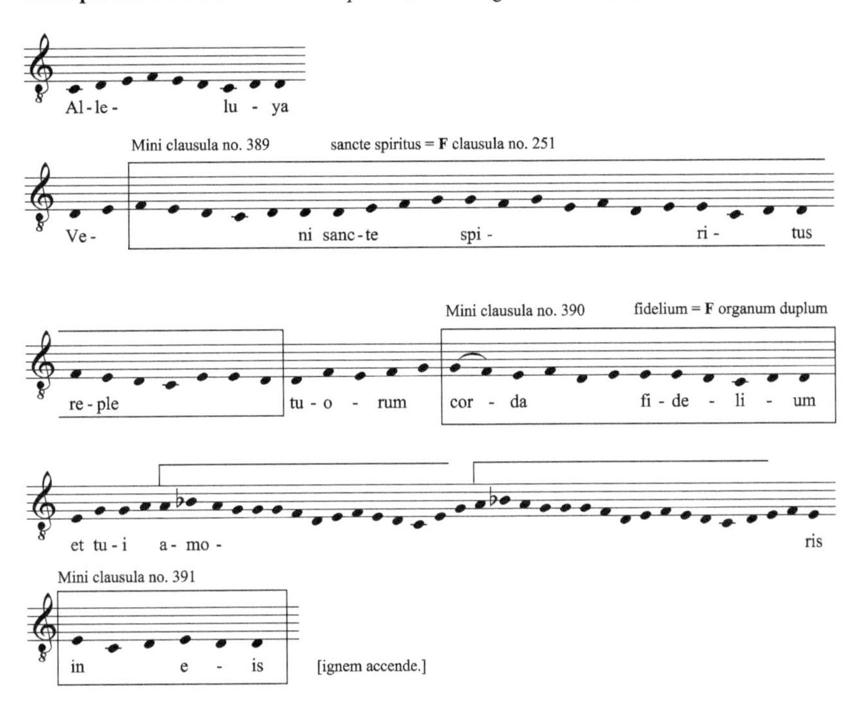

precise sections that they chose to cover are perplexing. Why does the first clausula start in the middle of the VENI melisma, rather than at the beginning, concluding not at the cadence on SPIRITUS, but continuing to REPLE?[31] Why is the short melisma on TUORUM omitted? And why do the second and third clausulae surround, but ultimately avoid, the conventional AMORIS tenor, which would be more appropriate for a discant setting?

This particular group of M 27 mini clausulae exhibits an unusually high level of external concordances with other conventional clausulae and organa in **F**. The first mini clausula (*Veni sancte spiritus reple*, no. 389; see Example 2.2) is one of only five to share a substantial part of its material (on SANCTE SPIRITUS) with an independent clausula. The conclusion of the second (*Corda fidelium*, no. 390; see Example 2.3) is almost identical to the relevant portion of the *organum duplum* in **F**. While the third

[31] A plausible answer only for the omission of the chant's first two notes on VENI is forthcoming: the very opening of a Gradual melody was often treated to an extended *organum purum* flourish, which would not be so suitable for inclusion among the mini clausulae. Yet elsewhere, the mini clausulae do provide discant settings for precisely these opening moments at which an *organum purum* flourish was usual; see n. 13 above.

Example 2.2 *Veni sancte spiritus reple* mini clausula (M 27), **F**, no. 389, fol. 181v–IV, 3.

VE - NI

Sancte Spiritus = F Clausula 251

Clausula 251 Duplum

SAN-CTE SPI - RI - TUS

RE - PLE

(*In eis*, no. 391; see Example 2.4) bears a more distant resemblance to the corresponding part of the **F** organum.

The first M 27 mini clausula, *Veni sancte spiritus reple*, is in fact longer than its exceptional clausula concordance (*Sancte spiritus*, **F**, no. 251, fol. 175r–3) extant outside this collection. The mini clausula surrounds the SANCTE SPIRITUS material with additional polyphony for VENI and REPLE (see Example 2.2), resembling an excerpt from a complete two-voice organum, comprising individual sections in different styles, rather than an individual discant clausula per se. Not only is the internal SANCTE SPIRITUS discant marked out by an acceleration of the tenor rhythm, but it is preceded and concluded by brief cadences in the *organum purum* style (marked by boxes in Example 2.2) that link together the three distinct units of the text and music (each corresponding to a system in Example 2.2).

The impression of an excerpt from a two-voice organum prevails in the following mini clausula on CORDA FIDELIUM (see Example 2.3).[32]

[32] In the mini clausula, a clef change has obviously been omitted in the duplum, since the duplum on FIDELIUM and of the following mini clausula on IN EIS are copied a third too high throughout. This is corrected in Examples 2.3 and 2.4.

Example 2.3 *Corda fidelium* mini clausula (M 27), **F**, no. 390, fol. 181v–V, 1.

Example 2.4 *In eis* mini clausula (M 27), **F**, no. 391, fol. 181v–VI, 1.

A unique setting of the chant on CORDA leads – after an organal-style close – into the passage of discant on FIDELIUM that is recorded also in the **F** organum (shown above the stave in Example 2.3). These two settings of FIDELIUM are almost identical, although the **F** organum has a more elaborate version of the cadential approach sung above the sustained tenor D. A connection between mini clausulae and the two-voice organum in **F** is apparent also in the final M 27 clausula on IN EIS (see Example 2.4), which shares its opening motive and (again slightly shorter) final cadence with the complete organum setting in the same source. Such common material between mini clausulae and two-voice organa is relatively characteristic: mini clausulae frequently deal in the same musical formulae, some constituting merely an established cadential figure or joining together several standard melodic gestures.[33]

Despite concrete concordances and traces of a shared melodic language, the mini clausulae for this Pentecost Alleluia do not align exactly with the wider clausula or organum treatments of this chant. The *Sancte spiritus* clausula is couched within a longer mini clausula setting in which the VENI and REPLE sections are unique. This first mini clausula could be declared an 'abbreviation' of the corresponding part of the two-voice organum in **F**, which – including the passage on SANCTE SPIRITUS – is in a much more extended *organum purum* style. While the same explanation could serve for the second mini clausula (whose setting of CORDA is noticeably shorter than that in the **F** organum), the third seems simply alternative rather than abbreviatory. And abbreviation cannot account for the different approach to the Alleluia chant; the way in which it is divided up in the mini clausulae; and the omission of the most popular discant tenor, AMORIS.

In the context of the collection, the mini clausulae for M 27 are exceptionally comprehensive in their coverage of the chant as a whole.[34] But if complete coverage was an aim, then why exclude the first two notes of the VENI melisma – which would surely complicate the process of substituting this clausula within an organum – and why not include a setting for the five notes of TUORUM, which would have made the first two mini clausulae continuous? These omissions cannot be put down to economy, since the scribe was content to copy the same basic cadence – over the sustained tenor D, marked by boxes in Examples 2.2–2.4 – four times across three mini clausulae for M 27.

In their use of such partial and atypical plainchant tenors and in combination with their musical characteristics, the majority of mini clausulae simply cannot stand alone as coherent pieces. They seem suitable for performance only as part of, or substituted within, a larger and implied organum context. Scholars have tended to assume that this context must be the *organa dupla* of the *Magnus liber* as recorded in **W1**, **F**, and **W2** – understandably so in the light of occasional concordances and stylistic similarities, and since no plausible alternative repertoire is extant. Yet even in the case of these M 27 mini clausulae, whose connections with surviving organa and clausulae are unusually pronounced, their tenor selection criteria and their genesis

[33] See, for instance, Baltzer's remarks in her commentary for, respectively, nos. 329 and 331; *Les clausules à deux voix*, p. 373.

[34] For M 26, a Pentecost Alleluia of similar length, there is just one mini clausula (no. 388, **F**, fol. 181v–IV, 2), providing only for the '-RA-' of PARACLITUS.

cannot be accounted for according to conventions of the *Magnus liber* as it now survives. Flotzinger previously suggested that the mini clausulae must have stemmed from and been used within a different repertoire from that represented elsewhere in **F**, but this convincing proposition has not yet been thoroughly investigated.[35] It remains overshadowed by Waite's more widely cited article on the mini clausulae as Anonymous IV's 'abbreviations', which situates them firmly *within* the *Magnus liber* repertoire itself. The following analyses aim to demonstrate pronounced incompatibilities between mini clausulae and the *Magnus liber* repertoire, in an attempt to highlight and explain their musical characteristics, and to imagine more precisely a lost wider musical tradition from which they might stem.

Mini Clausulae versus the *Magnus liber*: The Office Responsories *Non conturbetur* (O 10) and *Dum complerentur* (O 11)

The Office responsories *Non conturbetur* (O 10) and *Dum complerentur* (O 11), for use at first Vespers on the respective feasts of the Ascension and Pentescost, are closely related chant melodies. They receive polyphonic *organum duplum* settings copied side by side in **W1**, **F**, and **W2**,[36] and incomplete copies of *Dum complerentur* are additionally preserved in the Polish fragments **StS1** and – as a three-voice organum – in the Basel fragment, **Basel**.[37] Despite the fact that organum settings for both chants appear in all three of the principal *Magnus liber* sources, no independent clausulae for either O 10 or O 11 survive outside the mini clausula series.[38] Within the mini clausulae, both chants are relatively well represented, with short settings of two melismas from O 10 – from the verse (PARACLITUM, no. 292) and the *Gloria patri* doxology (ET FILIO, no. 293) – and of four portions of O 11: part of the respond ([COMPLEREN]TUR, no. 295) and

[35] See Flotzinger, *Der Discantussatz*, p. 59.

[36] **W1**, fols. 19r and 19r–v; **F**, fols. 71v–72r and 72r–v; **W2**, fols. 49v–50v and 50v–51r.

[37] On **StS1**, see Katarzyna Grochowska, 'Tenor Circles and Motet Cycles: A Study of the Stary Sącz Manuscript [PL-SS MUZ 9] and Its Implications for Modes of Repertory Organization in Thirteenth-Century Polyphonic Collections', Ph.D. diss. (University of Chicago, 2013), esp. pp. 68–9, 457. On **Basel**, see Wulf Arlt and Max Hass, 'Pariser Modale Mehrstimmigkeit in einem Fragment der Basler Universitätsbibliothek', *Formum musicologicum*, 1 (1975), 223–72, esp. pp. 266–8.

[38] This is typical for Office chants in the *Magnus liber*, in sharp contrast to those for the Mass. Of the forty different Office chants set in organa in **F**, only six have independent or 'substitute' clausulae outside the mini clausulae series.

of the verse (SPIRITU SANCTO, no. 296), and two sections of the *Gloria* (ET FILIO and SANCTO, nos. 297–8).

Although *organa dupla* settings of the O 10 and O 11 chants invariably appear as a pair, they are separated in the mini clausula cycle by another Ascension responsory, O 32 (*Omnis pulcritudio. A summo celo*).[39] Ludwig's numbering system for Office and Mass chants strictly follows the ordering of the *organa dupla* as recorded in **F**, even when this arrangement deviates from the liturgical calendar. The mini clausulae proceed in the numerically disjunct sequence O 10, O 32, O 11, but this order is technically more correct, since O 32 belongs, along with O 11, to the Ascension liturgy. In the **F** *organa dupla*, by contrast, O 32 appears at the beginning of an appendix, which is placed at the end of the third fascicle, following the complete Office organa series and several *Benedicamus Domino* settings. This appendix consists of three *organum duplum* settings – all unique to **F** – of Office responsories unrepresented in the preceding cycle: for Ascension (O 32), Pentecost (O 33), and the Finding of St Stephen (3 August, O 34). O 34 does not feature among the chants represented in the mini clausulae, but O 33 does, and once again it is here integrated within the mini clausula series at the correct liturgical juncture: following the Pentecost responsory, O 11. This section of the mini clausula cycle is, therefore, both comprehensive – providing for Office chants for which no polyphonic settings are recorded in **W1** and **W2** – and more precise in its liturgical sequence than the *organum duplum* collection preserved earlier in **F**.

A liturgical 'correctness' in the order of the mini clausulae seems to be complemented by the version of the tenor plainchant melodies employed for both O 10 and O 11. As noted above, O 10 and O 11 are very closely related musically, yet different parts of these chants are transmitted at different pitch levels in the organum repertoire. In his detailed analysis of O 10 and O 11 organa, Roesner commented on these quasi transpositions,

[39] The verse text beginning *A summo celo* – employed in both the **F** organum and the mini clausula – is unconventional, since Parisian chant sources typically use the verse *Nisi ergo* for this responsory; see Craig Wright, *Music and Ceremony at Notre Dame of Paris, 500–1500* (Cambridge, 1989), p. 257 n. 73. As Wright observed, however, the mid-thirteenth-century Parisian breviary Bibliothèque nationale de France, lat. 15613 adds the text *A summo celo* underneath *Nisi ergo* as an alternative on fol. 278r, suggesting either confusion or change in liturgical practice surrounding this responsory during the thirteenth century. Significantly, this breviary stems from the same atelier as **F** and has several connections with this source. See Mark Everist, *Polyphonic Music in Thirteenth-Century France: Aspects of Sources and Distribution* (New York, 1989), pp. 84–5; and Barbara Haggh and Michel Huglo, '*Magnus liber – Maius munus*: Origine et destineé du manuscrit F', *Revue de musicologie*, 90 (2004), 193–230, esp. pp. 207 n. 66, 226 n. 123.

noting that, for O 10, all of the extant organa begin the verse of the responsory down a fifth on F, rather than on C, as is more common in monophonic sources.[40] This is also the case in the verse of O 11 as recorded in **F**, **W2**, and **Basel**. But the O 11 organum in **StS1** and, on this occasion, in **W1** gives the responsory verse 'at pitch', beginning, like the chant sources, on C rather than F. Notably, the tenors of mini clausulae for both O 10 and O 11 consistently employ the 'untransposed' version of the responsory verse. It is striking that these clausulae should match the more conventional form of the chant as recorded in Parisian antiphoners. Furthermore, this difference in pitch level (as well as in ordering) indicates that the mini clausulae in **F** were copied from an exemplar independent of that used for the *organa dupla*, and without particular attention to the possible insertion of these mini clausulae within the host organa as recorded earlier in the same source.

A further lack of connection between the Office organa and mini clausulae in **F** is evident in their treatment of the doxology for O 10 and O 11.[41] The organa in **W1**, as is typical, do not include a setting of the *Gloria patri* for either chant. In **W2**, the doxology for O 10 is literally copied out again at the end of O 11, and **F** – in accordance with standard practice in the *organa tripla* and *dupla* collections – implies this repetition, economically presenting the *Gloria* only after the first responsory. By contrast, the mini clausulae include sections of the *Gloria* for each individual chant, providing two slightly different elaborations of the same tenor melisma on ET FILIO for the Ascension and the Pentecost responsory respectively (see Examples 2.5 and 2.6). These mini clausulae were evidently intended for an organum cycle in which O 10 and O 11 were treated, at least in part, to independent polyphonic doxologies.[42] Such an organum cycle could not have been exactly that found in the surviving *Magnus liber* manuscripts.

The provision of one particular mini clausula for O 11 may confirm a heightened sensitivity to the individuality of the two very similar responsories in this collection. A key difference between the two chants has been highlighted by Roesner, who underlined their identical opening responds, except in the treatment of the final syllable '-tur' (see Example 2.7). The

[40] Roesner, 'Who "Made" the *Magnus liber*?', p. 246.

[41] On the conventions for provision of doxologies in **W1**, **F**, and **W2**, see ibid., p. 247 n. 33.

[42] These mini clausulae may also have doubled as settings for the corresponding portions of their responsory verses, which share the music of the doxology. On the relationship between verse and doxology for O 10 and O 11, see Norman E. Smith, 'The Clausulae of the Notre Dame School: A Repertorial Study', Ph.D. diss., 3 vols. (Yale University, 1964), Vol. I, pp. 184 and 186 respectively. More generally, the extent to which mini clausulae provide for doxologies is notable: all but two (O 1 and O 32) of the Office chants represented include part of the *Gloria patri*.

Example 2.5 *Et filio* mini clausula (O 10), **F**, no. 293, fol. 178r–VI, 2.

Example 2.6 *Et filio* mini clausula (O 11), **F**, no. 297, fol. 178v–I, 3.

O 10 chant, *Non conturbetur*, sets the last syllable of the respond to a single note. The respond is extended in O 11, where the setting of the 'Dum complerentur' text ends with a five-note melisma. Significantly, the first mini clausula for O 11 – no. 295, texted simply 'TUR' – offers a setting of precisely the four extra pitches, found in *Dum complerentur* but absent from *Non conturbetur* (see Examples 2.7 and 2.8).[43]

As a result, the text cue for the mini clausula is technically incorrect: in the chant, the syllable '-tur' falls on the previous pitch, G, common to both O 10 and O 11 chants – a pitch not included in the mini clausula. Presumably, the syllable was here knowingly misplaced, but included to cue the identity of this section of the chant.[44] In setting only part of the -TUR melisma, the mini clausula – of which Roesner was apparently unaware – provides exclusively for the most musically divergent moment in the two responsories. Roesner demonstrated that these chants share significant portions of their polyphonic settings in the *Magnus liber*. And such musical overlap explains a curious feature of the **W2** organum for O 11 (see the final system of Example 2.7), where the tenor of *Dum complerentur* does not accurately reproduce its chant melody. As Roesner proposed, this must result from the fact that the O 11 organum in **W2** is a reworking of the O 10 setting, and – in its dependence on the O 10 chant – incorrectly omits the final melisma on -TUR unique to O 11.[45] Access to the -TUR mini clausula

[43] Example 2.7 adapts Example 3 from Roesner, 'Who "Made" the *Magnus liber*?', p. 248.

[44] Baltzer observed that, probably for the purposes of identification, the mini clauslae frequently include text-syllables that they properly should not. See *Les clausules à deux voix*, p. xlvi.

[45] Roesner, 'Who "Made" the *Magnus liber*?', pp. 247–8.

Example 2.7 The opening respond of O 10 and O 11 in chant and polyphony.

Example 2.8 [*Compleren*]*tur* mini clausula (O 11), **F**, no. 295, fol. 178v–I, 1.

for O 11 would have solved precisely this problem, to which the scribe or creator of the **W2** organum was insensitive. The mini clausula economically treats exactly the extra portion of chant that would have enabled the O 10 Ascension organum to be more successfully and correctly refashioned as a polyphonic setting of the O 11 Pentecost responsory.[46]

The inclusion of this -TUR mini clausula for O 11 suggests both care and insight in the selection of mini clausula tenor segments, as well as practicality and efficiency. This is at odds with the more inexplicable (even

[46] A comparison of the **F** and **W1** *organum duplum* settings of this -TUR melisma is given in ibid., p. 251. The mini clausula on -TUR is shorter than the discant in **F** and seems to be a compressed version of the **W1** discant. This undermines Roesner's view that the -TUR passage in **W1** may have been a new 'on the spot' composition undertaken by a local Scottish scribe (pp. 251–2).

insensitive) division of a plainchant melody in the case of the mini clausulae for the Pentecost Alleluia (M 27) discussed above. Such economy contrasts also with the seeming extravagance of copying the same cadence four times in the M 27 clausulae and of providing alternative settings of the identical ET FILIO melisma for the O 10 and O 11 responsories. The musical nature of the -TUR clausula itself may further complicate an understanding of its function. Perhaps a useful reminder that this section of the O 11 responsory differs from the O 10 chant, the polyphonic setting is otherwise so straightforward that it seems hardly worth committing to written record. The brief cadential gesture is just the sort of stock formula that one imagines singers or scribes could have supplied from memory or elaborated, even created anew, without much difficulty. And the two alternative settings of the ET FILIO melisma provided for O 10 and O 11 seem similarly unnecessary, since they constitute alternative approaches to the same basic cadence. Once again, it is difficult to posit a consistent function or rationale for the provision of mini clausulae for O 10 and O 11, and the intention and motivation for the collection recorded in **F** remains mysterious. It is perhaps remarkable that a written record of certain of these clausulae was considered necessary or desirable, all the more so since they could not easily have been employed within the *organum duplum* repertoire preserved elsewhere in the same source.

Independence and Awareness: Liturgical Ordering and Provision in the Mini Clausulae vis-à-vis the *Magnus liber*

Questions of purpose and context for the mini clausulae in **F** are complicated further still by additional aspects of their ordering and chant selection. On the one hand, the liturgical order of the mini clausula cycles confirms the impression given by the O 10 and O 11 responsories: that the mini clausulae are independent of and incompatible with the *Magnus liber* organa. Yet on the other hand, the compiler of the mini clausula collections in **F** seems simultaneously to be aware of the *Magnus liber* organum cycles, apparently prioritising, in the record of mini clausulae, plainchants and sections of plainchants that are least well represented in the surviving *Magnus liber* sources at large.

In terms of independence from the *Magnus liber*, the Office series of mini clausulae (shown in Table 2.1) contains a significant divergence (marked in bold) from the sequence of organa preserved earlier in **F**, in addition to the integration of Ascension and Pentecost responsories O 32 and

Table 2.1 Office mini clausulae (**bold** indicates a different order from the *Magnus liber*)

Office chant no.	Feast	Mini clausula nos.	Sources of 2vv organa	Sources of 3vv organa
O 1	Christmas	289	**W1, F, W2**	**F, W2**
O 2	Christmas	290–1	**W1, F**	**W1, F, W2, LoA**
O 10	Ascension	292–3	**W1, F, W2**	—
O 32	**Ascension**	**294**	**F**	—
O 11	Pentecost	295–8	**W1, F, W2, StS1**	**Basel**
O 33	**Pentecost**	**299–300**	**F**	—
O 13	John the Baptist	301–3	**W1, F, W2, StS1**	—
O 14	Peter and Paul	304–7	**F, StS1**	—
O 16	Assumption BVM	308–10	**F, W2**	**W1, F**
O 19	Nativity BVM	311–15	**F**	**Basel**
O 24	All Saints	316–17	**W1, F, W2, Ber**	—
O 27	**Martin**	**318–20**	**F**	**W1, F, W2, Mo**
O 25	Nicolas	321–4, 329	**W1, F, W2**	**F**
O 26	Common of an Apostle	325–8	**F, W2**	—
O 28	Common of confessor not bishop	330–2	**W1, F, W2**	—
O 29	Common of a virgin	333–8	**W1, F, W2**	—
O 30	Holy Trinity	339–42	**F**	—

O 33 within the liturgical cycle noted above. This involves the treatment of a responsory for the feast of a confessor bishop (O 27), a melody that features prominently in thirteenth-century polyphonic sources. O 27 serves as the tenor of a two-voice organum setting in **F**, and a three-voice organum in **W1**, **F**, **W2**, and the later-thirteenth-century Montpellier codex.[47] In the cycle of two-voice Office organa in **F**, O 27 is placed near the end, alongside other 'common' chants, since the responsory could be sung on about a dozen different individual feasts with the name of the appropriate confessor bishop substituted as required.[48]

[47] O 27 appears in **Mo** also among the group of five three-voice organa at the end of the first fascicle. The organa are (in their manuscript order): O 40, M 38, O 27, M 51, O 41.

[48] O 27 was sometimes used more than once on the same feast (as the ninth responsory of Matins and as a Processional responsory). For a list of the principal feasts in the Parisian liturgical calander see Rebecca A. Baltzer, 'Performance Practice: The Notre Dame Calendar and the Earliest Liturgical Motets' (unpublished paper presented at Das Ereignis Notre Dame, Wolfenbüttel, 1985), available online at *Archivum de musica medii aevi*, www.univ-nancy2.fr/MOYENAGE/UREEF/MUSICOLOGIE/AdMMAe/AdMMAe_index.htm (accessed 22 February 2018), pp. 34–7. All dates and ranks for feasts given here are taken from this calendar.

Despite the responsory's inherent functional flexibility, all sources of O 27 organa open with the text *Sancte Germane*, naming the dedicatee of Paris's oldest medieval abbey, whose feast was celebrated at semi-duplex rank on 28 May.[49] This departs from the convention of contemporary liturgical books, where the plainchant responsory text is usually given instead as *Sancte Marcellus*, for the confessor bishop whose feast on 3 November and Translation on 26 July were both celebrated at the higher duplex rank.[50] It is striking that sources of polyphonic organa should refer so consistently to St Germain, of lesser importance in the Parisian calendar. Moreover, the mini clausulae do not follow this polyphonic convention: the responsory is here texted *Sancte Martine*, for use at the duplex-ranked feast of St Martin of Tours (11 November). The O 27 mini clausulae are located at the appropriate juncture for this feast – as part of the Sanctorale rather than in the later group of common chants – placed between O 24 (for All Saints on 1 November) and O 25 (for St Nicolas, 6 December).

These differences in the specific saint named in the O 27 responsory among chant books, organa, and mini clausulae naturally reflect the multivalent nature of the melody. Even though all of the polyphonic organa explicitly name St Germain, this would by no means have prevented their performance also on the feast of St Martin. And while not explicitly present in the Office cycle, Martin features in the Mass organa of the *Magnus liber* repertoire (and also in the mini clausula Mass cycle), with a two-voice setting of the *Alleluia. Hic Martinus* (M 44) recorded in **F** and **W2**. Nevertheless, the difference in treatment of the O 27 responsory between the mini clausulae and the *organum duplum* repertoire is significant, especially since it affects the ordering of the two collections. In the **F** *organa dupla*, O 24 and O 25 appear in succession, reflecting a musical kinship between the two chants, which (like O 10 and O 11) are almost identical. In the mini clausulae, the musically related O 24 and O 25 responsories are separated by the interpolation of O 27, just as the musical pairing of O 10 and O 11 is disrupted by the presence of O 32. The grouping together of related chant melodies in the **F** *organa dupla* is further facilitated by the inclusion of O 32 in an appendix, where it appears alongside two other responsories – O 33 and O 34 – that share its same basic melody. Attention to such musical relationships among the Office chants, sometimes at the expense of the liturgical sequence, was evidently a concern in the Office

[49] On the use of the O 27 chant for St Germain, see Wright, *Music and Ceremony*, pp. 256–7.
[50] See Baltzer, *Les clausules à deux voix*, p. 371, no. 318.

organa dupla of **F**, but not in the mini clausula cycle. As a result, the two repertoires do not align straightforwardly.

The Mass cycle of the mini clausulae likewise displays some discrepancies when compared with extant *organa dupla*. This series of mini clausulae is larger than that for the Office, reflecting the conventional emphasis on Mass chants as polyphonic tenors evident also in the *Magnus liber*. Perhaps because of its increased size, there are seven occasions (italicised in Table 2.2) when the sequence of the mini clausula cycle seems genuinely to err, with the appropriate chant usually inserted shortly after the correct juncture.[51] Yet, just as in the Office cycle, there are also two occasions in the mini clausula Mass series where a difference in ordering has a convincing and alternative liturgical rationale from that in the *Magnus liber* repertoire. The first concerns a Gradual for the Feast of the Holy Trinity, Ludwig's M 56. An organum setting of M 56 is found only in **F**, and occurs here at the very end of the Mass series of *organa dupla*, after the liturgy for the dedication of a church. In the mini clausulae, however, M 56 is integrated within the liturgical year, correctly following the M 27 Alleluia for Pentecost week.[52] The second divergence involves the M 37 Gradual whose mini clausulae are discussed in further detail below. In *organa dupla* cycles in **W1** and **F**, this *Propter veritatem* Gradual is included alongside other Assumption chants. But in the mini clausula collection, M 37 follows M 54, treated instead as part of the common of virgins, as it is also in most thirteenth-century monophonic sources.[53]

Like that for the Office, the cycle of mini clausulae for the Mass differs in its precise liturgical conception from any surviving sources of *organa dupla*. Once again, the mini clausulae do not provide for any wholly new chants that are not already furnished with polyphony in the *Magnus liber*, but the particular feasts represented in both mini clausula cycles do not align exactly with the provision of Office and Mass organa in **W1**, **F**, or **W2**. It appears that both cycles of mini clausulae stemmed from, or were for use within, a sizeable collection of two-voice organa, smaller than that recorded in **F** but bigger than that in either **W1** or **W2**. **F** preserves a significantly

[51] The exception is M 25, which occurs at some remove from other Pentecost chants, but irregularities are evident also at this earlier point in the cycle.

[52] By contrast, the Office mini clausulae for the vespers responsory for Holy Trinity (O 30) occur at the end of the cycle (as they do in the *Magnus liber*); see Table 2.1.

[53] The two-voice organum cycle in **W2** also includes the M 37 organum in the section of common chants, between M 51 and M 54. As Baltzer has noted, the mini clausula ordering is unconventional, since M 37 here follows – rather than precedes, as it should – M 54. See her *Les clausules à deux voix*, p. 388, no. 436.

Table 2.2 Mass mini clausulae (*italics* indicate clausulae out of liturgical order; **bold** indicates a different liturgical order from the *Magnus liber organi*)

Mass chant no.	Feast	Mini clausula nos.
M 1	Christmas	343–4
M 2	Christmas	345–6
M 3	Stephen	347
M 4	Stephen	348–51
M 5	John Evangelist	352
M 6	John Evangelist	353–6
M 7	Holy Innocents	357–9
M 8	Holy Innocents	360
M 9	Epiphany	361
M 10	Epiphany	362–3
M 11	Purification BVM	364–5
M 12	Purification BVM	366
M 16	Easter week	367–71
M 18	Easter week	372–4, 376
M 19	Easter week	375
M 20	Easter week	377
M 22	Finding of the Holy Cross	378–9
M 24	Ascension	380–82
M 21	*Easter week*	*383–4*
M 23	*Ascension*	*385–7*
M 26	Pentecost	388
M 27	Pentecost week	389–91
M 56	**Holy Trinity**	**392–393b**
M 28	John the Baptist	394–5
M 30	Peter and Paul	396
M 31	Peter and Paul	397
M 32	Assumption BVM	398
M 34	Assumption BVM	399–400
M 33	*Assumption BVM*	*401–2*
M 25	*Pentecost*	*403–5*
M 38	Nativity BVM	406–9
M 39	Michael	410
M 41	Denis/All Saints/Common of Several Martyrs	411–12
M 40	*Common of Several Martyrs*	*413*
M 42	Denis/All Saints/common of several martyrs	414–16
M 44	Martin	417–19
M 45	Andrew	420
M 48	Common of a confessor not bishop	421–2
M 49	Common of a martyr	423–6

(*continued*)

Table 2.2 (*continued*)

Mass chant no.	Feast	Mini clausula nos.
M 46	*Common of an Apostle*	*427–9*
M 53	Common of a confessor	430–1
M 52	*Common of a martyr*	*432–3*
M 54	Common of a virgin	434–5
M 37	**Common of a virgin**	**436–9**
M 58	Dedication of a church	440–2

larger repertoire of Office and Mass *organa dupla* than **W1** and **W2**, and a substantial number of the Office and Mass chants in Ludwig's numbered sequences have polyphonic settings extant only in **F**. The **F** *organa dupla* for the Office provide for thirty-four different chants, **W2** for fifteen, and **W1** for thirteen. In the mini clausula series, seventeen individual Office chants are represented, including five that feature in two-voice organa in **F** but not in **W1** or **W2**.[54] For the Mass, several breaks in the sequence of chant numbers likewise indicate the mini clausulae's less extensive range of chants than the *organa dupla* earlier in **F**. Yet, as for the Office, the mini clausula Mass cycle is more comprehensive than the Mass organa in either **W1** or **W2**, including polyphonic settings of twelve chants unrepresented in these manuscripts.[55]

Despite their ample coverage, there is a notable gap in each of the mini clausula cycles. In the Office series, this occurs early in the liturgical sequence. Two-voice organa on O 4 and O 5 – responsories for the Epiphany and the Purification of the Blessed Virgin Mary respectively – are found in all of the major *Magnus liber* sources, but are absent from the mini clausulae, in which chants for the Christmas Office are immediately followed by those for the Ascension.[56] More remarkable is the complete lack in the Mass cycle of any mini clausulae on chant tenors for Easter (M 13, M 14, or M 15).[57] Only Ludwig commented on this lacuna, attributing it to

[54] These five are: O 14, O 19, O 30, O 32, and O 33.

[55] These twelve are: M 6, M 7, M 16, M 18, M 19, M 20, M 21, M 24, M 25, M 28, M 52, and M 56. Except for four organa represented also in the **Silos** fragments (M 18, M 20, M 21, and M 24), eight of these twelve organa are found uniquely in **F** and the mini clausulae.

[56] The cycle of two-voice Office organa in **W1** includes only two further chants absent from the mini clausula series: O 35 and O 36 (unrepresented also in **F** and **W2**). **W2** contains *organa dupla* for three further chants – O 18, O 22, and O 31 – absent from the mini clausula series but present elsewhere in **F**.

[57] The absence of Easter tenors from the Office cycle in the mini clausulae is not unusual, and is found also in the *organa dupla* of **W1** and **W2**.

the large number of (extended) clausula settings on these highly melismatic Easter tenors evident earlier in the fifth fascicle of **F**.[58] That the importance of these Easter tenors, and the very wide availability of polyphonic elaborations of M 13 and M 14 in particular, secured their exclusion seems plausible. Notably, the mini clausulae include settings for five considerably less widespread plainchant tenors for Easter week (M 16 and M 18–21) for which *organum duplum* settings are absent from **W1** and **W2**.[59] Perhaps mini clausulae were judged unsuitably simple for a feast as high as Easter. Alternatively, any modest polyphonic settings of Easter Day chants could already have been supplanted within this repertoire by the more extensive organum settings found in the *Magnus liber* and recorded earlier in **F**.

Since the mini clausulae represent parts of a liturgical cycle of organa, one usually more comprehensive than that of the *organa dupla* in **W1** and **W2**, the initial exemplar from which the collection in **F** was derived must surely have contained at least some polyphony for Easter Masses. The current sense of the mini clausulae as unique and unusual could, therefore, be the artificial result of a deliberate attempt on the part of the **F** scribe or compilers to record that which was atypical or *not* to be found elsewhere in the manuscript, omitting those pieces that were. This would account for some notable variations in the extent of mini clausula provision for different chants. In addition to the cases noted above, there are further instances when plainchants with organa extant in **W1**, **F**, and **W2** have fewer mini clausulae than those chants for which organa survive uniquely in **F**. The popular Gradual for the feast of John the Evangelist (M 5), with complete organum settings in **W1**, **F**, and **W2**, is represented by a single mini clausula. By contrast, the Alleluia for the same feast (M 6), for which an organum survives only in **F**, is furnished with four mini clausulae. In the case of the feast of the Holy Innocents, it is the Alleluia (M 8) that is more commonly set in polyphony and that receives just one mini clausula, but the less prevalent Gradual (M 7) is provided with three.

A desire to avoid duplication, and to give precedence to uncommon polyphonic settings not already recorded elsewhere, would explain also the unexpected and almost complete absence of popular and extended clausulae and motet tenors in the mini clausulae, in favour of unusually apportioned plainchant melodies that did not typically circulate independently of host organa. On only ten occasions do mini clausulae share the same tenors as independent

[58] Ludwig, *Repertorium*, Vol. I/1, p. 93.

[59] Only the **Silos** organum fragments also preserve the Easter organa M 18, M 20, and M 21, but they lack a setting for M 19, found in both **F** and the mini clausula cycle.

clausulae elsewhere in **F**.[60] In just one of these instances (discussed below) is the tenor (FILIA) a popular one, and these mini clausulae are mostly either exact or related concordances of stylistically straightforward and short independent clausulae – an overlap that could reasonably have escaped the notice of the **F** scribe given the large number of pieces involved.[61]

Just two mini clausulae could be proposed as 'simpler' alternatives to other independent clausulae, offering notably shorter polyphony for an established clausula tenor. The mini clausula *Donec veni[am]* (M 5) – **F**, no. 352, fol 180v–I, 3 – stands in stark contrast to the single earlier clausula on the same chant segment, which features five repetitions of the tenor chant and a highly decorated sixth-mode duplum (unique to **F**, no. 50, fol. 152r–3). Yet the second 'simpler' mini clausula – *Dum loqueretur* (M 16), no. 371, fol. 181r–IV, 2 – presents a more intriguing case. The DUM LOQUERETUR tenor, with a twenty-eight-note internally patterned melisma on the '-re' of *loqueretur*, received three independent clausulae earlier in **F** (nos 107–9, on fol. 159r). Remarkably, the mini clausula setting cuts precisely the long melisma that had inspired three independent clausulae, preceding from its first note (and corresponding syllable '-re') straight to its concluding three pitches (the second of which accompanies the syllable '-tur'). Such an unorthodox and unique tenor treatment could be the tantalising trace of a functional performance practice in which longer plainchant melismas were significantly curtailed.[62] But in any case, only the *Donec veni[am]* mini clausula can be straightforwardly rationalised as a shorter clausula substitute, and it does not appear that the consistent provision of simple single-tenor statement clausulae *and* more complex extended clausula settings for each chant tenor was a priority across the fifth fascicle of **F** as a whole.[63]

[60] Three of these tenors are for the M 37 chant discussed below.

[61] As in the case of the tenors OMNES (M 9), CAPTIVAM (M 23), SANCTE SPIRITUS (M 27), ANGELI (M 33), and VENI (M 54).

[62] Alternatively, the scribe of **F** may have been responsible, either accidentally or deliberately, for the mini clausula's plainchant 'cut'. Baltzer (*Les clausules à deux voix*, p. 379) noted that the third independent clausula found earlier in **F** (no. 109, fol. 159r–4) is on -RETUR only, containing the portion of the chant missing from the mini clausula. Since it is stylistically compatible (with a single-statement tenor in unpatterned duplex longs, unlike the preceding two clausulae) she proposed that the -RETUR clausula should have been combined with the mini clausula. If this were the case, however, one might expect the mini clausula to terminate just before -RE-, or for the shared final tenor pitches of the two clausulae to be accompanied by identical (rather than only broadly similar) dupla.

[63] The clausula fascicle of **F** does not invariably preserve straightforward settings for the extended tenor melismas lacking in the mini clausulae cycles. **F** does not record independent clausulae featuring a single statement of the chant melisma in unpatterned ternary or duplex longs for the extended melismas LUX MAGNA (M 2), ET ILLUMINARE (M 9), [CAPTIVI]TA[TEM] (M 23), VIRGO (M 32), and ET SPERABIT (M 49).

Although the scribe of **F** seems to have compiled the mini clausulae with an eye to the surrounding contents of his manuscript, therefore, the different types of clausulae in the fifth fascicle were evidently not intended to be complementary, and they represent instead genuinely different approaches to their plainchant foundations.

Plainchant Tenor Variants and the Gradual *Propter veritatem* (M 37)

Such fundamental conceptual differences between mini clausulae and independent clausulae, evident also between mini clausulae and the surviving *organum duplum* repertoire, are especially pronounced in the case of the M 37 Gradual *Propter veritatem*, the subject of the previous chapter. As noted above, the liturgical placement of this chant in the mini clausulae is not under the feast of the Assumption, where it is located in the *organa dupla* of **W1**, and **F**, and in certain chant books associated with Notre Dame Cathedral. M 37 appears instead among the common of virgins, as it does in the majority of thirteenth-century liturgical books (and, exceptionally, in the **W2** two-voice organum cycle). In addition, the initial three of the four mini clausulae for M 37 – on VERITATEM, FILIA, ET INLCINA AUREM TUAM, and CONCUPIVIT REX (nos. 436–9) – employ particular versions of their plainchant tenors that more closely resemble the typical thirteenth-century monophonic transmission of these chants than do the tenors of organa in the *Magnus liber*.

Unlike the M 37 organa in **W1**, **F**, and **W2**, the VERITATEM mini clausula (Example 1.4 in the previous chapter) employs a shorter version of this melisma that more faithfully reproduces the chant as conventionally transmitted in thirteenth-century monophonic sources (see Example 1.3). This shorter melisma is found in only one other thirteenth-century polyphonic source, a later and unique three-voice organum in the Spanish manuscript **Hu**. Similarly, the AUREM TUAM portion of the second M 37 mini clausula on ET INCLINA AUREM TUAM is shorter than the version found elsewhere in the *Magnus liber* (see Example 1.5), and relates more closely to the wider monophonic transmission of this melisma and the form in which it later appears as a motet tenor. The initial ET INCLINA portion of this mini clausula corresponds also with a composition outside the 'central' *Magnus liber* tradition, sharing its discant setting with a younger local Scottish organum composition in **W1**.[64] The third mini clausula, on the tenor FILIA, employs

[64] See Smith's comments on this concordance in 'Tenor Repetition', p. 333.

one of the two versions of this melisma circulating in *Magnus liber* organa, which matches that typically recorded in chant sources of the melody. And the final M 37 mini clausula on CONCUPIVIT REX once again resembles the discant of the Scottish organum in **W1** more closely than any of the *Magnus liber* settings.[65] All four of the M 37 mini clausulae, therefore, seem to stand outside the liturgical and musical conventions associated with the treatment of this chant in the organa of the *Magnus liber*, demonstrating a closer relationship with established monophonic traditions as well as 'peripheral' and 'later' polyphonic settings.

In addition to their pronounced independence from organa in **W1**, **F**, and **W2**, the mini clausulae for M 37 usefully challenge the pervading assumption that mini clausulae are always 'substitutes' for *organum purum* sections. Exceptionally, all four mini clausulae for this chant feature melismas conventionally treated in discant in the *Magnus liber*. Number 437, on FILIA, is unprecedented in its use of a tenor that features in extended clausula collections in **W1** as well as **F**, appearing also in the motet repertory. Perhaps owing to its uncharacteristically extended chant melisma, the FILIA setting is one of a total of only three mini clausulae that group their tenor pitches into a regular pattern (here of four notes).[66] Similarly, the AUREM TUAM section of the following M 37 mini clausula is atypically 'advanced', constituting one of only three mini clausulae to employ a tenor in the fifth rhythmic mode.[67] It is possible that the unusual inclusion of such conventional discant tenors among the mini clausulae was motivated by the recognition that the details of their plainchant foundations differed from other polyphonic settings in **F**.

Stylistically more akin to other independent clausulae, the M 37 mini clausulae nonetheless offer strong evidence in favour of the conception of this repertoire within a liturgical and musical tradition that was not that of the *Magnus liber organi*. An emphasis on specific plainchant variants as identifiable with particular churches or religious orders in the thirteenth century is problematic: Craig Wright convincingly questioned Heinrich Husmann's efforts in this regard, undermining also any attempts to associate the tenor chants of the *Magnus liber* with a specific group of extant monophonic sources.[68] Yet Wright noted that 'there are, in fact, many variants in the tenors of the *Magnus liber organi* that are nowhere to be found in the manuscripts of Parisian chant'.[69] He suggested that certain

[65] See Baltzer, *Les clausules à deux voix*, p. 389, no. 439.

[66] See ibid., p. xliv.

[67] See ibid., p. xliv.

[68] Wright, *Music and Ceremony*, pp. 247–58.

[69] Ibid., p. 250. Wright's remarks were general and he listed just three isolated examples in n. 43.

'minor alterations' – of a much smaller magnitude than those evident in the *Propter veritatem* tenors, and often involving just a single pitch – were made 'for musical purposes' and become established in polyphonic transmission.[70] A natural flexibility and tendency to variation in both monophonic and polyphonic transmissions of chant melodies notwithstanding, there is scope for a larger comparative study that might establish consistent patterns in the versions of plainchant melodies recorded in the organa of the *Magnus liber*, the mini clausula repertoire, and monophonic sources.[71] It is significant that variants specific to and pervasive in the *Magnus liber* polyphony for *Propter veritatem* should be absent from the mini clausulae in **F**, and I have observed at least one further instance in which a mini clausula in **F** matches a chant melody as consistently transmitted in chant books, omitting an 'extra' pitch from the version of this chant tenor recorded in organa and motets.[72] This underlines the position of the mini clausula repertoire with respect to wider plainchant traditions in the thirteenth century, as seemingly closer to established monophonic practices than to the particular versions of and conventions for plainchant tenors observable within the organa of the *Magnus liber*.

Conclusions

Superficially, the mini clausulae of **F** appear functionally more straightforward than other examples of clausulae as a genre. There can be no doubt that these short snippets – often incomplete or incoherent – require a broader organum context in order to make musical sense. They must, therefore, accord with the 'substitute' function that offered the initial and perhaps still the most satisfactory explanation for the existence of clausulae. Thorny issues associated with other independent clausulae – such as the liturgical necessity for multiple different musical realisations of a single chant melisma and chronological relationships with motets – simply do not arise. Yet at an individual level, the substitution of mini clausulae

[70] Ibid, p. 250.

[71] Flotzinger lists twenty-six mini clausulae with 'variant' tenor melodies relative to extant *organa dupla*; Flotzinger, *Der Discantussatz*, p. 117 n. 48. How these variants relate to other polyphonic and monophonic sources merits further investigation.

[72] This is the plainchant melisma IUSTUS (M 49), **F** mini clausula no. 425, fol. 182v–VI, 1. See the comparison of monophonic and motet versions of this tenor in Mark Everist, *French Motets in the Thirteenth Century: Music, Poetry, and Genre* (Cambridge, 1994), pp. 94–5. Organum and motet tenors have an 'added' penultimate A absent from monophonic sources and the mini clausula tenor.

within the *organa dupla* recorded earlier in the same manuscript often proves difficult or even impossible, because of the use of unexpected tenor segments, with syllables of text unconventionally underlaid, and additionally employing different versions of chant melodies, sometimes at different transpositions.[73] Furthermore (and unlike the majority of other clausulae), their largely unique contents and liturgical and chronological relationship to the chief witnesses of the thirteenth-century organum repertoire that we now possess remain obscure. While there is much evidence to indicate that the mini clausulae stem from a polyphonic tradition that is not the same as that of the *Magnus liber organi*, no other traces of any such alternative tradition survive.

In addition, there are many apparently contradictory aspects of the mini clausula collection that demand explanation. Why do the mini clausula cycles offer, in general, a remarkably comprehensive coverage of different chants across the liturgical year, but fail to provide any polyphony for Easter Day Masses? And how can an at-once intimate familiarity with the details of plainchant tenors – the seeming awareness of their treatment and popularity in organa and clausulae in the *Magnus liber* repertoire, as well as the kind of sensitivity that encouraged the inclusion of the O 11 -TUR mini clausula – be reconciled with the somewhat insensitive selection of chant tenors in the mini clausulae for the M 27 Pentecost Alleluia?

A further paradox concerns the possible use and practicality of the repertoire. A short, economically presented, and comprehensive record of discant settings for a wide coverage of Office and Mass chants, sensitive to the potential for contrafaction (as in the case of the -TUR mini clausula), seems, on the face of it, a highly serviceable resource. Arguably, this functionality could explain the unique status of the repertoire as preserved in **F**, suggesting that small booklets of mini clausulae typically circulated separately, not as part of elaborate presentation codices, but as purely practical exemplars or performance manuscripts of a sort that were heavily used but not preserved for posterity. Yet, in fact, it is hard to imagine that a written document of this kind would have been of much help to a scribe, still less to a singer. In their tightly packed presentation in **F** – sometimes texted with only a single nondescript syllable or with an erroneous or missing initial – it is difficult to imagine that the collection of clausulae would be easily navigable, even with recourse to a corresponding written repertoire of *organa dupla* in exactly the same order and employing exactly the same chant

[73] On the potential difficulties of substituting mini clausulae, see Baltzer, *Les clausules à deux voix*, p. xlvi.

melodies. It is hard to see why many of the short and formulaic sections of discant, which often resemble each other or constitute conventional melodic gestures, could not instead have been supplied from memory or improvised rather than consulted in writing in a separate clausula collection.

All of these curious circumstances could be accounted for if the mini clausula collection as represented in **F** was the creation of this manuscript's single scribe, who was excerpting ad hoc from a complete organum cycle.[74] The scribe of **F** was intimately familiar with the contents of the *Magus liber*, recorded earlier in the same book, and would have been fully aware which chants and portions of chants were well represented there, and which were not. The scribe's expert knowledge would also justify the very intelligent plainchant treatment that apparently resulted in the -TUR mini clausula. At the same time, inevitable difficulties and complications in the process of excerpting from a large organum cycle would account for rather less explicable choice and division of plainchant melodies on other occasions, as well as for the inclusion of linking passages and cadences in the *organum purum* style interspersed with the predominantly discant idiom, and for the occasional duplication of material. This could also explain why the upper voices of mini clausulae whose tenors share the same chant melodies, but are texted for use on different feasts, can differ very slightly.[75] Had these short sections circulated independently as clausulae it is possible that such variants – presumably a response to the wider organum context in each particular case – would have been eliminated by the advent of a single standardised clausula version.

But why might the scribe of **F** undertake this task, especially given that the result does not seem wholly practical? The act of excerpting mini clausulae from organa was probably motivated by economy of space (accounting also to some degree for the omission of the unnecessary Easter Mass chants), since copying in its entirety a second complete collection of organa for Office and Mass would have taken up considerably more than seven folios. The mini clausulae may reflect a desire to preserve for posterity at least part – and perhaps especially the unique parts – of a different organum cycle from that recorded earlier in the manuscript. It is significant that these mini clausulae survive only in **F**, by far the most comprehensive of the *Magnus liber* manuscripts, and whose single scribe seems to have had

[74] Flotzinger suggested that occasional slips in the liturgical ordering of the mini clausulae cycles could be explained by a process of compilation from organa (rather than direct copying from an identical exemplar). See *Der Discantussatz*, p. 61.

[75] Such as nos. 393a and 396, discussed in n. 24 above.

a tendency towards the exhaustive, concerned to record as much music as possible. As demonstrated in Chapter 4, the scribe of **F** was no stranger to adjusting and reimagining his exemplars ad hoc: elsewhere in the clausula fascicle he apparently reworked motets as clausulae, translating them into modal notation as he copied, sometimes with limited success. To place excerpts from a different organum cycle at the end of the clausula fascicle was a sensible choice. Clausulae themselves are excerpts too, and the mini clausulae are chiefly in the fascicle's prevailing discant style.

Baltzer has underlined the practicality of the discant style over florid *organum purum*, suggesting that a simple note-aginst-note polyphonic idiom was preferred outside Paris.[76] Smith also noted the unusual preponderance of discant in the local Scottish organum setting of *Propter veritatem* in **W1**.[77] The mini clausula need not necessarily stem from a non-Parisian cycle of organa, but it seems likely that their host organa – wherever they came from – principally employed a functional and faster discant style. This style was punctuated by organal linking passages and cadences, but was chiefly lacking in the extended melismatic *organum purum* flourishes that accompanied many of their same tenor segments in the *Magnus liber*. Perhaps these were older and less developed organa that preceded those subsequently created for Notre Dame. Alternatively, they could have been a contemporary, even a newer, repertoire, created for and within a musical context where extended clausulae and motets were not part of compositional activity, but where there was a need for liturgical polyphony that was basically similar to that at the Parisian Cathedral, but notably shorter and less ambitious.

The mini clausulae, despite their very limited manuscript survival, may represent a significant trace of the kinds of functional polyphony that were presumably widely performed and in principally oral circulation in the thirteenth century, but for which little other written musical evidence is extant. Viewed from the new perspective of the mini clausulae, certain musical features of organa in the *Magnus liber* seem all the more outstanding. In comparison, one realises how polished, sophisticated, and heavily reworked the organa of the *Magnus liber* may be; how extravagant they are in terms of length, *organum purum* flourishes, internal tenor repetitions, and tenor manipulations in complex rhythmic patterns. Remarkable in the extended clausulae and motets of the *Magnus liber* is the intense compositional focus

[76] See Rebecca A. Baltzer, 'Review of Jutta Pumpe, *Die Motetten der Madrider Notre-Dame-Handschrift* (Tutzing, 1991)', *Notes*, 51 (1994), 579.

[77] See Smith, 'Tenor Repetition', p. 332.

on particular and carefully chosen chant segments – often Alleluia melismas with internally repetitive melodic structures – which, as shown in Chapter 3, are subjected to multiple different rearrangements and elaborations. In comparison to the mini clausulae, other musically and compositionally motivated aspects of the *Magnus liber organi* also come more clearly into focus: the potential for establishing the kinds of new and extended variants of plainchant quotations explored in the previous chapter, for instance, as well as the tendency among **F** Office organa to group related chant melodies together in contravention of a strict liturgical sequence. That the mini clausulae, on the other hand, use more conventional versions of chant melodies and enforce the ordering principles of the liturgical calendar more rigorously seems to be a mark of their more quotidian character, their greater functionality and practicality. In sum, therefore, the mini clausulae serve as a useful and challenging reminder that the *Magnus liber* organa that do survive may represent an almost ideal and monumental musical repertoire – one whose sounding reality could have been much more rarefied and limited than this long-overlooked collection of tiny and modest polyphonic excerpts, which is now unique and seemingly marginal.

3 Texting Clausulae: Repetition and Regularity on the REGNAT Tenor

Which Came First: Clausula or Motet?

The poet could not simply arrange words freely according to his instincts or his ear, rather they had to be painstakingly accommodated to a given melody ... As was first the case in Notker's sequences, so it was later in many motets. I have finally found a satisfactory solution to the puzzle that has long troubled me: the [poetic] form of motets.

Wilhelm Meyer, *Der Ursprung des Motets*, 1898.[1]

Dominating discussions of the origins of the thirteenth-century motet has been the question of its chronological relationship to another genre, the clausula. It was the philologist Wilhelm Meyer who in 1898 first noted that a significant proportion of motets – particularly those in the earliest surviving sources and with Latin texts – shared their musical material with melismatic clausulae. Meyer's explanation was that the motets had been created through the addition of syllabic texts to the pre-existent music of their related clausulae, a plausible hypothesis for several reasons. The idea that clausulae should 'come first' chronologically was compatible with their apparent heritage within the liturgical practice of organum that pre-dated any motet compositions. Furthermore, the compositional process Meyer proposed had an established pedigree. In the late ninth century, Notker of St Gallen explained that he had added texts ('proses') to the extended melismas ('sequences') of plainchant Alleluias, texts whose rhymes and syllables assisted in the memorisation of the long melismas.[2] Poetry fashioned for existing melodies in the so-called sequences and prosulae of

[1] 'Die Wörter sind ja nicht nach dem Gehör und Gefühl des Dichters frei gefügt, sondern sie müssen mühsam einer gegebenen Melodie angeschmiegt werden ... Was das einst bei den Sequenzen Notkers der Fall war, so später bei vielen Motetten. So habe ich endlich eine mich befriedigende Lösung des Rätsels der Motettenformen gefunden, das mich lange beunruhigt hatte.' Wilhelm Meyer, 'Der Ursprung des Motett's: Vorläufige Bemerkungen', in *Nachrichten von der königlichen Gesellschaft der Wissenschaften zu Göttingen: Philologisch-historische Klasse, 1898* (Göttingen, 1898), Vol. II, pp. 113–45; repr. in *Gesammelte Abhandlungen zur mittellateinischen Rhythmik* (Berlin, 1905), Vol. II, pp. 303–41 (pp. 311–12).

[2] For reflections on Meyer's parallel with Notker's prosulae see Susan Rankin, 'Thirteenth-Century Notations of Music and Arts of Performance', in Andreas Haug and Andreas Dorschel

the ninth century and beyond often expanded upon or troped the contents of the original plainchants, from which they began to circulate independently. The genesis of the sequence, therefore, overlapped on multiple levels with Meyer's view of the motet: not only did motets seem to originate in the creation of texts for clausulae, but these new texts frequently invoked the immediate and wider plainchant contexts of their older clausula tenors, while simultaneously defining the autonomous new genre of the motet, self-sufficient outside clausula and plainchant contexts.

Meyer's initial observation has justifiably stood the test of time, and it remains the accepted view that many motets with related clausulae (especially early Latin motets) did indeed derive from these clausulae. Nevertheless, the clausula–motet relationship prompted heated debate throughout the twentieth century, and its historiography is well documented.[3] The tone was set when what was a general chronological theory assumed the status of objective fact. Designating individual clausulae related to motets simply as *Qu.* (*Quelle*, or source), Friedrich Ludwig inscribed the chronology into the fabric of his 1910 *Repertorium* – the monumental catalogue, still in current use, of almost all extant thirteenth-century polyphony.[4] This practice persisted in later scholarship, and it seems to have fostered an unusually strong attachment to the status quo.[5] Yvonne Rokseth's suggestion, in a 1939 footnote, that clausulae accompanied by vernacular motet incipits in the anomalous St Victor manuscript might be motet transcriptions, received a book-length riposte from Jürg Stenzl in 1970.[6] Similarly, William Waite's passing proposition in 1954, that twenty-one irregularly notated clausulae

(eds.), *Vom Preis des Fortschritts: Gewinn und Verlust in der Musikgeschichte*, Studien zur Wertungsforschung 49 (Vienna, 2008), pp. 110–41 (pp. 122–3).

[3] See, for example, Norman E. Smith, 'The Earliest Motets: Music and Words', *Journal of the Royal Musicological Association*, 114 (1989), 141–63 (pp. 141–6).

[4] Friedrich Ludwig, *Repertorium organorum recentioris et motetorum vetustissimi stili*, ed. Luther A. Dittmer, 2 vols. in 3 (New York, 1964–78 [1910]). In his 1957 reformulation of Ludwig's *Repertorium* as a motet catalogue, Friedrich Gennrich retained the designation *Quelle* for clausulae. See his *Bibliographie der ältesten französischen und lateinischen Motetten*, SMMA 2 (Frankfurt, 1957).

[5] Gordon A. Anderson, for instance, indicated clausulae concordances with 'S.' for 'source' in his 1968 edition of Latin motets in **W2**. See the editorial commentary to Gordon A. Anderson (ed.), *The Latin Compositions in Fascicules VII and VIII of the Notre Dame Manuscript Wolfenbüttel Helmstadt 1099 (1206)*, Musicological Studies 24, 2 parts (New York, 1968–76), Part I.

[6] See Yvonne Rokseth (ed.), *Polyphonies du XIIIe siècle: Le manuscrit H196 de la faculté de médecine de Montpellier*, 4 vols. (Paris, 1935–9), Vol. IV, pp. 70–1. For a rejection of Rokseth's hypothesis, see Jürg Stenzl, *Die vierzig Clausulae der Handschrift Paris, Bibliothèque nationale, latin 15139 (Saint Victor-Clausulae)*, Publikationen der schweizerischen musikforschenden Gesellschaft, series 2:22 (Bern, 1970), pp. 113–25. The priority of St Victor clausulae (following Stenzl) remained the default assumption. See, for instance, Emma Dillon, *The Sense of*

in the Florence manuscript could derive from motets, prompted Gordon A. Anderson's article sixteen years later, devoted to rejecting Waite's claim.[7] By contrast, Wolf Frobenius's arguments for a general motet priority received no such detailed consideration, and his radical 1987 article was by and large tacitly disregarded.[8] Only in recent decades have these 'clausula first' detractors met with a more sympathetic reception. Fred Büttner's 2012 monograph on the St Victor clausulae confirmed Rokseth's early suspicions.[9] Building on the work of Wulf Arlt and Büttner,[10] I have offered further evidence in support of Waite's hypothesis as well as certain of Frobenius's findings, advocating openness to local reversals of the conventional clausula-before-motet chronology.[11]

Understandings of clausula–motet interactions have arguably been poorly served by the general nature and the straightforwardly linear chronological preoccupations of the debate. In consequence, scholars writing after Frobenius have tended to avoid direct engagement with chronological questions. Mark Everist, for example, realistically emphasised the 'spectacular explosion of experimental procedures', while Susan Rankin underlined the 'changes and exchanges … fundamental to musical activities' in the twelfth and thirteenth centuries.[12] This book explicitly foregrounds such complexity and multi-directionality in thirteenth-century

Sound: Musical Meaning in France 1260–1330, New Cultural History of Music Series (New York, 2012), pp. 161–3. Fred Büttner has now convincingly demonstrated the motet origins of the St Victor clausulae in his *Das Klauselrepertoire der Handschrift Saint-Victor (Paris, BN, lat. 15139): Eine Studie zur mehrstimmigen Komposition im 13. Jahrhundert* (Lecce, 2011).

7 See William G. Waite, *The Rhythm of Twelfth-Century Polyphony: Its Theory and Practice*, Yale Studies in the History of Music 2 (New Haven, 1954), p. 101; and Gordon A. Anderson, 'Clausulae or Transcribed Motets in the Florence Manuscript?', *Acta musicologica*, 42 (1970), 109–28.

8 Wolf Frobenius, 'Zum genetischen Verhältnis zwischen Notre-Dame-Klauseln und ihren Motetten', *Archiv für Musikwissenschaft*, 44 (1987), 1–39. On the reception of Frobenius's theory, see Franz Körndle, 'Von der Klausel zur Motette und zurück? Überlegungen zum Repertoire der Handschrift *Saint-Victor*', *Musiktheorie*, 25 (2010), 117–28 (p. 118).

9 Büttner, *Das Klauselrepertoire der Handschrift Saint-Victor*. See n. 6 above.

10 See especially Wulf Arlt, 'Zur frühen Geschichte der Motette: Funktionen – historische Schichten – Musik und Text – Kriterien der Interpretation' (unpublished paper presented at Das Ereignis Notre-Dame, Wolfenbüttel, 1985); and Fred Büttner, 'Weltliche Einflüsse in der Notre-Dame-Musik? Überlegungen zu einer Klausel im Codex F', *Anuario musical*, 57 (2002), 19–37. Another key text is Klaus Hofmann's *Untersuchungen zur Kompositionstechnik der Motette im 13. Jahrhundert durchgeführt an den Motetten mit dem Tenor 'In seculum'*, Tübinger Beiträge zur Musikwissenschaft 2 (Neuhausen-Stuttgart, 1972).

11 Catherine A. Bradley, 'Contrafacta and Transcribed Motets: Latin Motets and Clausulae in the Florence Manuscript', *Early Music History*, 32 (2013), 1–70.

12 Mark Everist, *French Motets in the Thirteenth Century: Music, Poetry, and Genre* (Cambridge, 1994), p. 29; and Rankin, 'Thirteenth-Century Notations', p. 134.

chronologies: from clausula to motet, from motet to clausula, or from organum to motet with apparently no intervening clausula tradition (not to mention the equally complex chronological relationships between motets and vernacular songs explored in Chapter 4, and between motets and rhymed Offices considered in Chapter 6). Yet it does so by establishing and examining chronological relationships in particular cases, exploring the consequences of these relationships for processes of composition. While subsequent chapters demonstrate the de-texting and reworking of motets as clausulae, the traditional 'clausula-to-motet' progression is the focus here. Compositionally, the consequences of this chronological relationship – exemplified in this chapter by two Latin motets on the tenor REGNAT – are significant. What are the skills and priorities involved in creating a text for an existing melody? And how might this process of creation affect the character of the new text, as well as the older music?

This chapter shows ways in which internal chronological clues may be read from surviving musical and textual materials. It argues for the importance of apparently insubstantial musical variants that have been overlooked by scholars, even dismissed as inconsistencies or copying errors. Significantly, such small variants can serve not only as chronological indicators – suggesting the accommodation of music to text or vice versa – but also as aesthetic ones. I demonstrate an instance in which clausula and motet versions of the same musical material exhibit alternative compositional preferences, the former favouring harmonic consonance over the more literal melodic repetition preferred in the latter. This offers rare concrete evidence in practice of a compositional issue – the relationship between harmonic dissonance and melodic repetition – addressed in theoretical treatises. Close readings of a pair of REGNAT clausulae and their related motets underline the subtlety, complexity, and mutually enhancing nature of relationships between text and music. These examples serve also to unsettle two fundamental preconceptions of early Latin motets derived from clausulae: first, that motets invariably reproduce literally the music of their clausula models;[13] and second, that the poetic irregularity characteristic of thirteenth-century motet texts, both Latin and vernacular, was a necessary consequence of the genre's prosula origins.[14]

[13] This is Smith's thesis in 'The Earliest Motets'.

[14] This hypothesis, which originated with Meyer, is still widely accepted. For a recent example, see Leofranc Holford-Strevens, 'Latin Poetry and Music', in Mark Everist (ed.), *The Cambridge Companion to Medieval Music* (Cambridge, 2011), pp. 225–40 (p. 234).

Making Clausulae: Repetition and the REGNAT Tenor

To understand the process of conversion from clausula to motet, I first examine the musical construction of a pair of melismatic two-voice clausulae, before demonstrating how syllabic texts were added to their upper voices to make a pair of two-voice motets.[15] This pair of clausulae – designated *Reg*[*nat*] *6* (no. 164) and *Reg*[*nat*] *8* (no. 165) – is copied side-by-side, over the turn of folio 166 of **F**. While *Reg*[*nat*] *8* is unique to **F**, *Reg*[*nat*] *6* is also transmitted among the clausulae of **W1** (no. 77, fol. 59r–4). In **F**, these two clausulae occupy an important position at the head of a group of thirteen different two-voice elaborations of the same tenor melisma. The liturgical importance of the REGNAT tenor, drawn from the *Alleluia. Hodie Marie* for the feast of the Assumption (M 34), may explain its status as the premier clausula tenor in the thirteenth century.[16] But the melisma itself surely had a further, primarily musical, attraction as a polyphonic foundation. Example 3.1a shows the REGNAT tenor in the version in which it is typically found as a tenor in **F**. This forty-four-note melisma has its own intricate melodic design, a tripartite AAB structure, in which the A sections themselves also have a tripartite xx′y structure (where each internal section concludes with a repetition of the final pitch, G).

REGNAT clausulae arrange the pitches of this pre-existent chant melisma in rhythmically patterned tenors. Both *Reg*[*nat*] *6* (Example 3.2) and *Reg*[*nat*] *8* (Example 3.3) have tenors in the fifth rhythmic mode, consistently assigning the length of a long to each individual note of the chant. These successive longs are punctuated by rests and are grouped differently in the two clausulae, which also adjust the length of their REGNAT tenors in slightly different ways (compare Examples 3.1a–c). In *Reg*[*nat*] *8* (Example 3.1c) the tenor melisma ends early, omitting the final four notes of the chant (which effectively repeat the melisma's B–A–G closing figure) and their accompanying syllable of text (-NAT).[17] This leaves forty pitches to be arranged in multiples of four and eight (six groups of four-note tenor

[15] Only Frobenius, as part of his more widespread reversal of the traditional clausula–motet relationship, challenged the chronological priority of the *Reg*[*nat*] *6* and *Reg*[*nat*] *8* clausulae. See 'Zum genetischen Verhältnis', p. 24. I challenge the evidence for Frobenius's hypothesis below (see n. 29).

[16] In total, twenty different discant/clausula compositions on the REGNAT tenor are extant across **W1**, **F**, and **W2**. See Norman E. Smith's table detailing the rhythmic arrangements of REGNAT tenors in discant/clausulae in 'An Early Thirteenth-Century Motet', in Mark Everist (ed.), *Models of Musical Analysis: Music before 1600* (Oxford, 1992), pp 20–40 (p. 25).

[17] The omission of the final four pitches on '-NAT' is common in *Regnat* clausulae. See Smith, 'An Early Thirteenth-Century Motet', p. 25.

Example 3.1a Structure of the REGNAT melisma.

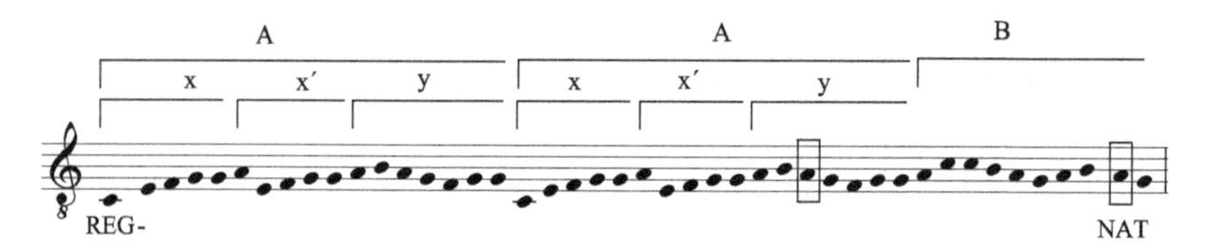

Example 3.1b Arrangement of the REG[NAT] melisma in *Reg[nat] 6*.

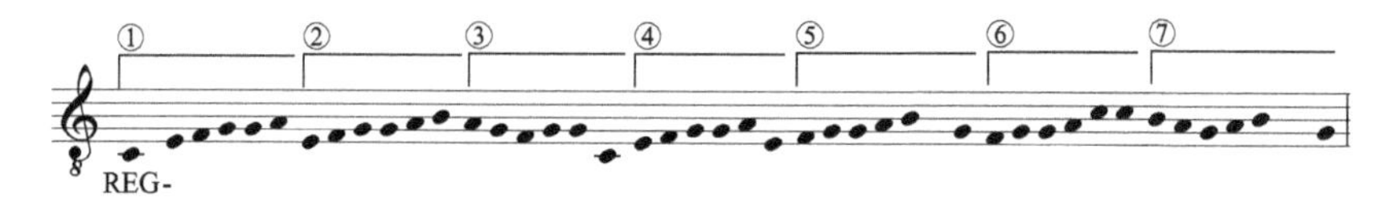

Example 3.1c Arrangement of the REG[NAT] melisma in *Reg[nat] 8*.

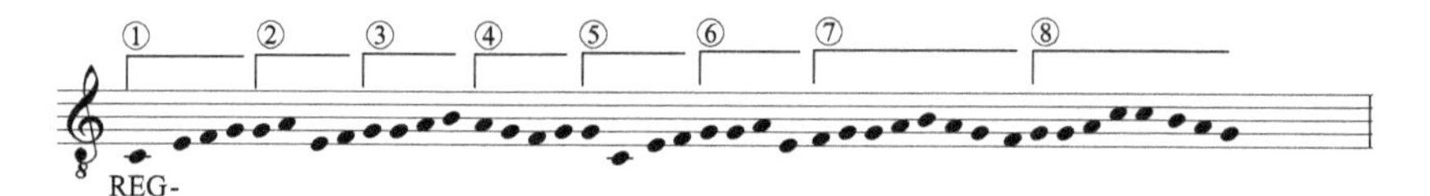

ordines, followed by two eight-note ordines). *Reg[nat] 6* (Example 3.1b) organises the REGNAT melisma into seven six-note groups, a design that requires the exclusion of two pitches. In this instance, and for reasons explored below, the chant was not simply curtailed. Instead, two internal pitches were excised (marked by boxes in Example 3.1a): two As appearing in similar melodic contexts.[18] Significantly, both clausula tenors cut directly across all of the existing large-scale melodic patterns within the chant.[19] For *Reg[nat] 6* and *Reg[nat] 8* regular tenor groupings of pitches – into units of six or four/eight notes, respectively – were evidently a priority, upheld at the expense of melodic repetitions inherent in the plainchant itself.

[18] That these two pitches were deliberately excluded in *Reg[nat] 6* is confirmed by the fact that they are included in all nineteen other extant clausulae on REGNAT. It seems unlikely that the tenor of *Reg[nat] 6* simply employed a different version of this chant, because the pitch A omitted from the second presentation of the A section of the melisma is included in the first presentation of this A section. That the tenor was subjected to unusual manipulation in *Reg[nat] 6* could also explain the copying error in the tenor of the **F** version of this clausula. In **F**, the mistaken omission of the penultimate pitch B results in the conclusion of the tenor with the pitches A–G, the more typical ending for the REGNAT melisma.

[19] None of the extant clausulae on REGNAT complements exactly patterns in the chant melisma. However, the tenor arrangement of *Regnat 7* seems to follow the chant's xx'y groupings in the opening A section. The initial five-note groupings in the chant's x material may have ensured the popularity of five- and ten-note ordines in clausula tenors.

Example 3.2 *Reg[nat] 6* clausula **F**, fol. 166r–6 (with **W1**, fol. 59r–4 variants shown).

The upper voices, or dupla, of the two-voice clausulae *Reg[nat] 6* and *Reg[nat] 8* reflect the interest in regularity evident in their tenor designs. Both pieces have dupla in the first rhythmic mode, that consistently respect the phrase structure of their underlying tenors: the end of each tenor group is marked by a simultaneous break in both voices. In addition to a regular and

Example 3.3 *Reg*[*nat*] *8* clausula, **F**, fol. 166r–7.

repetitive phrase structure, the clausula dupla are preoccupied with melodic repetitions. This is particularly marked in *Reg*[*nat*] *6*, where each duplum phrase employs exactly the same conventional pattern of the first rhythmic mode, and all duplum phrases (with the exception of the last) incorporate two literally repeated motivic units (assigned letters in Example 3.2).[20]

[20] Example 3.2 shows all variants in the **W1** version of this clausula. The two versions of it are very closely related: there are only two differences of pitch between them (in perfections 32

Such repetitions occur not only within but also across the six-perfection phrases: perfections 7–12 repeat perfections 1–6 (two statements of motive a) down a tone, while perfections 19–24 (two statements of motive c) are repeated down a third in perfections 25–30 and (with a single statement of this transposed motive) in perfections 40–2. The sense of motivic economy in *Reg[nat] 6* is further enhanced in the remaining six-perfection phrases, which appear only once. Motive b is similar in profile and pitch content to motive a, while the opening of motive d strongly resembles that of motive c, transposed up a tone.

Melodic repetition is central also to the duplum of *Reg[nat] 8*, though it is less obviously literal here than in *Reg[nat] 6*. The shorter four-perfection phrases of *Reg[nat] 8* are also internally repetitive, through a continued emphasis on the successive repetition of individual pitches. Large-scale repetitions are evident too: the initial four-perfection motive of *Reg[nat] 8* (labelled a) is immediately presented down a tone in perfections 5–8 (labeled a'). Perfections 9–12 introduce new material, b, also with an emphasis on descending repeated pitches, which is then restated down a third, as b', in perfections 13–16. Another motive, c – again related in range with internally repeating pitches – is employed in perfections 17–20 and 21–4. The c motive additionally serves as the beginning of a final pair of extended eight-perfection phrases (perfections 25–32 and 33–40, labelled d and d'), which begin identically, but ultimately lead towards different cadences.

The insistent upper-voice repetitions in these two clausulae seem highly appropriate for an intricately patterned tenor such as REGNAT. Yet, as emphasised above, the arrangement of this chant melisma as a clausula tenor in *Reg[nat] 6* and *Reg[nat] 8* obscures melodic repetitions within the chant. Upper-voice repetitions do not simply correlate directly with those in the underlying REGNAT melisma: though this would have required irregular tenor groupings, it could have been an effective and straightforward compositional ploy. Instead, and paradoxically, the clausulae seem actively to avoid or forgo any obvious coincidence of tenor and duplum repetitions. The four- and eight-note groupings of chant pitches in *Reg[nat] 8* produce tenor ordines of diverse contours, which are nonetheless accompanied by similar duplum motives. Conversely, the six-note tenor groupings in *Reg[nat] 6* highlight certain small-scale motivic recurrences within the chant melody. This notwithstanding, these tenor repetitions were typically

and 35), and the **W1** clausula has an additional decorative plica (at perfection 17) absent from the version in **F**.

treated to different duplum motives.[21] Upper-voice repetitions in *Reg[nat] 6* and *Reg[nat] 8*, therefore, were not obviously suggested or facilitated by the underlying tenor melisma but are achieved almost in spite of it.

It is striking that tenor and upper-voice repetitions align on just a single occasion across these two clausulae. This occurs in *Reg[nat] 6*, where the final three perfections of the clausula tenor and duplum are identical to perfections 28–30 (marked by boxes in Example 3.2, the second half of ordines 5 and 7). The moment constitutes an exceptional repetition that seems to have been deliberately cultivated, since the recurrence of the underlying tenor progression was made possible by the omission of two internal pitches of the REGNAT melisma in the motet tenor.[22] Furthermore, in order to facilitate the final appearance of the upper-voice motive c′, the hitherto consistent repetition of two internal units within a phrase was compromised. Motive x (perfections 37–9) closely resembles motive c′, but its first three notes are transposed down a tone, presumably to avoid the dissonance that would have sounded had the phrase begun (at perfection 37) with C in the duplum against the B in the tenor.[23] Such a coincidence of repetition in both tenor and duplum voices at perfections 40–2 arguably contributes to a sense of closure at the end of the clausula. It may also draw attention to a crucial aspect of the compositional game of *Reg[nat] 6* (and of its neighbouring clausula in **F**, *Reg[nat] 8*), namely that all previous melodic repetitions had been achieved in the face of the changing harmonic context of a borrowed and rhythmically patterned tenor melisma.

Reg[nat] 6 and *Reg[nat] 8* are indicative of a creative culture in which makers of clausulae relished and even engineered compositional challenges, deliberately eschewing a straightforward correlation of tenor and upper voices to achieve repetition 'against the odds'. Such compositional game-playing involving repetition is evident not only at a local level within individual clausulae, but also across groups of clausulae on a shared tenor. As noted above, *Reg[nat] 6* begins a series of thirteen reworkings of the same chant melisma in **F**. Ten of these clausulae undertake their own unique

[21] Tenor ordines 2 and 4 open with the pitches E–F–G, and while this opening accompanies motive a' in the duplum at perfections 7–9, it appears in conjunction with motive c at perfections 19–21. Similarly, the successive tenor ordines 5 and 6 share an F–G–G opening, but the duplum motive c' at perfections 25–7 is transposed and reworked (as motive d) at perfections 31–3.

[22] Had the melisma been borrowed literally, perfections 28–30 would have consisted of the tenor pitches A–B–A and perfections 40–2 of G–A–B.

[23] There are five occasions when a stressed dissonant interval of a second occurs between the tenor and the upper voice (at the beginning of perfections 26, 29, 35, 38, and 41). However, all five occur within the middle of a phrase, rather than at the beginning or end.

arrangement of the REGNAT tenor: there are various groupings of the chant pitches, regular and irregular, in several modal patterns, from duplex longs, to the longs and breves of the third rhythmic mode.[24] In contrast to this marked variety in their treatment of the shared tenor, every clausula in the group opens with a duplum motive that descends through the pitches C–B–A. In eight cases, the first upper-voice phrase specifically explores the descending C–G fourth so prominent in *Reg[nat] 8*. Of course, this may partly be the result of practicality: for a tenor that opens by rising from C to G, a duplum that descends from C to G is the obvious choice, beginning on the consonant harmonic interval of an octave and moving in contrary motion. It is not surprising that such a strong opening gesture could have become conventional, even to the exclusion of all others. Nevertheless, it seems remarkable that thirteen individual clausulae should confine themselves so strictly to the raw material of tenors and dupla, then proceed to demonstrate how this material could be arranged and worked out in very different ways. This stands as evidence, on a grand scale, of an interest in creative recasting within self-imposed compositional parameters.

A certain playfulness in balancing repetition and variety – a concern shared by many clausulae – seems especially central to the compositional aesthetic of these REGNAT pieces. And near-contemporary theoretical evidence suggests that repetition was key also to the aesthetic experience of this music in sound. John of Garland, an Englishman who studied and taught in Paris in the early thirteenth century, expounded the concept of *color* in his mid-thirteenth-century treatise *De mensurabili musica*.[25] For Garlandia, *color* was akin to the 'beauty of sound' and the 'object of hearing, by which hearing takes pleasure'.[26] *Color* could be achieved or inspired by the familiarity of a

[24] The remaining three clausulae – *Regnat 14, Regnat 15,* and *Regnat 16* (**F**, fol. 167v) – constitute a trio of reworkings of an idiosyncratic third-mode tenor whose ordines close with an unusually extended period of silence.

[25] See Erich Reimer, *Johannes de Garlandia: 'De mensurabili musica'*, 2 vols., Beihefte zum Archiv für Musikwissenschaft 10–11 (Wiesbaden, 1972), Vol. I, p. 95. Scholars conventionally attribute these remarks on *color* to Garlandia, although Reimer has questioned the authenticity of the chapter (15) in which they appear (see ibid., Vol. I, pp. 18–32). Chapter 15 of Garlandia's treatise is transmitted only in the version in Paris, Bibliothèque nationale de France, lat. 16663, compiled by Jerome of Moravia, and Reimer suggests that this could indicate a date of post-1272 for the chapter in question. On the identity of John of Garland, see Constant J. Mews, John N. Crossley, Catherine Jeffreys, Leigh McKinnon, and Carol J. Williams (ed. and trans.), *Johannes de Grocheio: 'Ars musice'* (Kalamazoo, 2011), pp. 8–9.

[26] See Reimer, *Johannes de Garlandia*, Vol. I, p. 95. For a detailed discussion of the relevant passages, see Guillaume Gross, 'Organum at Notre-Dame in the Twelfth and Thirteenth Centuries: Rhetoric in Words and Music', *Plainsong and Medieval Music*, 15 (2006), 87–108 (pp. 92–6). See also Mary Channen Caldwell, 'Singing, Dancing, and Rejoicing in the

melody arising from its repetition (*repetitio*). At a macro level, the repeated and increasingly recognisable 'stock' opening of the *Regnat* clausulae seems to exemplify precisely the effect Garlandia described. At a micro level, *Reg[nat] 6* and *Reg[nat] 8* epitomise local forms of *repetitio* outlined in detail in *De mensurabili musica. Sonus ordinatus* – the restatement of short motives – is the fundamental technique of both clausulae, while *Reg[nat] 8* showcases (albeit on a much more modest scale) what Garlandia dubs *florificatio vocis*, the immediate repetition of single pitches. The carefully wrought repetition in these clausulae, therefore, presumably delighted the ears of listeners and singers, and perhaps readers too, just as much as it provided a pleasurable compositional challenge to their creators.

Making Motets: Textual Responses to Repetition

The two motets *Deus omnium* and *Infidelem populum* add an additional sonic and semantic layer to the music of *Reg[nat] 6 and Reg[nat] 8*, respectively.[27] Like their related clausulae, *Deus omnium* and *Infidelem populum* appear as a pair, recorded side by side, and uniquely, on either side of fol. 403 in the collection of two-voice motets in **F**.[28] Unsurprisingly, repetition and regularity remain the central principles of these motet texts, which respond to and enhance the musical structures and patterns of their inherited clausula material through poetic syllable counts, stresses, and rhymes. At first glance, both motets seem to reproduce verbatim the music of their clausula models. Yet the close comparison of motets and clausulae offered below reveals certain slight variants between them. Although these small differences of rhythm and phrasing are of minimal impact in purely musical terms, I argue that they have a clear poetic motivation, and that the case for their introduction in a motet to facilitate particular features of its accompanying text is therefore strong. If – as only Frobenius has proposed – the REGNAT clausulae instead derived from parent motets, it would be difficult to explain why these minor alterations were made when

Round: Latin Sacred Songs with Refrains, circa 1000–1582', Ph.D. diss. (University of Chicago, 2013), pp. 96–101.

[27] The discussion of *Reg[nat] 8* and *Deus omnium* draws on material previously published in Catherine A. Bradley, 'Comparing Compositional Process in Two Thirteenth-Century Motets: *Deus omnium/REGNAT* and *Ne m'oubliez mie/DOMINO*', *Music Analysis*, 33 (2014), 263–90.

[28] While *Reg[nat]* 6 precedes *Reg[nat] 8* in the clausula fascicle of **F**, the related motets appear in reverse order: *Infidelem populum* (related to *Reg[nat]* 8) precedes *Deus omnium* (related to *Reg[nat]* 6).

motet texts were removed.[29] Such inexplicable alterations in the process of creating clausulae from motets seem increasingly unlikely in view of the potential for a text to stabilise the transmission of rhythmic and structural elements in a composition. Just as Notker's sequence prosulae could function as memory aids for a long Alleluia melisma, so it seems that the existence of motet texts would probably serve to solidify the details of melismatic clausulae to correlate with associated textual material.[30]

Deus omnium/REGNAT

Deus omnium/REGNAT is given as Example 3.4, and the motet text and its translation follow in Table 3.1.[31] *Deus omnium* very closely resembles *Reg[nat] 6* (compare Example 3.2), but one aspect of this clausula is consistently reworked in the motet version. In the third perfection of each of the seven phrases, the motet has a decorative figure in place of a long and a breve in the clausula model. This is a so-called *longa florata*, a common device by which a note is ornamented by reiteration and the addition of a passing (literally 'folded') *plica*, the three pitches conventionally sung as a short melisma on the same syllable of text. In *Deus omnium*, *longae floratae* link the first presentation of each three-perfection motive to the second, supporting a single syllable in the motet instead of the two syllables that would have been required had the clausula been texted literally.[32] Such alterations, though relatively unobtrusive, have a significant impact on the

[29] Significantly, Frobenius did not note these musical variants between clausula and motet versions in his cursory notes on *Reg[nat] 6* and *Reg[nat] 8* ('Zum genetischen Verhältnis', p. 24). He proposed that the regular 'four-square nature' (*Quadratismus*) of these clausulae seemed to be motivated by textual concerns, indicating a motet origin. This argument is problematic, since – as discussed further below – *Quadratismus* is fairly common in clausulae without any extant motets, but textual regularity is a less common feature of motet texts in general.

[30] I have argued that this is the case in the clausula *[Immo]latus est 4* in **F** (no. 103, fol. 158v–1), related to the motet *Homo quam sit pura/[IMMO]LATUS* (Mt231). 'Extra' notes absent from the version of the *Latus 4* clausula in **W1** (no. 56, fol. 57r–3) are introduced to facilitate a regular motet text. Presumably owing to the influence of this associated motet text, these 'extra' notes are present in the **F** clausula. See Catherine A. Bradley, 'Origins and Interactions: Clausula, Motet, Conductus', in Jared C. Hartt (ed.), *A Critical Companion to Medieval Motets* (Woodbridge, 2018), pp. 43–60 (pp. 46–57).

[31] Round brackets in Example 3.4 indicate erasures still visible in **F**. Many of these lines of punctuation were unsystematically removed from the motets in **F**. See the discussion of this phenomenon in Catherine A. Bradley, 'New Texts for Old Music: Three Early Latin Motets', *Music and Letters*, 93 (2012), 149–69 (pp. 164 n. 35). I thank Eleanor Giraud for her assistance with the Latin translation in Table 3.1.

[32] If the *Reg[nat] 6* clausula were a motet transcription, there would be no compelling notational reason to exclude the motet's *longae floratae*. In fact, the clausula notation could arguably be

Table 3.1 Text and translation of *Deus omnium*

1.	Deus omnium,	**5a**	-ium	**pp**	O God of all,
2.	turba gentium	**5a**	-ium	**pp**	a crowd of people
3.	circumstantium	**5a**	-ium	**pp**	gathering round
4.	sanctuarium	**5a**	-ium	**pp**	your sanctuary
5.	tuum polluit,	**5b**	-uit	**pp**	has polluted it,
6.	nec exhorruit	**5b**	-uit	**pp**	and [the people] did not tremble
7.	nomen Domini.	**5c**	-ini	**pp**	at the name of the Lord.
8.	Tuo nomini	**5c**	-ini	**pp**	Your name
9.	gens improperat,	**5d**	-erat	**pp**	the people has insulted,
10.	si hic auferat	**5d**	-erat	**pp**	if now [your right hand] were to remove
11.	gentis scelera,	**5e**	-era	**pp**	the sins of the people,
12.	tua dextera	**5e**	-era	**pp**	your right hand
13.	arcum conterat	**5d**	-erat	**pp**	would break the bow
14.	quem tetenderat.	**5d**	-erat	**pp**	which they had stretched.

Example 3.4 *Deus omnium/REG[NAT]*, **F**, fol. 403v.

added motet text: they permit an isosyllabic poetic structure of five syllables per line (Table 3.1). On two occasions (perfections 12 and 36) *longa florata* figures are also introduced at the end of a six-perfection phrase, making the motivic repetition in each half of the phrase an exact one, and both times joining together lines that are linked syntactically in the motet text (lines 4–5 and 12–13).

Such minor musical alterations in *Deus omnium* facilitate the text's consistent line lengths, which are matched by a constant proparoxytonic stress throughout (designated **pp** in Table 3.1), thereby heightening the regularity of phrasing and motivic economy of the clausula model. This poetic uniformity also reinforces the internal repetitions in the clausula duplum, as the kinship between the three-perfection units is strengthened through their identical syllable count. Internal repetitions are further underscored by the use of rhyme in the motet text, where every pair of five-syllable lines shares the same end rhyme, thereby emphasising the lines' status as a pair.[33] In addition, the reuse of certain pairs of rhymes corresponds with large-scale melodic repetitions. The two opening six-perfection phrases (lines 1–4) share the '-ium' rhyme (designated **a** in Table 3.1), highlighting the fact that perfections 7–12 are a transposed repetition of perfections 1–6. The separate identity of the two pairs of lines is nonetheless maintained: each line of the opening pair is made up of a two-syllable word, followed by a three-syllable one ('Deus omnium / turba gentium'), while the second pair is characterised by two five-syllable words ('circumstantium / sanctuarium'). Similarly, the '-erat' rhyme (designated **d** in Table 3.1) is first employed in perfections 25–30 (lines 9–10) and reappears in perfections 37–42 (lines 13–14). This underlines the shared closing gesture of perfections 25–7 and 37–9, perhaps even helping to disguise the fact that their opening pitches are not identical. The reuse of the '-erat' rhyme also complements the literal repetition of both motetus and tenor parts between perfections 28–30 and 40–2.

Infidelem populum

The motet *Infidelem populum* given as Example 3.5 presents a similar, if slightly less clear-cut, case. Once again, this motet text is highly regular (see

clarified by the inclusion of these decorative figurations, since the ligations of both iterations of each repeated motive would then be identical.

[33] This correspondence between musical and poetic structure has also been noted by Rebecca A. Baltzer, 'Notation, Rhythm, and Style in the Two-Voice Notre Dame Clausula', Ph.D. diss., 2 vols. (Boston University, 1974), Vol. I, p. 341; and Hendrik van der Werf, *Hidden Beauty in Motets of the Early Thirteenth Century: XXV Vignettes* (Tucson, 1999), p. 3.

Example 3.5 *Infidelem populum/REG[NAT]*, **F**, fol. 403r–v.

Table 3.2). Every four-perfection musical phrase corresponds to a seven-syllable poetic line (lines 1–6). In the final two eight-perfection phrases, the first line of each phrase (lines 7 and 10) continues the seven-syllable pattern, but the second half of each musical phrase is made up of a pair of four-syllable lines each beginning on an anacrusis (lines 8 and 9 and lines 11 and 12). Syllabic consistency was evidently a priority for the creator of the motet text, since the two eight-perfection phrases themselves have matching poetic structures, and each preserves the initial seven-syllable

unit of the earlier phrases. In view of this consistency, it is significant that the motet creator did not affect slight musical adjustments in the closing pair of phrases to achieve an isosyllabic text. In the middle of the two eight-perfection phrases (perfections 28 and 36) a single pitch could simply have been omitted, or enveloped within a *longa florata*. Instead, and arguably more effectively, the creator of the motet chose not to compromise the reiteration of individual pitches and the scalic descent of these final phrases. In consequence, the text maintains its characteristic syllabic setting, and the change in the length of poetic lines – especially the introduction of shorter lines with up-beats – contributes to a sense of momentum towards the closing cadences.

Poetic rhymes and stresses in *Infidelem populum* complement its syllabic regularity. Throughout, each simultaneous tenor and motetus cadence is matched by the same rhyme, '-um'. The only prominent variation in rhyme occurs within the final two eight-perfection phrases (lines 7–9 and 10–12). The introduction of new rhymes here ('-ulo' and '-ice', labelled **b** and **c**, respectively, in Table 3.2) enhances the forward motion within these phrases, both of which close with a return to the established '-um' rhyme. That the same new rhyme is shared between a seven-syllable line and a shorter four-syllable unit (lines 7 and 8, and lines 10 and 11) also creates continuity across these exceptional breaks in the syllabic pattern. Economy of rhyme is matched by a total consistency of proparoxytonic end stress, the same stress employed in *Deus omnium* and one particularly well suited to the profile of the first rhythmic mode.[34] Even the short four-syllable lines in *Infidelem populum* are proparoxytonic, resulting in a noticeable intensification in frequency of this stress in the two extended phrases that further contributes to a sense of acceleration and arrival in the final pair of cadences.

Comparing *Infidelem populum* and its clausula *Reg*[*nat*] *8* (Examples 3.3 and 3.5) rhythmic variants are slight. Nevertheless, the motet's treatment of the groups of two brief moments of *fractio modi* in the clausula – breaking down the conventional two-note long-breve pattern into three separate breves in perfections 9 and 13 – is telling. The usual procedure of matching a single syllable to a single pitch is suspended in perfections 9 and 13 to maintain regular seven-syllable text lines. In perfection 9, the motet assimilates the clausula's 'extra' middle pitch into the final breve, such that the second syllable of the phrase is sung to a pair of semibreves. In perfection 13, the motet omits the clausula's extra breve altogether, creating a small melodic

[34] In accordance with musical setting, the text stress in the first part of each seven-syllable line is typically also paroxytonic. In line 3, the proparoxytonic 'suspenditor' is misaccentuated musically as 'suspenditor'.

Table 3.2 Text and translation of *Infidelem populum*

1.	Infidelem populum!	**7a**	-ulum	**pp**	Unfaithful people!
2.	Haman ad patibulum	**7a**	-ulum	**pp**	Haman from his own gallows
3.	suspenditor proprium.	**7a'**	-ium	**pp**	was suspended.
4.	Apprehende gladium	**7a'**	-ium	**pp**	Seize the sword
5.	frange manus hostium.	**7a'**	-ium	**pp**	break the hordes of enemies.
6.	Veni in auxilium	**7a'**	-ium	**pp**	Come to the aid
7.	naufraganti seculo	**7b**	-ulo	**pp**	of the shipwrecked world
8.	et populo	**4b**	-ulo	**pp**	and people
9.	fidelium.	**4a'**	-ium	**pp**	of the faithful.
10.	Iebuseos erice!	**7c**	-ice	**pp**	Master the Jesubites!
11.	Non respice	**4c**	-ice	**pp**	Respect us
12.	per filium.	**4a'**	-ium	**pp**	through your Son.

inconsistency between its pair of b and b′ phrases as a result. Yet this new version of perfection 13 arguably highlights a different motivic aspect of the b′ motive, emphasising the leap of a third from A to C, prominent in the subsequent c and d phrases.

A third and final difference in rhythm between *Infidelem populum* and *Reg[nat] 8* seems similarly motivated by both motivic and textual concerns. In perfection 20, the motet links the two c phrases separated by a rest in the clausula with a decorative *longa florata*. Musically, this connects the composition's most literally repetitive pair of four-perfection phrases. As in *Deus omnium*, such a slight decorative addition to the clausula's musical material might also have been prompted by a further component of the motet's poetic design, its syntax. *Longae floratae* joined grammatical text units in *Deus omnium*. But in *Infidelem populum* the linking melodic decoration at perfection 20 arguably underlines a significant disjunction evident throughout the motet: a pervasive disconnection between the sense units of its text (clarified here by editorial punctuation) and its pairs of musically repetitive phrases. Unlike all other poetic features of *Infidelem populum* – rhyme, syllable count, and stress – syntactical structures within the text actively cut across musical ones.[35] Spatially, the layout of Table 3.2 groups lines of text by their musical pairings, but grammatically the first line of *Infidelem populum* is a stand-alone exclamation ('Unfaithful people!'), while it is lines 2 and 3 that form a poetic unit. Similarly, lines 4 and 5

[35] Van der Werf also observed this syntactical feature of *Infidelem populum*. See his *Hidden Beauty*, p. 9.

belong together grammatically, as do lines 6 and 7–9. All these syntactic groupings conflict with musical ones, and the final eight-perfections of the motet (lines 10–12) mark the first occasion on which a musical phrase aligns with a discrete sense-unit. It is telling that this coincidence of syntactic and musical unity is reserved until the very end of *Infidelem populum*. When finally achieved, the coincidence effectively resolves the earlier conflict between musical phrases and poetic syntax.[36]

Tension between poetic syntax and musical repetitions in *Infidelem populum* stands in stark contrast to the wholly complementary behaviour of text rhymes, stresses, and line lengths. As a result, the relationship between music and text in this motet is both varied and complex in a manner that suggests careful cultivation on the part of the motet creator. The subversive syntactic structure of *Infidelem populum* arguably serves as a foil to what might otherwise have become a relentlessly repetitive and predictable motet. Interestingly, however, this foil operates at a purely semantic level. Sonically, the aurally perceptible patterns of text rhymes, stresses, and line lengths – what Leo Treitler has called the 'phonetic level of poetic expression' – serve straightforwardly to reinforce musical repetitions.[37] Only a more careful consideration of the text's grammar and meaning reveals a dichotomy between music and text that coexists but does not interfere with their sounding unity and regularity. Although Garlandia speaks of *color* in exclusively musical terms, the addition of words to the melody of a clausula duplum might constitute a further facet of its *color*: a motet text offers a new layer of sound, in which poetic repetitions may heighten, perhaps even beautify, musical repetitions and familiarity.

Color, Consonance, and Dissonance

Extant theoretical documents do not describe or offer guidance for the setting of texts to clausulae, nor do they indicate – as suggested above – that the added words of a motet could be considered an aspect of *color*. Yet poetic characteristics of both *Deus omnium* and *Infidelem populum* confirm the

36 This technique is arguably analogous to the coincidence of musical repetition in tenor and motetus voices that is reserved for the closing cadence of *Deus omnium*. The eventual alignment of repetitions in this case similarly serves retrospectively to recast repetitive relationships earlier in the motet.

37 Leo Treitler, 'The Marriage of Poetry and Music in Medieval Song', in *With Voice and Pen: Coming to Know Medieval Song and How It Was Made* (Oxford, 2007 [1995]), pp. 457–81 (p. 460).

perceived centrality of repetition as a compositional feature in their model clausulae: whether or not the creators of these motet texts were familiar with *color* as a theoretical concept, their sensitivity to repeated *colores* in practice is clearly evident. Moreover, both motets offer additional insights into the practical handling of a further dimension of *color* as outlined in Garlandia's treatise.[38] Garlandia forges a connection between *color* and dissonance, noting that discords can be written 'for the sake of *color* or for musical beauty' ('causa coloris sive pulchritudinis musicae').[39] Additional evidence from a later theorist, the Englishman Walter of Odington writing around 1300, clarifies Garlandia's connection.[40] Odington highlights an exceptional circumstance in which the usual requirement for a consonant harmonic interval on a strong beat is waived, in order to facilitate the linear repetition of a melodic unit or *color*.[41] He cites a musical example – the opening of the two-voice motet *De penetractoribus/AGMINA* (see Example 3.6) – where literal repetition in the upper voice (marked by boxes) is pitted against the underlying tenor chant quotation.[42] This produces a dissonant second between the two parts at the return of the opening motetus melody (marked by a dashed box), since the initial pitch, C, of the upper-voice phrase now sounds, not in unison with the tenor, but against a B flat in the chant quotation.

Two moments in the motet *Infidelem populum* and its related clausula *Reg[nat] 8* (marked by dashed boxes in Examples 3.3 and 3.5) closely resemble Odington's special circumstance for stressed dissonance. The

[38] This observation is found in Chapter 10 of the treatise, transmitted in all manuscript sources, unlike the later remarks on *color* from Chapter 15 discussed above. See n. 25.

[39] See Reimer, *Johannes de Garlandia*, Vol. I, p. 74.

[40] Odington writes that 'Dissonance is excused in other ways in *moteti colorati*, when some part of a melody is repeated over a given tenor' ('Alio modo excusatur discordia ut in motetis coloratis quum [*sic*] scilicet super certum tenorem aliqua pars cantilenae iterator'); see Frederick H. Hammond, *Walteri Odington: 'Summa de speculatione musicae'*, CSM 14 (Rome, 1970), p. 140. The translation is adapted from Jay A. Huff, *Walter Odington: 'De speculatio musicae' Part VI*, Musicological Studies and Documents 31 (Rome, 1973), p. 28.

[41] On the permission in theoretical treatises of dissonance on weak beats see the summary in Hans Tischler, 'The Evolution of Harmonic Style in the Notre-Dame Motet', *Acta musicologica*, 28 (1956), 87–95 (pp. 90–1).

[42] This example is transcribed from Cambridge, Corpus Christi College, MS 410, fol. 34v, the only complete surviving source of Odington's *De speculatione musicae*. On sources, see Elina Grace Hamilton, 'Walter of Evesham Abbey and the Intellectual Milieu of Fourteenth-Century English Music Theory', Ph.D. diss. (Prifysgol Bangor University, 2014), pp. 113–27. Odington's example (Mt540) survives in full only in **Mo** (fols. 148v–151v), in a three-voice form with different texts (Mt538–9). For a discussion of Odington's example and an annotated transcription of the complete host motet, see Gaël Saint-Cricq, 'Formes types dans le motet du XIIIe siècle: Etude d'un processus répétitif', Ph.D. diss. (University of Southampton, 2009), Vol. I, pp. 93–4 and Vol. II, pp. 111–12 respectively.

Example 3.6 Illustration of dissonance in *motetus coloratus* from Walter Odington's *De speculatione musicae.*

first involves a harmonic second at perfection 23 – in the repetition of the c motive – where B in the upper voice eventually resolves onto a unison with the accompanying tenor A before the cadence in perfection 24. The second is more striking, since it occurs at the beginning of a phrase, the outset of the d motive in perfection 25. The start of the upper-voice phrase on G sounds against a tenor F rather than in unison with a tenor G, as on the two previous appearances of this motive (perfections 17 and 21) and in the subsequent repetition of the d phrase (as d' in perfection 33). These two dissonances are clearly motivated and justified by the same preoccupation with upper-voice repetition evident in Odington's example.

A third and final example of stressed dissonance 'for the sake of *color*' is found only in the motet *Infidelem populum* and is notably absent from its related clausula. This constitutes the most significant musical variant between the two extant versions. The dissonance exclusive to *Infidelem populum* is reminiscent of perfection 23 in both clausula and motet: it occurs mid-phrase at perfection 35 (marked by a box in Example 3.5), where the motetus again sounds B against the tenor A, resolving onto a C–A chord in perfection 36. This dissonance arises because of an exact musical repetition in the motet. The motet's final d′ phrase (perfections 33–7) reiterates verbatim the same musical material of perfections 25–9, with the opening G–A–C gesture characteristic of the c motive followed by a repeated-note descent from C to F found also in the opening phrase, a. The final two phrases of the clausula do not feature such exact repetition, however. The d′ phrase here eliminates the repetition of the pitches C and B in perfection 34, with the result that the initial melodic descent occurs more quickly. In consequence, the rest of the d material until the beginning of perfection 38 (marked by a box in Example 3.3) is transposed down a tone, producing a phrase composed only of stressed perfect consonances: unisons, fourths, or fifths sound between the upper voice and tenor at the beginning of each perfection. In the motet, the upper-voice insistence on repeated C and B pitches in perfections 34 and 35 produces not only a dissonant second with the tenor in perfection 35, but also the weaker consonance of a third between tenor and motetus in perfection 36.

In consequence, the motet version of this phrase was presumed to be erroneous by Hans Tischler, who in his edition of *Infidelem populum* substituted the more consonant clausula reading instead, proposing that the motetus had simply been copied a second too high.[43] Yet scribal error seems unlikely here. The motet dissonance in perfection 35 is in keeping with the idiom of the piece as a whole, it has an obvious motivic rationale, and the phrase as copied is complete and of the required duration.[44] There seems little reason to doubt that the motet's version of the d′ phrase was intentional and that the two versions of the same phrase extant in motet and clausula are genuine alternatives. They occur in the face of an otherwise stable transmission, betraying subtly different attitudes to melodic and harmonic parameters – a preference for literal repetition on the one hand and for consonance on the other. Such variant readings, easily overlooked at a superficial glance, offer revealing insight into the sorts of compositional choices with which the creators of motets and clausulae played. The *Reg[nat] 8* clausula demonstrates just how a *color* could – if desired – be unobtrusively manipulated to avoid dissonance against a given tenor.[45]

Harmonic dissonance 'excused' by melodic repetition, sanctioned by Garlandia and Odington, was not therefore an option invariably exploited. Although consonance gives way to exact repetition on some occasions, repeated motives are manipulated to avoid dissonance on others. These circumstances do not seem to be chronologically or generically contingent, and they underline a fundamental flexibility in attitudes towards repetitive *color* and consonance, a flexibility tellingly evident across the two extant versions of the *Reg[nat] 8* material.[46] Such flexibility becomes apparent only when different versions of the same material are scrutinised closely, and

[43] See Hans Tischler, *The Earliest Motets (to circa 1270): A Complete Comparative Edition* (New Haven, 1982), Vol. I, p. 378, no. 44. Van der Werf also adjusts the final phrase of *Infidelem populum* to match its related clausula. See the edition in *Hidden Beauty*, pp. 10–11.

[44] The accelerated descent from F to D in perfection 38 of the motetus compensates for its extended repetitions in perfections 34–5.

[45] A similar instance in the neighbouring pieces *Reg[nat] 6* and *Deus omnium* was discussed above: the interval of a second between upper voice and tenor is avoided (at perfection 37) by the reworking of motive c′ as motive x (see Example 3.2). In this case, both clausula *and* motet reveal a preference for and means of achieving consonance through a small compromise in motivic repetition.

[46] See also the discussion in Chapter 5 of a circumstance in which a French motet is rendered more dissonant but more literally repetitive in its clausula transcription.

when alternative manuscript readings – particularly the more dissonant ones – are considered seriously, not simply dismissed as errors. This pair of compositions on the REGNAT tenor presents unusually clear and concrete evidence of the ways in which theoretical precepts codified in treatises might relate to and operate in musical practice – practice in which the compositional priority of harmonic and melodic components, of consonance or *color*, was evidently in flux.

Challenging Conceptions of Clausula-Derived Motets

In many respects, *Deus omnium* and *Infidelem populum* are typical of early Latin motets derived from clausulae. These characteristically brief pieces on a popular Assumption tenor make only very minor adjustments to their clausula models, and they add an additional and complementary textual dimension to pre-existing musical material. Yet textually, the REGNAT compositions defeat conventional expectations for motets of this type in two regards. The first involves semantic relationships between motetus texts and their accompanying tenor text and liturgical context, while the second concerns their poetic regularity.

Scholars have long acknowledged the importance of assonance in motet texts, which frequently borrow and elaborate vowel sounds prominent in an underlying tenor chant text, and sometimes open or close with direct reference to their complete tenor word.[47] Interest in the textual sounds of a tenor quotation is compatible with the derivation of motets from clausulae, where single syllables are treated to long melismatic elaborations, the character of their extended vowel sounds presumably infusing the musical texture. Typical of early Latin motets, in particular, is a deeper semantic engagement with the tenor word, and additionally with broader contexts of the host chant, the liturgy, and even the original biblical text from which the tenor's plainchant is drawn. In consequence, many of these troping motets have been considered suitable for liturgical use. Rebecca A. Baltzer, strictly limiting her selection to motets that make explicit reference to the tenor

[47] See, for example, Hans Nathan, 'The Function of Text in French 13th-Century Motets', *Musical Quarterly*, 28 (1942), 445–62. Examples of motets that open with complete tenor words include *Mors a primi/Mors que stimulo/Mors morsu/MORS* (Mt254–6) and *Nostrum est impletum/NOSTRUM* (Mt216). The motet *Homo quam sit pura/[IMMO]LATUS* (see n. 30 above) closes with the word 'immolatus'.

feasts and host plainchants in question, deemed 72 per cent of the exclusively Latin motet collection in **F** as appropriate for liturgical performance.[48]

Notably, both *Deus omnium* and *Infidelem populum* lack any explicit connection to the *Alleluia. Hodie Marie* chant from which the REGNAT melisma is drawn. These two motets refer neither to the specific feast of the Assumption, nor even to the Virgin Mary. The closing rhyme, '-erat', of *Deus omnium* is surely an assonant allusion to the tenor word, employing the initial and final consonants of REGNAT as well as its opening vowel sound. But the rhymes ('-um'; '-ice'; '-ulo') of *Infidelem populum* seem independent of their accompanying tenor text. Both motet texts intersect only broadly with the local textual message of the word REGNAT ('reigns'), referring in its original chant context to Mary, but here emphasising God's power and strength in militaristic language reminiscent of crusade poetry.[49] *Deus omnium* employs relatively familiar biblical lexis, such as the opening invocation 'God of all', the concept of 'trembling at the name of the Lord', and the idea of God 'breaking the bow'.[50] Similar imagery is at play in *Infidelem populum*, which also makes reference to the Old Testament story of the treacherous Haman, who prepares for the hanging of his rival for royal favour, Mordecai, but whose betrayal is discovered and who is instead hanged himself.[51] These two narrowly focused semantic responses to the REGNAT tenor – taking the word's immediate meaning, but neglecting any wider liturgical connotations – invite a parallel with the isolation of the REGNAT melisma from its surrounding chant or organum context in clausulae.

As the thirteenth century's most popular clausula tenor, it was in this genre that the REGNAT melisma enjoyed its polyphonic heyday. Twenty different discant or clausula settings of this tenor are recorded across **W1**, **F**, and **W2**, while there are only ten extant REGNAT motets – six Latin, four

[48] See Rebecca A. Baltzer, 'Performance Practice: The Notre-Dame Calendar and the Earliest Latin Liturgical Motets' (unpublished paper presented at Das Ereignis Notre Dame, Wolfenbüttel, 1985), available online at *Archivum de musica medii aevi*, www.univ-nancy2.fr/MOYENAGE/UREEF/MUSICOLOGIE/AdMMAe/AdMMAe_index.htm, p. 32 (accessed 1 March 2018). See also the discussion of a possible liturgical performance for Latin motets in **F**, in Catherine A. Bradley, 'Ordering in the Motet Fascicles of the Florence Manuscript', *Plainsong and Medieval Music*, 22 (2013), 37–64 (pp. 52–5).

[49] The reference in *Infidelem populum* to overthrowing the Jesubites – the inhabitants of Jerusalem – seems especially significant in this context.

[50] 'Trembling at the name' as employed in Isaiah 59:19 or Psalm 102; 'breaking the bow' as found in Jeremiah 49:53 or Psalm 46:10 (Vulgate Psalm 45), a text that also emphasises God's ability to end conflict.

[51] Esther 5:8–7:10.

French – in the entire thirteenth-century corpus.[52] Strikingly, all six of the Latin REGNAT motets are found in **F** and all apparently derive from related discant or clausula compositions recorded earlier in this manuscript, yet just half of them seem suitable for liturgical use.[53] The four French motets on REGNAT – lacking any clausula concordances in **W1**, **F** or **W2** – are recorded among the earliest layers of vernacular motet composition (in the mid-century sources **Her**, **N**, **R**). In sharp contrast, new compositions on REGNAT are completely absent from later-thirteenth-century motet collections (such as **Mo** and **Ba**), suggesting that interest in this tenor did not persist in the motet genre and tailed off as the century progressed. Such intense concentration on the REGNAT tenor in clausulae of the early thirteenth century seems indicative of a compositional climate driven, less by an explicitly textual interest or liturgical need, than by predominantly musical experimentation with the rich possibilities – which creators of dupla played with and against – presented by this substantial and intricate chant melisma.

This creative context would account for the fundamentally structural rather than exegetical nature of text–music relationships in *Deus omnium* and *Infidelem populum*. The REGNAT tenor here functions more as a musical foundation and inspiration for repetitive play, motivic and poetic, than a key to the motets' thematic content. It seems that the marked preoccupation with musical repetition and regularity in both *Reg*[*nat*] *6* and *Reg*[*nat*] *8* clausulae motivated their two such unusually regular motet texts. Stereotypical motet texts – of the kind that puzzled Meyer – may feature a wide variety of poetic line lengths, sporadically mixing very short text units with longer ones.[54] As an isosyllabic text, *Deus omnium* is unique in the context of the sixty-nine motets in the collection in **F**. And although the final phrases of *Infidelem populum* briefly interrupt its regular seven-syllable pattern, this text still stands out as remarkably consistent. Though unusual, the fact that such poetic regularity is achievable in clausula-derived motets raises larger questions, explored below, about the conventional narrative of motet development inherited from Meyer.

[52] Clausula and discant settings are listed in Smith, 'An Early Thirteenth-Century Motet', p. 25. The ten motets are Mt437–447a. As a counter-example to REGNAT, the IN SECULUM tenor received fifteen different clausula or discant settings across **W1**, **F**, and **W2** and was the basis of forty-six different motets.

[53] Baltzer considers *Flos de spina rumpitur*, *Hodie Marie concurrant*, and *Rex pacificus* as liturgically appropriate, but not *Ad solitum vomitum*, *Infidelem populum*, and *Deus omnium*. See 'Performance Practice', p. 43.

[54] See, for instance, the example discussed in Holford-Strevens, 'Latin Poetry and Music', pp. 234–5.

Conclusions

In examining the creation of two REGNAT motets from clausulae, this chapter has sought to tease out various strands and challenge several assumptions encapsulated in the epigraph from Meyer. A deeper understanding of the 'painstaking' process of crafting texts for given melodies, and its impact on poetry and music alike, goes some way to addressing later scholarly perceptions and valuations of this process. Meyer, for instance, pays respect to the difficulties of the poet's task, but at the same time one senses his unease that a poet must subordinate his instincts to the demands of a melody. More telling still is the troubling puzzle that seemingly motivated the philologist to investigate these creative circumstances: that motet texts did not have coherent or conventional forms in themselves, and thus – by implication – lacked poetic merit. Interestingly, musicologists such as Everist have revealed the opposite anxiety, suggesting that the purely musical 'sophistication' of clausulae may have been compromised by 'poetic exigencies' of the texting process.[55] I argue instead for a fundamentally productive and dynamic music–text relationship, showing how a new text may respond to, enhance, and recast a pre-existing musical structure often at multiple levels. I underline the symbiosis of music and text in clausula-derived motets and the possible artistry of their combination. Above all, this chapter has sought to highlight the inherent flexibility in relationships between text and music, and between melodic repetition and harmonic consonance in the early thirteenth century. While its focus has been restricted to clausulae that have priority over their related motets, subsequent chapters make the case for the opposite chronological relationship, underlining the possibility of multi-directional interactions also at the level of genre.

As motet texts, *Deus omnium* and *Infidelem populum* are exceptional in their lack of liturgical engagement and especially in their highly regular poetry, apparently crafted in response to their musically repetitive clausula models. Yet though exceptional, these two case studies have important consequences for understandings of clausula-derived motets more generally. This pair of compositions demonstrates that poetic regularity is eminently possible when texting a pre-existent melody. A motet creator just needs to select a regular clausula model, or one that can be easily and unobtrusively manipulated to support regular poetic lines. In *Reg[nat]* 6 this is achieved simply by encompassing 'extra' clausula pitches within melodic embellishments on a single syllable. Other Lain motets apparently derived

[55] Everist, *French Motets in the Thirteenth Century*, p. 27.

from clausulae standardise the number of notes per phrase by comparable means: breaking down longer notes into several shorter components, for instance, or regularising cadence types to include or omit repeated pitches as necessary.[56] Textual regularity or irregularity in clausula-derived motets, then, seems determined not by practical necessity but by choice as to the type and treatment of clausula models. This contradicts Meyer's still prevalent belief that the origin of motets in clausulae was necessarily the impetus for the genre's poetic irregularity.

Significantly, though, motet creators working with pre-existing clausulae rarely availed themselves of possibilities to create regular texts, eschewing opportunities for regularity in both their selection and handling of clausula models. In terms of available clausula models, Baltzer identified a group of nineteen especially regular clausulae with highly consistent phrase lengths, noting with some surprise that not one of these clausulae had a motet concordance.[57] There are also multiple examples of clausula models that could easily have been regularised to promote more regular syllable counts in their related motets but were not.[58] Furthermore, there exist motets in which clausula models seem actively to have been made less regular: through deliberately variable approaches to texting fast notes (at times syllabic, at times melismatic);[59] through reparsing musical phrases;[60] and even, in one

[56] I show how these straightforward musical adjustments to clausulae facilitate a more uniform motet text, in Catherine A. Bradley, 'Re-workings and Chronological Dynamics in a Thirteenth-Century Latin Motet Family', *Journal of Musicology*, 32 (2015), 153–97. Significantly, variants of this kind are not apparent between French motets and their extant clausula transcriptions in **F**: in these cases, clausula and motet tend to match up exactly in terms of the number of pitches they contain.

[57] See Baltzer, 'Notation, Rhythm, and Style', Vol. I, pp. 256–7. Although Baltzer draws attention to the brevity of these clausulae and their preponderance of duplex longs as features possibly unattractive to motet creators, the complete lack of extant motet concordances for such highly regular clausulae remains striking. Susan A. Kidwell analysed a group of clausulae with related motets against a 'control' group of clausulae without extant motets in 'The Selection of Clausula Sources for Thirteenth-Century Motets: Some Practical Considerations and Aesthetic Implications', *Current Musicology*, 64 (1998), 73–103. Although Kidwell's methodology, relying heavily on statistical comparisons, is problematic, she concludes that motet creators favoured clausula models that had 'irregularities of design' (p. 94), acknowledging that irregularities in Latin motets may reflect 'artistic choice' (p. 95).

[58] In *Factum est salutare/DOMINUS* (Mt43), for instance, clausula pitches could have been subsumed within melismas to facilitate a text of regular seven-syllable lines throughout. In *Qui servare puberem/*[*DOMI*]*NE* (Mt59), clausula anacruses could simply have been omitted to permit a more regular alteration of seven- and five-syllable lines.

[59] On flexibility of syllabification when texting short-note (or *fractio modi*) passages in clausulae, see Smith, 'The Earliest Motets', pp. 151–4.

[60] See my discussion of *Formam hominis/GLORIA* (Mt643), in 'New Texts for Old Music', pp. 162–8.

case, by introducing cadential inconsistencies where the extant clausula is consistent.[61] All this confirms not merely that poetic regularity was generally of little concern to motet creators, but that irregularity was prized and deliberately cultivated.[62] If irregularity in motet texts was not an inevitable consequence of the texting of clausulae but rather an aesthetic choice, this offers a new perspective on early motets and promotes reconsideration of the origins of the genre.

For Meyer and Ludwig the priority of clausulae and the Latin liturgical heritage of motets was unquestionable, a presumption that went hand in hand with the hypothesis that irregularities in motet texts stemmed from their initial conception as prosulae for clausulae. Considered in a broader generic context, however, the number of thirteenth-century motets with extant/known related clausulae in **W1**, **F**, and **W2** is relatively modest: 104 individual pieces, which equates to approximately 20 per cent of the entire thirteenth-century motet corpus.[63] At a generous estimate, only around sixty-five mainly Latin-texted motets genuinely derive from their related clausulae, constituting about 15 per cent of the repertoire as a whole. Vernacular motets, which represent the majority of the thirteenth-century corpus, are overwhelmingly newly composed works.[64] Notwithstanding the fact that genres may undergo multiple and seemingly unaccountable transformations, it is perhaps surprising that motet's supposed original impetus, the art of prosula, did not persist. And if poetic irregularities were simply a prosaic consequence of the prosula process, it seems remarkable that they

[61] Compare *Virgo singularis*/[*DOMINO*] (Mt655), recorded uniquely in **F** (fol. 414r–v), and its related clausula *Domino 11*, also unique to **F** (fol. 88v–3).

[62] Kidwell previously underlined the preference for irregular clausula models in her 'The Selection of Clausula Sources'. Similarly, David Maw has emphasised the importance of poetic irregularity in Petronian motets, proposing that this was a quality also deliberately sought in earlier pieces. See his '"Je le temoin en mon chant": The Art of Diminution in the Petronian Triplum', in Catherine A. Bradley and Karen Desmond (eds.), *The Montpellier Codex: The Final Fascicle. Contexts, Contents, Chronologies* (Woodbridge, 2018), pp. 161–83 (p. 174 n. 35).

[63] These numbers were calculated with reference to Norman E. Smith's catalogue in 'From Clausula to Motet: Material for Further Studies in the Origin and Early History of the Motet', *Musica disciplina*, 34 (1980), 29–65 (pp. 38–65), taking account of concordances reported since then by Saint-Cricq ('Formes types', Vol. I, p. 146) and Robert Michael Curry ('Fragments of *Ars antiqua* Music at Stary Sącz and the Evolution of the Clarist Order in Central Europe in the Thirteenth Century', Ph.D. diss. (Monash University, 2003), p. 158). I take the roughly 460 individual motet families catalogued in Gennrich's *Bibliographie* to represent the size of the thirteenth-century motet repertoire (I do not count contrafacta or motets with added voices as separate pieces).

[64] See the discussion of the relationship between vernacular motets and clausulae in Chapter 4. I argue elsewhere (in 'Contrafacta and Transcribed Motets', p. 69) that no more than half – and probably considerably fewer – of the sixty-one French-texted motets with related

should continue to characterise texts in both Latin and vernacular motets long after concrete connections with clausulae diminished.

What, then, might have encouraged an aesthetic preference for poetic irregularity in motets if the process of creating prosulae for pre-existing clausulae was not responsible? In fact, and as Richard Crocker has emphasised, a similarly irregular kind of Latin poetry is frequently evident in earlier, and newly composed, Aquitanian versus.[65] It is possible that this set the precedent for textual irregularity exploited also in motets, although it seems curious that the more direct descendant of the versus – the conductus – tended, by contrast, towards a more conventional form of Latin poetry. Crocker rightly observed that there was no comparably irregular precedent in vernacular polyphony, and the poetry of high-register romances and trouvère songs is, too, noticeably more conventional than that of motets. Nevertheless the proposition that motets owed their characteristic poetic irregularity to a more informal textual ethos that was predominantly vernacular merits consideration, since it has effectively been precluded until now by conventional historiographical narratives. French arguably permits a more flexible kind of text declamation than Latin: it is less strictly accentual, and presents various options for elision and for the sounding (or not) of feminine end-rhymes, possibilities exploited especially in vernacular motets that declare their texts at a fast rate.[66] Furthermore, the characteristic quotation of refrains in French motets – incorporating snatches of text (and music) borrowed from different host contexts, explored in the following chapters – further heightens their tendency towards poetic irregularity. Unlike prosula techniques, an interest in quotation, and especially the quotation of plainchant tenor melodies, remains central to French and Lain motets throughout the thirteenth century. Clausulae such as *Reg[nat]* 6 and *Reg[nat]* 8, although they do not quote refrains, play with and against different kinds of quotational constraints, insistently repeating, developing,

clausulae in **W1**, **F**, and **W2** are genuinely derived from these clausulae. Furthermore, in around twenty cases where clausulae do seem to have chronological priority over related vernacular motets, these vernacular texts are probably contrafactum reworkings of earlier Latin motet texts.

[65] See Richard Crocker, 'French Polyphony of the Thirteenth Century', in Richard Crocker and David Hiley (eds.), *The Early Middle Ages to 1300*, NOHM 2 (Oxford, 1990), pp. 636–78 (p. 663).

[66] See, for example, the comparison of the suitability of Latin and vernacular textual responses to the same fast-note musical declamation in my 'Contrafacta and Transcribed Motets', pp. 8–22. On the flexibility of elisions in French motet texts, see p. 18 n. 57. It must be acknowledged that Latin declamation in early motets evidently had some degree of flexibility also, since what might be considered misaccentuations of Latin words are fairly common in motet texts (see the example of misaccentuation in *Deus omnium* discussed in n. 34 above).

and twisting melodic ideas above a pre-determined tenor. The possibility for short and variable text lines in motets undoubtedly complements and enhances such musical impulses. Musical games of quotation and repetition perhaps encouraged the motet's freer approach to poetic conventions, which allowed texts fully to engage in play with musical elements with fewer external constraints of their own.

4 Transcribing Motets: Vernacular Refrain Melodies in *Magnus liber* Clausulae

The appearance within Latin liturgical clausulae of melodies associated with secular vernacular refrains – short phrases of music and French text circulating across and within romance, chanson, and motet repertoires – has long proved difficult to reconcile with conventional historiographical narratives for thirteenth-century polyphony. The previous chapter explored the conversion of clausulae into Latin motets, while Chapters 1 and 2 highlighted more unusual clausulae behaviours: the marked independence of clausulae and motets on *Propter veritatem* tenors, and the status and function of the atypical mini clausulae. In all cases, however, these various types of clausulae had an essentially sacred identity, as polyphonic elaborations of plainchant tenors that could plausibly be used in the liturgy. Given this strongly religious and Latinate context, the presence within certain clausulae of musical phrases that elsewhere have the status of worldly French refrains is perplexing: how did such refrain melodies – characteristic of monophonic *rondeaux* and *pastourelles* and often circulating as quotations across several different songs – come to be present within this polyphonic liturgical genre; and what might their presence reveal about the conception of such clausulae?

Vernacular motets constitute the crucial link between clausulae and refrains. Since melismatic clausulae may share the music of French-texted motets employing refrains, such clausulae offer additional, purely musical, refrain concordances. The accepted answer to the questions posed above, therefore, is that melodies associated with refrains were conceived within the sacred clausula context, the clausulae were later texted to make French motets, and only subsequently did certain melodic phrases attain refrain status, at which point some of these refrains went on to permeate the world of monophonic chansons.[1] Such a chronology fits happily with established

[1] For examples of recent scholarship that expound or subscribe to this chronology, see Mark Everist, *French Motets in the Thirteenth Century: Music, Poetry, and Genre* (Cambridge, 1994), pp. 66–71; Suzannah Clark, '"S'en dirai chançonete": Hearing Text and Music in a Medieval Motet', *Plainsong and Medieval Music*, 16 (2007), 31–59 (p. 46 n. 32); and Jennifer Saltzstein, *The Refrain and the Rise of the Vernacular in Medieval French Music and Poetry* (Cambridge, 2013), pp. 15–16.

models of motet development: a general progression from clausula to motet, and from polyphonic musical practices associated with Notre Dame Cathedral to those of the more popular, vernacular realm. Through detailed analyses of musical and notational aspects of refrain transmission, this chapter offers substantial evidence against the current default presumption that clausulae containing refrain melodies are the sources of these refrains. I explore the consequences of this chronological reversal for current understandings of clausulae, motets, chansons, refrains, and their interactions, as well as of refrain origins and circulation more generally. This opens up wider questions about the conceptualisation of genres as liturgical, sacred, and secular, and the nature and functional consequences of musical exchange between sacred and secular, Latin and vernacular spheres.

A Clausula-Refrain Corpus

Yvonne Rokseth, in 1939, was the first to voice a challenge to the perceived origins of refrain melodies within clausulae, with specific reference to the St Victor manuscript.[2] Dated to the 1270s, the forty clausulae in **StV** are exceptionally accompanied by corresponding vernacular motet incipits. To account for the presence both of motet incipits and of refrain melodies, Rokseth proposed that these clausulae did not pre-date their related vernacular motets as hitherto presumed, but were instead textless transcriptions of these motets. Her hypothesis, contrary as it was to the chronology enshrined within Friedrich Ludwig's monumental catalogues, was not universally accepted, and until recently scholars continued to assume that the normal 'clausula-to-motet' progression applied also in **StV**.[3] In 2011, Fred Büttner finally and convincingly proved, through comprehensive analysis of each of the **StV** clausulae, their consistent origins in motets.[4] Büttner proposed that this coherent collection of transcribed motets represented a deliberately conservative attempt to reform worldly songs into a supposedly

[2] Yvonne Rokseth (ed.), *Polyphonies du XIIIe siècle: Le manuscrit H196 de la faculté de médecine de Montpellier*, 4 vols. (Paris, 1935–9), Vol. IV, pp. 70–1.

[3] See, for example, Emma Dillon, *The Sense of Sound: Musical Meaning in France 1260–1330*, New Cultural History of Music (New York, 2012), pp. 161–3. See also Clark, 'S'en dirai chançonete', pp. 55–6.

[4] Fred Büttner, *Das Klauselrepertoire der Handschrift Saint-Victor (Paris, BN, lat. 15139): Eine Studie zur mehrstimmigen Komposition im 13. Jahrhundert* (Lecce, 2011).

purer sacred state, imitating the early- and mid-thirteenth-century *Magnus liber* sources, **W1**, **F**, and **W2**.

Since **StV** undeniably represents a special case, it is perhaps understandable that the older *Magnus liber* sources it may have sought to imitate typically continue to be excluded from **StV**'s revised chronological narrative, which grants French motets and refrains priority over their related clausulae. In 1987, Wolf Frobenius called attention to the presence of refrain melodies also in *Magnus liber* clausulae, proposing that these clausulae must, like those in **StV**, also represent transcribed motets.[5] Yet Frobenius's widespread reversal of the traditional clausula-to-motet chronology met with resistance, and scholars were reluctant to accept that a source such as **F**, with its close ties to Notre Dame, might intersperse vernacular motet transcriptions with true 'substitute' clausulae and motet sources of the sort discussed in the preceding chapters.[6] I have argued elsewhere that Frobenius's hypothesis is convincing in several individual cases.[7] This chapter places such claims in a broader context, defining and scrutinising a corpus of *Magnus liber* clausulae that contain refrain melodies.

Comprehensive assessment of the relationship between refrains and clausulae has long been impeded by the state of published catalogues. This results partly from the exclusively textual bias of the standard refrain inventories by Friedrich Gennrich and Nico van den Boogaard: since these resources contained no musical information, they did not acknowledge the purely musical concordances of refrains within clausulae.[8] And while all catalogues of clausulae and organa detail motet concordances as a matter of course, they are universally silent on the subject of any refrain melodies transmitted within them. A new online refrain database with melodies, compiled by Mark Everist and Anne Ibos-Augé, is the first explicitly to include a category for clausula concordances, but even here it remains

[5] Wolf Frobenius, 'Zum genetischen Verhältnis zwischen Notre-Dame-Klauseln und ihren Motetten', *Archiv für Musikwissenschaft*, 44 (1987), 1–39.

[6] Gordon A. Anderson rejected outright the priority of motets over clausulae in **F** in his 'Clausulae or Transcribed Motets in the Florence Manuscript?', *Acta musicologica*, 42 (1970), 109–28. See also Franz Körndle's comments on the reception of Frobenius's reversal of the clausula-to-motet chronology in 'Von der Klausel zur Motette und zurück? Überlegungen zum Repertoire der Handschrift *Saint-Victor*', *Musiktheorie*, 25 (2010), 117–28 (p. 118).

[7] Catherine A. Bradley, 'Clausulae and Transcribed Motets: Vernacular Influences on Latin Motets and Clausulae in the Florence Manuscript', *Early Music History*, 32 (2013), 1–70.

[8] The refrain catalogues are Friedrich Gennrich, *Bibliographisches Verzeichnis der französischen Refrains des 12. und 13. Jahrhunderts*, SMMA 14 (Frankfurt, 1964); and Nico van den Boogaard, *Rondeaux et refrains du XIIe siècle au début du XIVe*, Bibliothèque française et romane, Série D: Initiation, textes et documents 3 (Paris, 1969).

difficult to assess precisely how many clausulae contain refrain melodies and to survey details of their manuscript transmission.[9]

To that end, Table 4.1 offers a complete list of refrain melodies in *Magnus liber* clausulae.[10] Crucially, it also implements Jennifer Saltzstein's recently established distinctions between different types of refrain. Circulation as a musical and/or textual quotation has long been considered central to the identity of a refrain. Although quotation was fundamental also to Van den Boogaard's understanding of refrains, this did not prevent him from including in his catalogue many 'unique' refrains: those, that is, surviving only in the context of a single motet or chanson.[11] Scholars such as Ardis Butterfield and Everist have since rightly queried whether these unique refrains can properly be classified as such.[12] Saltzstein has instituted the category of the intertextual refrain to distinguish those with more than one extant concordance (text and/or music) whose status as quotations is substantiated.[13] She also usefully distinguishes intertextual refrains transmitted only within the motet repertoire ('intertextual motet refrains') from those circulating across motet and chanson repertoires (designated here as intertextual motet and chanson refrains). Although the term intertextual is often employed somewhat loosely (encompassing a variety of purely textual, purely musical, and both textual and musical concordances), its unqualified use here is reserved for refrains extant with the same text *and* music in more than one host source. These intertextual refrains – musico-textual units known in multiple contexts and whose status as true refrains is therefore certain – are shown in bold in Table 4.1. They form the principal focus of the current chapter, in which intertextuality that is exclusively textual or exclusively musical is always specified as such.[14]

[9] Mark Everist and Anne Ibos-Augé, *REFRAIN: Musique, poésie, citation: Le refrain au moyen âge/Music, Poetry, Citation: The Medieval Refrain*, at http://medmus.soton.ac.uk/view.html (accessed 4 March 2018).

[10] Table 4.1 includes a new concordance for vdB 310 that I have discovered in Mt402. It also includes a concordance for vdB 1157 in Mt81 identified by Hans Tischler in 1985 but omitted from any of the published or online resources. See his *The Style and Evolution of the Earliest Motets (to circa 1270)*, 4 vols., Musicological Studies 40 (Ottawa, 1985), Vol. II, p. 131, no. 365.

[11] See the discussion of Van den Boogaard's unique refrains in Ardis Butterfield, 'Repetition and Variation in the Thirteenth-Century Refrain', *Journal of the Royal Musical Association*, 116 (1991), 1–23 (pp. 1–3).

[12] See ibid.; and Everist, *French Motets in the Thirteenth Century*, pp. 54–7. See also Robyn E., Smith, 'Gennrich's *Bibliographisches Verzeichnis der französischen Refrains*: Tiger or Fat Cat?', *Parergon*, 8 (1990), 73–101; and Clark, 'S'en dirai chançonete', pp. 47–8.

[13] Jennifer Saltzstein, 'Relocating the Thirteenth-Century Refrain: Intertextuality, Authority and Origins', *Journal of the Royal Musical Association*, 135 (2010), 245–79 (p. 251).

[14] Saltzstein offered a selective list of six intertextual motet refrains found in clausulae in *The Refrain and the Rise of the Vernacular*, p. 15 n. 35. Four of the six entries in her list contain

Table 4.1 *Magnus liber* clausulae containing refrain melodies

Clausulae MS sources	Clausula title	Clausula or passage of discant within organum	Related motet(s)	Refrain vdB	Refrain type	Irregular clausula notation
F, fol. 10v	*Tanquam 12* (O 2) (triplum staves blank, with traces of erasure)	C	Mt636	—	—	
			Mt 637	—	—	
			Mt638	300	U	
F, fol. 11r	*Virgo* a3 *2* (M 32)	C	Mt414	—	—	
			Mt415*	1154	U	
F, fol. 11r	***Flos filius eius* a3 *3* (O 16)**	C	Mt647	—	—	
			Mt648	—	—	
			Mt649	—	—	
			Mt650	—	—	
			Mt651	338	**IMC**	
			Mt652	—	—	
			Mt653	—	—	
			Mt654	—	—	
F, fol. 42v	*Domino* a3	D	Mt762	—	—	
W1, fol. 12r	(BD VI)	D	Mt763	—	—	
W2, fol. 29r–v		D	Mt764	343	U	
F, fol. 45r	*In odorem* a3 *2*	C	Mt495	—	—	
W1, fol. 91v	(M 45)	C	Mt496	247 & 547	U & U	
			Mt497	244	U	
F, fol. 45r–v	*Et illuminare* a3 (M 9)	C	Mt101	—	—	
			Mt104	21 & 199	U & U	
			Mt105	—	—	
F, fol. 88v–4	***Domino 12* (BD I)**	**C**	**Mt754**	**287**	**IM**	**Waite**
				1361	**IM**	
F, fol. 89r–3	*Domino 16* (BD I)	C	Mt756	87	U	Flotz.
F, fol. 100v	*Viderunt omnes 3*	D	Mt5	1481	U	
W2, fol. 64r	(M 1)	D				
F, no. 25, fol. 149r–2	*Omnes 10* (M 1)	C	Mt8	364	U	
F, no. 38, fol. 150v–3	*Lux magna 4* (M 2)	C	Mt55	570	U	
F, no. 40, fol. 151r–2	*Domine 3* (M 3)	C	Mt63	852	U	
W1, no. 14, fol. 50r–4		C				
F, no. 41, fol. 151r–3	***Domine 5* (M 3)**	**C**	Mt60	—	—	**Waite**
			Mt61	—	—	
			Mt62	**314**	**IMC**	

(*continued*)

Table 4.1 (*continued*)

Clausulae MS sources	Clausula title	Clausula or passage of discant within organum	Related motet(s)	Refrain vdB	Refrain type	Irregular clausula notation
F, no. 46, fol. 151v–2	***Manere 7* (M 5)**	**C**	**Mt79**	**285**	**IM (Different text)**	
F, no. 59, fol. 152v–7 F, no. 60, fol. 152r–8	*Surge 4 &* *Et illuminare 6* (M 9)	C C	Mt100	210	T	Waite Waite
F, no. 63, fol. 153r–4	***Venimus 2* (M 10)**	**C**	**Mt54**	**310** 1018 1832	**IM** T U	**Flotz.**
F, no. 76, fol. 155r–3	*Hec dies 5* (M 13)	C	Mt122	135	U	Waite
F, no. 84, fol. 156r–4	*Domino-quoniam 8* (M 13)	C	Mt135	1110	U	Waite
F, no. 93, fol. 157r–4 **W2**, fol. 72r	*In seculum 3* (M 13)	C D	Mt165	553	T	
F, no. 104, fol. 158v–2	***Immolatus est 9* (M 14)**	**C**	Mt233 **Mt233a**	— **1699**	— **IM**	**Waite**
F, no. 105, fol. 158v–3	***Immolatus est 10* (M 14)**	**C**	**Mt235***	**1149**	**IMC**	**Waite**
F, no. 135, fol. 162v–3 **W1**, no. 25, fol. 53v–1	*Hodie perlustravit 2* (M 25)	C C	Mt337 Mt338 Mt339	— 106 1697 —	— U T —	
F, no. 140, fol. 163v–1	*Amoris 2* (M 27)	C	Mt360 Mt361 Mt364 Mt365	— 815 — —	— U — —	Waite
F, no. 149, fol. 164v–3	*Pro patribus 3* (M 30)	C	Mt397 Mt398 Mt400	411 — —	T	Waite
F, no. 150, fol. 164v–4	***Pro patribus 4* (M 30)** (incomplete)	C	**Mt402**	**237** **310**	**IM** **IM**	
F, no. 155, fol. 165v–1	*Virgo 8* (M 32)	C	Mt419 Mt420	1794 —	U —	Waite
F, no. 162, fol. 166r–4	***Flos filius eius 4* (O 16)**	C	**Mt663** Mt665	**595** —	**IMC** —	**Waite**
F, no. 188, fol. 169r–2	***Domine 2* (M 48)**	C	**Mt406/501a**	**237**	**IM**	

(*continued*)

Table 4.1 (*continued*)

Clausulae MS sources	Clausula title	Clausula or passage of discant within organum	Related motet(s)	Refrain vdB	Refrain type	Irregular clausula notation
F, no. 196, fol. 169v–7	***Qui conservaret 7*** **(M 50)**	**C**	**Mt515a**	**1157**	**IM**	
F, no. 207, fol. 171r–1	*Et tenuerunt 3* (M 17)	C	Mt250	701	U	
				1832	U	
F, no. 452, fol. 184r–4	*Immolatus est 12*[a] (M 14)	C	Mt241	189	T	
F, no. 462, fol. 184v–7	*Docebit 6* (M 26)	C	Mt347	749	U	
				1412	U	

Abbreviations

BD Ludwig Benedicamus Domino number
C Clausula
D Passage of discant within an organum
IM Intertextual motet refrain
IMC Intertextual motet and chanson refrain
T Text-only refrain concordance
U Unique refrain

* Transmitted also as a monophonic chanson

[a] This clausula-motet concordance was recently discovered by Gaël Saint-Cricq. See his 'Formes types dans le motet du XIIIe siècle: Etude d'un processus répétitif', 2 vols., Ph.D. diss. (University of Southampton, 2009), Vol. I, p. 146.

Table 4.1 (with an accompanying list of abbreviations) records all *Magnus liber* clausulae known to contain melodies accorded the status of a refrain by Van den Boogaard. Ordered according to their appearance in **F**, Table 4.1 specifies extant manuscript sources for these clausulae, indicating whether they constitute true clausulae copied in separate fascicles devoted to this musical type (C), or passages of discant transmitted within an organum (D). Two-voice clausulae located in separate clausula fascicles in **F** were individually numbered in series by Ludwig, and these numbers are given

errors: one entry combines two motets – Mt402 and Mt403 – that are in fact separate pieces; two refrains – vdB 1157 and 1361 – are listed alongside host motets in which they appear, but these are not the motets with related clausulae; and one refrain – vdB 1671 – occurs in the triplum voice of a motet whose musical material is absent from the related two-voice clausula. Such small, but nonetheless significant, errors illustrate the difficulty of establishing clausula-refrain concordances from published catalogues.

(along with folio numbers) to clarify the sequence of clausulae in **F**. The final column indicates clausulae independently identified as notationally irregular by William Waite, including also Rudolf Flotzinger's additions to Waite's list.[15]

Patterns of Transmission

The majority of the thirty-three clausulae in Table 4.1 contain refrains that are unique, and whose status as quotations is unsubstantiated by external evidence. Yet eleven clausulae – a third of the total – feature intertextual refrain melodies (four of which circulate within monophonic chansons as well as motets), and an additional five clausulae have refrains for which independent text-only concordances survive. These different types of refrain notwithstanding, coherent patterns of transmission for their host clausulae are evident. The vast majority of refrain clausulae, and all of those containing intertextual refrains, are preserved uniquely in **F**: only six have concordances in **W1** and/or **W2**. Within **F**, these clausulae are overwhelmingly true clausulae – rather than passages of discant located within organa, as in only two cases – and they are often clustered together. Clausulae transmitting refrain melodies are heavily concentrated in the first liturgically ordered series of the manuscript's fifth fascicle (from *Omnes 10* on fol. 149r to *Qui conservaret 7* on fol. 169v), while the final three clausulae in Table 4.1 appear as part of an appendix to this fascicle. Clausulae transmitting refrain melodies are entirely absent from the second clausula series, or from the mini clausula collection (the third and fourth series).

Significantly, refrain clausulae on the same tenor chant always appear side by side.[16] And they tend to be transmitted at or near the end of a group of pieces based on a particular tenor.[17] In portions of the manuscript that are not strictly ordered liturgically, these clusters are even more pronounced. The first three clausulae in Table 4.1 form a group at the beginning of a small collection of nine three-voice clausulae appended to fascicle 1 of **F** (fols. 10v–13r). Similarly, the two three-voice clausulae containing refrains

[15] William G. Waite, *The Rhythm of Twelfth-Century Polyphony: Its Theory and Practice*, Yale Studies in the History of Music 2 (New Haven, 1954), p. 101; and Rudolf Flotzinger, *Der Discantussatz im 'Magnus liber' und seiner Nachfolge*, WMB 8 (Vienna, 1969), pp. 68–70.

[16] These clausulae are: **F**, nos. 40 and 41 on DOMINE; nos. 104 and 105 on IMMOLATUS EST; and nos. 149 and 150 on PRO PATRIBUS.

[17] *Manere 7* concludes the group of *Manere* clausulae on fol. 151r–v, and *Immolatus est 10* marks the end of the *Latus* clausulae on fol. 158v.

on fol. 45r open a set of five three-voice clausulae at the end of fascicle 2.[18] Such consistent patterns underline the validity of considering clausulae with refrain concordances as a meaningful sample, suggesting at the very least an awareness of a connection between these clausulae on the part of those planning and copying **F**. These pieces plausibly stemmed from a common exemplar, employed principally for the first clausula series, and turned to at the end of each group of clausulae on a particular tenor segment.

Notational Irregularities

Such trends alone cannot confirm the motet origins of clausulae containing refrains: they could reflect merely a desire to gather together clausulae in a style that later proved popular in melismatic sources for French motets, or to group clausulae already known to have inspired French motets. It is, however, significant that almost half of the clausulae in Table 4.1 were independently associated with notational irregularities that might result from the conversion of *cum littera* motet models – where each note is simply aligned with the text syllable to which it corresponds – into the ligature patterns of melismatic *sine littera* clausulae in modal notation. In 1954, Waite identified twenty-one clausulae in **F** as notationally irregular, highlighting their unconventional use of ligatures and improperly texted chant tenors (also lacking strokes articulating changes of syllable in the chant text). Waite proposed that these clausulae represented transcribed motets, without specifying the type of motets (French or Latin; motets with refrains or not) of which they were transcriptions. Of Waite's twenty-one clausulae, seventeen have extant related motets, and of these seventeen, twelve appear in Table 4.1, five containing intertextual refrains. Flotzinger disagreed with Waite's proposal that notational irregularities in these clausulae were brought about by motet transcription, but he added a further three similar clausulae with extant motet concordances to Waite's list, two of which additionally appear in Table 4.1.

F, no. 162 (fol. 166r–4), *Flos filius eius 4*, containing an intertextual motet and chanson refrain, admirably exemplifies Waite's notational irregularities

[18] *Domino 12* and *Domino 16* may frame a group of five transcribed vernacular motets at the end of the collection of two-voice DOMINO clausulae on **F**, fols. 88v–89r. *Domino 14* has a related French motet that does not feature a refrain melody catalogued in vdB. *Domino 13* and *Domino 15* do not have extant motet concordances, but both were considered notationally irregular by Waite and Flotzinger respectively. See also the discussion of connections between motets related to *Domino 12*, *Domino 14*, and *Domino 16* in the next chapter.

Figure 4.1 *Flos filius eius 4*, **F**, fol. 166r–4 (detail). Reproduced by permission of Florence, Biblioteca Medicea Laurenziana, MiBACT. Further reproduction by any means is prohibited.

(see Figure 4.1). Of the tenor text, only the initial 'F' is provided: the rest of the text is missing, as are any strokes to mark places where syllable changes should occur. These details were commonly overlooked in motet tenors, but usually punctiliously observed in clausulae, and of practical importance if the clausulae were to be substituted within organa. The duplum of this *Flos filius eius* clausula also posed problems for the scribe, who made several erasures and struggled to align the two voices. It seems that the tenor was copied first in its entirety and the scribe then fitted the duplum around it, copying, not from beginning to end, but working sectionally, combining short portions of the duplum with the tenor. The resulting clausula – with four gaps in the duplum, all exhibiting traces of erasure – suggests that the exemplar was neither in score nor in *sine littera* modal notation. It was, I propose, a *cum littera* motet, notated in parts, that the scribe was converting into a clausula in score as he copied.

The scribe inserted a stroke in the middle of the first line of the duplum to mark a point of congruence with the tenor at the end of a troublesome passage that he erased but never corrected. Similarly, he erased a stroke at the end of the first line of the duplum (in the middle of the refrain melody, vdB 595) presumably realising that the upper voice and tenor did not break together here, but unable to solve the problem of how the duplum should continue. While the beginning and end of the clausula were completed, internal sections proved more troublesome, suggesting attempts to locate and to work around points of coordination between the voices. It was not, therefore, that the exemplar contained lacunae, but rather that the scribe struggled to interpret it. This hypothesis is confirmed by erased passages, of which traces are still visible, that contained the appropriate pitches but aligned or ligated in a manner evidently identified as problematic.

Flos filius eius 4 is a particularly strong but not uncharacteristic example of apparently ad hoc notational translation. A pair of *Pro patribus* clausulae (nos 149–50, *Pro patribus 3* and *4*, fols. 164v–165r, shown in facsimile in Figure 4.2) just two folios earlier in **F** exhibits analogous processes. *Pro patribus 3* contains a refrain with a surviving independent text concordance. *Pro patribus 4*, had it been completed, would have transmitted two intertextual motet refrains (vdB 237 and 310 discussed further below; see Examples 4.3 and 4.7). Significantly, *Pro patribus 4* is the only clausula among the 462 of fascicle 5 to break off mid-piece (just after vdB 310, but before vdB 237), its allotted staves unfilled. *Pro patribus 3* (though not its successor) was included on Waite's list of notationally irregular clausulae. Its tenor is correctly texted – with the appropriate syllable strokes for '-tri-' and '-bus' – but the alignment of voices again posed problems. There are two substantial erasures in the tenor part (the second never refilled with the appropriate music) as well as a large space in the middle of the second tenor system that facilitated realignment of the two voices. It seems that the scribe was here fitting the tenor around the duplum (the opposite of his procedure in *Flos filius eius 4*), as is evident also in *Pro patribus 4*, for which he never entered the tenor on fol. 165r.

The surviving portion of *Pro patribus 4* exhibits similar problems. Three notes of the duplum are erased in the first phrase, perhaps because the scribe was unhappy with the expression of their rhythm in ligatures (the appropriate pitches, as found in the motet concordance, are still perceptible). The ligation of this clausula duplum is complicated throughout by the presence of many small note decorations and embellishments, common in *cum littera* French motets and easily expressed in this notation, but relatively rare and cumbersome in the context of *sine littera* clausulae.[19] Although alignment between the voices is satisfactory for the few ordines of the tenor that were copied, the fact that the tenor voice breaks off before the duplum once again points towards an exemplar in parts rather than score, and to the adaption of materials undertaken, and eventually abandoned, by the scribe himself. A prevalence of erasure and problems of layout and alignment between voices might, therefore, be added to the notational irregularities

[19] See my more extended discussion of this phenomenon in 'Clausulae and Transcribed Motets', pp. 57–61.

(a)

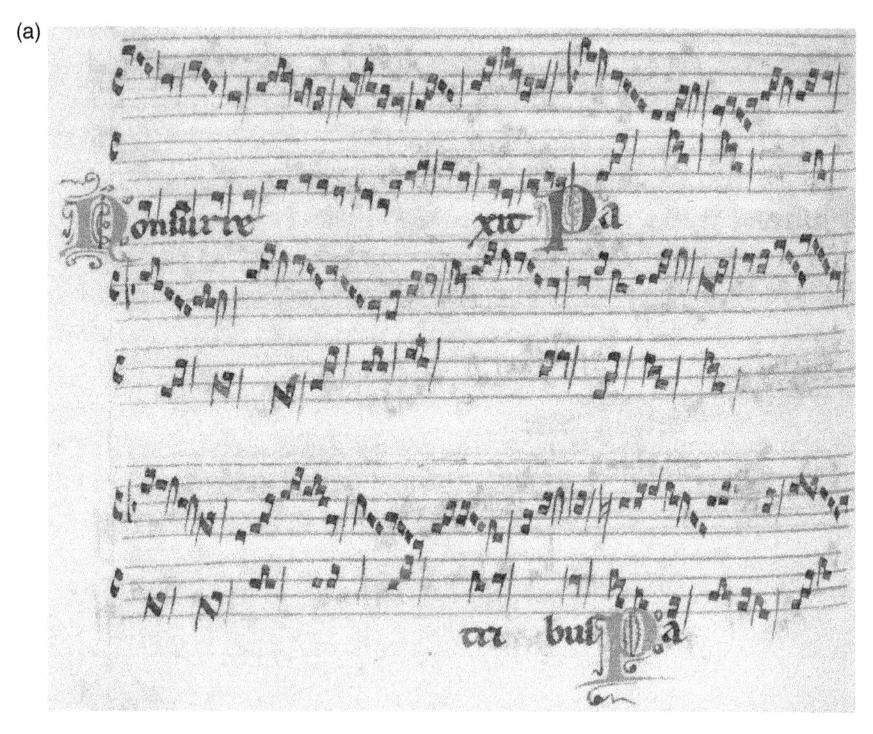

(b)

Figure 4.2 (a) **F**, fol. 164v (bottom half); (b) continued, fol. 165r (top half). Reproduced by permission of Florence, Biblioteca Medicea Laurenziana, MiBACT. Further reproduction by any means is prohibited.

observed by Waite as indicative of motet transcription, a process that could apparently be carried out by a scribe in real time, directly creating clausulae in **F** from motet exemplars.

An unusual feature of the relationship between such clausulae and their corresponding motets is further evidence of such a transcription process. Details of pitch remain very stable between clausula and motet versions, but the clausula notation frequently implies a different rhythmic reading from that found in related motets. This disjunction between the stability of transmission of pitch and rhythm is easily accounted for in a process of notational translation. When converting motets into clausulae pitch requires no manipulation, but rhythmic information must be converted from either unrhythmicised *cum littera* or rhythmically prescriptive mensural notation into the ligature patterns of *sine littera* modal notation. A tendency to assume the priority and 'authority' of clausulae over related motets has encouraged the preservation of their alternative rhythmic readings in modern editions: the rhythms of supposedly later motets are not typically imposed on their 'source' clausulae, even in cases where clausula ligature patterns are seemingly erroneous, or almost impossible to reconcile with any conventional modal interpretation.[20]

Yet it must be acknowledged that certain rhythmic alternatives cannot straightforwardly be dismissed simply as the result of irregularities in clausula notation, because a more conventional way of recording motet rhythms in *sine littera* notation would have been possible. This applies in two cases where a normal interpretation of ligature patterns in clausulae identified by Waite as irregular – *Domino 12* and *Immolatus est 9* – produces rhythmic readings for their respective intertextual refrains (vdB 287 and 1699) that differ from the rhythms securely established in their wider motet transmission. In the case of vdB 287 (see Example 4.1a), the rhythm implied by the *Domino 12* clausula in **F** is at odds with that in its related motet, *Ne m'oubliez mie*/*DOMINO* (analysed in detail in the next chapter), and all other versions of the refrain. Yet the established motet rhythm for vdB 287 could have been expressed more clearly in the **F** clausula, as indeed it was – albeit still somewhat unconventionally – in the **StV** clausula transcription of another motet containing this same refrain, *Mainte dame*/*IOHANNE* (see Example 4.1b).[21] The alternative clausula rhythm in **F** may

[20] For analysis of a particular instance, see ibid., pp. 59–61.

[21] Clausulae in **F** occasionally feature formulaic closing melismas over held tenor notes in the *organum purum* style. These appended melismas – discussed in detail in Chapter 5 – are part of the house style in **F**. They are omitted here, but are indicated by a single (rather than a double) bar-line at the end of the transcription.

Example 4.1 (a) intertextual motet refrain vdB 287 in *Domino 12* and related motet.

Domino 12 Clausula, **F**, fol. 88v-4

Ne m'oublie mie/DOMINO, **Mo**, fols. 261v-262r

(b) VdB 287 in **StV** clausula transcription of *Mainte dame/IOHANNE*, fol. 290v.

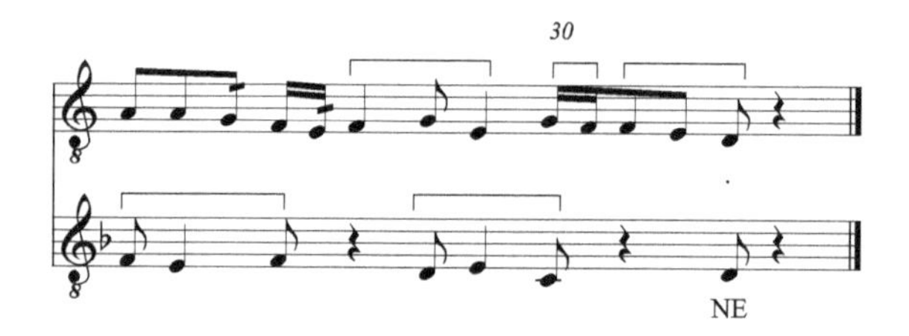

perhaps have been intentional, producing a more consonant combination with the tenor. Nonetheless, this rhythmic variance in contrast with stable pitch content is telling, as is the fact that the two clausulae versions of this refrain prompted two different ligations. This suggests the lack of any stable transmission for vdB 287 in modal notation and the possible conception of the musical phrase in association with a different, *cum littera*, notational system.

The appearance of vdB 1699 in the *Immolatus est 9* clausula presents a similar circumstance, also suggestive of notational translation (see Example 4.2). The tenor and duplum parts are misaligned in the **F** clausula, and although the melodic shape of the refrain is maintained, it is difficult to interpret and to understand the rationale behind the clausula ligature patterns. Why is the initial C not ligated within the following two-note D–E ligature? And why is the refrain's final C not also included within its preceding two-note ligature? The peculiar clausula notation actively prevents the imposition of the corresponding motet rhythms and again suggests a

Example 4.2 Transmission of vdB 1699: in *Immolatus est 9* clausula and related motets; in *L'autrier en mai/TANQUAM*.

Immolatus est 9 Clausula, **F**, no. 104, fol. 158v-2

Mout soloie chant/LATUS, **Mo**, fol. 263r-v

In modulo sonet letitia/LATUS, **F**, fol. 407v

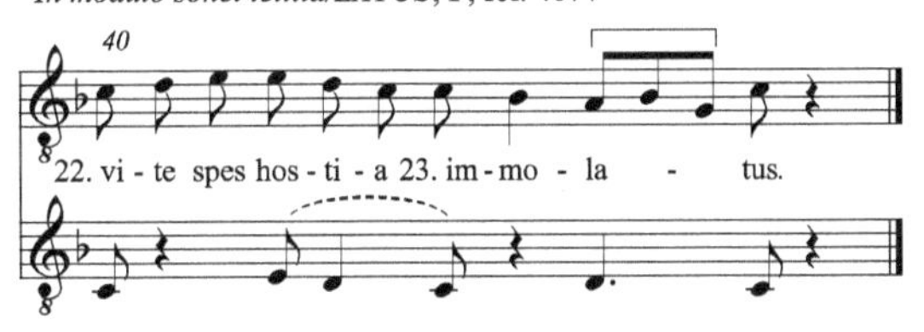

---

vdB 1699 Concordance in *L'autrier en mai/TANQUAM*
N, fols. 188v-189r (tenor incomplete) and **R**, fols. 208v-209r

more consonant version of the refrain, but it is difficult to know whether the different rhythmic reading is intentional.[22] In the face of ambiguities in

[22] My transcription of this clausula matches the unanimous rhythmic interpretations of Rebecca A. Baltzer and Hans Tischler. See Rebecca A. Baltzer (ed.), *Le 'Magnus liber organi' de Notre-Dame de Paris V: Les clausules à deux voix du manuscrit de Florence, Biblioteca*

sine littera notation, one naturally relies more heavily on clues offered by the harmonic context; in consequence, it is unsurprising that an interpretation of ambiguous clausula notation should produce a highly consonant reading. An increase in consonance cannot, therefore, in itself validate a particular rhythmic interpretation.

Translation from motet to clausula accounts unequivocally for a curious notational feature of another intertextual refrain, vdB 237, as transmitted in the clausula *Domine 2* (see Example 4.3).[23] The version of the refrain melody in the **F** clausula has a stroke in the middle of the duplum that creates notational confusion: the stroke divides the phrase in the middle of a perfection, giving the erroneous impression that the second half of the refrain – with its pair of two-note ligatures, followed by a three-note ligature – may suddenly be in the second rhythmic mode. The articulating stroke does not mark a rest or a point of congruence between duplum and tenor. Its presence in the clausula is, instead, most convincingly explained with reference to the associated French motet text, where it conventionally corresponds to a separation of the two text lines of the refrain, the second line beginning on an anacrusis.[24] The *Domine 2* clausula was not on Waite's list, yet it too exhibits irregularity in ligature patterns as well as problems of alignment, with a noticeable gap in the duplum in the middle of the final system to facilitate the realignment of the two voices at the beginning of the concluding refrain (see the facsimile in Figure 4.3).

Remarkably, the motet concordance – in which the tenor is alternatively designated BENEDICTA (M 32) – does not commence at the beginning of the clausula. Instead, it begins (as marked by an arrow in Figure 4.3) following an initial cursus of the short tenor melody in a polyphonic setting that is uniquely preserved in **F**, with no extant concordances in the clausula or motet repertoire. Motets occasionally combine two or more independent

Medicea-Laurenziana, Pluteus 29.1, fascicule V (Monaco, 1995), p. 85, no. 104; and Hans Tischler (ed.), *The Earliest Motets (to circa 1270): A Complete Comparative Edition*, 3 vols. (New Haven, 1982), Vol. I, p. 438, no. 58.

[23] In the *Domine 2* clausula and its related motet in **W2**, the tenor's regular rhythmic pattern of successive ternary longs breaks down at the point of the refrain. This irregularity in the tenor seems to accommodate the refrain quotation. Significantly, the final tenor cursus of the same motet in **Cl** has been altered: the tenor retains its regular rhythmic pattern but departs from the literal quotation of the chant melisma.

[24] In this instance, none of the extant motet sources happens to preserve this stroke, but there was evidently some flexibility in this regard: in the case of vdB 338 (see Example 4.8) two of its six extant motet sources have a stroke (here interpreted as a rest) between the two halves of the refrain. A further example where the scribe of **F** confusingly retained, in a clausula transcription, strokes associated with the text of a related French motet is offered by Büttner. See his *Das Klauselrepertoire der Hanschrift Saint-Victor*, pp. 153–4.

Example 4.3 Transmission of vdB 237: in *Domine 2* clausula and related motets; in *L'autrier quant me chevauchoie/PRO* [*PATRIBUS*].

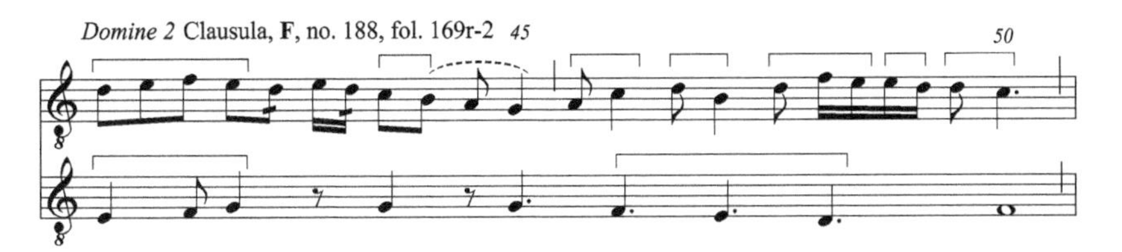

---

vdB 237 Concordance in *L'autrier quant me chevauchoie/PRO [PATRIBUS]*, **N**, fol. 193r-v

Related to Clausula *Pro patribus 4* Clausula, **F**, no. 150, fol. 164v-4 (incomplete—lacking refrain)

clausulae, but it is almost unheard of for a motet to be only partially concordant with a larger clausula.[25] The relationship between *Domine 2* and its corresponding motet was sufficiently unusual that Frobenius, though

[25] Only one other case is known to date: the concordance discovered by Robert Michael Curry ('Fragments of *Ars antiqua* Music at Stary Sącz and the Evolution of the Clarist Order in Central Europe in the Thirteenth Century', Ph.D. diss. (Monash University, 2003), p. 158)

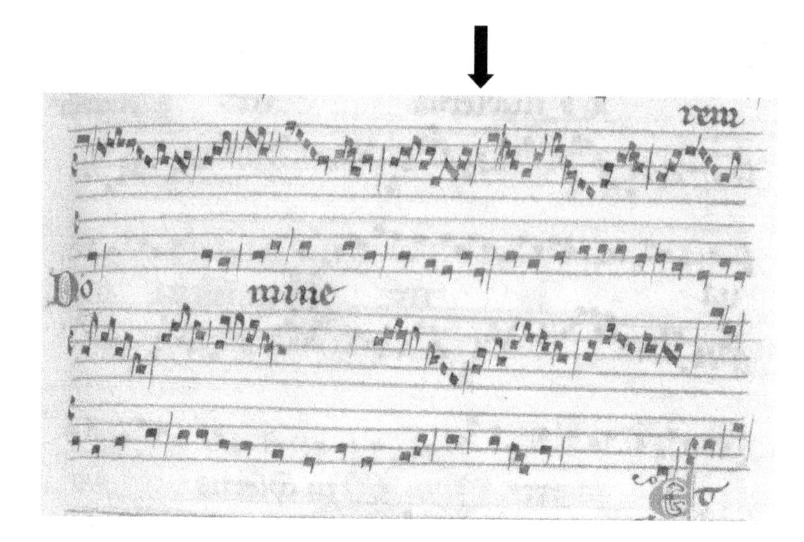

Figure 4.3 *Domine 2*, **F**, fol. 169r (detail). Reproduced by permission of Florence, Biblioteca Medicea Laurenziana, MiBACT. Further reproduction by any means is prohibited.

he acknowledged the concordance as documented in Norman E. Smith's catalogue, was 'unable to recognise' it (presumably because he did not expect the motet to begin in the middle of the clausula).[26] The anomalous nature of *Domine 2* could indicate an unusual and intriguing genesis, in which a 'genuine' clausula (with an *organum purum*-style opening) and a transcribed motet may have been tacked together, raising questions about the possible status and function of such a clausula, explored further below.[27]

Tenor–Refrain Relationships: Musical Evidence of Quotation

In addition to notational irregularities, there are also several clausulae in **F** in which refrain melodies may be identified on purely musical grounds as genuine quotations. The successful simultaneous combination in polyphony of a pre-existent refrain melody with a pre-existent tenor chant melisma might, understandably, require some manipulation of either or

between the motet *Quod promisit/LATUS* (unique to **StS1**, fol. 4v) and the second cursus of the *Immolatus 8* clausula (unique to **F**, no. 102, fol. 158r–4).

[26] See Frobenius, 'Zum genetischen Verhältnis', p. 7 n. 30 ('Nicht anerkennen können wir Sm[ith] Nr. 83'). Norman E. Smith's catalogue is 'From Clausula to Motet: Material for Further Studies in the Origin and Early History of the Motet', *Musica disciplina*, 34 (1980), 29–65.

[27] That *Domine 2* is a combination of two separate clausulae is suggested by a stroke added in the duplum after the initial F at the second tenor statement (the first note of the motet). This is surely a syllable stroke, matching that at the very start of the clausula after the initial F on 'Do-' (though the second cursus lacks a reiteration of the tenor text or an accompanying stroke in the tenor).

both quotations. Tenor manipulations are readily verifiable: as melodic deviations from the version of the plainchant melisma usually employed in organa, clausulae, and motets; and/or as disruptions in an otherwise regular rhythmic pattern. In instances where an intertextual refrain survives in multiple different host sources, it is similarly possible to identify divergences from a standard version of the refrain melody, and to assess whether these changes were motivated by its particular tenor context. Yet even when extant refrain concordances are limited, evidence in favour of quotation – such as an uncharacteristic increase in dissonance against the tenor – can be gleaned from the broader musical context. Two examples discussed in detail here exemplify these diagnostic methods.

The first concerns the clausula *Qui conservaret 7* and its related motet *Quant l'aloete saut*/*QUI CONSERVARET*. In this clausula and motet, a quotation of the widely disseminated refrain vdB 1157 was apparently altered to sound in consonant combination with a chant tenor. The terminal refrain vdB 1157 is found in three additional motet contexts, all of which employ the tenor MANERE (see Example 4.4). This refrain occurs in the motetus of the three-voice *L'autrier m'esbatiue*/*Demenant grant joie*/*MANERE*;[28] with an alternative text for the first half of the refrain in *Aveques tel Marion*/*MANERE*; and the same refrain melody appears with an entirely different refrain text (that of vdB 285) in *Manoir me fet en folie*/*MANERE*, which is related to the clausula *Manere 7*.[29] In contrast to its textual instability, the refrain's melody is subject to only minimal variations in decoration between sources, and it appears at the same point and in identical combination with its tenor in all three MANERE motets, the motetus and tenor beginning on a unison E.

Quant l'aloete saut/*QUI CONSERVARET* and its related clausula in **F** employ a slightly different version of this refrain melody. The refrain starts on A in perfection 54, before falling a fourth to E, and the opening A is accompanied by an additional text syllable, 'O', absent from all other versions of vdB 1157 (see Example 4.5). This extra A seems to have been introduced in *Quant l'aloete* in order to fit with the QUI CONSERVARET melisma. In the MANERE motets, where vdB 1157 begins over E in the tenor, either an opening E or A for this refrain would produce a satisfactory harmonic interval (a unison or a fourth). By contrast, the underlying

[28] At the close of *L'autrier m'esbatiue*/*Demenant grant joie*/*MANERE*, vdB 1157 is presented in textual unison. The motetus contains the intertextual refrain melody, while its triplum (Mt83) sets the refrain text to different music.

[29] The melody accompanying refrain text vdB 1008 in the motet *Amours m'a asseure*/*AMORIS* (Mt366) also resembles that of vdB 1157 (in an extended form).

Example 4.4 VdB 1157 in three MANERE motets.

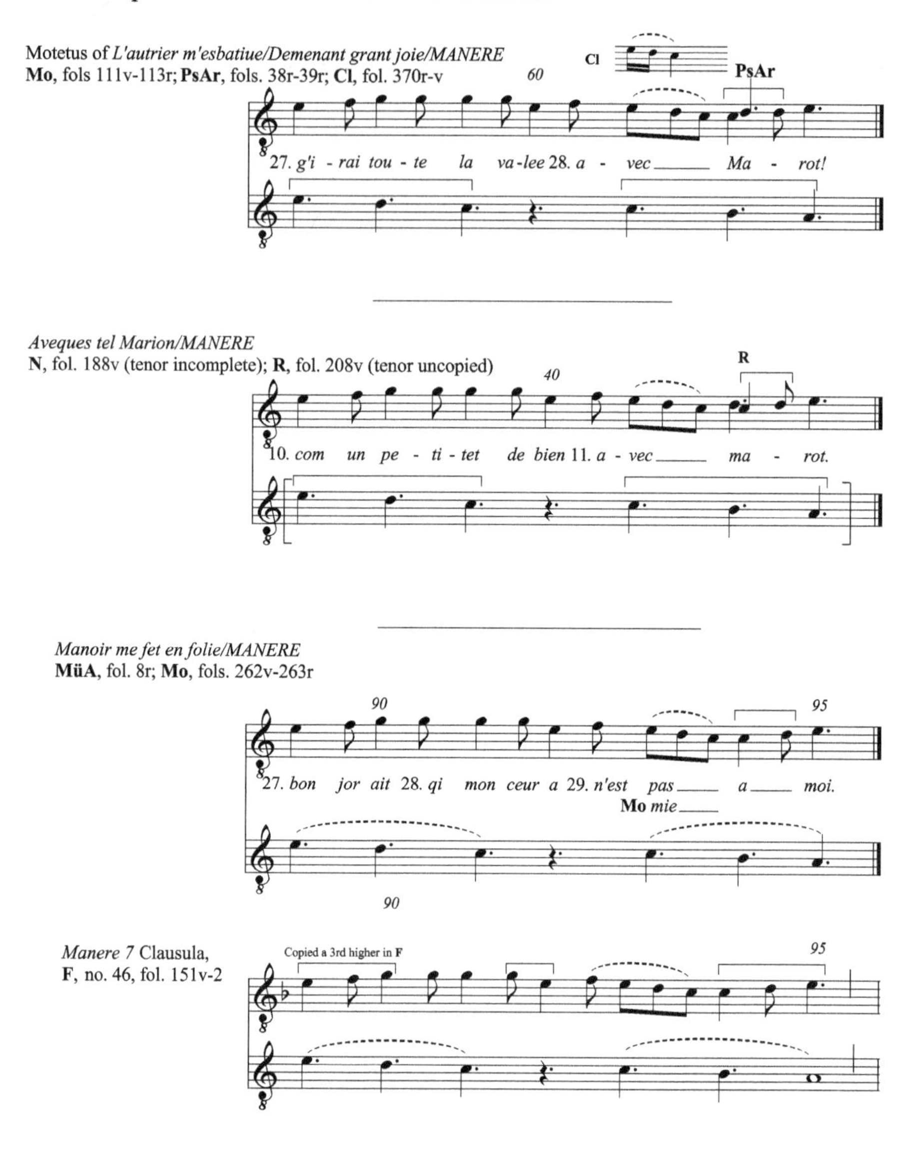

D in the QUI CONSERVARET tenor at the beginning of the refrain would create a dissonant second if the refrain melody were to begin, as it typically does, on E. To open the refrain on A, by contrast, results in the concordant interval of a fifth. The phrase immediately preceding the appearance of vdB 1157 in *Quant l'aloete* confirms its conscious alteration in this motet. A shortened version of the usual form of the refrain melody prefigures vdB 1157, beginning on E at perfection 50, in unison with the tenor, and accompanied by a text ('who sang in a loud voice') that serves also to prepare

Example 4.5 VdB 1157 in *Qui conservaret 7* clausula and related motet.

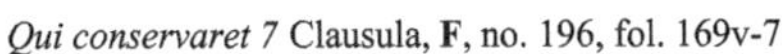

Qui conservaret 7 Clausula, **F**, no. 196, fol. 169v-7

the refrain.[30] As well as its ameliorative harmonic purpose, therefore, the introduction of an extra A at perfection 54 effectively draws attention to the beginning of the refrain proper, the additional declamatory 'O' enhancing further its explicitly song-like nature.

Significantly, the clausula notation of this refrain melody in *Qui conservaret 7* is ambiguous, and has prompted several alternative rhythmic realisations in modern editions.[31] In **F**, the clausula tenor and duplum are misaligned, with the melody of vdB 1157 copied above just the final three tenor pitches, widely spaced, although the refrain actually corresponds with the last seven tenor notes. In the clausula, the descending plicated A at the start of the refrain stands alone and unligated, with no clear indication of its rhythmic relation to the surrounding pitches. This could confirm the status of this initial A as an addition, especially since the refrain in *Qui conservaret 7* then continues – in ignorance of the preceding plicated A – with the expected opening three-note ligature of the first rhythmic mode. In consequence, the refrain melody is ligated exactly as in its other clausula

[30] The prefiguring of refrain melodies is a fairly common technique. It may echo the repetition of refrain melodies within monophonic *rondeaux*, serving also to underline the refrain status of certain melodies (see, for example, the discussion of vdB 287 as transmitted in Mt754 in Chapter 5).

[31] These ambiguities principally concern the refrain's opening. Baltzer interprets the opening A plica differently from Tischler and Everist. Baltzer, in *Les clausules à deux voix*, p.161, no. 196, adds the plica to the end of the previous phrase. Tischler and Everist – in *The Earliest Motets*, Vol. II, p. 1420, no. 269, and *French Motets in the Thirteenth Century*, p. 161, respectively – place the plica at the beginning of the refrain but with a rhythm that differs from that suggested in the related motet.

appearance in **F** (*Manere 7*; compare Example 4.4). As concerns the end of the refrain melody, which is fairly straightforward in its mode-one rhythmic profile, this is both unsurprising and appropriate.[32] Yet such notational consistency at its opening is misleading, since *Qui conservaret 7* (with its extra A) initially differs rhythmically from the version of the refrain in *Manere 7*. Notational evidence, therefore, further confirms that the melody of vdB 1157 already had the status of a refrain before its appearance in the *Qui conservaret 7* clausula: a phrase conceived *cum littera*, it later proved difficult to express in the ligature patterns of *sine littera* notation.

In my second example – the clausula *Venimus 2* and its related two-voice motet *Ja pour longue demouree* – grounds for establishing refrain quotations depend on an understanding of the composition as a whole and on signs of tenor manipulation. This clausula and motet tenor is drawn from an Alleluia melody used on several liturgical occasions in conjunction with different plainchant texts. While the clausula is designated VENIMUS (M 10), the extant copies of the motet *Ja pour longue demouree* in **MüA** and **Mo** have the respective alternative tenor texts HODIE (M 2) and DIES (imprecisely referring to the longer version of this melisma earlier in the M 2 Alleluia). *Ja pour longue demouree* is a so-called cento motet, a short patchwork piece created by joining together several independent refrains.[33] This practice is strongly associated with vernacular motets, and *Ja pour longue demouree* is the only extant cento motet to share its musical material with a clausula, whose unconventional *sine littera* notation caught Flotzinger's attention.

This cento motet is made up of four separate refrains (see Example 4.6 and the text and translation in Table 4.2).[34] Each refrain is textually independent, with its own rhymes and syllable counts, and there is also little correspondence of melodic motive or phrase length and structure between

[32] The notation of this phrase in both **F** clausulae offers the clearest expression possible in *sine littera* notation of the refrain rhythm as transmitted in its related motets. A completely conventional ligation of this refrain melody is prevented by the repetition of the pitch C towards the end of the refrain (in perfections 58–9 of *Qui conservaret 7*). Had they not shared the same pitch, these two notes could have been combined within a five-note conjunctura, and the last note of this ligature would then have fallen, more conventionally, at the beginning of a perfection. Baltzer, Tischler, and Everist (see n. 31 above) offer an alternative rhythmic interpretation of perfections 57–9 of *Qui conservaret 7* that respects this rule and differs from extant motet concordances: placing the final C of the conjunctura at the beginning of a perfection.

[33] For a discussion of the nineteen French motets identified as refrain centos, see Mark Everist, 'The Refrain Cento: Myth or Motet?', *Journal of the Royal Musical Association*, 114 (1989), 164–88.

[34] The translation is adapted from Joel C. Relihan and Susan Stakel (eds.), *The Montpellier Codex, Part IV: Texts and Translations*, RRMMA 8 (Madison, 1985), p. 80.

Example 4.6 *Ja pour longue demouree/DIES*, **Mo**, fols. 267v–268r.

Refrain 1 vdB 1018

Refrain 2 vdB 1382

1. Ja pour lon - gue de - mou - re - e 2. n'iert bone a - mors ou - bli - e - e 3. n'oub - li mi - e 4. mes a - mours

DIES

Refrain 3 vdB 310

Refrain 4 Gennrich 1360

5. car si dou - ce-ment 6. m'a na - vre la be - le 7. que nus maus ne sent 8. je muir si vif en mou - rant.

II

Table 4.2 Text and translation of *Ja pour longue demouree*

Refrain 1 – vdB 1018				
1.	Ja pour longue demouree	**8a**	-ee	Long delay has never caused
2.	n'iert bone amors oubliee	**8a**	-ee	true love to be forgotten
Refrain 2 – vdB 1382				
3.	n'oubli mie	**4b**	-ie	do not forget me
4.	mes amours	**3c**	-ours	my sweetheart
Refrain 3 – vdB 310				
5.	car si doucement	**5d**	-ent	for so sweetly
6.	m'a navre la bele	**6e**	-ele	the fair one has wounded me
7.	que nus maus ne sent	**5d**	-ent	that I feel no pain
Refrain 4 – Gennrich 1360				
8.	je muir si vif en mourant.	**7f**	-ant	I die and yet I live in dying.

the individual refrain units. The motet, therefore, conveys a strong cento character, even though it is unlikely that all four of its refrains constitute genuine quotations. The closing refrain, for instance, is unique to this motet, and though it was included in Gennrich's catalogue, Van den Boogaard did not consider it to be a refrain. The second refrain is even more doubtful as a quotation. 'N'oubli mie mes amours' (vdB 1382, transmitted as 'n'oblie mie bele amie' in **MüA**), is a highly generic turn of phrase, as the interchangeability of stock vocabulary in **Mo** and **MüA** confirms. Though found in many motets, it is never consistently linked to an accompanying musical phrase. Yet the motet's first and third refrains are apparently more in keeping with the characteristic cento practice of quotation.

The opening refrain, *Ja pour longue demouree* (vdB 1018), has an independent text concordance in a monophonic *chanson avec des refrains*.[35] It appears as the refrain at the end of the second stanza in the version of *Pour ce que mes cuers souffre grant dolour* recorded in **Trouv. C**, a source whose musical staves were never filled with notation.[36] While it is therefore

[35] Typically, vdB 1018 circulates as *Ja pour longue demouree*, rather than with the variant *desiree* found in **MüA**. This refrain appears also in related forms as vdB 1079, found (without music) in a motet enté in **Douce 308**, and in the works of Guillaume de Machaut. See the discussion of this refrain in Yolanda Plumley, *The Art of Grafted Song: Citation and Allusion in the Age of Machaut* (Oxford, 2013), pp. 286–7.

[36] This chanson is no. 1975 in Hans G. Spanke, *Raynaud's Bibliographie des altfranzösischen Liedes neu bearbeitet und ergänzt* (Leiden, 1955). It is transmitted, without musical notation, in **Trouv. C** (fols. 183v –186r) and in **Trouv. U** (fol. 140r–v), which lacks the stanza and refrain in question. The start of vdB 1018 also opens the chanson *Ja pour longue demouree* (Spanke no. 504, attributed to Gautier d'Espinau), again transmitted in **Trouv. C** (fol. 100r) and in **Trouv. U** (fol. 135r), lacking music in both cases.

Example 4.7 A new motet and clausula concordance for vdB 310 in *L'autrier quant me chevauchoie/PRO [PATRIBUS]*. (Related to *Pro patribus 4* clausula, **F**, no. 151, fol. 164v–4: incomplete, lacking refrain).

L'autrier quant me chevauchoie/PRO [PATRIBUS], **N**, fol. 193r-v, Perfections 33-41

Pro patribus 4 Clausula, **F**, no. 150, fol. 164v-4, Perfections 33-41 (tenor incomplete)

impossible to establish conclusively whether or not the motet and the chanson employed the same melody for their common refrain, internal evidence suggests that vdB 1018 is indeed a musical quotation in *Ja pour longue demouree/DIES*. The seconds between motetus and tenor in perfection 4 are uncharacteristically dissonant within the context of the piece as a whole, and the motet's initial sonority of a fourth between motetus and tenor (rather than a unison, fifth, or octave) is also atypical.[37] Had the creator of the motetus had free rein to write an opening melody against the tenor, it seems unlikely that he would have fashioned this one.

I have identified a new concordance for the motet's third refrain (*Car si doucement*, vdB 310), which confirms that this melody and text – previously thought to be unique to *Ja pour longue demouree* – circulated as a quotation. It also appears, with minor textual and musical variants, in the middle of the motet *L'autrier quant me chevauchoie/PRO PATRIBUS* (unique to **N**, see Example 4.7). This motet additionally contains the closing intertextual motet refrain vdB 237 (see Example 4.3), and it is related to the incomplete clausula *Pro patribus 4* (see Figure 4.2). A slight difference in vocabulary in the opening line of text of vdB 310 – the synonymous 'si mignotement' rather than 'car si doucement' – could explain

[37] In *The Earliest Motets*, Vol. II, p. 1373, no. 249, Tischler either mistranscribed or silently corrected the opening motetus G to A, thereby creating a more conventional fifth with the tenor D, even though all extant sources clearly indicate G.

why the concordance in *L'autrier quant me chevauchoie* has previously been overlooked. But its existence underlines the need to take seriously apparently unique refrains, which are plausibly quotations for which concordances are now lost or not yet discovered.

The treatment of this intertextual refrain in *Ja pour longue demouree* suggests that it did not originate within the cento motet, since the motet's tenor is altered to accommodate it. An extra A (marked by a box in Example 4.6), absent from both the established chant melody and the first tenor cursus of the motet, is added in the second tenor cursus at perfection 17. It is not only unusual for chant tenors to be altered (especially in a clausula), but even more so for two statements of the same chant melisma to differ from each other within a single composition. Tellingly, this extra A is mistakenly omitted in two of the piece's three manuscript sources (in **F** and **MüA**) even though it is required to make musical sense of the piece, whose tenor is otherwise one note too short. This alteration to the pre-existent chant melody facilitates its more consonant combination with the refrain quotation, avoiding what, in perfection 20, would otherwise have been a stressed dissonant second between a tenor F and motetus G.

The new concordance for vdB 310 in the motet *L'autrier quant me chevauchoie* likewise bears signs of musical accommodation that indicate quotation. In the version of this refrain in the cento motet *Ja pour longue demouree*, its musical material has an internal ABA form (marked in Example 4.6), and the first A phrase – rising from G up to C – is repeated literally at the close of the refrain. Significantly, the appearance of vdB 310 in *L'autrier quant me chevauchoie* obscures this symmetry, because the repetition of the A material now starts on A rather than G (marked by a dashed box in Example 4.7). It seems that this change in the refrain material in *L'autrier quant me chevauchoie* is a response to the tenor context, once again avoiding what would have been a dissonant second between tenor A and motetus G in favour of a unison A. The accommodation here is made in the refrain, rather than in the tenor's plainchant quotation, but it similarly confirms the pre-existent status of both melodies.

The *Pro patribus 4* clausula related to *L'autrier quant me chevauchoie* also records the melody of vdB 310 just before its duplum notation breaks off. Remarkably, and unlike its related motet, *Pro patribus 4* preserves the refrain melody's internal ABA form. The A material (marked by boxes in Example 4.7) is literally repeated, despite the dissonance that would presumably have resulted with an accompanying tenor.[38] It is striking that the

[38] While the pitch content of the two A sections is identical, their ligation is not, and the scribe's first notation of the A material (though unusually featuring a plica within a conjunctura) is

clausula's version of the refrain is therefore closer, not to the motet to which it is directly related, but to an independent quotation of vdB 310 in *Ja pour longue demouree*. This seems incontrovertible evidence that – like *Venimus 2 – Pro patribus 4* contained melodies that already had the status of genuine refrains, which, in the case of vdB 310, must have originated in another lost or still unidentified song or motet context. The circumstances of vdB 310 – previously presumed unique and therefore of dubious refrain status – confirm that close engagement with surviving musical evidence can facilitate a knowledge of hypothetical sources, either now unknowable or as yet unknown.

Performative Traces

All of the refrains analysed above evince a largely stable transmission in written documents. Nevertheless, slight differences in poetic vocabulary and musical decoration (in vdB 237 in Example 4.3, or vdB 310 in Examples 4.6 and 4.7) may represent traces of a fundamentally performative refrain culture, involving the quotation, variation, and adaptation of particular musical and textual phrases across a variety of contexts. These short melodic and poetic units must additionally have circulated orally, as familiar phrases that singers and composers knew well and plausibly in multiple different versions and/or host contexts. The case of vdB 338 confirms that several distinct versions of the same refrain could circulate concurrently, even within a polyphonic context that should naturally constrain any significant variation of individual parts. This refrain is found in a monophonic *rondeau*, in two different chansons, and its melody is in the three-voice *Flos filius eius* clausula in **F** (fol. 11r–v). The clausula shares its musical material with a motet whose music is transmitted across eleven manuscript sources, and associated with three different Latin texts, in addition to the vernacular motetus *L'autrier jour mon alai*, which incorporates vdB 338.[39] As Everist has previously noted, there is some discrepancy as to the repetition of the words 'la fin' in the text of this refrain.[40] Example 4.8 shows all motet versions of this refrain text, while Example 4.9 records all concordances for this refrain outside the context of the motetus

less ambiguous than the second. These different ligations of the same phrase confirm that rhythmic notation in clausulae evidently converted from motets ad hoc could be inconsistent or erroneous, a consequence of challenges faced in transcription.

[39] I have argued that this **F** clausula represents a vernacular motet transcription; see Bradley, 'Clausulae and Transcribed Motets', pp. 40–57.

[40] Everist, *French Motets in the Thirteenth Century*, p. 67.

Example 4.8 Transmission of vdB 338 in the vernacular motetus *L'autrier jour mon alai* (Mt651).

Example 4.9 External concordances (outside Mt651) for vdB 338.

vdB Rondeau 92 (attributed Guillaume d'Amiens)

Vat, fol. 119v, opening and closing refrains

End First Stanza *Belle m'est la revenue* (Spanke no. 2072)

Trouv. C, fol. 31v (text only)
'C'est la fin cai ke nuls die j'amerai'

End Third Stanza *Amours me semoit et prie* (Spanke no. 1197)

Douce 308, fol. 212r (text only)
'C'est la fins lai fins c'ai ke nuns die j'amerai'

L'autrier jour.[41] In all of its vernacular motet versions in **W2**, **Mo**, **Cl**, and **Ca** (see Example 4.8) and in the chanson *Amours me sermoit* (the final item in Example 4.9), vdB 338 appears with an internal text repetition as '*C'est la fin, la fin que que nus die j'amerai*'. But in Guillaume d'Amiens's *rondeau* and in the chanson *Bele m'est la revenue* it is simply '*C'est la fins koi que nus die j'amerai*' (see Example 4.9). Guillaume d'Amiens's *rondeau* – the only extant musical concordance for this refrain outside its motet network – lacks two additional pitches that consistently accompany the repeated '*la fin*' in its motet contexts.[42]

The repetition of '*la fin*' in the motet versions may have imitated a form of the refrain derived from the chanson *Amours me sermoit*. Yet it seems more likely that *Amours me sermoit* – of which only the text is uniquely preserved in the fourteenth-century manuscript **Douce 308** – bears the influence of the motet version of this refrain.[43] In the motet context, it is probable that

[41] For the sake of concision, the numerous versions of the vdB 338 melody with Latin contrafactum texts, as well as the untexted clausula version, are not included here.

[42] See also the edition of Guillaume d'Amiens's *rondeau* in Everist, *French Motets in the Thirteenth Century*, p. 67.

[43] A variant version of the motet text *L'autrier jour mon alai* appears also in **Douce 308** (fol. 243v). This motet text correctly and conventionally contains the repetition of the words '*la fin*', matching the extended form of the vdB 338 refrain in the unique copy of the chanson *Amours me sermoit* earlier in the same source. The refrains share the orthography '*c'ai ke nuns die*

the refrain's internal repetition of '*la fin*', along with its two extra pitches, was introduced to lengthen the melodic quotation, thereby increasing its compatibility with the FLOS FILIUS EIUS tenor. Significantly, two vernacular motet versions of this refrain in **R** and **N** do not repeat the words '*la fin*' (see the bottom two systems of Example 4.8). In **R**, the two notes usually accompanied by the second '*la fin*' simply lack any corresponding text syllables. The motet in **N** omits not only the textual repetition of '*la fin*' but also the two pitches associated with it, resulting in a version of the motetus that is too short to fit with its underlying tenor.[44] Both **R** and **N** are principally monophonic chansonniers, additionally containing motets, while the remaining sources that correctly include the '*la fin*' repetition – **W2**, **Mo**, **Cl**, and **Ca** – are all polyphonic motet collections.[45] It is remarkable that **R** and **N**, two manuscripts associated with the 'trouvère' tradition, should record in motet versions a variant of vdB 338 that matches its typical monophonic transmission, particularly since this variant has a disruptive influence in its polyphonic context.

Such awareness of multiple incarnations of a particular refrain, or of established possibilities for its variation, is evident also in the melody of vdB 1699 as found in the Latin motet *In modulo sonet letitia*/*LATUS*. Uniquely preserved in **F**, this Latin motet shares the music of *Mout soloie chant*/*LATUS* in **Mo** and of the *Immolatus est 9* clausula, whose problematic notation was discussed above (see Example 4.2). In *Mout soloie chant*/*LATUS* and its related clausula, the refrain closes with the conjunct ascent of a third (A–B–C). There is an external concordance for vdB 1699 in the motet *L'autrier en mai*/*TANQUAM* in **N** and **R**, where it appears transposed down a fifth, and with an alternative closing gesture, outlining a concluding ascending fourth (from C to F). *In modulo sonet letitia*/*LATUS* seemingly combines both versions of the refrain's ending: it has a three-note A–B–G melisma on its penultimate text syllable, interrupting the rising conjunct

j'amerai'. These matching and late copies of the vdB 338 refrain in **Douce 308** plausibly reflect its established and widely attested thirteenth-century motet transmission.

44 Alejandro Enrique Planchart offers a rhythmic interpretation for this final phrase of the motet in **N** that allows a satisfactory combination between motetus and tenor. See his 'The Flower's Children', *Journal of Musicological Research*, 22 (2003), 303–48 (p. 339). While Planchart's solution is ingenious, it differs rhythmically from all established transmissions of these pitches in the refrain, and it seems unlikely that such an interpretation was the scribe's intention. It is evident that the scribe of **N** was not particularly sensitive to the combination of tenor and upper voices here, since he mistakenly appended an extraneous ordo at the end of the tenor chant.

45 The exception is the text-only source of this motetus in **Douce 308**, which contains the '*la fin*' repetition. See the discussion in n. 43 above.

third (A–B–C) of its related vernacular motet and clausula, with a dip down to the lower fourth (G) before arriving on the C final.

This combination of two different refrain endings is all the more notable for its occurrence, independently of any associated vernacular refrain text, within a Latin motet in **F**. Deviating also from its related clausula copied in the same manuscript, this Latin motet incorporates a musical feature of the refrain recorded only within the context of an otherwise unrelated French motet preserved in **N** and **R**. While the hybrid version of vdB 1699 in *In modulo sonet* may well have been (or become) part of a written transmission process, it is nonetheless suggestive of an oral musical practice, in which refrains could alter over time, and where different incarnations of the same refrain were known to scribes, composers, and singers. It may be testament to the strength of such oral practices that the potential for refrain reinterpretation should be evident in two versions of the same musical material copied by the same scribe in the same manuscript source, and furthermore in the non-vernacular genres of Latin motet and clausula. This confirms that refrains retained aspects of their performative culture and their refrain status, even when divorced from associated vernacular texts and contexts.

Conclusions

Notational and musical evidence presented above suggests that *Magnus liber* clausulae containing intertextual refrain melodies represent transcriptions of French motets.[46] These refrain melodies did not, therefore, derive from clausulae; rather they entered clausulae in **F** (as they did those in **StV**) via related vernacular motets. The question of where the refrain quotations themselves originated remains equivocal: were these musical and textual phrases conceived within the polyphonic motet repertoire, or did they stem from monophonic trouvère chansons? The earliest studies of refrains presumed their origins in vernacular song – specifically within the *rondeaux* in which refrains play such a vital formal role – proposing that refrains circulating in oral and popular monophonic contexts

[46] Two of the eleven clausulae containing intertextual refrains have not been closely examined here. *Domine 5*, containing vdB 314, was convincingly established as a transcribed motet by Fred Büttner in his 'Weltliche Einflüsse in der Notre-Dame-Musik? Überlegungen zu einer Klausel im Codex F', *Anuario musical*, 57 (2002), 19–37. *Immolatus est 10*, transmitting vdB 1149 and whose entire motetus is elsewhere recorded as a monophonic song in trouvère sources, is also a strong candidate, bearing signs of tenor manipulation and notational translation.

only later infiltrated polyphonic motets.[47] This chronology has now been convincingly challenged, most notably by Saltzstein, who drew attention to the paucity of intertextual refrains found in extant *rondeaux* and *rondets de carole* and to a small corpus of thirty-seven intertextual motet refrains, for which there are no surviving chanson concordances and that were apparently devised and quoted exclusively in polyphonic motet contexts.[48] As will be demonstrated in the next chapter, refrains could indeed be newly created in motets – rather than invariably constituting (song) quotations – and a linear conception of refrains invariably travelling from chanson to motet repertoires is undoubtedly problematic.

Yet revisionist responses to a presumed chanson-to-motet progression were additionally motivated by a need to reconcile connections between clausulae and chansons within other and more established historiographical narratives: proceeding from clausula to motet, and from sacred to secular. Relying on precisely these established narratives, Saltzstein adduced the very presence of refrain melodies within sacred clausula sources as additional evidence that they could not possibly have come from chansons.[49] And Richard Crocker, Everist, and Clark all cited vdB 338 as an important example of a refrain melody, which originated in a source clausula and motet, only afterwards permeating the realm of trouvère song.[50] Now that such clausula–motet–refrain chronologies have been challenged, evidence against a chanson origin for refrains is weaker than currently supposed. There is also scope for further investigation of clausulae whose upper voices are widely transmitted as monophonic songs in trouvère sources: songs whose inevitable clausula genesis continues to be assumed.[51]

Magnus liber clausulae transmitting unique refrains present a somewhat less clear-cut case. Sixteen of the thirty-three clausulae in Table 4.1 are linked only to unique refrains, whose very classification as

[47] See, for example, Alfred Jeanroy, *Chansons, jeux partis et refrains inédits du XIIIe siècle* (Toulouse, 1902), p. 51.

[48] Saltzstein, *The Refrain and the Rise of the Vernacular*, pp. 11–16.

[49] Ibid., p. 15.

[50] See Richard Crocker, 'French Polyphony of the Thirteenth Century', in Richard Crocker and David Hiley (eds.), *The Early Middle Ages to 1300*, NOHM 2 (Oxford, 1990), pp. 636–78 (p. 652); Everist, *French Motets in the Thirteenth Century*, p. 71; and Clark, 'S'en dirai chançonete', p. 46 n. 32.

[51] Davide Dalomi, for instance, recently and misleadingly stated that 'it is well known that many *chansons* stemmed from polyphonic *clausulae*'. See his 'Notre Dame's New Clothes', *TRANS – Revista transcultural de música/Transcultural Music Review*, 18 (2014), 2–26 (p. 5). There are two clausulae whose upper voices circulated as monophonic songs in Table 4.1: *Virgo* a3 *2* and *Immolatus est 10* (marked by asterisks in Table 4.1).

refrains might occasionally be dubious.[52] Yet the consistent transmission patterns amongst these clausulae in Table 4.1, coupled with the fact that almost half of them exhibit notational irregularities independently associated with motet transcription, must undermine the presumption that unique refrain melodies are any more likely to have originated in clausulae than intertextual ones. Admittedly, the proportion of clausulae representing transcribed French motets in **F** remains small: only sixty-four independent clausulae out of 476 in **F** have related French motets.[53] Even if all sixty-four represented motet transcriptions (which is unlikely) this would account for about a tenth of the clausulae in the entire manuscript. But *within* this sample of clausulae related to vernacular motets, the proportion of clausulae that appear to be vernacular motet transcriptions is large. Of the thirty-three clausulae containing refrains in Table 4.1, for example, initial notational and musical investigations indicate that at least twenty (that is, about 60 per cent) represent transcribed motets.[54] As for refrains, the origins of particular clausulae must be assessed individually. But the evidence presented here indicates that the current tendency to presume that French motets and their refrains post-date related clausulae and Latin motets is, as Frobenius argued in 1987, misleading. Any vernacular tradition of fashioning motets through adding texts to pre-existent clausulae appears, in contrast to the creation of early Latin motets (*pace* Frobenius), to have been minimal.

The origin of many early Latin motets in clausulae does not exclude the possibility that certain newly composed Latin motets may, like their French counterparts, have received clausula transcriptions. The identification of transcribed Latin motets requires additional and alternative methods of investigation that merit a separate study, since the question of refrain concordances naturally does not arise. It seems reasonable to posit that clausulae transcriptions may draw on sources extending beyond the vernacular motet repertoire, given that this practice was apparently fairly widespread. The presence of transcribed motets in both **F** and **StV** confirms

[52] The status of vdB 343 as a true refrain, and the priority of any related motets (Mt762–4) over the three-voice *Domino* discant (transmitted within organa in **F**, **W1**, and **W2**) is, for example, improbable.

[53] In three instances, two clausulae are combined in a single corresponding French motet; thus the number of French motets with related clausulae is sixty-one. It should be noted that around twenty of these French motets are probably contrafacta retextings of extant Latin works originally created through the addition of texts to clausulae.

[54] These include the fourteen clausulae whose notational irregularities attracted the attention of Waite and Flotzinger, plus five further clausulae transmitting intertextual refrains discussed above, and the first two clausulae in Table 4.1, for whose status as part of a group of transcribed motets I have argued in 'Clausulae and Transcribed Motets', pp. 53–7.

that this activity was not confined to a single scribe or a single manuscript. Furthermore, since so few extant sources preserve collections of clausulae – only **W1**, **F**, and **StV** (with clausula fascicles notably absent from **W2** and **Ma**) – those including motet transcriptions among their clausulae are in a majority.

The conspicuous absence of transcribed motets from **W1** and their typical location in **F** (as in **StV**) as independent clausulae, rather than as passages of discant recorded within organa, is significant. **W1** seems to preserve the earliest layers of the *Magnus liber*, and the repertoire of organa is generally considered to pre-date that of extended independent or so-called substitute clausulae. This suggests that the transcription of motets occurred as a relatively 'late' phase in the history of the clausula. I have speculated elsewhere as to the reasons why this development in clausula creation may have occurred.[55] Although definitive answers remain elusive, scribes evidently went to some trouble to craft these motet transcriptions.

As proposed above, a genuine clausula and a textless vernacular motet were apparently combined within the *Domine 2* clausula in **F**, underlining the creative and innovative nature of the scribe's motet transcription process. *Domine 2* also confirms a lack of concern to segregate different types of clausulae in **F**, in which – although French texts are removed – musical connections to the world of vernacular motets and songs remain plainly evident. This suggests a much more complex and fluid relationship between materials and genres that are often now regarded as distinctly sacred or secular, and it may point towards the possibility that transcribed motets were sung in liturgical contexts. After all, motets with sacred Latin contrafactum texts were not, presumably, disqualified from any religious or devotional purpose because their melodies had originated as, or been tainted by association with, vernacular love songs.

Yet the already extensive provision of clausulae in **F** makes it unlikely that the transcription of French motets as clausulae (tellingly placed near the end of groups of compositions on a particular tenor chant) was undertaken expressly for their practical use in the liturgy. Did this process serve also, perhaps principally, as an intellectual exercise in notational translation? Or was the scribe just indulging his penchant for filling in empty space in the clausula fascicle? Conversely, motets may have been presented as clausulae for reasons of space efficiency, the melismatic clausula in score requiring less parchment than the syllabic motet in parts. Or – as in the case of the mini clausulae discussed in Chapter 2 – the motet transcriptions could have

[55] Ibid., pp. 63–7.

been a means of preserving music, this time vernacular music, for posterity, recording motets as clausulae without their associated vernacular texts (or any French incipit cues), in keeping with the otherwise exclusively Latinate contents of **F**.

The number of motet transcriptions amongst the clausulae of **F** may, in fact, be greater than is suggested by both surviving evidence and its current state of scholarly understanding. Table 4.1 documents refrain concordances for those clausulae known to have related French motets, but it is likely that additional clausulae in **F** may be transcriptions of vernacular refrain motets now lost, and there is scope for a widespread investigation of this possibility, particularly among the clausulae in the first series of fascicle 5.[56] While Gennrich and Van den Boogaard were in many respects overzealous in their identification of refrains, they were (as I suggest in the following chapter) in other respects too reticent: unknown concordances may exist with musical and textual phrases unidentified as refrains in present catalogues. To accept that the presence of a refrain melody within a *Magnus liber* clausula – particularly when accompanied by notational irregularities – probably indicates its derivation from a parent motet offers fertile ground for the location of refrains in previously unsuspected contexts and for the reclamation of lost vernacular motet melodies within an ostensibly liturgical corpus of clausulae.

[56] Büttner suggested, for instance, that **F**, no. 445 (*Patribus* 6, fol. 183v–5) is a transcription of a French motet, now lost. See *Das Klauselrepertoire der Handschrift Saint-Victor*, pp. 184–9. Other likely candidates are the clausulae identified by Waite and Flotzinger as notationally irregular but lacking motet concordances.

5 | Framing Motets: Quoting and Crafting Refrains against Plainchant Tenors

The designation 'motet', a vernacular and diminutive term, is remarkable for a sophisticated polyphonic genre thought to originate within the sacred and Latinate context of Notre Dame clausulae.[1] 'Motet' had an additional connotation in the thirteenth and fourteenth centuries, where it was used – particularly within lyric romances – to describe the brief vernacular phrases or 'mottoes' also known as refrains.[2] As Klaus Hofmann proposed in 1970, an overlap in terminology between motets and refrains is etymologically significant, and in keeping with the predominance of refrains in the vernacular motet repertoire.[3] Hofmann's conclusions are advanced by evidence presented in the previous chapter: if refrain melodies do not typically derive from clausulae, then a vernacular origin for refrains and their status as genuine quotations within French motets is more widespread than currently presumed. And the fact that several clausula-related Latin motets are typically labelled not as motets but as *tropus* or *prosa* in thirteenth- and fourteenth-century sources strengthens the possibility that an early and comparatively modest tradition of creating Latin motets through texting pre-existent clausulae was somewhat independent, compositionally, of its vernacular, often refrain-dependent, counterpart.[4]

While Chapter 3 examined the making of Latin motets from clausulae, this chapter considers a parallel creative process for vernacular motets, exploring the role of refrains in the construction of two 'newly composed' two-voice motets, *Ne m'oubliez mie/DOMINO* and *Nus ne se doit/AUDI FILIA*. In addition to the terminal refrains so common in French

[1] See Christopher Page's summary of the etymology of 'motet' and his discussion of the significance of the diminutive suffix in *Discarding Images: Reflections on Music and Culture in Medieval France* (Oxford, 1993), pp. 59–60. See also Michael Beiche, 'Motet/motetus/mottetto/Motette', in Hans Heinrich Eggebrecht (ed.), *Handwörterbuch der musikalischen Terminologie*, Vol. XXXVI (Stuttgart, 2003/4), pp. 1–23, esp. pp. 6–7.

[2] See the recent discussion of 'motet' as a term for refrain in Judith A. Peraino, *Giving Voice to Love: Song and Self-Expression from the Troubadours to Guillaume de Machaut* (Oxford, 2011), pp. 195–7. See also Beiche, 'Motet/motetus/mottetto/Motette', pp. 7–8.

[3] Klaus Hofmann, 'Zur Entstehungs- und Frühgeschichte des Terminus Motette', *Acta musicologica*, 42 (1970), 138–50.

[4] See ibid., pp. 145–6.

motets – and that typically comprise a pair of short, complementary phrases – both pieces also open with a refrain. These surrounding refrains not only enclose but also seem to generate much of the motets' internal musical and poetic material. This framing technique is reminiscent of the more common motet enté practice, in which music and text are 'grafted' between the two halves of a refrain that is split to form the opening and closing phrases of a piece.[5] Yet working with two separate refrains, as opposed to two halves of a single refrain, presents a rather different compositional situation: the opening and closing refrains may be independent quotations selected and combined in a motet, or one or both of the refrains could be newly crafted to create a complementary pair. In the latter instance, such 'refrains' might not be considered refrains in the strictest sense, since they do not meet the traditional requirement of quotation. Nevertheless, as I shall argue, the formal function, compositional treatment, and musical and poetic characteristics of apparently newly created 'refrains' in *Nus ne se doit* are strikingly analogous to those of the genuine refrain quotations in *Ne m'oubliez mie*. These two motets raise questions, not only about how the category of refrain might be defined and understood, but also about the complex and intricate relationship between plainchant tenors and refrain melodies. How were chant and refrain quotations combined; how were refrains selected or crafted for particular tenor contexts; and might particular tenor melodies have encouraged certain types of refrain behaviour and vice versa?

Combining Quotations in *Ne m'oubliez mie/DOMINO*

The two-voice French motet *Ne m'oubliez mie/DOMINO* is preserved uniquely in the sixth fascicle of the Montpellier Codex (see Example 5.1).[6] Its tenor DOMINO is drawn from a Benedicamus Domino melody (BD I), and is musically identical to the EIUS melisma from the Assumption

[5] The medieval term 'motet enté' has been the subject of debate. Mark Everist, *French Motets in the Thirteenth Century: Music, Poetry, and Genre* (Cambridge, 1994), pp. 75–89, challenged the established definition of the enté practice as described above. Ardis Butterfield discussed further possible meanings for the term, but reinstated the idea of a split refrain as central to a motet enté. See her '"Enté": A Survey and Reassessment of the Term in Thirteenth- and Fourteenth-Century Music and Poetry', *Early Music History*, 22 (2003), 67–101. See also the response to Everist and Butterfield in Peraino, *Giving Voice to Love*, pp. 208–12.

[6] The analysis of *Ne m'oubliez mie* draws on material previously published in Catherine A. Bradley, 'Comparing Compositional Process in Two Thirteenth-Century Motets: *Deus omnium/REGNAT* and *Ne m'oubliez mie/DOMINO*', *Music Analysis*, 33 (2014), 263–90.

Example 5.1 *Ne m'oubliez mie/DOMINO*, **Mo**, fols. 261v–262r.

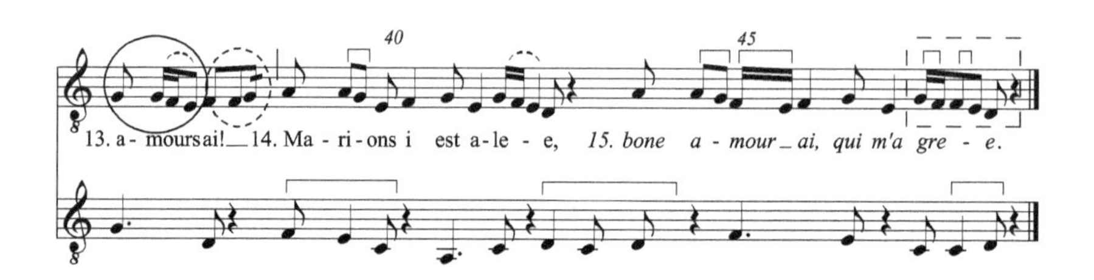

responsory *Stirps Iesse* (O 16), one of the most popular thirteenth-century motet tenors.[7] In *Ne m'oubliez mie*, this chant melisma is stated twice in the same rhythmic arrangement, one that is unique amongst all extant motets

[7] FLOS FILIUS EIUS is the second most popular motet tenor in the thirteenth century, employed in twenty-six different motets. See Klaus Hofmann, *Untersuchungen zur Kompositionstechnik der Motette im 13. Jahrhundert durchgeführt an den Motetten mit dem Tenor 'In seculum'*, Tübinger Beiträge zur Musikwissenschaft 2 (Neuhausen-Stuttgart, 1972), p. 11. An additional nine motets use this tenor melody under the label DOMINO.

and clausulae on DOMINO or EIUS.[8] The plainchant quotation is subject to a small but significant alteration from the established version of the chant consistently employed in polyphonic settings: on both occasions the penultimate note C is repeated, and this extra pitch allows the end of the tenor's melodic cursus to coincide with the end of its rhythmic pattern. As a result, both tenor statements are identically rhythmicised, but since the end of the first tenor statement occurs in the middle of a motetus phrase (at perfection 24), phrase endings in the motetus fall at different points in the tenor restatement.

Ne m'oubliez mie is framed by the presentation of two intertextual refrain melodies and texts in the motetus voice. These refrains are extant exclusively within motets: the unusually extended opening refrain (vdB 1361) is found at the close of another **Mo** motet, *La plus bele/[PACEM]*, while the shorter closing refrain, vdB 287, is more widely transmitted, appearing in two further motets across four different sources (see Table 5.1). In *Ne m'oubliez mie* the melody of refrain 287 is presented twice in succession: its appearance with the associated text '*bone amour ai, qui m'agree*' is preceded by a slightly less embellished presentation of the same melody with the text 'Marions i est alee' at perfections 39–43.[9]

Although refrains 1361 and 287 evidently circulated as quotations in the motet repertoire, their status as pre-existent material in *Ne m'oubliez mie* has been called into question because this motet has a related clausula on DOMINO, preserved uniquely in **F** and designated *Domino 12* (see Example 5.2). In accordance with the general view (challenged in the preceding chapter) that clausulae pre-date their related motets, *Domino 12* has typically been regarded as the initial incarnation of this musical material, to which a French text was subsequently added.[10] The melodies of refrains 1361 and 287, therefore, have until now been thought to originate in the melismatic *Domino 12* clausula; they were then furnished with

[8] The same basic tenor rhythm is employed, but not strictly throughout, in *S'amour souspris m'a/EIUS* (Mt676) and *Dame je pens fors/Souffert 'ma en esperance/EIUS* (Mt688–9).

[9] This varied repetition does not seem to have been demanded by the underlying tenor in *Ne m'oubliez mie*. Perfections 39–43 resemble the melody of the version of refrain 287 employed in *Quant voi yver/Au douz tans/HODIE PERLUSTRAVIT*, where the difference in decoration *is* demanded by the tenor (see Table 5.1). This may suggest that the creator of *Ne m'oubliez mie* knew a number of different versions of vdB 287, including the one in *Quant voi yver/Au douz tans*.

[10] See, for example, Gordon A. Anderson, 'Clausulae or Transcribed Motets in the Florence Manuscript?', *Acta musicologica*, 42 (1970), 109–28; and Rebecca A. Baltzer, 'Notation, Rhythm, and Style in the Two-Voice Notre Dame Clausula', Ph.D. diss., 2 vols. (Boston University, 1974), Vol. I, p. 106.

Table 5.1 Refrains 1361 and 287 and their motet concordances

vdb 1361: *Ne m'oubliez mie, bele et avenant/Quant je ne voz voi, s'en sui plus dolens*

Opening of *Ne m'oubliez me/DOMINO*
Mo, fols. 261v–262r

Close of *La plus bele/[PACEM]*
Mo, fol. 253r–v

vdB 287: *Bone amour ai, qui m'agree*

Close of *Ne m'oubliez mie/DOMINO*
Mo, fols. 261v–262r

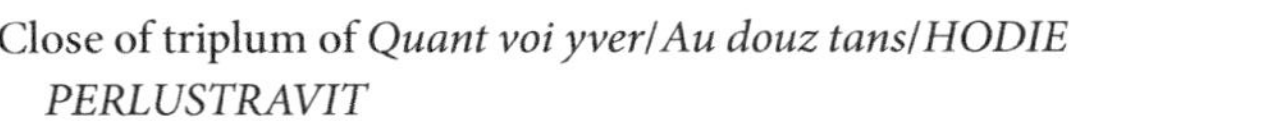

Close of triplum of *Quant voi yver/Au douz tans/HODIE PERLUSTRAVIT*

Mo, fols. 190v–191v and **MüB**, fol. B6

Close of *Mainte dame/IOHANNE*

N, fol. 191r

R, fol. 209v[a]

[a] The music of the tenor of *Mainte dame* is not copied in **R**, though the tenor word IOHANNE (with a space for accompanying music) appears at the end of the motet. The editorial tenor provided here follows that of the IOHANNE clausula in **StV** (fol. 290v), which shares the music of this motet, see Example 4.1b.

Example 5.2 *Domino 12* clausula, **F**, fol. 88v–4.

their accompanying texts in *Ne m'oubliez mie*/*DOMINO* and only after that circulated as refrains with this text among other motets.[11]

Yet even before the challenge voiced in Chapter 4, the chronological priority of *Domino 12* over *Ne m'oubliez mie* was questioned on notational

[11] See Everist, *French Motets in the Thirteenth Century*, p. 108; and Jennifer Saltzstein, *The Refrain and the Rise of the Vernacular in Medieval French Music and Poetry* (Cambridge, 2013), pp. 15–16.

grounds by William Waite in 1954, an hypothesis later reinforced by Wolf Frobenius and more recently by Fred Büttner, both of whom emphasised the presence of widely circulating refrain melodies in this clausula as indicative of its motet origin.[12] Waite's notational argument is highly convincing. As he observed, the tenor of *Domino 12* is improperly texted (it lacks the final two syllables of the word 'Domino' and any accompanying syllable strokes), and the duplum is ligated irregularly.[13] This irregular ligation is chiefly the result of decorative figurations, very typical of French motets but hard to express in *sine littera* clausula notation. The possible validity of alternative rhythmic interpretations of the closing refrain in clausula and motet (vdB 287, perfections 44–8) was discussed in the previous chapter. But in perfections 34–5 (marked by a box in Example 5.2), the difference in rhythm between clausula and motet versions, and the clausula's modally unconventional notation, seems more straightforwardly to result from the difficulty of replicating the decorated motetus line *sine littera*. Furthermore, a number of the notational anomalies in the clausula duplum (marked by dashed boxes in Example 5.2) apparently arise from the preservation of ligature patterns employed in the related motet (compare the same passages in dashed boxes in Example 5.1). In the clausula, the final pitch (D) of these cadence figurations should conventionally be subsumed within the preceding two-note ligature, since it is to sound on a strong beat. It is telling that this pitch instead stands alone – as it does in the motet notation – where it is accompanied by a new syllable of text.

Directly responding to Waite, Gordon A. Anderson was puzzled by the presence of new 'closing melismas', absent from motet versions, at the end of thirteen of Waite's notationally irregular clausulae proposed as transcribed motets. 'How', Anderson asked, 'could a [clausula] transcription by a redactor who did not understand the notation have had appended an entirely new melisma not known in the original [motet]?'[14] The seven-note melisma over a held tenor note at the end of *Domino 12* is typical of such closing gestures, and it has been described by Norman E. Smith as a 'simple and frequently used cadential formula found throughout the

[12] William G. Waite, *The Rhythm of Twelfth-Century Polyphony: Its Theory and Practice*, Yale Studies in the History of Music 2 (New Haven, 1954), p. 101; Wolf Frobenius, 'Zum genetischen Verhältnis zwischen Notre-Dame-Klauseln und ihren Motetten', *Archiv für Musikwissenschaft*, 44 (1987), 1–39 (p. 20) (Frobenius refers to *Domino 12* as **Sm 104**); and Fred Büttner, *Das Klauselrepertoire der Handschrift Saint-Victor (Paris, BN, lat. 15139): Eine Studie zur mehrstimmigen Komposition im 13. Jahrhundert* (Lecce, 2011), pp. 161–4.

[13] See also the comments on the notational ambiguity of this clausula in Baltzer, 'Notation, Rhythm, and Style', Vol. I, p. 106.

[14] Anderson, 'Clausulae or Transcribed Motets?', p. 112.

Magnus liber'.[15] It is not, therefore, an 'entirely new melisma' at all, and its addition to the end of *Domino 12* is conventional in the context of the clausula collection in **F**.[16] Notational evidence undermines the presumption that this clausula–motet pair must enact the typical chronological progression from clausula to motet, and this is reinforced by the analysis of *Ne m'oubliez mie*, which further underlines its conception as a refrain motet.

Yet, even if we dismiss the idea that refrains 1361 and 287 originated in a clausula, it remains uncertain whether they represent pre-existent materials quoted in *Ne m'oubliez mie*, or whether this motet was instead the source of newly created refrains later employed in other compositions. Several features point towards the status of both refrains 1361 and 287 as genuine quotations in *Ne m'oubliez mie*. Büttner, discussing refrain 287, reached this conclusion on harmonic grounds.[17] He observed that the combination of refrain 287 with the tenors DOMINO and IOHANNE resulted in contrapuntal progressions and sonorities that would surely have been avoided had the motetus melody been newly created in these motets, and that these infelicities were all the more remarkable given the harmonically unambiguous D-mode profiles of both the refrain and the tenor melismas. Büttner drew attention to the unusual opening interval of a third at the beginning of the refrain in *Mainte dame/IOHANNE* (perfection 27) and at the first appearance of the melody of refrain 287 in *Ne m'oubliez mie* (perfection 39), which also features the stressed interval of a dissonant seventh between motetus and tenor in perfection 41. Noting the doubling of pitches (F and E) between motetus and tenor in perfections 45–6 of *Ne m'oubliez mie*, and the interval of a fourth (rather than the expected fifth) between triplum and tenor on the final note of *Quant voi yver/Au douz tans/HODIE PERLUSTRAVIT*, Büttner concluded that, in all three of its motet appearances, refrain 287 functioned as a quotation.[18]

A similar case can be made for the pre-existence of refrain 1361 in *Ne m'oubliez mie*. Only two phrases in this motet open with the interval of a third between motetus and tenor, all others beginning on stronger consonances of unisons, fifths or fourths. One is, as noted, on the first appearance of refrain melody 287 at perfection 39, and the other is in perfection 10, at the

[15] Norman E. Smith, 'Some Exceptional Clausulae of the Florence Manuscript', *Music and Letters*, 59 (1973), 405–14 (p. 409).

[16] Büttner noted that closing melismas over a held tenor note are very often included at the end of clausulae in **F**, but omitted from copies of these same clausulae in **W1**. See *Das Klauselrepertoire der Handschrift Saint-Victor*, pp. 157–8.

[17] Ibid., p. 162.

[18] Ibid., p. 165.

start of the final section of refrain 1361. Immediately following the presentation of refrain 1361, the motetus proceeds in a similar vein: perfections 13–14 employ the same rising-fifth gesture from D to A as the opening of the motet, with the accompanying text, 'car je n'oubli mie', a clear reference to the start of the refrain. However, the musical parallel is not exact, since the rhythm of this rising-fifth gesture differs in perfection 13, where the leap up to A is delayed until perfection 14 and is preceded by two repeated Ds. This delay was presumably demanded by the underlying tenor G in perfection 13, against which A in the motetus would have produced a dissonant second.[19] It is significant that the correspondence between the opening of *Ne m'oubliez mie* and perfection 13 could have been exact had the motet's creator employed the second (D–D–A) version of the rising-fifth motive on both occasions. If refrain 1361 were newly composed in this motet, then one would expect this later version of the opening motive to have been employed consistently throughout.

Notably, the related *Domino 12* clausula does indeed achieve this consistency of motive between perfections 1 and 13, but through exactly the opposite means: it is the refrain's opening D–A–A gesture that is employed twice, in spite of the resulting dissonance on its second appearance. A further variant between the clausula and motet versions arises when the clausula again utilises the rising-fifth motive in perfection 7 of the refrain. In perfection 7, *Domino 12* echoes the opening D–A fifth with a C–G leap in the duplum, producing a dissonant second with the underlying D in the tenor. On this occasion too, *Ne m'oubliez mie* has a more consonant version, since the motetus begins on D in perfection 7, in unison with the tenor, but echoing less exactly the opening of the refrain with the leap of a fourth.[20] The absence of these two clausula dissonances in the related motet suggests that they were considered undesirable and therefore either avoided or eradicated.[21] That such dissonances were tolerated in the clausula, though,

[19] Ibid., p. 164. Büttner also noted this varied repetition of the opening of *Ne m'oubliez mie* in perfection 13 and attributed it similarly to the underlying tenor pitch.

[20] The use of a fourth in perfection 7 of the motet complements the later return of this interval in perfection 16. It is possible, therefore, that the dissonant clausula C in perfection 7 may be a scribal error. Even in this case, the nature of the scribe's mistake – reflecting the prominence of the rising-fifth motive – is still revealing.

[21] This is a further example of the situation discussed in Chapter 3 for *Reg[nat] 8* and *Infidelem populum/REG[nat]*. Here a more literal approach to repetition, vis-à-vis the clausula *Reg[nat] 8*, was achieved at the expense of consonance in *Infidelem populum*. It is significant that this preference for literal repetition as opposed to consonance is not consistently linked to genre: in the case of *Domino 12* and *Ne m'oubliez mie* it is the clausula that is the more dissonant, while the *Reg[nat] 8* clausula offers a more consonant reading than its motet counterpart.

betrays a strong allegiance to the opening shape of refrain 1361, most plausibly explained by its status as a genuine quotation, accommodated within a new harmonic context.

It is evident from Table 5.1 that both refrains 1361 and 287 circulated with a considerable degree of musical and textual stability. In its two motet appearances refrain 1361 is subject to variations in spelling, and there is an additional decorative note in perfection 37 of *La plus bele*/[*PACEM*]. The moment of variance in this refrain between *Domino 12* and *Ne m'oubliez mie*, at perfection 7, is different again at perfection 35 of *La plus bele*, where the motetus has a leap of a third, E–G, which clashes with the tenor D. This could simply be scribal error (there is no clear motivic justification for the dissonance), but it is nonetheless noteworthy that this portion of the refrain melody is consistently unstable. The various appearances of refrain 287 also exhibit small differences in spelling, and the textual alternative 'haute amour' appears instead of 'bone amour' in the motet *Mainte dame*. Melodically, all quotations of refrain 287 are closely related, with only minor differences in plication or decoration occurring on the word 'amour'.

Both motet refrains appear in conjunction with various different tenor melismas: refrain 1361 over DOMINO and PACEM and refrain 287 over DOMINO, HODIE PERLUSTRAVIT and IOHANNE. Though these motets are based on different chants, the rhythmic arrangements of their various tenor melismas actually provide quite similar accompaniments for the corresponding refrains. The sections of DOMINO and PACEM above which refrain 1361 appears are in the same D mode, and strongly resemble one another in terms of range and pitch content, with a preponderance of D and F. The two motets have identical tenor-motetus sonorities for the opening three perfections of refrain 1361 (excepting the non-harmonisation of the syllable '-ez' of 'oubliez' in *Ne m'oubliez*), and the first half of the refrain also closes on a G–C cadence in both cases. The tenor sections supporting refrain 287 are likewise related. Again, all tenors are in the same mode, principally emphasising the pitches D, F, and C, and there are coincidences of melodic and harmonic details: the DOMINO and IOHANNE tenors both close with a C–D progression, and the refrain's initial A sounds against a D in the tenor in both *Ne m'oubliez mie* and *Quant voi yver*/*Au douz tans*.[22]

Refrains 1361 and 287 are combined only in the motet *Ne m'oubliez mie*, but as a pair they are well chosen. The two melodies are compatible

[22] The exception is the version of *Mainte dame* in **N**, where an 'extra' penultimate D is introduced in the tenor that is absent from the related clausula in **StV**.

modally, both closing on the final of the mode, D, and spanning essentially the same range (C–A in 1361 and D–A in 287). The overall shape of refrain 287 enacts the descent of a fifth, from A to D, the same shape outlined in the final three perfections of refrain 1361. This descending fifth, common to both refrain melodies, also balances the characteristic opening gesture of refrain 1361, a rising fifth from D to A. In addition, their texts are linked by a shared paroxytonic '-e' ending ('mie' in 1361 and 'm'agree' in 287), and by the common theme of courtly love, voiced by a first-person lover. The two refrains are nevertheless sufficiently different, musically and textually, to support the hypothesis that they are quotations from independent sources brought together in this motet. If they stemmed, for example, from a common monophonic *rondeau*, now lost, one would expect an even closer relationship between them, such as a shared internal rhyme, similar syllable count (refrain 1361 employs five- and six-syllable lines, while refrain 287 comprises an eight-syllable line) or common details of melodic decoration. Given also their consistently independent circulation in other contexts, it seems that these refrains represent autonomous musical and textual quotations selected by the creator of *Ne m'oubliez mie* because of their similarities to one another.

Melodic and poetic features of both refrains were apparently central to the construction of the motetus in *Ne m'oubliez mie*. As noted above, the initial presentation of refrain 1361 is followed by an imitation of its opening. At perfection 13, a phrase of six perfections (the same length as the phrases of refrain 1361) mimics the rising-fifth gesture of the opening of the refrain. This reference is reinforced by the use of a six-syllable line of text and the phrase 'car je n'oubli mie', with the word 'oubli' set (as in the refrain) to two repeated As, and the word 'mie' accompanied by the same falling melodic gesture (circled in Example 5.1) found in perfection 3. Perfections 16–18 resemble the second half of the refrain textually (setting a five-syllable line of text) and musically. Perfection 16 encompasses a rising fourth (just like perfection 7) and is followed by the descent of a fifth (marked by a box in Example 5.1), similar to that at the close of the refrain (in perfections 10–11). This decorated descending fifth in perfections 17–18 features in two further phrases, perfections 20–1 and 25–6, on these occasions with same pitch content (A–D) as at the end of refrain 1361.

Certain other musical features of the opening refrain reappear later in the motet. Perfections 33–6 resemble the opening of refrain 1361: the phrase turns around A and concludes (in perfection 36) with the same falling gesture that accompanied 'mie' (in perfection 3), at the same pitch and with a similar text (the syllables '-mee' of 'ramee'). The falling gesture is then

Table 5.2 Text and translation of *Ne m'oubliez mie*

1.	*Ne m'oubliez mie*	**6a**	-ie	*Do not forget me*
2.	*bele et avenant!*	**5b**	-ant	*lovely and fair one!*
3.	*Quant je ne voz voi,*	**5c**	-oi	*When I do not see you,*
4.	*s'en sui plus dolens.*	**5d**	-ens	*I am all the more saddened.*
5.	Car je n'oubli mie	**6a**	-ie	For I will not forget
6.	vostre grant valour	**5e**	-our	your great worth
7.	ne la compaignie	**6a**	-ie	nor your companionship
8.	a nul jour,	**3e**	-our	ever,
9.	n'avre mes envie	**6a**	-ie	I will not desire
10.	d'amors	**2e'**	-ors	the love
11.	d'autre feme nee.	**6f**	-ee	of another living woman.
12.	C'est la jus en la ramee,	**8f**	-ee	It is over there in the thicket,
13.	amours ai!	**3g**	-ai	I have love!
14.	Marions i est alee,	**8f**	-ee	Marion has gone there,
15.	*bone amour ai, qui m'agree.*	**4g + 4f**	-ai -ee	*I have a fine love, which holds me.*

Translation adapted from that in Joel C. Relihan and Susan Stakel (eds.), *The Montpellier Codex, Part IV: Texts and Translations*, RRMMA 8 (Madison, 1985), p. 77.

immediately repeated down a tone in perfection 37. Indeed, the following perfection (38) of the motetus seems also to refer to the opening refrain: it employs the same closing figure as perfection 9 (marked by a dashed circle in Example 5.1) over the same pitch, D, in the tenor. This figure, in both perfections 9 and 38, resolves to an F/A sonority, with the A in the motetus eventually descending to D. The reappearance of this melodic figure in perfection 38 therefore underlines the relationship between the close of refrain 1361 and the shape of refrain 287. The influence of refrain 1361 can also be observed poetically: the refrain provides the '-ie' rhyme that appears repeatedly in the first ten lines of the text (Table 5.2). These ten lines also employ six-syllable lines as the principal textual unit, mirroring the opening line of text in the refrain.

In a similar manner, details of the concluding refrain 287 are prefigured in the motetus of *Ne m'oubliez mie*. The final cadence of this refrain (perfections 47–8, marked by a dashed box in Example 5.1) is foreshadowed in perfections 27–8, over the same C–D progression in the tenor. This cadence appears again, in an inverted form, in perfections 31–2, where the same rhythm is employed but the motetus outlines a progression from D to G rather than G to D. The phrase length of refrain 287, five perfections in duration, is also anticipated in perfections 19–23 and 24–8. Indeed, this pair of five-perfection phrases resembles the pair of phrases made up of refrain 287 and the preceding quotation of its melody. Though they close differently, perfections 19–23 and 24–8 open with very similar melodic gestures (A–B–C in perfection 19 versus A–C–B in perfection 24). The kinship between these two pairs of phrases is also reinforced by the fact that perfections 19–28 and 39–48 are the only phrases in *Ne m'oubliez mie* to be joined together by the continuation of the tenor voice during a break in the motetus. In both instances the tenor progression is the same (C–D in perfections 23–4 and 43–4), and the exceptional continuation of the tenor voice seems to draw attention to the melodic repetition employed in both pairs of phrases that it links. The rhymes of refrain 287 are also introduced in advance: the '-ee' ending is employed from line 11 onwards (perfections 31–2) and the internal '-ai' rhyme of the refrain is also prepared in line 13 (perfection 38). In addition, the use of the eight-syllable line that characterises this refrain is prefigured in lines 12 and 14. The two refrains that frame *Ne m'oubliez mie* were, therefore, crucial in shaping the melodic and poetic details of its motetus, and the fundamental influence of these refrain quotations on this musical material confirms its conception as a French motet, rather than a clausula.

Not only is the combination of these two refrains in *Ne m'oubliez mie* effective, but their quotation in conjunction with that of a pre-existent chant melisma in the tenor is skilful.[23] It could have been the mode and pitch content of the DOMINO melisma that inspired these refrain quotations, and the strong resemblance between DOMINO and the very uncommon PACEM tenor also found in conjunction with vdB 1361 seems telling in this regard.[24] But it may equally have been the nature of one, the other, or both of the refrain melodies – or even the possibility for the direct repetition of melody 287 – that prompted the choice and rhythmic arrangement of the motet's underlying tenor. Given the essential similarities of the various chant melodies associated with refrains 1361 and 287, it seems realistic to imagine a two-way process in which the modal and melodic profile of a tenor chant might suggest a corresponding refrain melody, while particular refrains could also lead to the selection of certain types of tenors.

This two-way chant–refrain process is borne out by the circumstances of the distinctive D–A leap that opens refrain 1361. A preoccupation with this motive is evident throughout *Ne m'oubliez mie* and also in *La plus bele/ [PACEM]*: although vdB 1361 is quoted here as a terminal refrain, *La plus*

[23] Frobenius described the use of refrains in this motet as 'especially spectacular' (*besonders spektakulär*) in 'Zum genetischen Verhältnis', p. 20.

[24] In addition to *La plus bele*, the PACEM tenor (M 72) features in just one other motet, which is also a unicum (*Amours qui tant/PACEM*, Mt566). Unlike O 16 or BD 1, M 72 does not appear in any organa or clausulae in the *Magnus liber*.

Example 5.3 Similar motetus incipits in three DOMINO motets.

Opening of *Ne m'oubliez mie/DOMINO*, **Mo**, fols. 216v-262r

Opening of motetus and tenor of *Pucelete/Je lang[ui]/DOMINO*, **Mo**, fols. 193v-195r

Opening of *Hier mein trespensis/DOMINO*, **W2**, fol. 218va

bele additionally opens with the refrain's characteristic D–A gesture over a tenor D. Interestingly, two other motets on the DOMINO tenor, which do not include refrain 1361 – *Pucelete bele et avenant/Je lang*[*ui*] *des maus d'mours/DOMINO* and *Hier mein trespensis d'amour/DOMINO* – nonetheless feature its opening motive (see Example 5.3).[25] This D–A leap appears in a different rhythmic and harmonic context in *Hier mein trespensis*, where it is in the first rhythmic mode, and the A sounds, not over the opening tenor D, but in conjunction with the second pitch (F) of the chant melody. Yet the opening motetus phrases in these three DOMINO motets are further connected by their shared reiterations of the note A, from the starkly repetitive *Je lang*[*ui*] *des maus* to the more decorated *Ne m'oubliez mie* and *Hier mein trespensis*, both of which turn around this pitch in a similar manner.

The opening leap of a fifth from D to A is significantly absent from all other clausulae or Latin motets on DOMINO, and from the clausulae and

[25] Like *Ne m'oubliez*, both *Hier mein* and *Pucelete/Je lang*[*ui*] have related two-voice clausulae in **F**: *Domino 14* (fol. 89r–1) and *Domino 16* (fol. 89r–3) respectively. All three are preserved within a notationally irregular group of DOMINO clausulae that I have proposed as transcribed motets. See Chapter 4 n. 18.

numerous motets on the musically identical EIUS tenor, whose upper voices tend to begin either a fifth (on A) or an octave (D) above the tenor.[26] The D–A leap at the beginning of vdB 1361 in *Ne m'oubliez mie* may itself have established a conventional opening for vernacular motets on DOMINO, taken up in subsequent compositions. Alternatively, the decision to quote this refrain at the outset of *Ne m'oubliez mie* could have been inspired by the knowledge of other French DOMINO motets beginning in an identical fashion. Such a relationship between chant and refrain quotations is, in many respects, straightforwardly practical: particular motetus melodies and melodic gestures are effective, and thus reappear, in particular polyphonic contexts. At the same time, an awareness of both refrain and/or chant melodies in multiple host contexts may, in addition to the explicit reuse of musical and textual material, constitute another more subtle layer of quotation or allusion, indicating a fundamentally intertextual compositional culture for motets.

Crafting Refrains in *Nus ne se doit/AUDI FILIA*

The two-voice motet *Nus ne se doit* on the tenor AUDI FILIA, from the Assumption Gradual *Propter veritatem* (M 37), is also characterised by the use of framing refrains in its motetus, and stands in interesting relation to *Ne m'oubliez mie*. Similarly preserved in the sixth fascicle of **Mo**, *Nus ne se doit* additionally appears among the motet collections in the otherwise monophonic chansonniers **N** and **R**.[27] As I shall show, the opening and closing refrains here play a role comparable to the refrains of *Ne m'oubliez mie*, influencing much of the internal musical and textual material in the motetus. But although the framing phrases of *Nus ne se doit* have all the appearance and function of refrains, they are unique to this motet and their status as quotations is doubtful. I explore ways in which this compositional scenario, one in which the motet creator had greater control and flexibility, contrasts with that in *Ne m'oubliez mie*, a piece that is outwardly of the same mould.

A textual kinship between the initial and final phrases of *Nus ne se doit* – which share vocabulary, and rhymes, and a poetic topos – is immediately

[26] For incipits of all EIUS and DOMINO clausulae and motets, see Friedrich Ludwig, *Repertorium organorum recentioris et motetorum vetustisimi stili*, ed. Luther A. Dittmer, 2 vols. in 3 (New York, 1964–78 [1910]), Vol. II, pp. 95–101 (for O 16) and pp. 111–13 (for BD I).

[27] **Mo**, fols. 246v–247r; **N**, fol. 187v; **R**, fol. 208r.

Example 5.4 Opening and closing refrains in *Nus ne se doit/AUDI FILIA*, **Mo**, fols. 246v–247r.

apparent (see Example 5.4, where shared features are highlighted in bold). The opening refrain advocates that the pain of love should not dissuade the lover from loving, while the closing maxim denies the joy of love to those who have not suffered from it. Each conventionally comprising a couplet, the refrains are similar in length: the opening refrain has two seven-syllable lines, the closing a seven-syllable, six-syllable pair. Their near-identical beginnings – 'Nus ne se doit' and 'Nus ne doit' – lead to the same rhyme (-tir) in the middle of the refrains. The second lines of each couplet also start alike ('d'amors'), but the closing refrain adopts as terminal an internal rhyme in the opening refrain ('mal'), prefacing this with an allusion ('trait mal') to the opening refrain's terminal rhyme (-ait). Musically, these poetic similarities are complemented by a shared opening gesture, a repeated-note falling figure (marked by boxes in Example 5.4). Both refrains also cadence on the same final pitch, F, and they resemble one another in their range, tonal profile, and melodic decorations (particularly the conjunct falling third figures, marked by dashed boxes).

These phrases give the strong impression of a poetic and musical pair, and the fact that neither is found independently outside the context of this particular motet suggests they were conceived as such. Were both refrains newly created together here; or was one of the refrains indeed a quotation – for which other instantiations are now lost – and on which the other was modelled? These unique refrains are absent from Van den Boogaard's catalogue, but Friedrich Gennrich's earlier refrain *Verzeichnis* included the opening phrase.[28] The refrain status of the motet's closing phrase was recognised in the recent online refrain database by Mark Everist and Anne Ibos-Augé, who inserted it at the appropriate alphabetical juncture in Van den Boogaard's catalogue under the number 1395a.[29] In the copies of *Nus ne se doit* in **N** and **R**, the beginning of vdB 1395a is marked by a capital initial 'N', a convention to indicate a terminal refrain in these sources.

Although neither the opening nor closing phrases of *Nus ne se doit/ AUDI FILIA* concord directly with another extant refrain text or melody, both exploit highly generic refrain features. To open a refrain with 'Nus ne' is a typical poetic gesture found in eighteen additional refrains in Van den Boogaard's catalogue, the majority of which expound the same trope – the necessity of suffering for love. Gennrich observed an internal poetic similarity between the opening refrain and the refrain '*Fin cuers* ***ne se doit repentir*** */ de bien amer*' (vdB 755, shared vocabulary in bold) widely transmitted across chanson and motet repertoires.[30] Hans Tischler listed the closing refrain in *Nus ne se doit* (vdB 1395a) as a version of vdB 1351, which uses the alternative negative construction '*Ne … pas*': '***Ne doit*** *pas* ***le bien sentir / d'amour*** *qui* ***n'en*** *sent* ***mal***'.[31] I have additionally noted a musical and textual proximity between the closing refrain in *Nus ne se doit* (vdB 1395a) and the beginning of another 'Nus ne' refrain, vdB 1395, which appears uniquely at the end of the triplum voice in the four-voice motet *Celui de cui/La bele estoile/La bele en cui/IOHANNE* (see the comparison in Example 5.5).[32] In vdB 1395, the text incipit shared with vdB 1359a is accompanied by a similar opening melodic gesture at the same pitch level

[28] Refrain no. 221 in Friedrich Gennrich, *Bibliographisches Verzeichnis der französischen Refrains des 12. und 13. Jahrhunderts*, SMMA 14 (Frankfurt, 1964).

[29] See Mark Everist and Anne Ibos-Augé, *REFRAIN: Musique, poésie, citation. Le refrain au moyen âge/Music, Poetry, Citation: The Medieval Refrain*, at http://medmus.soton.ac.uk/view.html (accessed 4 March 2018).

[30] Friedrich Gennrich, *Rondeaux, Virelais und Balladen aus dem Ende des XII., dem XIII., und dem ersten Drittel des XIV. Jahrhunderts mit dem überlieferten Melodien 2*, Gesellschaft für romanische Literatur 47 (Göttingen, 1927), p. 204. This poetic similarity is not, however, matched in the refrain melody accompanying vdB 755 (Gennrich refrain no. 458) in chanson or motet sources.

[31] See Hans Tischler, *The Style and Evolution of the Earliest Motets (to circa 1270)*, 4 vols., Musicological Studies 40 (Ottawa, 1985), Vol. II, p. 110, no. 77. Tischler erroneously indicates 1351 as the refrain number in Gennrich's, rather than Van den Boogaard's, catalogue; vdB 1351 is transmitted in the text-only context of a *dit* by Baudouin de Condé, *La Prison d'amours*.

[32] This vernacular motet (Mt388–90) is also extant in two-voice (Mt388) and three-voice (Mt388–9) versions, as well as in two-voice (Mt391) and three-voice (Mt 391–2) versions with Latin contrafactum texts.

Example 5.5 Comparing vdB 1395a and refrains in *Celui de cui/La bele estoile/La bele en cui/IOHANNE*, **Mo**, fols. 24v–27r.

Ending of *Nus ne se doit/AUDI FILIA*, **Mo**, fols. 246v-247r

Ending of *Celui de qui/La bele estoile/La bele en qui/IOHANNE*, **Mo**, fols. 24v-27r

(marked by a dashed box in Example 5.5), while the close of the first half of both refrains (marked by boxes) is musically identical.

In the four-voice IOHANNE motet, vdB 1395 occurs at the same time as another refrain, vdB 1327. The text of refrain 1327 is employed in both motetus and quadruplum voices, but only the closing motetus phrase constitutes a true intertextual refrain, whose text *and* music also appear in another independent motet context.[33] Strikingly, the unique quadruplum melody for vdB 1327 matches the repeated-note opening motive of vdB 1395a (marked by a box in Example 5.5). Since an exact version of the opening motive of vdB 1395a appears in the polyphonic context of the musically and textually similar vdB 1395, it is possible that the creator of *Nus*

[33] As found in the motetus *La bele en cui*, vdB 1327 is concordant with the end of the motetus in *En tel lieu s'est entremis/VIRGO* (Mt424).

ne se doit/AUDI FILIA had the ending of this four-voice IOHANNE motet in mind.[34] Yet it seems more likely that, just as the refrain texts in *Nus ne se doit/AUDI FILIA* refer to a well-established refrain opening, their melodies likewise begin with a conventional melodic gesture common to other textually related refrains. The myriad partial similarities but lack of any exact matches between these framing refrains and various other refrain texts and melodies surely arise as the result of allusions to established musical and poetic refrain topics rather than any attempts at literal quotation.

These framing phrases clearly function as and allude to the musical and poetic conventions of refrains. That they were not quotations, but instead expressly crafted for the motet in question, is additionally supported by their musical context (see Examples 5.6 and 5.7: the layout of Example 5.6 is determined by the structure of the motetus, while Example 5.7 reflects that of the tenor). *Nus ne se doit* features two complete and unaltered tenor repetitions of the chant melody AUDI FILIA in an entirely consistent rhythmic pattern.[35] Unlike *Ne m'oubliez mie/DOMINO*, there is no noticeable increase in either dissonance or parallel motion during the opening or closing refrains. Although there are occasional dissonances in the combination of refrain and tenor material – notably the stressed appoggiatura-like seconds and sevenths at the end of the opening refrain (perfections 6–7) – these are by no means uncharacteristic of the motet as a whole. The phrase immediately following the opening refrain (perfections 9–12), for instance, is not obviously determined by reference to any refrain motives. Yet it features both unison motion between motetus and tenor (perfections 9–10) and movement in parallel seconds at the end of perfection 11.

The two refrains are also integral to large-scale formal procedures in the AUDI FILIA motet. *Nus ne se doit* is in two halves of equal length (20 perfections), each corresponding to an identical statement of the AUDI FILIA melody. In the first tenor statement, motetus and tenor phrase together, the motetus adopting the four-perfection units of the tenor's rhythmic pattern, to create an overall 8–4–8 perfection structure, initiated by the opening refrain (see Example 5.7). In the second half, by contrast, the motetus cuts across the tenor pattern. Initial four-perfection units are maintained, but the second part of each phrase is shortened, producing

[34] There are no other obvious musical correspondences between the two motets. Textually, they explore broadly similar poetic tropes (such as loyalty and the pain of love) but without any considerable overlap in vocabulary, rhyme, or poetic structure.

[35] As discussed in Chapter 1, *Nus ne se doit* uses version α′ of the FILIA melisma, which is shared by the two Latin motets on the FILIA tenor. See Chapter 1, Example 1.8.

Example 5.6 *Nus ne se doit/AUDI FILIA*, **Mo**, fols. 246v–247r (with selected variants shared by **N**, fol. 187v and **R**, fol. 208r shown above the stave).

a larger and independent 7–6–7 perfection structure, culminating in the final refrain. A shared tripartite symmetrical structure, enclosing a shorter middle phrase, creates a balance between the two halves of the motetus. At the same time, the subtle decrease in the length of the outer phrases from eight to seven perfections significantly recasts the relationship between

Example 5.7 Tenor–motetus relationships and phrase structures in *Nus ne se doit/AUDI FILIA*, **Mo**, fols. 246v–247r (lines mark ends of phrases, arrows indicate anacruses).

upper voice and tenor, facilitating a different motetus response to the same underlying chant arrangement.

This kind of compositional ploy, virtuosically displaying different polyphonic elaborations of a chant foundation within a single piece, is typical of many thirteenth-century motets. Apparent also in *Ne m'oubliez mie*, it seems even more central to the conception and compositional sophistication of *Nus ne se doit*. The change in motetus phrase structure in the second half of *Nus ne se doit* varies the phase and causes an enjambment of motetus and tenor endings. This effectively increases a sense of momentum towards the conclusion of the motet at which a clear simultaneous break in both voices is finally achieved. The drive towards the final cadence is complemented by the exploration of a new tonal area, facilitated also by the change in tenor–motetus alignment. Since each four-perfection tenor ordo ends alternatively on C or on F (the motet's final), the first tenor cursus exclusively employs cadences on these related tones, closing on a unison C or F, or on an F/C fifth. The second tenor cursus begins with two unison C cadences (in perfections 24 and 27), but a contrasting cadence on a unison A is introduced at perfection 31, and is exploited in two immediately following cadences at perfections 33 and 37 (marked by dashed boxes in Example 5.6). This insistence on a new and more 'open' sonority – exploiting the cadential possibilities of a pitch that falls in the middle and at the beginning of a tenor ordo – enhances the sense of conclusion at the motet's final return to a 'closed' F/C cadence.

Although the framing refrains of *Nus ne se doit* are probably not themselves quotations, the motet nevertheless exploits multiple internal opportunities to 'quote' this refrain material in deliberately varied combination with its tenor chant. The two halves of the motet's opening refrain (labelled a and b in Example 5.6) are redeployed in several contexts. A shortened version of the b phrase returns to close the first half of the motet in perfections 18–20, where it is introduced by a phrase similar in contour to that which prefigured it in the opening refrain (perfections 15–16, tracing a descent from F onto a C cadence). The restatement of the tenor melody at perfection 21 features a return to the motet's opening a material, but this time transposed down a fifth, beginning on B flat. This transposition is remarkable, since it avoids an obvious opportunity for literal repetition of the tenor-motetus beginning, demonstrating instead an alternative combination of the same basic melodic material. A return of the a material at pitch is, instead, postponed until the start of the next phrase (perfection 28) where it now appears in conjunction with a different segment of the tenor chant. This a material is redirected towards the new cadence on A at perfection 31, which foreshadows that of the terminal refrain at perfection 37, and thereby encapsulates a transition from the opening to the closing material.

As in *Ne m'oubliez mie*, the motetus of *Nus ne se doit* exhibits a concern for repetition throughout. A cadential figure at perfections 11–12 (marked by a wavy box in Example 5.6), for instance, recurs in a different tenor context at perfections 23–4. But, as demonstrated above, musical material is otherwise drawn principally from the motet's refrains, effectively 'developing' the opening refrain and 'preparing' for the closing one. This is complemented by the accompanying motetus text, clearly in the same semantic vein as its framing refrains, and with no obvious connections to the liturgical context of its Assumption tenor (see Table 5.3). The motetus shares much of its poetic vocabulary with these refrains, and its rhymes are drawn exclusively from refrain material. Following the opening refrain, line 3 immediately replicates the internal and terminal rhymes (labelled b and c respectively) of the refrain's second half, while lines 4 and 5 repeat the rhymes of the motet's opening couplet. Interestingly, line 4 adopts the words 'biens sentir' from the final refrain to accompany a new declamatory feature characteristic of this refrain and that prevails for the rest of the piece: this is the introduction of an anacrusis in the second half of each eight-perfection phrase. The final refrain is also prefigured by a change in rhyme scheme at line 9, where the opening refrain's '-ait' ending is abandoned in favour of the '-al' rhyme, which featured as an internal rhyme in the opening refrain, but now appears in a terminal position, as in the closing refrain. The general regularity of this poetic structure, in both syllable count and rhyme scheme, is in sympathy with the motet's balanced musical form.

The text and music of *Nus ne se doit* are saturated with references to its framing refrains, which themselves reference one another, and seem fundamental to the compositional impulse for this motet. Musically, however, the clarity and precise degree of motivic connections across the motetus varies slightly between its different extant versions. In **R** – but not in **Mo** or **N** – the transposed return of the a material at the beginning of the second tenor cursus (perfection 21) is obscured by a slightly different decoration of the melodic line, as is the connection between the cadence figure (marked by wavy boxes) in perfections 11–12 and 23–4. In the **Mo** motet, on the other hand, small-scale motivic consistency appears to have been of particular concern. Here perfections 24–6 prefigure the corresponding moment in the closing refrain, in perfections 37–9 (marked by boxes in Example 5.6), encompassing a repeated-note rising figure (G–G–A): an inverse of the refrains' opening motive. This correspondence is less obvious in the version

Table 5.3 Text and translation of *Nus ne se doit repentir* (vocabulary shared with refrains shown in bold)

1.	***Nus ne*** *se* ***doit*** *repentir*	**7a**	-tir	*No one should repent*
2.	***d'amors*** *por* ***mal****, qu'il en* ***ait***	**4b + 3c**	-al -ait	*of loving on account of his pain*
3.	qu'a chascun **mal** qu'il en **trait**,	**4b + 3c**	-al -ait	since for every pain that he suffers,
4.	en puet il cents **biens sentir**,	**7a**	-tir	he can have a hundred joys,
5.	se de ce pens ne le re**trait**.	**8c**	-ait	if his thoughts do not make him pull back.
6.	Et qui ne veut con**sentir**	**7a**	-tir	And he who does not wish to consent
7.	tout ce qu'**amors** l'en fet,	**6c'**	-et	to all love does to him,
8.	onques n'**ama** sans mentir	**7a**	-tir	in truth has never loved
9.	de cuer loial.	**4b**	-al	with a loyal heart.
10.	***Nus ne doit*** *les* ***biens sentir***	**7a**	-tir	*No one should ever feel the joys*
11.	***d'amours****, s'il n'en* ***trait mal****.*	**6b**	-al	*of love if he does not suffer its pain.*

Translation adapted from that in Relihan and Stakel, *The Montpellier Codex, Part IV*, p. 72.

of the closing refrain found in **N** and **R** (indicated above the stave in Example 5.6). And it is remarkable that the decorative cadence in perfection 33 of **Mo** features the same rising G–G–A figure, once again absent from **N** and **R**, which offer a more consonant and conventional reading. This recalls *Ne m'oubliez mie* and its related clausula, which provide comparable alternative readings of a shared musical text. Once again, it is difficult to ascribe authority or chronological priority to particular versions. The obfuscating decoration unique to **R** at the return of the opening motive in conjunction with the beginning of a new tenor statement, for instance, blurs what seems to be a crucial structural moment. It is probable, then, that this is a later corruption, but it is problematic to assume, more generally, that the most 'unified' version of the motet must be the 'original'. The extra layer of coherence in motivic details in the **Mo** version of *Nus ne se doit* could reflect the opportunistic innovations of a scribe or singer, exploring further a compositional inclination already inherent in this tightly controlled motet.

Even a motet with as consistent an identity as *Nus ne se doit* – which apparently received neither clausula transcription, contrafactum motet texts, nor additional voice parts – may have an essentially collective authorship; treated, not as the finished work of a single creator, but circulating in alternative forms within a repertoire in which recopying and reworking were the norm. A sense of *Nus ne se doit* as belonging within this broader repertorial context is confirmed by its relation to other motets on the FILIA and AUDI FILIA tenors, of which (in marked contrast to the EIUS/DOMINO tenor) there are only five in total. Margaret Bent observed that connections between motets are 'all the more convincing when the

Example 5.8 Similar framing refrains in AUDI FILIA motets.

tenor is unusual … than when it is a well-known chant', and this seems particularly applicable in the context of AUDI FILIA motets.[36] As discussed in Chapter 1, several versions of the FILIA chant melisma circulated concurrently, and *Nus ne se doit* employs a certain variant of the tenor found, not in any organa or clausulae, but in the two Latin motets on FILIA.[37] The remaining AUDI FILIA motets – *M'ocirres voz dous/AUDI FILIA* and *Biaus cuers/AUDI FILIA* – have in common the same basic version of the FILIA chant as *Nus ne se doit*, but in its more conventional, unaltered, form. Nevertheless the upper voices of these three two-voice vernacular settings share several striking features (see Example 5.8).

[36] Margaret Bent, 'Polyphony of Texts and Music in the Fourteenth-Century Motet: *Tribum que non abhorruit/Quoniam secta latronum/Merito hec partimur* and Its "Quotations"', in Dolores Pesce (ed.), *Hearing the Motet: Essays on the Motet of the Middle Ages and Renaissance* (New York, 1997), pp. 82–103 (p. 83).

[37] See Chapter 1, Example 1.8 and Appendix 1.2.

Gaël Saint-Cricq previously noted similarities in construction between *Nus ne se doit* and *M'ocirres voz dous* (unique to **Mo**).[38] *M'ocirres* likewise employs two framing refrains that serve as the basis for much of the motet's internal melodic material; these refrains are an even more closely related pair than in *Nus ne se doit*, since the closing refrain effectively repeats and extends the opening. *Biaus cuers desirres et dous/AUDI FILIA*, musically unique to **Mo** but whose text additionally appears among the motets in the text-only chansonnier **Douce 308** (fols. 244v–245r), differs slightly: a single refrain is here split in two in accordance with motet enté convention. Nevertheless, it is remarkable that all three of the AUDI FILIA motets, preserved in **Mo** within the space of eleven folios, use refrain material to frame their upper voices and, furthermore, that their opening refrains share the same melodic gesture: a repeated F, which immediately falls to E, and eventually to C.

The status of these additional framing refrains on the AUDI FILIA tenor, as quoted or newly composed, merits brief consideration here. Once again, and despite their use of stereotypical refrain vocabulary ('m'ocirres', 'fins cuers'), neither of the *M'ocirres* refrains was included in Van den Boogaard's catalogue, and both are apparently unique to this motet. Musically, however, their polyphonic treatment suggests that they do indeed constitute musical quotations (see Example 5.9). The motet's initial tenor pitches are rhythmically extended (marked by a box in Example 5.9), delaying the onset of its rhythmic pattern, to produce a more successful harmonic combination with the opening refrain (compare the dissonant alternative tenor rhythmicisation suggested below the stave). The established version of the AUDI FILIA tenor as employed in both *M'ocirres* and *Biaus cuers* is shown as Example 5.10. In *M'ocirres*, the chant quotation is melodically exact in the motet's first cursus, but is tellingly altered during the second cursus at the point of the closing refrain, in which the tenor's rhythmic pattern is also disturbed. Here two additional pitches (marked by a dashed box in Example 5.9) are introduced in perfections 54–5, necessarily lengthening the tenor to accommodate the refrain (compare the hypothetical alternative in Example 5.9).[39] And more cosmetic rhythmic and melodic alterations to the underlying chant melody at perfection 58 (marked by boxes and dashed

[38] See Gaël Saint-Cricq, 'Formes types dans le motet du XIIIe siècle: Etude d'un processus répétitif', Ph.D. diss. (University of Southampton, 2009), Vol. I, pp. 260–1.

[39] There may be corruption in the tenor at the moment that it deviates from the chant source. It seems likely that the new tenor pitch introduced in perfection 54 should be B, in unison with the motetus, rather than C, producing a dissonant second.

Example 5.9 Opening and closing phrases of *M'ocirres voz/AUDI FILIA*, **Mo**, fol. 250r–v (with hypothetical alternative tenor realisations).

Example 5.10 Established version of AUDI FILIA tenor melisma adopted (but altered) in *M'ocirres* and *Biaus cuers*.

boxes respectively) additionally strengthen the motet's final cadence (an unaltered version of the chant quotation is given above the stave).

Whether or not the split refrain in *Biaus cuers* (vdB 216) – once again lacking any extant musical concordances – constitutes a musical quotation is more equivocal.[40] In this motet also, both the beginning and end of the AUDI FILIA tenor exhibit irregularities, but these cannot be so straightforwardly explained in terms of accommodating a refrain (see Example 5.11). Like

[40] Van den Boogaard lists an independent text concordance in the religious treatise *Le livre d'amoretes* (Paris, Bibliothèque nationale de France, lat. 13091). Certain variants in the text as found in *Le livre d'amoretes* – notably the omission of the opening words 'Biaus cuers desirres' – may render this concordance doubtful.

Example 5.11 Opening and closing phrases of *Biaus cuers desires/AUDI FILIA*, **Mo**, fols. 255v–256r (with hypothetical alternative tenor realisations).

M'ocirres, Biaus cuers presents the initial two tenor pitches, corresponding to the AUDI portion of the melisma, in longer note values, that stand outside the tenor's fast-moving pattern (alternating between modes one and six). In this case, by contrast, the elongation of the opening chant pitches has little impact on the combination with the motetus refrain. Remarkably, the initial tenor–refrain combination would not have been radically different had the tenor's rhythmic pattern been imposed from the outset (see the hypothetical tenor reworking below the stave in Example 5.11).[41] Similarly, another break in the tenor's rhythmic pattern in its final ordo need not necessarily have been prompted by any refrain quotation: two additional longs (marked by a box in Example 5.11) are introduced in a broadening towards the final cadence, which would otherwise fall in the middle of an ordo. It is likewise difficult to account for the alteration of the motet tenor's penultimate tenor note, the only chant pitch modified in the motet, purely in terms of the closing refrain. The AUDI FILIA tenor terminates early in this motet, omitting the final four notes of the chant melody (compare

[41] It is significant that the two notes corresponding to the AUDI portion of the chant melisma are omitted from the second tenor cursus, which repeats only the FILIA melody. This tenor treatment is comparable to that in the enté motet *Puis que bele dame/FLOS FILIUS EIUS* (Mt671), where the initial FLOS FILIUS section of the melisma is also initially stated in long notes, outside the tenor's rhythmic pattern, and is omitted from the second tenor cursus, which begins at the EIUS portion of the chant.

Example 5.10). An inconclusive E–C tenor progression is here amended to D–C, creating a more compelling final cadence against B–C in the motetus refrain. Since this closing motetus gesture would have been both expected and desirable in a motet that cadences on C, it is problematic to ascribe the tenor alteration purely to the demands of a pre-existent refrain.

Although the status of the *Biaus cuers* refrain as a quotation remains inconclusive, investigation of the broader intertextual tenor–refrain context for *Nus ne se doit* is revealing in two principal respects. First, the literal quotation of the AUDI FILIA melisma in an entirely consistent rhythmic pattern was of greater concern in *Nus ne se doit* than in the other two motets on this tenor. Such unusual fidelity to the tenor melisma and its pattern seems, therefore, all the more likely to have been facilitated by the creation of a pair of refrains for and within this particular motet context. Second, I have demonstrated that, at the opening of *Biaus cuers*, the AUDI FILIA tenor could have been alternatively rhythmicised to produce an equally successful combination with its motetus refrain. This circumstance underlines the inherent polyphonic potential and flexibility of the AUDI FILIA melisma itself, the ease with which it can be manipulated to combine in various ways against a given upper voice. This is a result of the chant's flat and repetitive melodic profile, which consistently emphasises just four main pitches. Three of these – F, A, and C – are relatively interchangeable, since all can harmonise effectively with each other, and combine successfully with a motetus melody based around F and C. The fourth tenor pitch, D, can work against F (and A) when necessary, but it also facilitates an alternative G–B–D tonality as a contrast to the F-based sonorities. It is hardly surprising that such a repetitive tenor foundation – itself repeating both individual/related pitches as well as certain melodic cells – might promote melodic repetition in an upper voice. Similarities between the opening and closing of the chant melisma in particular (see the passages marked by boxes in Example 5.10) could further account for the consistent use of framing refrain gestures in AUDI FILIA motets. The final portion of the melisma, with its string of repeated Fs followed by an A–C–D ascent – the point at which concluding refrain material appears in all three motets – offers exactly the same tonal possibilities as the chant's beginning.[42] These matching gestures at either end of the chant melisma strongly complement the matching openings characteristic of framing and enté refrains.

[42] Given that closing refrains of different length are involved, and *Biaus cuers* ends before the completion of its second tenor cursus, it is all the more remarkable that concluding refrains invariably occur in conjunction with the same portion of the AUDI FILIA melisma.

All three surviving AUDI FILIA motets exploit the repetitive potential of their tenor, but none does so in a straightforward fashion. Upper-voice repetitions in direct coincidence with the chant melody seem deliberately to have been avoided, and all of these two-tenor-statement motets actively recast the tenor melody on its second appearance (facilitated in *M'ocirres* and *Biaus cuers* by a different alignment of tenor pitches and rhythms). A desire to explore the different possibilities of the AUDI FILIA melisma is perceptible too across the three motets as a group, since each imposes upon the chant a new rhythmic pattern.[43] Repetition and allusion operate, therefore, at multiple levels in *Nus ne se doit*. Within this piece, a pair of framing refrains generates much of the motet's internally repetitive musical and poetic material. These refrains themselves point outwards, alluding textually to established topics, as well as invoking the broader context of AUDI FILIA motets, which employ melodically similar refrains, over similar portions of the chant tenor, to similar framing effect.

Conclusions

Ne m'oubliez mie and *Nus ne se doit* exemplify the compositional importance of refrains in vernacular motets, a connection so fundamental that 'motet' was often synonymous in medieval vocabulary with what would now be labelled a 'refrain'. Although the refrains have a different genesis in these two pieces, their essential function and handling is superficially indistinguishable, framing and generating the musical poetic content of the motetus in both cases. *Nus ne se doit* thereby problematises current scholarly tendencies to place quotation at the forefront of refrain definition, accepting as true refrains only phrases for which concordances survive in independent host contexts. Not only does this accord excessive significance to what might constitute the vagaries of source survival, but it also discourages the analysis of unique refrains in context, creating a marked distinction between newly created and intertextual refrains that – as a comparison of *Ne m'oubliez mie* and *Nus ne se doit* reveals – does not necessarily reflect their status or treatment in practice.

[43] The consistently different rhythmicisations of AUDI FILIA are noteworthy, since motets and clausulae on the same tenor (for example, LATUS, M 14) often establish standard rhythmicisations of a chant melody that are employed across several different pieces. On the other hand, the AUDI FILIA motets resemble the group of REGNAT clausulae discussed in Chapter 3, which explored a variety of tenor patterns in conjunction with a consistent opening gesture in the duplum. These similarities are discussed in detail below.

Nevertheless, at a compositional level, the creation rather than quotation of refrains against a pre-existent tenor melody naturally resulted in different kinds of challenges – often, it seems, self-imposed ones. The composer of *Nus ne se doit* had the freedom to fashion an opening refrain with the potential simply to be repeated in, for instance, perfections 21–7 (along with the restatement of the tenor opening) or at the close of the motet. He did not choose to do this, preferring to allude to and recast the music and text of the opening refrain in subsequent phrases, deliberately eschewing an opportunity to reprise the beginning of the motet at perfection 21. Remarkably, the literal repetition of a refrain melody (vdB 287) occurs instead in *Ne m'oubliez mie*, where it is considerably more difficult to achieve because the motet creator is working here with two pre-existent quotations. Both *Nus ne se doit* and *Ne m'oubliez mie* strictly enforce a rhythmic pattern on their underlying chant melismas, displaying varied motetus responses to an unaltered restatement of the same tenor material. At the same time, the decision to employ framing refrains creates additional musical restrictions in the motetus voices – restrictions of a kind specific to the status of these refrains as quoted or crafted, but containing (in every sense) the invention of internal musical material.

Perhaps because of these additional restrictions, the selection of tenor chants in *Ne m'oubliez mie* and *Nus ne se doit* seems to have been driven primarily by musical, rather than textual, concerns: by the potential to combine particular refrain quotations with a particular tenor, or the capacity of a certain chant melody to support similar opening and closing refrains. While many Latin motet texts draw principally on their tenor words and associated liturgical or biblical contexts, the poetic idiom in these vernacular motets was apparently determined instead by their generic refrains and associated topoi. All the same, both *Ne m'oubliez mie* and *Nus ne se doit* seem *musically* to engage with and even allude to polyphonic possibilities and conventions more broadly associated with their chant tenors in other vernacular motets. A further layer in an already multi-faceted quotational game, this is indicative, not only of a fundamentally intertextual motet culture, but also of one deeply preoccupied with its own craft. It seems realistic to imagine, therefore, a contemporary appraisal of motets such as *Ne m'oubliez mie* and *Nus ne se doit* that extended, not just to the recognition of their refrains either as genuine quotations or as newly created with only the appearance of quotations, but also to attendant compositional contexts, challenges, and subtleties.

It is a paradox that, although this chapter seeks to demonstrate the centrality of refrains in French motets created from scratch without any reference to clausula models, in fact the handling of such refrains chimes in many ways with the ludic compositional practices in clausulae and their related motets outlined in Chapter 3. In the French AUDI FILIA motets in particular, one observes very similar characteristics to thirteen REGNAT clausulae grouped together in **F** (fols. 166r–168r): creators of both motets and clausulae are aware of other compositions on the same chant, and of their conventional or characteristic opening gestures. The quotation or creation of similar refrains for vernacular motets on the AUDI FILIA tenor is equivalent to the exploration of a stock duplum beginning for families of clausulae. In both cases, this is a form of compositional play, an allusion to wider polyphonic conventions for a given tenor melody, and a self-imposed creative constraint. At the same time, there is an undeniably practical aspect: certain tenor openings naturally invite certain compositional responses – at intervals strongly consonant with the chant quotation, and/or moving in contrary motion – and the existence of established openings for the REGNAT or AUDI FILIA tenors, may have aided singers in recalling their polyphonic elaborations, as well as guiding composers in the selection of suitable refrain material. Analogous too, is the permission of harmonic dissonance for the sake of repetition or quotation of a given melodic idea (*color*) in both clausulae and motets.

Probably the greatest difference in the compositional characteristics shared by vernacular motets and clausulae, however, lies in the nature of the given upper-voice material itself, and the repetition to which it is subjected. In the REGNAT clausulae, short duplum motives are intensely reworked and frequently transposed and transformed. In *Ne m'oubliez mie* and *Nus ne se doit*, the framing refrains are more substantial and melodic, and their treatment too has a more obviously songlike effect. Refrain material is typically re-presented at pitch, the same musical phrases reappear in differently decorated forms, and shared phrase openings lead to alternatively 'open' and 'closed' cadences. The distinct characteristics and treatment of given upper-voice materials in clausulae as opposed to vernacular motets make the two genres sound noticeably different, and of course motets have an additional textual dimension that has no obvious corollary in clausulae. Nevertheless, both genres evidently operated in the same creative environment. Thus, even if the motet originated, not through the addition of Latin texts to clausulae, but principally as a newly created vernacular-texted genre in which refrains were a central component, motets still operated within a wider musical and quotational practice of which clausulae were also part: both sacred and secular genres were governed and motivated by the same kinds of compositional interests, techniques, and challenges in working with pre-existing plainchant foundations.

6 Intertextuality, Song, and Female Voices in Motets on a St Elizabeth of Hungary Tenor

A creative culture fundamentally rooted in practices of quotation, and in which borrowed materials may recall the contexts of their various instantiations, offers particularly rich and subtle semantic possibilities. Medieval literary, philosophical, and theological texts relied on the quotation of ancient, biblical, and patristic authorities. This was a means of displaying learning, and of validating new texts through their situation within established traditions. In the music of the thirteenth century, the quotation of pre-existent plainchant melodies in both liturgical and vernacular genres had similar effects. In French motets in particular, the combination of these sacred melodies with secular song topics and refrain quotations offered – as scholars such as Sylvia Huot, Gerald Hoekstra, and Suzannah Clark have shown – especially complex and multi-layered fields of allegorical reference.[1] Specific interpretative circumstances for any artistic or literary object in the past are naturally difficult, even impossible, to reconstruct. Not only do these circumstances change and become obscured over time, but even within a circumscribed time-period a musical composition is inevitably received differently by individuals, whose perception may be further influenced by a particular performance or by the medium (oral, written, remembered) through which it is accessed. Nevertheless, one may still seek to establish what Hans Robert Jauss defined as an *Erwartungshorizont*: a 'horizon of expectations' that arises from pre-existing understandings of genre, form, and theme shared by an audience in the historical moment of a work's appearance.[2] For later musics, the availability of precise biographical and chronological information is invaluable in this regard, but the almost complete lack of such readily available testimony for the thirteenth

This chapter reworks material previously published as Catherine A. Bradley, 'Song and Quotation in Two-Voice Motets for Saint Elizabeth of Hungary', *Speculum*, 92 (2017), 661–91.

[1] Sylvia Huot, *Allegorical Play in the Old French Motet: The Sacred and the Profane in Thirteenth-Century Polyphony* (Stanford, 1997); Gerald R. Hoekstra, 'The French Motet as Trope: Multiple Levels of Meaning in *Quant florist la violete/El mois de mai/Et gaudebit*', *Speculum*, 73 (1998), 32–57; and Suzannah Clark, ' "S'en dirai chançonete": Hearing Text and Music in a Medieval Motet', *Plainsong and Medieval Music*, 16 (2007), 31–59.

[2] Hans Robert Jauss, *Toward an Aesthetic of Reception*, trans. Timothy Bahti (Minneapolis, 1982), p. 22.

century makes any frame of reference much more difficult to construct. How can it be ascertained with certainty the particular musical texts – other motets, songs, refrains, and their various host contexts – to which a medieval motet creator had access or might have referred? What kinds of quotations or allusions might a singer, reader, or listener have recognised and interpreted? How, furthermore, might one account for or imagine any texts and performative practices that are not explicitly documented in surviving written records?

By exploring a body of musical, poetic, and hagiographical texts associated with the exceptional plainchant tenor DECANTATUR, this chapter addresses these difficulties. Twelfth- and thirteenth-century creators of organa, clausulae, and motets handled their plainchant tenors with creativity and ingenuity, but in their selection of tenor sources they remained deeply rooted in convention. In the liturgical genre of organum, polyphonic elaborations were understandably confined to well-known and widely transmitted plainchant melodies for the Mass and, to a slightly lesser degree, for the Office. This persisted in clausulae – almost all of which were restricted to the same plainchant melodies that feature in organa – as well as in motets. Despite the improbability of a liturgical function for many thirteenth-century vernacular motets, their tenor foundations largely continued to be those of the earlier sacred organa in the *Magnus liber* repertoire. The selection of the motet tenor DECNATATUR – a passive form of the verb *decantare*, to sing, chant, or recite – not from the established stock but from a much more obscure host plainchant, was therefore a recognisably special circumstance. The origins of this plainchant tenor were unknown to a thirteenth-century scribe of the Montpellier codex, and also eluded scholars until Barbara Haggh-Huglo's 1995 identification of the melisma within an inconspicuous Office responsory for St Elizabeth of Hungary.[3]

This chapter traces a new network of interrelated motets, refrains, and chansons, whose shared musical, semantic, and geographical contexts resonate strongly with those of their associated St Elizabeth plainchant. Because of the situation of these texts within such a highly particular and atypical interpretative framework, grounds on which chronological relationships and connections between them may be established and explored are unusually secure. I argue that the DECANTATUR tenor could function as a cue, prompting a listener, reader, singer, or composer to think

[3] See Barbara Haggh (ed.), *Two Offices for Saint Elizabeth of Hungary: 'Gaudeat Hungaria' and 'Letare Germania'* (Ottawa, 1995), p. xv.

not only about acts of singing and song-making, but summoning a specifically female persona and voice, potentially bringing into play the wider content of the host responsory from which the DECANTATUR melody is just a short snippet; the Office of which this responsory is a part; the place – Cambrai – at which it was conceived and presumably performed; and, perhaps most importantly, the life and cult of St Elizabeth herself. The DECANTATUR network, therefore, offers a remarkable glimpse into the kinds of rich intertextual and compositional cross-references that probably also existed for many other motets in the thirteenth century, but that – owing to the lack of such a specific evidence base – remain more resistant to detailed and precise reconstruction.

Singing about Song in Thirteenth-Century Cambrai: An Early Elizabeth Office

Elizabeth of Hungary, canonised in 1235, was venerated throughout late medieval Europe.[4] St Elizabeth (1207–31) was of noble birth (daughter of King Andrew II of Hungary) and married Ludwig IV, landgrave of Thuringia. Following her husband's death, Elizabeth sent her children away and renounced her wealth and position in society. She cared for the sick in a hospital that she founded in Marburg, dedicated to St Francis, where she died aged twenty-four. The pan-European popularity of Elizabeth's cult may be explained by several aspects of her life and identity, which powerfully encapsulated new types and aspects of sainthood emerging in the late twelfth and thirteenth centuries. Perhaps most important among these is her femininity, at a time when there occurred radical changes in literacy and in formalised devotion for women, principally through the foundation of the all-female lay devotional communities of Beguines in northern Europe.[5] Simultaneously responding to and inspiring such female devotion, there was a surge in the number of female saints between 1100 and 1400, with the percentage of women saints almost doubling in the thirteenth

[4] See, for instance, Dieter Blume and Mathias Werner (eds.), *Elisabeth von Thüringen: Eine europäische Heilige. Aufsätze* (St Petersburg, 2007); and Christa Bertelsmeier-Kierst (ed.), *Elisabeth von Thüringen und die neue Frömmigkeit in Europa* (Frankfurt, 2008).

[5] See the discussion and historiographical overview of a 'woman's movement' in the thirteenth century in Jocelyn Wogan-Browne and Marie-Elisabeth Henneau, 'Liège, the "Medieval Woman Question", and the Question of Medieval Women', in Juliette Dor, Lesley Johnson, and Jocelyn Wogan-Browne (eds.), *New Trends in Feminine Spirituality* (Turnhout, 1999), pp. 1–32.

century.[6] Like the majority of late medieval sainted women, Elizabeth was aristocratic and she was a lay woman, more unusually a married one. Her sanctity lay in the renunciation of these worldly attributes, choosing instead a life of humility and suffering. The emphasis on Elizabeth's body and physicality, her attitudes to food, to dress, and especially her desire for mortification of the flesh, is typical of the lives of female saints. This bodily focus represents a tension inherent in the fact that the *vitae* of saints such as Elizabeth were principally stories told by men, just as sensual Marian motets were composed by clerics.[7]

Elizabeth's spiritual confessor, Master Conrad of Marburg, who was renowned for his advocacy of physical mortification, instigated her canonisation. He at once wielded authority and power over Elizabeth, and demonstrated a fascination with her potent spirituality, stemming in large part from the 'otherness' of her womanhood.[8] Conrad's initial efforts in promoting her canonisation ensured the longevity and vitality of Elizabeth's cult, which is underlined by the existence of several thirteenth-century lives in the vernacular, most notably *La vie sainte Elysabel*, in rhyming couplets by the Parisian trouvère Rutebeuf.[9] In addition to her shrine at Marburg, devotion to Elizabeth was strong in France, particularly in the north, and also in the neighbouring Low Countries, where, upon her canonisation, Elizabeth was honored as a patron saint of the Beguines.

It is therefore unsurprising that the earliest extant plainchant Office, or *Historia*, for Elizabeth emanated from northern France. More notable is the fact that the Office seems principally to have been confined to this region. *Gaudeat Hungaria* was quickly supplanted by later alternative Offices, which enjoyed a much wider dissemination: a complete copy of *Gaudeat Hungaria* with musical notation survives only in an antiphoner from Cambrai, dated to the 1290s (Cambrai, Bibliothèque municipale, MS 38). Haggh-Huglo has uncovered evidence in the contemporary writings

[6] See Caroline Walker Bynum, *Holy Feast and Holy Fast: The Religious Significance of Food to Medieval Women* (Berkeley, 1987), pp. 13–30, esp. p. 20.

[7] On the writing of female saints' lives by men, see John W. Coakley, *Women, Men, and Spiritual Power: Female Saints and Their Male Collaborators* (New York, 2006).

[8] Conrad addressed a *Summa vitae* to Pope Gregory IX in 1232. See the translation in Kenneth Baxter Wolf, *The Life and Afterlife of Saint Elizabeth of Hungary: A Testimony from Her Canonization Hearings* (Oxford, 2010), pp. 91–5.

[9] See the edition of Rutebeuf's *Vie* and of his Latin models in Edmond Faral and Julia Bastin (eds.), *Œuvres complètes de Rutebeuf*, 2 vols. (Paris, 1960), Vol. II, pp. 60–166. A translation of Elizabeth's canonisation documents is available in Wolf, *The Life and Afterlife*, pp. 83–216. Portions of Rutebeuf's *Vie* and two further vernacular lives of St Elizabeth – one from Cambigneul, near Arras – are translated in Brigitte Cazelles, *The Lady as Saint: A Collection of French Hagiographic Romances of the Thirteenth Century* (Philadelphia, 1991), pp. 151–71.

of the monk Henry of Brussels that securely links the conception of this Office specifically to Cambrai, even identifying its creators by name. Henry of Brussels states that Brother Gerard, monk of Saint-Quentin-en-Isle near Cambrai, 'composed elegantly worded antiphons and responsories' to be sung on Elizabeth's feast day (17 November), while 'neumas [i.e. melodies] were joined to the same antiphons and responsories' by Peter, canon of Saint-Aubert of Cambrai.[10]

The composition of Elizabeth's first Office for use at Cambrai seems particularly appropriate. Elizabeth's heart was sent there as a relic, while her skull went further south, to Besançon. *Gaudeat Hungaria* is recorded with melodies only in the Cambrai antiphoner, but the text of this Office circulates without musical notation in three additional sources, one of which is a fifteenth-century breviary from Besançon (Paris, Bibliothèque nationale de France, lat. 10487). The two remaining text-only records of the Office are also chronologically later than the Cambrai antiphoner, and they stem from places without such an explicit Elizabeth connection: a fourteenth-century breviary from Mons (Douai, Bibliothèque municipale, 146) and a Franciscan breviary from Rouen dated to 1412 (Baltimore, Walters Art Museum, MS W 300).[11] Nonetheless, the northern French and Flemish provenance of the manuscripts, copied outside Paris and in relative proximity to Cambrai, may explain the presence of *Gaudeat Hungaria* in these breviaries, further strengthening the geographical identity of this Office as a particular manifestation of Elizabeth's cult.

The fifth matins responsory of the *Gaudeat Hungaria* Office, *Ante dies exitus*, is the source of the polyphonic tenor quotation DECANTATUR (see Example 6.1).[12] The significance of a long and florid 'sung' melody accompanied by the text 'decantatur' could not have been lost on medieval composers. More broadly, the text of the tenor's host responsory exhibits a preoccupation with ideas of song and singing (see Table 6.1).[13] *Ante dies exitus* focuses on a notably musical miracle that reportedly occurred on

[10] I quote Haggh-Huglo's translation, in Haggh, *Two Offices for Saint Elizabeth of Hungary*, p. xiv. Haggh-Huglo suggests that the 'neumas' mentioned here refer, in the more specific sense of the term, to extended concluding melismas (like that on DECANTATUR), which were occasionally furnished with syllabic texts (or prosulae); see p. xvi.

[11] The sources of *Gaudeat Hungaria* are listed in Clemens Blume and Guido M. Dreves (eds.), *Historiae rhythmicae: Liturgische Reimofficien des Mittelalters, fünfte Folge*, Analecta hymnica 25 (Leipzig, 1897), p. 263. I thank Lynley Herbert of the Walters Art Museum for her help in identifying MS W 300 as the 1412 breviary listed by Blume and Dreves as being in a private collection.

[12] Example 6.1 is reproduced from Haggh, *Two Offices for Saint Elizabeth of Hungary*, p. 13.

[13] I thank Henry Parkes and Eleanor Giraud for their assistance with the translation in Table 6.1.

Table 6.1 Text and translation of *Ante dies exitus*

Respond	
Ante dies exitus	Before the day of her departure
eius collo celitus	from her throat
avis modulatur.	a bird sings divinely.
A qua voce modula	By which musical voice
dulce cum avicula	with the little bird
melos decantatur.	a sweet melody is sung.
Verse	
Iam vicino transitu	With her passing already approaching,
prophetali spiritu	with the breath of the prophets
Eliyzabeth donatur.	Elizabeth is given up.

Example 6.1 Responsory *Ante dies exitus* from *Gaudeat Hungaria*.

Elizabeth's deathbed: the singing of a bird that the saint joined in song. This moment is described in detail in Rutebeuf's *Vie*,[14] which itself is closely modelled on the earlier account of the occurrence in the Latin deposition of 1235, *Dicta quatuor ancillarum*, offered by four of Elizabeth's female companions in the process of her canonisation:

When my lady blessed Elizabeth lay on her deathbed, I heard the sweetest voice, which seemed to come from within her sweet neck as she lay facing the wall. After an hour she turned and said to me: 'Where are you my beloved?' I responded: 'Here I am' and then I added: 'Oh my lady! You were singing so sweetly!' She asked me if I had heard the singing and I said that I had. She said: 'I tell you, a little bird

[14] Faral and Bastin, *Œuvres Complètes de Rutebeuf*, Vol. II, p. 160, lines 1979–94.

situated between me and the wall was singing most joyfully to me. Inspired by its voice, it seemed fitting for me to sing along.' This happened only a few days before her death.[15]

Although at some chronological and geographical distance, the rhymed text of *Ante dies exitus* accurately reflects the content of this official report – details that may also have been known to Brother Gerard (the creator of its text) through Rutebeuf's vernacular paraphrase. Gerard's responsory describes how, before the day of her death, a bird sang from Elizabeth's throat, producing a seemingly hybrid voice, described both as 'dulce' (sweet) and 'modula' (suggesting something like musical, melodic, or modulated).[16] The word 'decantatur' – the crucial verb, which later became a self-sufficient melodic unit in its own right – falls at an important structural moment in its host responsory: it marks the close of the opening respond, a juncture at which an extended musical elaboration is conventional. The melisma on the penultimate syllable of 'decantatur' (marked by a box in Example 6.1), however, is noticeably more expansive than any other moment in *Ante dies exitus*, or indeed, as Haggh-Huglo noted, within the entire *Gaudeat Hungaria* Office.[17]

This reflects the explicitly musical nature of the DECANTATUR text, as does the character of the melisma itself, which is strikingly lyrical, initially playing with trios of pitches that explore the interval of a third. It is significant also, that this DECANTATUR melody expands and elaborates musical material that was previously heard in conjunction with the words 'a qua voce modula' (the musical correspondence is marked by a dashed box in Example 6.1). The two portions of this chant most explicitly concerning voice and song, therefore, receive similar and highly song-like settings. The effect of musical repetition at DECANTATUR underlines a listener's consciousness of the act of singing further still, so that this long and lyrical melisma constitutes a direct musical expression of its text.

The Hagiographical Motet *Un chant renvoisie/DECANTATUR* in Context

Despite the limited transmission for the earliest St Elizabeth Office as a whole, this most elaborately musical responsory, *Ante dies exitus*, had a

[15] Wolf, *The Life and Afterlife*, pp. 214–15.

[16] The precise meaning of the term is unclear, but see the entries for 'modula' and its derivatives in Michael Bernhard (ed.), *Lexicon musicum latinum medii aevi*, available online at http://woerterbuchnetz.de/cgi-bin/WBNetz/wbgui_py?sigle=LmL (accessed 18 March 2018).

[17] Haggh (ed.), *Two Offices for Saint Elizabeth of Hungary*, p. xv.

continued and independent existence. Haggh-Huglo discovered the music and text of this responsory in a sixteenth-century processional from Bruges (Brussels, Bibliothèque royale, MS IV 210), a source used by the Beguines.[18] This is the only musical concordance for any complete chant from the *Gaudeat Hungaria* Office outside the Cambrai antiphoner. That said, the *Ante dies exitus* responsory appears in the Bruges processional, not in the context of *Gaudeat Hungaria*, but alongside two antiphons for Elizabeth from the later and more popular Office, *Letare Germania*.

Just as *Ante dies exitus* was excerpted from its host Office here, so the melisma accompanying the final syllables '-tatur' of DECANTATUR was in turn excerpted from this host responsory as an independent thirteenth-century motet tenor. The selection of this particular tenor is unconventional in three principal respects. First, and as emphasised above, it stems from a narrowly disseminated and specialised saint's Office, rather than a standard Mass or Office chant. Second, it is the concluding responsories of a nocturn – the third, sixth, and ninth, but not the fifth – that are typically treated in polyphony in the twelfth and thirteenth centuries. Third, the DECANTATUR melisma is part of a choral portion of the respond, again breaking established liturgical conventions in earlier genres of organa and clausulae that polyphonic tenors should be drawn only from the sections of plainchant sung by soloists.

Such an unusual tenor choice must have been motivated by the specific circumstances of the two-voice motet *Un chant renvoisie*/*DECANTATUR*, where the DECANTATUR melody is complemented by an upper voice, whose text in praise of Elizabeth is equally atypical in being hagiographical (see Example 6.2).[19] This vernacular motetus makes explicit reference to two events in the saint's life (see Table 6.2). The first is another occurrence involving both song and birds that reportedly occurred just after Elizabeth's death; it is surely related to, but nonetheless distinct from, the earlier

[18] Barbara Haggh, 'The Beguines of Bruges and the Procession of the Holy Blood', in M. Jennifer Bloxham, Gioia Filocamo, and Leofranc Holford-Strevens (eds.), *Uno gentile et subtile ingenio: Essays in Honour of Bonnie J. Blackburn* (Turnhout, 2009), pp. 75–85 (pp. 78–9).

[19] Hagiographical aspects of this motet were discussed by Mark Everist, *French Motets in the Thirteenth Century: Music, Poetry, and Genre* (Cambridge, 1994), pp. 137–8, although the source of the DECANTATUR tenor was still unknown. Haggh-Huglo suggested that Peter of Cambrai may have been the composer of this motet, as well as of the Office *Gaudeat Hungaria*: Henry of Brussels described him as a composer of 'condictus' (*sic*), opening the possibility that Peter was skilled in polyphony as well as monophony. See Haggh, *Two Offices for Saint Elizabeth of Hungary*, p. xvi. I thank Huw Grange for his assistance with the transcription and translation of the text in Table 6.2, which is adapted from that in Everist, *French Motets in the Thirteenth Century*, p. 137.

Example 6.2 *Un chant renvoisie/DECANTATUR*, **ArsB**, fol. 14r.

a

1. Un chant_ ren-voi - sie et_ bel_ 2. di - rai_ de sainte_ Y - sa - bel_ 3. de cui_ fi- sent_ li_ oi - sel

DECANTATUR

b

4. en lour_ cans feste_ a sa_ mort. 5. A li ser - vir_ mais m'a - cort_ 6. car - des_ ver - tus me re - cort_

a

7. c'a Cam - brai fait_ de nou - vel_ 8. la pe - rent si biau_ jou - el_ 9. ou sont re - ve - scu troi_ mort.

II

40
45
10. Tort dame ai, quant vo - stre con - fort 11. re - quis n'ai, par ma fo - li - e, 12. du mal
50
55
qui me contr-a - li - e 13. dont sans vous ne vi - vrai mi - e, 14. pour che vous re - quier et
III
vdB 623
60
65
pri - e 15. de cuer en - tier et loi - al 16. *Dous cuers a - le - gies mon mal* 17. *qu'i ne m'o - chi - e.*

Table 6.2 Text and translation of *Un chant renvoisie*

1.	Un chant renvoisie et bel	**7a**	-el	A merry and beautiful song
2.	dirai de sainte Ysabel	**7a**	-el	I shall sing about St Elizabeth
3.	de cui fisent li oisel	**7a**	-el	whom the birds celebrated
4.	en lour cans feste a sa mort.	**7b**	-ort	in their songs at her death.
5.	A li servir mais m'acort	**7b**	-ort	I accord myself to serving her henceforth
6.	car des vertus me recort	**7b**	-ort	for I recall the miracles
7.	c'a Cambrai fait de nouvel	**7a**	-el	that she performs of late in Cambrai
8.	la perent si biau jouel	**7a**	-el	there such fine treasures are on show
9.	ou sont revescu troi mort.	**7b**	-ort	where three are raised from the dead.
10.	Tort dame ai, quant vostre confort	**8b**	-ort	I am wrong, Lady, when your comfort
11.	requis n'ai, par ma folie,	**8c**	-ie	I have not requested, by my folly,
12.	du mal qui me contralie	**8c**	-ie	from the pain that afflicts me
13.	dont sans vous ne vivrai mie,	**8c**	-ie	that without you I shall never survive,
14.	pour che vous requier et prie	**8c**	-ie	and so I beg and beseech you
15.	de cuer entier et loial	**7d**	-al	wholeheartedly and loyally
16.	*Dous cuers alegies mon mal*	**7d**	-al	*Sweet heart, ease my pain*
17.	*qu'i ne m'ochie.*	**5c**	-ie	*so that it doesn't kill me.*

deathbed-birdsong moment described in the responsory *Ante dies exitus*.[20] *Un chant renovisie* refers instead to the occasion when a large group of birds on the roof of the church in which Elizabeth's body reposed reportedly burst into song, as if performing funeral rites for her, and the motet additionally mentions a posthumous triple resurrection miracle, which occured at Cambrai.[21] *Un chant renvoisie* appears uniquely in **ArsB** (fol. 14r), a manuscript dated to the 1270s.[22] This manuscript was long thought to have been copied in northern France, and in Picardie in particular,

[20] Previous discussions of this motet have conflated these two miracles: see Everist, *French Motets in the Thirteenth Century*, p. 137; and Haggh, *Two Offices for Saint Elizabeth of Hungary*, p. xv. I believe that the stated time of the miracle as *after* Elizabeth's death, the use of the plural (birds), and the lack of any reference to the saint herself singing (so carefully described in the *Ante dies exitus* responsory), establish the miracle described in *Un chant renvoisie* as distinct from that in *Ante dies exitus*.

[21] This second birdsong miracle is recounted in the *Dicta quatuor ancillarum*: see Wolf, *The Life and Afterlife*, pp. 215–16. It does not, however, appear in Rutebeuf's *Vie*. Neither does Rutebeuf (nor any of his Latin models) make specific reference to a triple resurrection at Cambrai. Yet Elizabeth was well known for resurrection miracles more generally, and Rutebeuf speaks of the many resurrections that occurred after Elizabeth's own death. See the translation in Cazelles, *The Lady as Saint*, p. 168, lines 2147–8.

[22] See Alison Stones, Appendix IV, in Kathy M. Krause and Alison Stones (eds.), *Gautier de Coinci: Miracles, Music and Manuscripts* (Turnhout, 2006), p. 374.

but Alison Stones has recently proposed that it emanated instead from a more northeasterly centre of manuscript production in the Artois region: perhaps from Thérouanne, St-Omer, or Arras.[23] This proximity to plainchant sources for the *Gaudeat Hungaria* Office and – particularly if **ArsB** was copied in Arras – to Cambrai is significant, as is the nature of **ArsB** itself and the position of *Un chant renvoisie* within it.

A manuscript largely devoted to vernacular poetry rather than a polyphonic *liber motetorum*, **ArsB** contains two clusters of polyphonic motets. Both are groups of very widely disseminated Latin Marian motets, and *Un chant renvoisie* is not among them.[24] Instead, this vernacular motet comes at the end of a short collection of monophonic devotional songs in French and Latin located between the Latin and the vernacular tables of contents for Gautier de Coinci's *Miracles de nostre dame*. This seems to confirm the place of the motet within a more popular devotional and a Marian milieu: it is vernacular hagiography of a sacred woman, of a kind steeped in the idioms of courtly love song. Like the connection between the Virgin Mary and the secular Marion, or the dual religious and courtly connotations of 'dame' on which Gautier played, Elizabeth also has a worldly parallel as *Ysabelle* in motets and songs.[25] Elizabeth is never explicitly mentioned in Gautier's *Miracles*, but Nancy B. Black has noted that Gautier celebrated a very similar type of holy woman, one possibly even modelled on Elizabeth, in his *Noble fame de Rome* story.[26] In this narrative – which may have been conceived as an independent text but later circulated in the second part of the *Miracles* – Gautier's Empress is, like Elizabeth, both married and of noble birth. The Roman Empress does not simply use her wealth for the benefit of the poor but, in the emerging mode of female sainthood of

[23] See ibid.

[24] See Friedrich Ludwig's description and inventory of this source in his *Repertorium organorum recentioris et motetorum vetustissimi stili*, ed. Luther A. Dittmer, 2 vols. in 3 (New York, 1964–78 [1910]), Vol. I/2, pp. 594–602. The first cluster of motets is apparently a later addition to **ArsB**, inserted at the opening of the manuscript. The second group of polyphonic pieces is, however, germane to the collection, appearing in the second volume (lat. 1518) – a continuation of the manuscript containing *Un chant renvoisie* (lat. 1517).

[25] Ysabelle features in the incipits of two motets, both uniquely recorded in **Mo**: *Ma loyaute m'a nusi/A la bele Yzabelot/OMNES* (fols. 225v–227r, Mt25–6) and *Entre copin et bourgeois/Je me cuidoie/BELE YSABELOS* (fols. 277v–279r, Mt866–7). This flexible vernacularisation of Elizabeth as Ysabelle, rather than the more correct Elysabel, is not unusual. Yet it may be significant in the light of Rutebeuf's life of the saint, which was written for Queen Isabelle of Navarre, and therefore encouraged a flattering conflation between the names of its subject and its dedicatee.

[26] See Nancy B. Black, *Medieval Narratives of Accused Queens* (Gainesville, 2003), p. 31. Gautier's *Noble fame de Rome* is, not, however, included within the *Miracles* as recorded in **ArsB**.

which Elizabeth is a notable example, actively denies privilege to embrace suffering in poverty.[27]

As emphasised above, motets that might be described as hagiographical, those referring to specific details of a saint's life rather than simply offering directed praise or petition, are extremely rare in the wider corpus. Mark Everist has demonstrated that just one other thirteenth-century motet text, the quadruplum of *De la vierge Katherine/Quant froidure trait a fin/Agmina militiae/AGMINA*, resembles *Un chant renvoisie* in its explicit engagement with the *vita* of a particular saint.[28] This text for St Katherine also honours a female saint in the vernacular, and it is uniquely preserved in a strikingly similar source context, the 'La Clayette' manuscript (**Cl**, fol. 377r–v).[29] *De la vierge* appears here among the collection of polyphonic motets that constitutes the codex's only musical section. Otherwise, **Cl** is chiefly an anthology of religious vernacular texts, containing the rhymed *Vie de sainte Catherine*, as well as an incomplete copy of Gautier's *Miracles*.[30] Vernacular, devotional, and principally non-musical books, then, seem to have been the natural context for hagiographical motets, which enjoyed a comparatively more limited and apparently different kind of circulation on the fringes of the polyphonic motet as a genre.

Songs upon and within Songs in *Un chant renvoisie/ DECANTATUR*

The presence of *Un chant renvoisie* in the feminine context of Gautier's *Miracles* and in **ArsB** – a devotional manuscript produced at a time and place close to that of the Cambrai Office for St Elizabeth – goes some way to explaining the unprecedented appearance of the DECANTATUR melody in the context of a polyphonic motet. Nevertheless, musical and textual characteristics of this tenor itself surely rendered it attractive to a motet

[27] See Black, *Medieval Narratives of Accused Queens*, p. 26.

[28] Everist, *French Motets in the Thirteenth Century*, pp. 135–8.

[29] The AGMINA motet tenor, while more widely employed than DECANTATUR, is also similarly unconventional in its musical context. AGMINA is derived from the choral portion of the responsory *Virgo flagellatur* for St Katherine, which does not feature in organa or clausulae in the *Magnus liber* repertoire.

[30] See the recent study of this manuscript by Sean Paul Curran: 'Vernacular Book Production, Vernacular Polyphony, and the Motets of the "La Clayette" Manuscript (Paris, Bibliothèque nationale de France, nouvelles acquisitions françaises, 13521)', Ph.D. diss. (University of California, Berkeley, 2013).

Example 6.3 Three versions of the DECANTATUR melody.

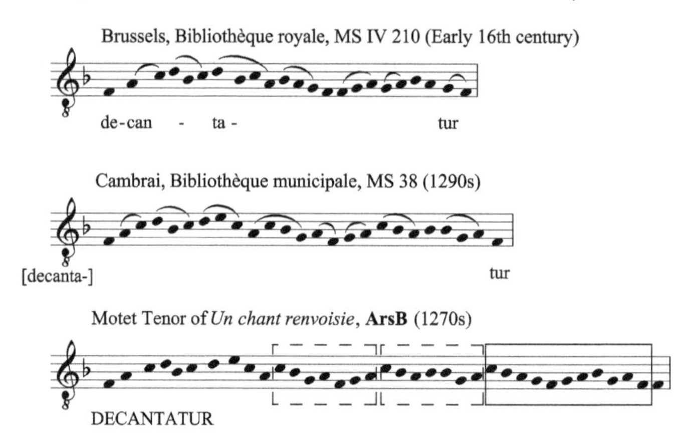

creator. In addition to the lyricism of its melody, the tenor quotation from the *Ante dies exitus* responsory has a very clear and conventional fifth-mode tonal profile. Opening and closing with the final pitch, F, the melisma remains within an octave above this pitch, principally exploring the space between F and its co-final C, which is clearly delineated at the outset of the melody by the rising F–A–C gesture. Example 6.3 shows the relevant portion of all extant versions of the DECANTATUR melody.[31] The melisma as recorded in the sixteenth-century processional from Bruges differs in many details – as does the responsory as a whole – from the earlier copy of the chant in the Cambrai antiphoner.[32] The tenor of *Un chant renvoisie*, however, precisely matches this Cambrai version of the chant, save the addition of eleven additional pitches before the final note of the melody (marked by a box in Example 6.3), a point at which an extended melodic insertion – a neuma – would be conventional in monophonic practice. Possibly, the creator of *Un chant renvoisie* adopted a different and longer alternative version, perhaps an earlier form of the chant of which no other record survives. Yet given the otherwise exact correspondence with the later Cambrai version of the DECANTATUR melody, the motet creator plausibly extended the chant quotation to suit its new polyphonic context, adding a passage sympathetic

[31] Transcriptions of the Bruges and Cambrai sources are reproduced from Haggh, 'The Beguines of Bruges and the Procession of the Holy Blood', p. 79. Her transcription of the DECANTATUR tenor erroneously gives F, rather than G, as its twenty-third pitch.

[32] See the complete transcriptions of the Bruges and Cambrai versions of *Ante dies exitus*, in ibid., p. 79.

to the character of the preceding melodic units (marked by dashed boxes in Example 6.3).[33]

Textually, *Un chant renvoisie* not only engages with the implied broader responsory context and connotations of the DECANTATUR melisma, but also plays on the isolated local meaning of its tenor word.[34] This motet literally adds a song on top of a song. Now with two singing voices in polyphony, it opens self-referentially with the declaration that a 'merry and beautiful song' is to be sung, additionally alluding to the birdsong that had previously occurred at Elizabeth's death. The beginning of the motet seems musically to be self-consciously song-like (see Example 6.2). The upper voice is initially remarkably florid – perhaps even an attempt to mimic the birdsong – and the first nine lines of the text are part of a rounded tripartite musical structure, an aba form (each section corresponding to a system in Example 6.2), where the first three lines of text are set to a melody that recurs in a decorated form for lines 7–9. This musical structure is complemented by the poetic rhyme scheme: the a sections are characterised by an '-el' rhyme (labelled a in Table 6.2), while the b section introduces a new rhyme, '-ort', which returns at line 9 to close the repetition of the opening a material.

A highly decorated upper voice featuring prominent musical and poetic repetitions creates a strong song-like identity for the opening of the motet. The aba structure, however, does not correspond exactly to a conventional chanson or motet form. Monophonic chansons of the troubadours and trouvères typically had, instead, a tripartite AAB, or *pedes cum cauda*, structure, frequently adopted also in motets, featuring the repetition of an initial music *pes*, or foot (A), followed by a longer coda (B). Yet each foot, or A section, was itself typically made up of two contrasting musical ideas (a and b). It is therefore probable that the beginning of *Un chant renvoisie* could have been understood as the beginning of an internal abab form (corresponding to the AA sections of a larger AAB design) but cut off before the final b section.[35]

[33] The extension of tenor plainchant quotations in this manner is very unusual, but not unprecedented. See Hans Tischler, *The Style and Evolution of the Earliest Motets (to circa 1270)*, Musicological Studies 40 (Ottawa, 1985), Vol. I, p. 147 n. 18.

[34] DECANTATUR is the only tenor in the thirteenth-century motet repertoire explicitly to refer to or describe the act of singing. Before its plainchant source was identified, therefore, Everist plausibly proposed that this text might have been a simple canon. See Everist, *French Motets in the Thirteenth Century*, p. 138.

[35] For a study of the AAB form in song and motets, see Gaël Saint-Cricq, 'A New Link between the Motet and Trouvère Chanson: The *pedes cum cauda* Motet', *Early Music History*, 32 (2013), 179–223.

The resulting sense of disruption – of a conventional abab chanson and motet opening unexpectedly curtailed and interrupted – is strongly underlined by the status of the initial section (perfections 1–36, text lines 1–9) of *Un chant renvoisie* as a musical and textual entity that is curiously set apart from the rest of the piece. From perfection 37 onwards, the point at which a listener might have expected the b material of the opening section to return, the musical idiom of the upper voice instead becomes noticeably plainer, and any large-scale formal repetition ceases. The beginning of this second section is additionally marked by an elongated first note accompanying the word 'tort', resulting in an extended five-perfection phrase that disturbs the motet's previously regular four-perfection units, as well as the synchronisation of its upper-voice and tenor phrase endings. Furthermore, a fundamental change in the underlying rhythmic pattern in the tenor at perfection 36 – from three-note to seven-note groupings in the chant – straddles this formal juncture. This rhythmic alteration in the middle of a melodic statement of the DECANTATUR plainchant is both striking and atypical in a motet.[36]

A musical disruption at perfection 37 is matched poetically by an abrupt shift at line 10 of the text from the very specific details of Elizabeth's miracles to the much more generic idiom of a courtly love song. A male protagonist addresses directly a beloved (unnamed) 'dame', for the love of whom he is suffering. Like Elizabeth, she is clearly a noble lady, rather than any lowly shepherdess. New rhymes (labeled c and d in Table 6.2) are introduced in this new section, and the regular seven-syllable lines of the motet's opening are superseded by eight-syllable ones. Significantly, the beginning of text line 10, 'Tort dame', is also marked by a small coloured initial 'T' in its manuscript source, confirming its separation from the motet's opening. But despite their differentiation, the two halves of the motet are undeniably part of the same piece. It does not appear, for instance, that the second section represents genuinely independent material that was simply combined with the opening of a motet crafted specifically for the St Elizabeth tenor. Musically, the change in the motetus at perfection 37 falls in the middle of a statement of the tenor melisma, and exhibits none of the typical signs of a pre-existent song or motetus accommodated to a new plainchant context. Poetically, the different structural moments in *Un chant renvoisie* are similarly integrated by rhyme: the '-ort' rhyme at the end of the first section in line 9 is taken up in line 10, just as the internal '-al' rhyme of the motet's concluding refrain in line 16 is prepared in line 15.

[36] See Tischler, *The Style and Evolution of the Earliest Motets*, Vol. I, p. 148.

The beginning of this terminal refrain, '*Dous cuers alegies mon mal/qu'i ne m'ochie*' (vdB 623), is similarly treated to an internal coloured initial in **ArsB**.[37] This is a much more conventional scribal practice, observable also in the chansonniers **N** and **R**. It reflects – as in this case, a degree of poetic integration notwithstanding – the often musically and textually disruptive character of refrains that may serve to highlight their special status as refrains or refrain quotations. It seems possible, therefore, that the marked shift in poetic and musical voice at perfection 37, to which the manuscript scribe also drew attention, functioned in analogous fashion: the new and more generic character of this material was intended to break the motet's narrative frame, playing further on ideas of singing by creating the sense of different songs within a song.

A sense of disruption was surely also the intended effect of the motet's closing refrain, vdB 623, but is here both a symptom and an aural signal of quotation. The final refrain couplet features a change of rhyme and shorter poetic lines, and musically it initiates a new motetus phrase unit of six perfections, accompanied by an interruption in the rhythmic pattern of the DECANTATUR tenor. This alteration of the established tenor rhythm in perfections 59–63 tellingly caused the scribe some difficulties, and he mistakenly omitted three notes of the tenor chant quotation (supplied in square brackets in Example 6.2). This change in the tenor pattern produces, in perfection 61, a rare simultaneous break in both voices (the first since perfection 20) just before the refrain commences. In addition simply to drawing attention to the refrain, the rhythmic manipulation of the tenor chant, in combination with an abnormal moment of dissonance between motetus and tenor in perfection 65 (marked by a dashed box in Example 6.2), strongly indicates that vdB 623 must constitute a musical quotation in *Un chant renvoisie*.[38]

[37] The appearance of vdB 623 in *Un chant renvoisie* was not listed in Nico van den Boogaard's catalogue of refrain texts, *Rondeaux et refrains du XIIe siècle au début du XIVe*, Bibliothèque française et romane, Série D: Initiation, textes et documents 3 (Paris, 1969), p. 148. Tischler previously noted the musical and textual concordance for vdB 623 in *Un chant renvoisie* (see *The Style and Evolution of the Earliest Motets*, Vol. II, p. 122, no. 265), as did Everist (see *French Motets in the Thirteenth Century*, p. 137) in a purely textual context.

[38] The 'extra' pitches of the DECANTATUR melisma exclusive to the motet version almost correspond with the presentation of the refrain (compare perfections 61–7 of Example 6.2 and the passage marked by a box in Example 6.3). However, the dissonance here, and the need to break the tenor's rhythmic pattern (as well as the omission of the melisma's final F), indicate that, if the DECANTATUR melisma was indeed extended by the motet creator, then this extension was not undertaken with the express purpose of accommodating the refrain quotation, and/or that the extension prioritised instead the near replication of preceding melodic figurations in the chant melisma.

Textually, the refrain's poetic material seems a fitting quotational choice for the motet context. The apostrophe 'douce coeurs' could have been a subtle reference to the location of Elizabeth's heart as a relic at Cambrai, the place specifically mentioned in the motet text and from which its tenor chant originated. Moreover, the refrain's plea to be spared from pain and death seems appropriate for a motet in praise of a saint whose physical suffering, though willing and in the service of God, was nonetheless extreme, and who eventually gave her life to caring for the sick. As Brigitte Cazelles observed, the 'ideology of suffering' is fundamental both to narratives of vernacular hagiographies (particularly of female saints) and to secular romances, for which the common experience of love – human and divine – 'seems inevitably grounded in pain'.[39]

Quotational Contexts for a Closing Refrain

The probability that the closing refrain of this hagiographical Elizabeth motet would have been recognised as such – as a borrowed snatch of song, sounding in combination with the end of the borrowed DECANTATUR plainchant – is corroborated by the circulation of its text and melody in the context of another, much more widely transmitted motet, *Douce dame sanz pitie/SUSTINERE* (see Example 6.4).[40] Unlike *Un chant renvoisie*, uniquely transmitted in the 'peripheral' manuscript **ArsB**, *Douce dame sanz pitie* appears in **W2** and **Mo**, as well as in the chansonniers **N** and **R**, and in a clausula transcription (with the motet incipit cued) in **StV**. Not only did the latter motet evidently circulate more widely, then, but it also appears in earlier and more mainstream polyphonic manuscript contexts. The refrain vdB 623 exhibits a very stable transmission across its various appearances. Poetically the appearance of the refrain in *Douce dame sanz pitie* differs from that in *Un chant renvoisie* only in its use of the plural 'maus' (pains),

[39] See Cazelles, *The Lady as Saint*, p. 75.

[40] Example 6.4 offers a transcription of *Douce dame sanz pitie* (Mt272) as recorded in **W2**, where perfections 13–30 of the upper voice are erroneously copied a tone too high (corrected in Example 6.4). The indication of B flats is sporadic (as it is also in the versions of the motet in **N** and **R**): these sources never notate flats in the tenor here, but **W2** provides a B flat signature only from perfection 31 onwards of the upper voice. The question of accidentals does not arise in the versions of the motet in **Mo** and **StV**, which are copied a fifth higher, beginning their tenor chant on C, the more typical pitch level for the SUSTINERE melody. It may be significant that the transposed version of the motet in **W2**, **N**, and **R** facilitates the presentation of vdB 623 at the same pitch as in *Un chant renvoisie*.

Example 6.4 *Douce dame sanz pitie/SUSTINERE*, **W2**, fols. 228v–229r.

rather than singular 'mal'.[41] Musically, the various versions of *Douce dame sanz pitie* themselves vary slightly in their decorations and figurations, but without obscuring the refrain's basic melodic contour and identity.

The possibility that the creator of *Un chant renvoisie* was familiar with *Douce dame sanz pitie*, so well represented in extant manuscript sources, is strengthened by several further similarities between the two motets, in addition to their shared refrain. *Douce dame* is on the Marian tenor SUSTINERE (also associated with the alternative text, PORTARE), and it exploits the same trope of devotion addressed to a beloved lady: a male narrator here complains of his unrequited love, once again referring explicitly to the song he is singing.[42] Musically, the rhythmic treatment of the SUSTINERE tenor also recalls that of DECANTATUR in *Un chant renvoisie*, in that both pieces unusually vary the rhythmic patterns in which their repeated chant melismas are presented. Although the phase of melodic and rhythmic tenor repetitions can shift to produce variety in motets, alterations to the profile of a rhythmic pattern itself are much less common.[43] *Douce dame sanz pitie* plays not only with this rhythmic pattern but also, and more unusually, with the rhythmic mode of its underlying tenor. Each of the three statements of the SUSTINERE melisma corresponds to a different rhythmicisation in a different mode (as shown by the layout of Example 6.4), enacting a gradual acceleration from groups of fifth-mode ternary longs, to the longs and breves of mode two, and finally to the successive breves of mode six.

This tenor acceleration, moving through three different rhythmic modes, is surely the most distinctive compositional feature of *Douce dame sanz pitie*, for which only one comparable example exists in the entire thirteenth-century corpus.[44] It is rendered especially striking by the concluding tenor

[41] In their online refrain database, Mark Everist and Anne Ibos-Augé list an additional text-only concordance for refrain 623 (in *Le livre d'amoretes*, Paris, Bibliothèque nationale de France, lat. 13091); see *REFRAIN: Musique, poésie, citation: Le refrain au moyen âge/Music, Poetry, Citation: The Medieval Refrain*, http://medmus.soton.ac.uk/view/abstract_item/623.html (accessed 4 March 2018).

[42] On the interchangeability of the texts SUSTINERE and PORTARE for this tenor melisma, see Dolores Pesce, 'Beyond Glossing: The Old Made New in *Mout me fu grief/Robin m'aime/PORTARE*', in Dolores Pesce (ed.), *Hearing the Motet: Essays on the Motet of the Middle Ages and Renaissance* (New York, 1997), pp. 28–51, esp. pp. 38–41. See the translation of *Douce dame sanz pitie* in Joel C. Relihan and Susan Stakel (eds.), *The Montpellier Codex, Part IV: Texts and Translations*, RRMMA 8 (Madison, 1985), p. 68.

[43] See Tischler, *The Style and Evolution of the Earliest Motets*, Vol. I, p. 148. Tischler notes that changes in tenor pattern are most common in two-voice French motets, but even here they occur only in around one in four cases.

[44] This is *Amours qui tant m'a greve/Des confortes ai este longuement/ET SUPER* (Mt544–546a), whose tenor employs fifth, first, and sixth modes. See the overview of tenor patterns offered by Tischler, ibid., *The Style and Evolution of the Earliest Motets*, Vol. I, pp. 132–42.

statement in the sixth rhythmic mode, so rarely employed in a tenor voice.[45] This fast-moving tenor accompanies the motet's terminal refrain in a near note-for-note combination that seems particularly virtuosic if both of the melodies involved – SUSTINERE and refrain 623 – are genuine quotations. Remarkably, this appears to be the case. Wolf Frobenius noted in a brief evaluation of this motet that its closing refrain has an unusual propensity to parallel octaves with the tenor (marked by dashed lines in Example 6.4).[46] The voices additionally sound the interval of a ninth in perfection 45, and move in uncharacteristic parallel seconds at the end of perfection 46 (marked by dashed boxes in Example 6.4). This confirms the impression that two pre-existent melodies, tenor and refrain, are being combined and quoted simultaneously here.

Since vdB 623 was apparently quoted in *Douce dame sanz pitie* as well as in *Un chant renvoisie*, this therefore indicates a larger circulation for the refrain than extant written sources currently attest. Even though vdB 623 probably did not originate in *Douce dame sanz pitie*, it remains possible that the creator of *Un chant renvoisie* knew the refrain in the context of this frequently copied motet, and that his rhythmic treatment of the DECANTATUR tenor could have been inspired by the more spectacular arrangement of SUSTINERE in *Douce dame sanz pitie*. Whatever its origins, in vernacular monophony or in polyphony, the refrain shared by these motets must have been a well-known musico-textual unit, widely disseminated in writing since at least the mid-thirteenth century. Those encountering the Elizabeth motet *Un chant renvoisie* – whether or not they were alert to highly specific connections with *Douce dame* – could, therefore, have recognised the refrain text and melody at its conclusion, realising that the close of this song about song on the pre-existing DECANTATUR tenor, with of all its musical connotations, was marked by another sung quotation.

In addition to playing with ideas of song at multiple levels – through quotation, explicit textual reference, musical depiction, and formal disruptions that signal songs-within-songs – *Un chant renvoisie* demonstrates a similar complexity with regard to voice. The tenor quotation DECANTATUR arguably evokes Elizabeth's own voice, since it describes and depicts a melody sung by the saint herself. Simultaneously, the motetus begins with what

[45] Only 13 motets out of a sample of over 350 pieces feature tenors that are entirely or partially in the sixth rhythmic mode. See Tischler, *The Style and Evolution of the Earliest Motets*, Vol. I, pp. 119–31.

[46] See Wolf Frobenius, 'Zum genetischen Verhältnis zwischen Notre-Dame-Klauseln und ihren Motetten', *Archiv für Musikwissenschaft*, 44 (1987), 1–39 (p. 16).

might be safely assumed to be the male first-person protagonist typical of vernacular motets, a singer adding his song to sing about Elizabeth. After this self-contained song, the motetus voice shifts to become that of an incontrovertibly masculine lover in a more conventional love song whose object is a noble lady – whether an earthly one or an allegory for the heavenly Elizabeth remains ambiguous, perhaps deliberately. Finally, this motetus closes with a third shift in voice marked by the quotation of a well-known refrain, which could be read as the culminating expression of a male lover, but might also – given the refrain's theme, and like its accompanying tenor quotation – invoke the voice and expression of Elizabeth.

A Hidden DECANTATUR Motet: *Amis, vostre demoree*

I have argued that the unusual choice of the DECANTATUR melisma as a polyphonic motet tenor was motivated by the exceptional circumstances of the hagiographical motet *Un chant renvoisie*. This tenor, however, unexpectedly reappears in one other motet context, in conjunction with the motetus *Amis, vostre demoree*, which lacks any explicit reference to St Elizabeth. The use of DECANTATUR here is perplexing, and it has not yet been properly acknowledged or investigated, since the chant melody is wrongly labelled as PRO PATRIBUS in the only surviving copy of *Amis, vostre demoree* recorded in **Mo** (see Example 6.5).[47] Melodically, its tenor is identical to that in *Un chant renvoisie*, matching exactly the latter's extended version of the DECANTATUR plainchant. That the **Mo** scribe misidentified it is understandable: PRO PATRIBUS is a very common motet tenor, in the same F mode, and that shares its opening three pitches (F–A–C) with DECANTATUR. Evidently this Parisian scribe did not know the unexpected Cambrai chant, and he supplied or corrected the tenor text as PRO PATRIBUS either in error (after a cursory glance at the melodic incipit) or owing to the lack of any convincing alternative identification.

[47] The musical concordance of the mislabelled PRO PATRIBUS tenor in *Amis, vostre demoree* with the DECANTATUR tenor in *Un chant renvoisie* was first noted by Hendrik van der Werf in his *Integrated Directory of Organa, Clausulae, and Motets of the Thirteenth Century* (Rochester, 1989), p. 135. When the plainchant source of the DECANTATUR melisma was later identified by Haggh-Huglo, she remained unaware of the additional appearance of this melody in *Amis, vostre demoree*. In their edition of the text *Amis, vostre demoree*, Eglal Doss-Quinby, Joan Tasker Grimbert, Wendy Pfeffer, and Elizabeth Aubrey acknowledged that it shared its tenor melody with *Un chant renvoisie* but did not know of Haggh-Huglo's identification of the DECANTATUR source. See their *Songs of the Woman Trouvères* (New Haven, 2001), p. 202.

Example 6.5 *Amis, vostre demoree/PRO PATRIBUS* (*sic*), **Mo**, fol. 249r.

This scribe's unfamiliarity with the DECANTATUR melody is revealing, and is further confirmation of the tenor's unusual status. But the creator of *Amis, vostre demoree* must have been aware of the connotations of this atypical chant melisma when he selected it as the basis of his motet. A shared musical incipit, which has previously escaped scholarly notice, confirms that the composer of *Amis, vostre demoree* knew the hagiographical motet on the same tenor. The motetus of *Amis, vostre demoree* is in the first, rather than the second, rhythmic mode, but its opening phrase nonetheless clearly invokes the beginning of *Un chant renvoisie* (see Example 6.6). Although the decoration of pitches differs slightly between the two motets, the melodic outline is incontrovertibly the same. And since this melody appears in conjunction also with the same chant tenor, in both cases arranged in groups of three pitches, the harmonic relationship between motetus and tenor is identical in both contexts (save at the beginning of perfection 3, marked by a box in Example 6.6). This consistency in both melodic and harmonic details, in addition to the fact that the quotation very obviously occurs in the same place, at the opening of both pieces, renders it particularly audible. The correspondence does not end there. As noted above, the opening phrase of the upper voice returns in *Un chant renvoisie* (creating its initial aba form) in conjunction with the repetition of the tenor melody. Remarkably, this is also the case in *Amis, vostre demoree*, where – although its first two pitches are altered (marked by a dashed box in Example 6.6) – the initial phrase is reprised along with the DECANTATUR melisma in the tenor.[48]

In considering the direction of influence between these two motets, I have argued that the uncharacteristic selection of DECANTATUR as a tenor in the motet repertoire must have been instigated by *Un chant renvoisie*, to complement its text about St Elizabeth. This hagiographical motet is also, therefore, the logical progenitor in terms of the musical incipit shared by *Amis, vostre demoree* – an hypothesis confirmed by considering the quoted opening melody, and its repetition along with that of the tenor chant, in context (see Example 6.5). In *Amis, vostre demoree*, these phrases are noticeably more florid than the rest of the motetus, which otherwise only rarely sub-divides longs into breves. The beginning of the motet and of its second statement of the tenor chant also has a different character that is aurally very noticeable: the quoted incipits have a higher concentration

[48] The only further variant in this motetus repetition is the omission in perfection 28 of the A passing tone previously heard in perfection 3 of *Amis, vostre demoree*, thereby matching the version of this phrase found in *Un chant renvoisie* more exactly.

Example 6.6 Comparison of motetus openings in *Amis, vostre demoree* and *Un chant renvoisie.*

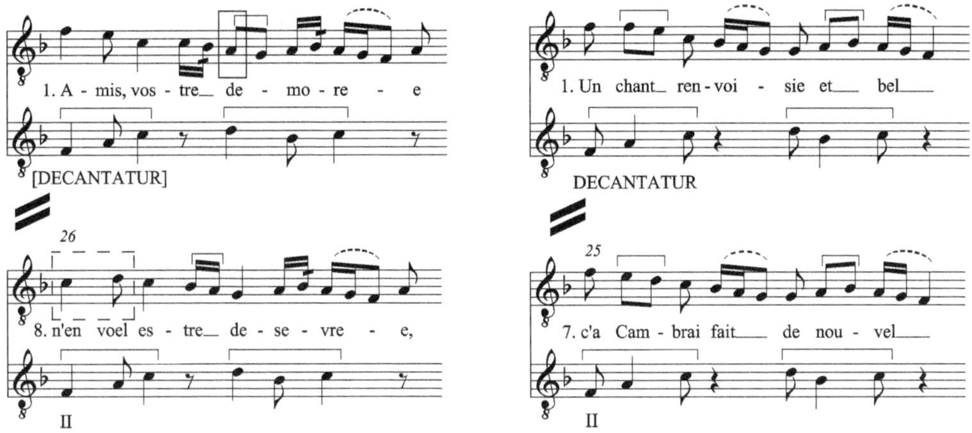

of contrary motion between voices, of voice-crossing between motetus and tenor, and of variety in the intervallic combination of the two voices.

The Gendered and Geographical Resonances of a Closing Refrain

It is certain, then, that the composer of *Amis, vostre demoree* knew *Un chant renvoisie*, adopting the unusual plainchant tenor of this hagiographical motet (and its extended version of the chant melisma) as well as parts of its motetus. Although the accompanying text in *Amis, vostre demoree* makes no specific reference to St Elizabeth, several of its characteristics now emerge as significant in this interpretative context. *Amis, vostre demoree* is one of just 23 out of over 300 motets in **Mo** that are in the female voice (see Table 6.3).[49] The gender of the complaining 'je' – once again bemoaning the pain of love – is clear from the outset, since the text immediately addresses a male beloved, 'amis', and feminine participles ('desevree' and 'donee' in lines 8 and 9, respectively) are used to refer to the speaker. From its opening word, this motet differentiates itself from the typical masculine love songs, probably composed and performed by men. That it is the expression of a woman's love is not merely an allusion to its tenor quotation, but profoundly

[49] See Anna Kathryn Grau, 'Representation and Resistance: Female Vocality in Thirteenth-Century France', Ph.D. diss. (University of Pennsylvania, 2010), p. 184. The text and translation in Table 6.3 are reproduced from Doss-Quinby, Grimbert, Pfeffer, and Aubrey, *Songs of the Woman Trouvères*, p. 202.

Table 6.3 Text and translation of *Amis, vostre demoree*

1.	Amis, vostre demoree	**8a**	-ee	Beloved, your absence
2.	me feit d'amours a celee	**8a**	-ee	makes me feel the pains
3.	sentir les dolours,	**5b**	-ours	of secret love,
4.	car vostres est toz	**5b**	-oz	for my heart is yours
5.	mes cuers, s'il tant voz agree,	**8a**	-ee	entirely, if it should please you,
6.	et sera tous jors.	**5b**	-ors	and always will be.
7.	Ne ja se ce ne'st par voz	**7b**	-oz	And never unless it is by you
8.	n'en voel estre desevree,	**8a**	-ee	do I wish to be parted from it,
9.	puis qu'a vos me sui donee.	**8a**	-ee	since I have given myself to you.
10.	Et biax cuers douz,	**4b**	-ouz	And fair sweet heart,
11.	*quant plus me bat et destraint li jalous*	**10b**	-ous	*the more the jealous one beats and oppresses me*
12.	*tant ai ge miex en amor ma pensee.*	**11a**	-ee	*all the more do I have love in my thoughts.*

reflects the agency inherent in the DECANTATUR tenor, as depicting and re-enacting a miraculous melody sung by Elizabeth.

As an expression of love, however, *Amis vostre demoree* is not straightforward, since it soon becomes evident that the lady is addressing a beloved who is not her husband. This is made explicit in the motet's terminal refrain, which refers to the woman's jealous husband ('li jalous') and his attempts to punish her for her infidelity: '*quant plus me bat et destraint li jalous / tant ai ge miex en amor ma pensee*' (vdB 1555; 'the more the jealous one beats and oppresses me / all the more do I have love in my thoughts'). In association with the DECANTATUR plainchant, the vernacular trope of an unfaithful *mal mariée* complaining about her jealous husband invites several possible allegorical interpretations. Since Elizabeth was a married saint – sacrificing herself to good works only after her husband's death – the conflicting demands of a husband and distant lover in the motet could suggest a parallel conflict between Elizabeth's marital duties and her love of God.[50] Yet in the context of Elizabeth's *vita*, the refrain's reference to beatings seems especially significant. As was well known, Elizabeth had a spiritual guardian, Master Conrad of Marburg, to whom she had sworn obedience and by whom she was encouraged in vows of poverty and chastity, and in self-flagellation. In the Cambrai Office *Gaudeat Hungaria*, from which the DECANTATUR tenor is drawn, Conrad's relationship to the saint is the topic of the second responsory (*Sub Conrad, Dei viro*), which describes Elizabeth's fear of her master and the abstinence he enforced.[51] References

[50] I thank Professor Sylvia Huot for this suggestion.

[51] See Haggh, *Two Offices for Saint Elizabeth*, p. 9.

specifically to beatings encouraged or sanctioned by Conrad are also found in many accounts of Elizabeth's life. The *Dicta quatuor ancillarum* records both occasions on which Elizabeth asked to be beaten, and a specific instance when Master Conrad ordered that she be whipped for disobedience.[52] Rutebeuf's *Vie* also emphasises Conrad's power over Elizabeth and her resulting desire to 'chastise her flesh'.[53] The very widely disseminated *Legenda aurea* – a late-thirteenth-century collection of hagiographies by Jacobus de Voragine – underlined the severity of the lashes inflicted on Elizabeth by Conrad, marks of which were reportedly still visible after three weeks had passed.[54] Iconographically, this aspect of Elizabeth's devotion was characteristic also: a psalter (Paris, Bibliothèque Sainte-Geneviève, 2689), considered by Alison Stones to record 'one of the earliest manifestations in France of the cult of Saint Elizabeth of Hungary', contains a full-page miniature of the saint being flagellated.[55]

In this context, is seems most unlikely that a reference to beatings in an atypically female-voiced refrain concluding a motet on the (albeit mislabelled) DECANTATUR tenor is a coincidence. The complex mix of sacred and secular materials in *Amis, vostre demoree* invites engagement and reflection, since allegorical readings cannot always be mapped directly: the worldly lady's jealous husband seems to have more in common with Master Conrad than Elizabeth's own husband. Unlike Conrad, however, although the husband in the motet beats his wife in order to obstruct her illicit desires, he succeeds, unintentionally, in fuelling them. Nevertheless, the refrain's dictum that the more one is beaten the more one loves operates powerfully in the context of its St Elizabeth tenor. While the refrain's beatings are physical and worldly, its loving is abstract in thought, just as Elizabeth's bodily mortifications served the purpose of bringing her closer to God in prayer and soul.

The closing motto '*quant plus me bat*' is drawn to a listener's attention in the motet *Amis, vostre demoree* by its clearly defined musical character as a refrain. Conventionally, a complementary pair of musical phrases accompanies the refrain's poetic couplet. Beginning identically, each phrase leads to a different cadence, the first ending on a tonally open sonority, which is effectively closed by the second (see Example 6.5). This song-like repetition

[52] See Wolf's translation in *The Life and Afterlife*, pp. 198, 212.

[53] See Cazelles's translation in *The Lady as Saint*, p. 158, lines 700–12.

[54] See William Granger Ryan (trans.), *Jacobus de Voragine, 'The Golden Legend': Readings on the Saints* (Princeton, 1993), Vol. II, no. 168, pp. 302–18.

[55] Alison Stones, 'Notes on the Artistic Context of Some Gautier de Coinci Manuscripts', in Krause and Stones, *Gautier de Coinci*, pp. 65–98 (p. 88 n. 33. See also p. 86).

in itself enhances the refrain's status as a self-consciously 'sung' musical unit, and there are contextual indications that the refrain additionally constitutes a genuine melodic quotation. The two stressed dissonant seconds between motetus and tenor in perfections 38 and 43 contrast with the harmonic grammar of the motet as a whole, as does the seventh created between the two voices at the end of perfections 36 and 41 (marked by dashed boxes in Example 6.5). Though uncharacteristic in *Amis, vostre demoree* and a likely consequence of combining musical quotations, these dissonances nonetheless reveal a careful treatment by the motet creator: they not only make the refrain stand out, but they also accentuate its paired phrase structure. The shared opening portion of each refrain phrase is presented in a near-identical harmonic combination with the tenor quotation, and the recurrence (in perfections 41 and 43) of the very same unusual harmonic dissonances (heard in perfections 36 and 38) calls attention to the refrain's repeated melodic material and song-like structure.[56]

The refrain's status as a genuine quotation is confirmed also by external evidence: '*quant plus me bat*' circulated widely as a musico-textual unit independently of the motet *Amis, vostre demoree*, attested in several contexts that pre-date Elizabeth's death.[57] The refrain probably originated in a monophonic chanson by Monios d'Arras, a monk-turned-trouvère who was active in Artois and in the courts of northern France in the first half of the thirteenth century. '*quant plus me bat*' concludes every one of the six stanzas of his song *Amours me fait renvoisier et chanter*, a chanson consistently attributed to him in all three of its surviving manuscript sources.[58] Monios's song is an unambiguously female-voiced *chanson de femme*, a poetic conceit in which male trouvères occasionally indulged.[59] The text of its entire first stanza appears also in the context of the romance *Roman de la violette* (dated to the late 1220s) and the refrain text is quoted within a

[56] The only harmonic discrepancy between the matching melodic portions of the refrain's pair of phrases is found at the start of perfections 36 and 41: perfection 36 opens on an F octave between tenor and motetus, while perfection 41 begins on the interval of a fifth (between B flat and F).

[57] Mark Everist offers a brief overview of the transmission and a comparative transcription of this refrain in 'The Thirteenth Century', in Mark Everist (ed.), *The Cambridge Companion to Medieval Music* (Cambridge, 2011), pp. 67–86 (pp. 82–3).

[58] Monios's song is recorded with music in **R**, fol. 118v. Its text only is preserved in Bibliothèque nationale de France, fonds fr. 12615, fol. 118r, and in **Vat**, fol. 44r.

[59] On *chansons de femmes* by male trouvères see Wendy Pfeffer, 'Complaints of Women and Complaints by Women: Can One Tell Them Apart?', in Barbara K. Altmann and Carlton W. Carroll (eds.), *The Court Reconvenes: International Courtly Literary Society 1998* (Cambridge, 2003), pp. 125–32.

mid-thirteenth-century Latin commentary by Gérard de Liège on illicit and Godly love, where it serves as a vernacular gloss to illustrate 'amor fortis'.[60]

The authorial association of this refrain with Monios d'Arras is geographically significant, constituting yet another link to the northern French region in with the DECANTATUR plainchant and the hagiographical motet *Un chant renvoisie* seem to have been both conceived and disseminated. It is tempting to make a further connection between the first line of Monios's song *Amours me fait renvoisier et chanter* and the incipit of the hagiographical motet *Un chant renvoisie*, quoted musically in *Amis, vostre demoree*. Although employing conventional vocabulary, this textual similarity between a host chanson and a motet model could have further encouraged the choice of Monios's refrain in *Amis, vostre demoree*. In any case, such traces of a northern French heritage for all three quoted components of the motet – plainchant, motet model, and refrain – underline a tradition of polyphonic composition outside the Parisian contexts with which polyphony is more usually associated.

Carol Symes and Jennifer Saltzstein have recently explored the sophisticated intellectual and cultural milieu in the city of Arras, where highly educated cleric-trouvères such as Adam de la Halle turned to polyphonic composition in the later thirteenth century.[61] These northern French musicians were often educated in Paris and well acquainted with the city's musical practices: the motet *Un chant renvoisie*, though itself unrecorded in manuscripts of the 'central' Parisian repertoire, nonetheless quoted a refrain that circulated in precisely such contexts. Conversely, several other identifiably northern French compositions made their way into Parisian compilations. Like *Amis, vostre demoree*, Adam's Arrageois motets are recorded in **Mo**, which also contains the curious and unique motet *A Cambrai avint l'autrier* – the only other thirteenth-century motet, along with *Un chant renvoisie*, to mention this city by name – whose tenor is designated SOIER.[62] Surely a local joke, this short and rather bawdy piece describes the

[60] For editions of these texts see Douglas Labree Buffum (ed.), *Gerbert de Montreuil: Le Roman de la violette ou de Gerart de Nevers*, Société des anciens textes français (Paris, 1928); and André Wilmart (ed.), *Gérard de Liège: Quinque incitamenta ad Deum amandum ardenter*, Analecta reginensia, Studi e testi 59 (Vatican City, 1933), pp. 205–47.

[61] See Carol Symes, *A Common Stage: Theater and Public Life in Medieval Arras* (Ithaca, 2007); and Jennifer Saltzstein, *The Refrain and the Rise of the Vernacular in Medieval French Music and Poetry* (Cambridge, 2013), pp. 80–113 (on song culture in Arras) and pp. 114–48 (on Adam de la Halle).

[62] *A Cambrai/SOIER* is recorded in an appendix of four motets (two Latin, two French) at the end of fascicle 3 of **Mo** (fols. 83v–86v). See Thomas Walker, 'Sui *Tenor* Francesi nei motetti del "200"', *Schede medievali: Rassegna dell' officina di studi medievali*, 3 (1982), 309–36 (pp. 322–4). A tradition of referring to home towns and cities is also evident in several Parisian motets, most notably *On parole/A Paris/FRESE NOUVELE*. See the discussion of this motet in Emma

actions of Sohiers the cooper, who left Cambrai to become mixed up with the Beguines at nearby Campître. As noted in Chapter 1, Thomas Walker observed that the SOIER melody closely resembles the more conventional tenor melisma on ET VIDE ET AUREM TUAM from the *Propter veritatem* Gradual.[63] That it is oddly labelled instead with the name of the motet's protagonist may indicate a lack of concern for, or a different approach to, the texting of tenor chants in these non-Parisian compositions, attested also by the misidentification of the unfamiliar DECANTATUR tenor in *Amis, vostre demoree*. Within this northern French context, the emphasis on the woman's heart given to her beloved in *Amis, vostre demoree* could have encouraged an allegorical reading: that of St Elizabeth – whose voice is summoned in the motetus, its closing refrain, and its accompanying tenor – literally offering her heart for the veneration of the people of Cambrai.

Conclusions

Thirteenth-century motets on the plainchant tenor DECANTATUR invite interpretation, since the quotation of this melody from a short-lived Cambrai Office for St Elizabeth of Hungary was an unconventional choice of semantic significance. In the hagiographical motet *Un chant renvoisie*, not only are the symbolic associations of the DECANTATUR tenor with Elizabeth and Cambrai made explicit in the vernacular upper-voice text, but – as a musical and poetic whole – the motet plays also on ideas of song, singing, and voice in ways that evoke the saint's *vita* and persona. The only other motet to use the DECANTATUR tenor, *Amis, vostre demoree*, has never previously been considered in the liturgical context of its plainchant quotation or in relation to *Un chant renvoisie*. Although *Amis, vostre demoree* does not name Elizabeth, it opens in the female voice with a direct musical reference to the beginning of the hagiographical motet *Un chant renvoisie*, and closes with another female-voiced refrain quotation from a song by Monios d'Arras, which powerfully encapsulates a defining aspect of the saint's identity, as a woman subjected to masculine violence. In tracing the provenance of plainchant sources for the DECANTATUR tenor, investigating refrain concordances and their host contexts, reading motets against their broader manuscript contents, and with reference to contemporary

Dillon, *The Sense of Sound: Musical Meaning in France 1260–1330*, New Cultural History of Music Series (New York, 2012), pp. 86–90.

[63] See Chapter 1, p. 31, n. 51.

accounts of Elizabeth's life, this chapter has established concrete quotational and semantic connections, positing a new intertextual network of musical compositions and delineating their *Erwartungshorizont*, or wider frame of reference.

The clarity of the links and intertextual connections in this DECANTATUR network goes some way to dispelling Christopher Page's doubts about the validity of uncovering allusions in thirteenth-century motets, and his provocative charge of overinterpretation.[64] Such concerns, which have been much disputed by musicologists in the intervening decades since the publication of Page's *Discarding Images* in 1993, pertained principally to close-readings of polytextual pieces, in which the simultaneous presentation of multiple texts in performance might impede their comprehensibility.[65] Questions of audibility do not apply to the two-voice motets as discussed here, since there is little difficulty in distinguishing a single syllabic upper-voice text above a melismatic tenor chant. Nevertheless, Page's sense that the strongly generic poetic character of vernacular motets could allow seemingly meaningful connections to be drawn between almost any given texts cannot be readily dismissed.[66] I have, therefore, placed the heaviest interpretative burdens on characteristics that, when judged against the extensive motet repertoire at large, emerge as genuinely unusual or in need of explanation: the nature of the plainchant tenor itself, for instance; the strange formal shifts that draw attention to acts of singing in *Un chant renvoisie*; the striking changes in tenor mode in *Douce dame sanz pitie/SUSTINERE*; or the uncharacteristic use of the female voice in *Amis, vostre demoree*. The fact that these features are unusual in themselves renders especially significant the added fact that they are often shared by pieces associated with the DECANTATUR melody, thereby strengthening the coherence of the whole network.

No other plainchant tenor in the thirteenth century can be so neatly connected to a particular time and place as DECANTATUR. The responsory *Ante dies exitus* must post-date Elizabeth's canonisation in 1235, and the excerption of the DECANTATUR tenor clearly occurred before its host Office (*Gaudeat Hungaria*) was largely supplanted by the more popular Elizabeth Office (*Letare Germania*) in the later thirteenth century.

[64] See Christopher Page, *Discarding Images: Reflections on Music and Culture in Medieval France* (Oxford, 1993), pp. 65–111.

[65] See also Christopher Page's later development of these arguments in 'Around the Performance of a Thirteenth-Century Motet', *Early Music*, 28 (2000), 343–57; and Clark's summary of the debate and response to Page in 'S'en dirai chançonete', pp. 31–5.

[66] See Page, *Discarding Images*, pp. 84–95.

Geographically, the connection of this chant to Cambrai and its surrounding regions depends, not on the problematic identification of any Parisian or 'peripheral' musical style, but rather on documentary evidence from Henry of Brussels and on the dissemination of *Un chant renvoisie* and its explicit reference to Cambrai. The quotation of a well-known refrain by an Arrageois trouvère in *Amis vostre demoree* is additionally significant, and this motet offers proof that the DECANTATUR tenor was not immediately recognisable to the Parisian scribe of **Mo**. Despite multi-directional musical exchanges between Paris and northern France, then, the DECANTATUR tenor evidently remained a somewhat local phenomenon. Its unusual specificity – geographical and chronological – usefully enables interpretative parameters to be drawn with uncharacteristic precision.

This intimate knowledge of the DECANTATUR tenor additionally allows us to glimpse contexts and practices for this melody that can no longer be accessed. It is almost unprecedented that the two motets citing the DECANTATUR melisma in fact constitute the earliest witnesses to their plainchant source. These motets pre-date by around two decades the first surviving manuscript of the Office *Gaudeat Hungaria*, which must previously have circulated either orally or in records that are now lost. The refrain vdB 623 presents a similar case. It is apparently quoted in both of its extant instantiations, and tantalisingly this invites speculation about the refrain's unknown origins, and their possible semantic significance in the context of the hagiographical DECANTATUR motet. Was this refrain also, for instance, associated with a woman's voice or with a 'local' northern French trouvère? Might its original lost host chanson or motet have chimed with any details of Elizabeth's life? Even in a network such as this one – where the surviving evidence seems unusually propitious and complete – there exists the potential for yet further intertextual subtleties that remain beyond the possibilities of current knowledge.

The polyphonic genre of the motet facilitates a remarkably sophisticated kind of simultaneous intertextuality. Two different types of song – a liturgical plainchant and a vernacular refrain – may clearly be heard and quoted at the same time, exploiting the potential of individual melodies and texts to recall almost instantly all manner of varied contexts and instantiations. Such quotations can additionally draw attention to the act of singing within a motet, which may also self-consciously evoke and play with ideas of song through self-referential texts or through particular repetitive, formal, and melodic procedures. This underlines the rich semantic potential of a two-voice motet, which is polyphonic, not just in its combination of individual voices, but also in its ability to conjure, through sound, additional and external musical and poetic contexts, genres, and performative acts. This is, in essence, a kind of polytextuality or polyvocality, but one that has attracted considerably less attention than the three- and four-voice motets with multiple syllabic texts to which this label is usually and more literally confined, and that remain shrouded by debates about the relationship between the semantic and the sonic.[67] Such debates have complicated, perhaps unhelpfully, discussions of meaning in thirteenth-century motets, nearly half of which are, in fact, two- rather than three- or four-voice compositions.[68] I have deliberately isolated here issues of interpretation from those of comprehensibility. Nonetheless, the DECANTATUR case study itself constitutes substantial evidence in favour of interpretative readings of literally polytextual motets, whatever their aural impact: if sophisticated allusions and cross-references can be convincingly demonstrated in two-voice works, then it is logical to conclude that such practices applied also in motets combining up to three different syllabic texts, which offered even greater scope for multi-layered meanings. Offering new evidence for musical evocations and venerations of St Elizabeth of Hungary in the thirteenth century, this chapter has underlined the potential of allusive and interpretative practices that must have been commonplace in the thirteenth-century motets and songs – practices whose effects and networks of meaning are often otherwise obscured, in some cases irrevocably, by the passing of time and the loss or lack of written sources.

[67] Two recent interpretative discussions of two-voice motets by Edward H. Roesner and Sean Curran are notable exceptions. See Edward H. Roesner, '*Subtilitas* and *Delectatio*: *Ne m'a pas oublié*', in Jane Burns, Eglal Doss-Quinby, and Roberta L. Krueger (eds.), *Cultural Performances in Medieval France: Essays in Honor of Nancy Freeman Regalado* (Cambridge, 2007), pp. 25–43; and Sean Curran, 'Feeling the Polemic of an Early Motet', in Almut Suerbaum, George Southcombe, and Benjamin Thompson (eds.), *Polemic: Language as Violence in Medieval and Early Modern Discourse* (Farnham, 2015), pp. 65–94.

[68] See the analysis of the proportion of two-voice versus polytextual thirteenth-century motets in Catherine A. Bradley, 'Seeking the Sense of Sound', *Journal of the Royal Musical Association*, 139 (2014), 405–20 (pp. 407–8).

7 From Florence to Fauvel: Rereading Musical Paradigms through a Long-Lived IOHANNE Motet

What might ensure the long life – in performance, in memory, and in written records – of a musical object? This chapter takes as its focus a short piece of two-voice polyphony that constituted some of the most regularly recopied, reworked, and updated musical material throughout the thirteenth and fourteenth centuries. This composition on the IOHANNE tenor – which circulated variously as a clausula, two-voice Latin and French motets, and as the basis of a three-voice French double motet – achieved a status as memorable and exemplary in its own lifetime that has been echoed in modern scholarship. Cited by the medieval theorist Franco of Cologne, these pieces have served more recently as a textbook paradigm of the development of both medieval musical notations and genres.[1] I offer a rereading of the IOHANNE network here, to reveal musical behaviours and chronological relationships that recast and challenge conventional models of generic and notational developments in the thirteenth century. At the same time, I shed new light on questions that have previously been overshadowed by a preoccupation with developmental trajectories. The 'catchy' and memorable nature of these enduring motets is probably their most obvious feature, but probably also that which is most difficult to talk about. This chapter seeks to explore the identity and appeal of this musical and poetic material: to think about why it was an attractive locus for recopying and reworking throughout the thirteenth century and beyond; how this polyphonic composition circulated; and what aspects of its musical fabric may have rendered it, and continue to render it, so aurally unforgettable.

[1] This motet family was used to illustrate the development of the motet, notationally and as a genre, in Ernest H. Sanders and Peter M. Lefferts, 'Motet: 1. Middle Ages, France, Ars antiqua', in Stanley Sadie and John Tyrrell (eds.), *The New Grove Dictionary of Music and Musicians*, 2nd edn (Oxford, 2001), Vol. XVII, pp. 190–5. It is similarly employed as the principal example in Rebecca A. Baltzer, 'The Thirteenth-Century Motet', in Mark Everist and Thomas Forrest Kelly (eds.), *The Cambridge History of Medieval Music* (Cambridge, 2018), pp. 1004–29. I am grateful to Professor Baltzer for sharing this material in advance of publication.

The IOHANNE Network: The Conventional Story

Drawn from the *Alleluia. Inter natos* (M 29) for the Nativity of John the Baptist (24 June), the IOHANNE melisma was of about average popularity as a choice for polyphonic elaboration in the thirteenth century. It flourished most obviously in the motet family in question, for which the earliest records are found in the Florence manuscript.[2] Two different versions of the same IOHANNE material are preserved in **F**, both in forms unique to this source: a two-voice melismatic clausula and a two-voice Latin motet, *Clamans in deserto*. As a motet, the musical material circulated more widely with the French text *Ne sai que je die* (in **W2**, **LoC**, **Bes**, and **Mo**). And this two-voice vernacular setting became the basis of a later three-voice double motet in the seventh fascicle of **Mo** and in **Ba**, with an added triplum, *Quant vient en mai*, that took full advantage of new possibilities for shorter rhythmic values characteristic of the later thirteenth century. Finally, the motet reappeared in its two-voice form in a copy with musical interpolations, dated to 1317, of the *Roman de Fauvel*, an allegorical satire about the rise to power of a human-equine hybrid. Here it was accompanied by another Latin text, *Veritas arpie*, which previously featured also in a second version of the motet recorded in the mid-thirteenth-century manuscript **W2**.[3]

This musical material on IOHANNE was not only recopied, but was also reshaped in various forms and contexts: as an untexted clausula, associated with three different motet texts, and with an added triplum. Further testament to its prominence is the appearance of this motet as a musical example in Franco of Cologne's treatise dated to the 1270s, *Ars cantus mensurabilis musicae*. The motet incipit appears with the text *Arida frondescit*, which invokes John the Baptist preparing the way for Christ in the desert, a contrafactum otherwise unknown in any complete form. *Arida frondescit* is offered in the treatise as an illustration of discant that opens with voices at the octave.[4] Both the nature and choice of Franco's example are significant.

[2] All sources are listed with folio numbers in Table 7.3.

[3] Translations of all texts are available in Gordon A. Anderson (ed.), *The Latin Compositions in Fascicules VII and VIII of the Notre Dame Manuscript Wolfenbüttel Helmstedt 1099 (1206)*, Musicological Studies 24, 2 parts (New York, 1968–76), Part I, pp. 376–82. See also the interpretation of this IOHANNE network in a recent study of motet texts for John the Baptist by Michael Alan Anderson: 'Fire, Foliage, and Fury: Vestiges of Midsummer Ritual in Motets for John the Baptist', *Early Music History*, 30 (2011), 1–54 (esp. pp. 29–33 and 39–46).

[4] See André Gilles and Gilbert Reaney (eds.), *Franco de colonia: Ars cantus mensurabilis musicae*, *CSM* 18 (Rome, 1974), p. 70.

First, it seems that yet another alternative Latin text existed for this motet, and that the IOHANNE material was even more widely disseminated than surviving musical sources attest. Second, the appearance of the motet in this context is revealing. Franco would surely have known a great many motets that opened with the highly conventional interval of an octave. With a wide range of available pieces to choose from, and in order to exemplify a very straightforward concept, it is reasonable to conclude that he selected an obvious one, a motet of the kind of classic status that would be readily familiar to the eyes and ears of his readers.[5]

These IOHANNE pieces – encompassing various genres and musical notations – have retained their exemplary status as a theoretical illustration in recent times. As conventionally told, the evolutionary narrative begins with the untexted IOHANNE clausula in *sine littera* modal notation, intended for substitution within a liturgical organum for its host Alleluia. Syllabic text is then added to the pre-existing music of the clausula. First comes the sacred Latin text for John the Baptist, *Clamans in deserto*, troping its liturgical tenor and recorded in unmeasured *cum littera* notation in the earliest extant motet manuscript, **F**. The motet then enters the secular realm, with a vernacular contrafactum text *Ne sai que je die*. In **Mo** and **LoC**, *Ne sai que je die* is presented in a new rhythmically prescriptive mensural notation, employing tails to indicate long notes. The motet's notational advance concludes with the addition of a vernacular triplum, which avails of the new rhythmic possibilities outlined in Franco's treatise, whereby breves can be divided into up to three shorter semibreves. The chronological progression outlined for this motet family neatly encapsulates the full range of available notational technologies in the thirteenth century, and it is in line with accepted clausula-to-motet, Latin-to-vernacular, and sacred-to-secular progressions.[6]

Yet even a case as seemingly archetypal as this one cannot be reconciled within any straightforwardly linear trajectory. For this IOHANNE network and more generally, narratives of development in the thirteenth century necessarily encompass what seems to be a regression in rhythmic notation.

[5] As explored further below, the choice of musical examples that are otherwise widely disseminated is common in Franco's treatise more generally, and was presumably a pedagogical ploy.

[6] This is the narrative outlined in Sanders's and Baltzer's discussions of these pieces (see n. 1 above). It is also fundamental to Gordon A. Anderson's observations on this motet family, in *The Latin Compositions in Fascicules VII and VIII*, Part I, pp. 376–82. Michael Alan Anderson likewise assumes the origins of this motet family in a source clausula, in 'Fire, Foliage, and Fury', pp. 30, 39.

The addition of a syllabic text in *cum littera* motets prevents the use of modal ligatures previously possible in the melismatic clausulae, which sometimes served as the musical basis to which motet texts were added. Before the advent of stems to distinguish long notes from short, motets in manuscripts such as **F** and **W2** lacked a means of explicitly communicating precise rhythmic information.[7] Although the earliest motets may generically be more modern and up to date than any clausula models, this modernity of genre was initially achieved at a cost of notational specificity. A sense that motets move from sacred to secular spheres, with Latin tropic texts giving way to vernacular ones, is similarly complicated. Motets frequently received multiple contrafacta in both languages, including apparently 'late' Latin reworkings of French texts. In the IOHANNE network, *Ne sai que je die* is (as will be demonstrated) a much more probable model, poetically and thematically, for the Latin text *Veritas arpie* found in **W2** and **Fauvel** than *Clamans in deserto*. The creation of *Veritas arpie*, therefore, and possibly also of *Arida frondescit*, constitutes an apparent return to the music's perceived Latinate and even liturgical origins via a vernacular intermediary.

Chronological narratives for this repertoire are further confounded by a complicated relationship between the age of a manuscript source and the relative age of the music it contains. I have previously challenged the assumption that motets in **F** should assume priority simply because they are contained within the earliest extant manuscript to record pieces in this genre. And I have stressed that the exclusively Latinate contents of this particular source do not necessarily constitute evidence that Latin motets preceded those in the vernacular.[8] At the other end of the spectrum, a fundamental gap between manuscript date and musical chronology is clearly evident in **Fauvel**. This manuscript included conducti and motets that must have been over a century old at the time of copying, and its compilers deliberately intermingled perceptibly outmoded pieces with those in a much more up-to-date *Ars nova* style. The IOHANNE motet *Veritas arpie* appears in **Fauvel** without the fast-moving triplum recorded in late-thirteenth-century sources. This two-voice form is consciously archaic not only in the context of **Fauvel**, but also when considered against notationally and musically more advanced versions of the piece preserved in earlier manuscript

[7] This is not to suggest that rhythmic information cannot be intuited from motets in **F** and **W2**, where aspects of text declamation, general modal conventions and patterns, and consonance against a rhythmically prescribed tenor serve (often comprehensively) as a guide.

[8] See Catherine A. Bradley, 'Contrafacta and Transcribed Motets: Vernacular Influences on Latin Motets and Clausulae in the Florence Manuscript', *Early Music History*, 32 (2013), 1–70.

contexts. In order to begin to catalogue and edit even this single motet family there is an understandable need to rationalise its multiple versions in some way: to sort by genre, by manuscript source, or by language, and to align these details with a chronology, either implicitly or explicitly. The challenges faced in working with such complex material may account for the persistence of conceptualising thirteenth-century clausulae and motets in a fundamentally linear fashion, despite problems and complications inherent in the application of such paradigms.

A Clausula Source for a Latin Motet? Tenor Manipulation and a Song-Like Duplum

The clausula *Iohanne 3* – recorded uniquely in **F** – is unanimously considered to represent the earliest form of this widely transmitted IOHANNE material.[9] This clausula has no obvious features that would conventionally encourage doubt of its chronological primacy and liturgical function as a 'substitute' clausula, for use within a two-voice organum setting of the *Alleluia. Inter natos*. Wolf Frobenius, in his provocative attempt to challenge the origins of motets in clausulae, did not propose *Iohanne 3* as a motet original (later transcribed without its text as a clausula), probably because of its lack of association with any vernacular refrain melody.[10] Notationally, the clausula itself displays little sign of irregularities associated with the transcription of a motet. The straightforward rhythmic profile of the duplum, in the first rhythmic mode is – with the exception of a single phrase – consistently rendered in conventional ligature patterns.[11]

In context, however, several aspects of *Iohanne 3* emerge as unusual. In the organa and clausulae of the so-called *Magnus liber*, the IOHANNE tenor was by no means uncommon, but neither did it inspire a noticeably large number of polyphonic settings (see Table 7.1). Two IOHANNE

[9] In addition to Sanders, Baltzer, Gordon Anderson, and Michael Anderson (see nn. 1 and 3 above), Wyndham Thomas also considered *Iohanne 3* automatically to be a clausula 'source'. See Wyndham Thomas, 'The *Iohanne* Melisma: Some Aspects of Tenor Organization in Thirteenth-Century Motets', *The Music Review*, 54 (1993), 1–13.

[10] Wolf Frobenius, 'Zum genetischen Verhältnis zwischen Notre-Dame-Klauseln und ihren Motetten', *Archiv für Musikwissenschaft*, 44 (1987), 1–39.

[11] Rebecca A. Baltzer previously noted – in 'Notation, Rhythm, and Style in the Two-Voice Notre Dame Clausula', Ph.D. diss. (Boston University, 1974), Vol. I, p. 250 – that the clausula's six-note ligature in perfections 21–3 is unconventional (see Example 7.3).

Table 7.1 Polyphonic elaborations of IOHANNE in the *Magnus liber*

Version number	Manuscript sources	Folio number	Context
1	**W1**	54v–3	Clausula (no. 33)
	F	121r	Discant in organum
2	**W1**	58r–3	Clausula (no. 66)
	F	164r–3	Clausula (no. 146)
	W2	76r–v	Discant in organum
3	**F**	164v–1	Clausula (no. 147)
4	**F**	175v–4	Clausula (no. 258)

clausulae are recorded in **W1**, but no host organum for the M 29 Alleluia. Two-voice organa on this chant are found in **F** and **W2**, where each organum has a different passage of discant on IOHANNE, each concordant with an alternative **W1** clausula. In addition to the M 29 organum, **F** records three independent clausulae on IOHANNE. One is found also in **W1** and within the M 29 organum in **W2**, and the other two are unique to this manuscript.

None of these clausulae or discant passages except *Iohanne 3* featured in the motet repertoire: the additional six motet families on IOHANNE tenors lack any connection to *Magnus liber* settings.[12] Significantly, *Iohanne 3* is also the only clausula or discant passage in the *Magnus liber* to adopt an unusual version of its chant melody. Like the REGNAT tenor discussed in Chapter 3, IOHANNE is another example of an Alleluia melisma with its own clearly defined tripartite melodic form (see Example 7.1). In this instance, its conventional AAB form is more properly expressed as AA'B, since the two A sections differ in their opening gesture: D–A–A at the melisma's outset, versus D–F–A upon the repetition of this A material. With the exception of *Iohanne 3*, the transmission of the chant melody as a polyphonic tenor in organa and clausulae is entirely stable.[13] This stability of transmission matches that in contemporary Parisian chant books, which likewise agree exactly on the melodic content of this melisma as shown in Example 7.1.

Two minor divergences from the conventional tenor melody apparent in *Iohanne 3* are marked by boxes in Example 7.2, which compares this clausula and motet tenor against the established form of the IOHANNE

[12] A complete list of motets on the IOHANNE tenor (Mt379–93) is available in Anderson, 'Fire, Foliage, and Fury', pp. 51–4.

[13] In later motet transmissions the IOHANNE tenor is more freely treated, as discussed below, n. 34.

Example 7.1 Conventional form of IOHANNE melisma.

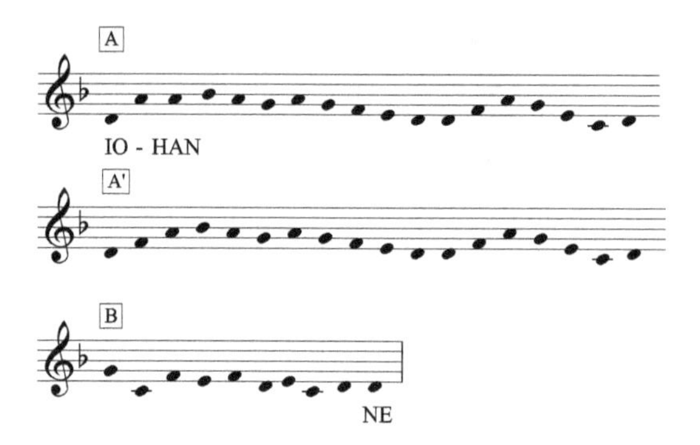

melisma.[14] The first divergence occurs at the outset of the tenor, where the clausula and motets have an additional iteration of the opening pitch D.[15] The second affects the beginning of the A' material: a repetition of the pitch D is here omitted in the clausula and motet tenor and an extra A is added. This reading of the IOHANNE melody differs from established monophonic transmissions and all other polyphonic practices in organa and clausulae. But its variants are absolutely in character with the melody of the *Alleluia. Inter natos* from which the IOHANNE melisma stems. The added D at the beginning of the IOHANNE tenor in fact matches the opening of the second principal discant and motet tenor drawn from this Alleluia – that is MULIERUM, which also opens with a D–D–A gesture.

Tellingly, the record of the two-voice motet *Ne sai que je die*/*IOHANNE* in fascicle 6 of **Mo** (fol. 234v) erroneously gives MULIERUM as its tenor designation. The designation is incorrect, because the MULIERUM and IOHANNE melodies diverge after their similar openings, but the scribe was understandably misled by his immediate recognition of the D–D–A opening as the conventional beginning of the MULIERUM tenor, though not of IOHANNE (which should begin simply D–A). What was ultimately a scribal error paradoxically reveals a very detailed knowledge of plainchant

[14] A copying error in the *Iohanne 3* clausula is corrected in Examples 7.2 and 7.3. The scribe of **F** replicated the melisma's opening D–D–A ordo (rather than D–F–A) at the beginning of the A' material in the seventh ordo (perfections 25–8). This is clearly erroneous, since all other motet sources have F as the second note of the seventh ordo, rather than D, which produces a dissonant seventh with the accompanying duplum C. That this mistake by the clausula scribe occurred at a moment of departure from the conventional chant melody is telling.

[15] Thomas, in 'The *Iohanne* Melisma', p. 5, also noted this variant opening for the IOHANNE melisma. However, he accepted the authority of this version, owing to its presence in the clausula 'source', and believed the *Alleluia. Inter natos* to be a chant unknown outside the context of the polyphonic *Magnus liber*.

Example 7.2 Comparison of *Iohanne 3* clausula and motet tenor with the conventional IOHANNE melisma. Square brackets show ordines groupings; ordo numbers are circled.

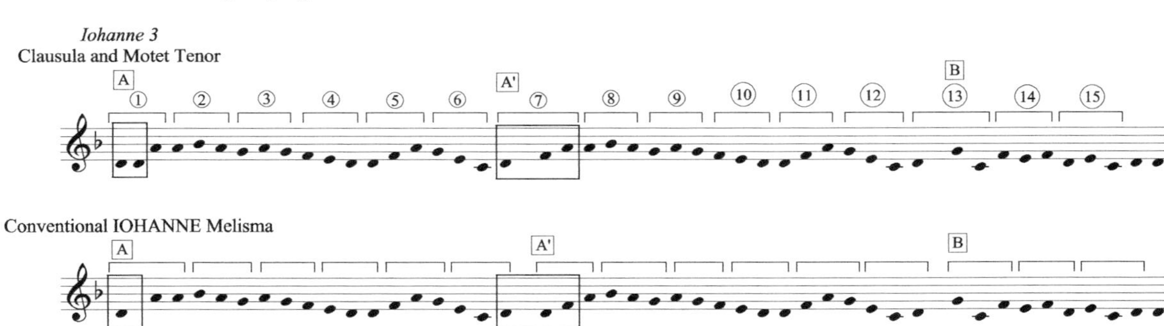

tenor melodies. And this underlines a well-established identity for the IOHANNE and MULIERUM melismas in the thirteenth century, such that an added opening pitch D was a recognisable difference between them.

The tenor of the musical example in two copies of Franco's treatise is significant also in this regard. The extra D found in other all sources of *Iohanne 3* and its related motets is omitted in the opening tenor ordo of two copies of Franco's treatise, where the tenor of *Arida frondescit* is given instead as D–A–A, replicating the chant's true beginning.[16] At least one copyist either judged the tenor opening here to be improper, or automatically 'corrected' the motet opening, suppling from memory a version more in keeping with the conventional form of the IOHANNE quotation. These scribal responses to the tenor incipit confirm that deviations from the established chant melody in *Iohanne 3*, though small, were identifiable as such: several thirteenth-century scribes were aware that a IOHANNE tenor should not begin D–D–A, and, in the case of **Mo**, that MULIERUM should. It is, therefore, most unlikely that the composer of the *Iohanne 3* polyphony simply confused his tenor openings – rather his echo of the MULIERUM beginning was surely deliberate – or that his manipulations of the established chant melody were unconscious.

That such manipulations were intentional and carefully considered is corroborated by their significant compositional impact on the musical material as a whole. *Iohanne 3* groups the pitches of its chant tenor in sets of three (marked by square brackets in Example 7.2). In a conventional fifth-mode tenor rhythm, each note is sustained for the length of a ternary long and the third pitch is followed by a rest of the same duration. In fact, the A sections of the unaltered IOHANNE tenor – each comprising eighteen notes – are already very amenable to a ternary division (as shown by square brackets in the bottom system of Example 7.2). There was no need, therefore, for the creator of *Iohanne 3* to add an extra pitch at the beginning of the chant in order to ensure that both the A and the A′ sections of the chant melody fell at the beginning of a rhythmic ordo. Furthermore, the added opening pitch in *Iohanne 3*, and the resulting shift in pitch groupings, essentially caused both A sections to conclude a note early, ending on C, rather than their final pitch – and the final of the melisma as a whole – D.

[16] Only three extant manuscripts of Franco's treatise transmit this example with the appropriate music. Paris, Bibliothèque nationale de France, fr. lat. 16663 and Saint-Dié, Bibliothèque municipale, 42 give the first tenor ordo as D–A–A. The motet's second tenor ordo (A–B–A) is unaltered, therefore introducing an extra A (rather than an extra opening D) in the IOHANNE chant. Oxford, Bodleian Library, Bodley 842 gives the tenor opening correctly (as D–D–A), and adds an otherwise unknown triplum above the motetus.

Yet in other respects the introduction of an extra opening D affected the groupings of pitches in such a way as to create a greater coherence and consistency between the individual tenor ordines. In *Iohanne 3*, the opening and closing pitches of each three-note ordo are noticeably more circumscribed than those of the unaltered melody would have been, and they define the piece's tonal palate more clearly. As arranged in *Iohanne 3*, the tenor foundation gives almost exclusive prominence to two contrasting tonal areas a tone apart: a 'closed' D/A sonority versus an 'open' alternative of C/G. This is heightened by a particular symmetry that emerges between ordines 5 and 6 (and 11 and 12), where a rising D–F–A triad is answered by the triadic descent, G–E–C. A desire to reprise this triadic shape seems additionally to have motivated the second alteration to the IOHANNE melisma at the beginning of the A' section. Unaltered, this seventh ordo would have been D–D–F, instead of the more obviously 'closed' reiteration of the D–F–A progression.[17]

Two slight changes effected in the tenor quotation in *Iohanne 3*, therefore, have a notable impact on its character and pitch groupings, not only with a view to the shape and symmetry of its ordines, but crucially also simplifying and strengthening its tonal identity as a polyphonic foundation. Unsurprisingly, the accompanying clausula duplum exploits to the full these aspects of its underlying tenor design (see the transcription of *Iohanne 3* in Example 7.3). Upper voice and tenor largely phrase together and, although the duplum sometimes fills the silence between two tenor ordines, it always leads towards a cadence either on A or G. Opening sonorities are likewise highly consistent: upper-voice phrases typically begin also either on A or G, or their related pitches, D and C. A sense of alternate tonal poles is additionally evident in the duplum response to the triadic tenor ordines, facilitated by the manipulation of the chant quotation (marked by boxes in Example 7.3). In perfections 17–24, the duplum accompanies the D–F–A tenor ordo with a corresponding phrase that begins and ends on A, and that is then repeated down a tone – beginning and ending on G – to complement the tenor's G–E–C descent. These tenor ordines receive a similar treatment on their second appearance in perfections 41–8. The duplum once again phrases with the tenor ordines in four-perfection units to produce a pair of phrases, the first enacting the descent of a fourth from D to A, the second

[17] As Büttner observed (*Das Klauselrepertoire der Handschrift Saint-Victor*, p. 147), the repetition of the D–F–A ordo in the IOHANNE tenor caused the scribe of *Ne sai que je die/IOHANNE* in **LoC** to mistake ordo 5, the first D–F–A ordo, as the beginning of the A' material. He therefore omitted ordines 5 and 6 of the tenor, proceeding straight from ordo 4 to ordo 7.

Example 7.3 *Iohanne 3* clausula, F, fol. 164v–1.

circling around G. In addition, the upper voice responds to the artificially achieved reiteration of the D–F–A tenor ordo in perfections 25–7, matching this tenor repetition with a reprise of the corresponding duplum material from perfections 17–19.

Tonally closed versus open cadences in the upper voice are complemented by the interchange of two types of rhythmic cadence: a stressed cadence – articulated on the strong beat as a single ternary long and followed by a rest of the same duration – versus an unstressed phrase ending on the weak beat, often a repeated-note cadence (see Example 7.4, which presents the IOHANNE material in the form of the motet *Ne sai que je die*/*IOHANNE*).[18] Stressed cadences are marked by boxes in Example 7.4. With just one exception (at perfection 47), they are reserved for the closed sonority, A (at perfections 15, 31, 43, and 61). The sense of closure – tonal and rhythmic – at these four moments is heightened by the fact that they occur at the end of phrases that are extended in length, breaking the regular four-perfection units of the tenor ordo. Stressed cadences in perfections 15, 31, and 43 mark the end of two tenor ordines that have been joined by the upper voice (shown by an arrow in Example 7.4), while the motet's final cadence concludes a closing six-perfection unit. The single stressed cadence on G that occurs at perfection 47 is also the only occasion in the motet where one stressed cadence follows another and concludes a four-perfection phrase. This one exception to the established rhythmic and tonal pattern might be understood as a means of creating variety, marking the first of a series of three open G cadences (perfections 47, 51–2, and 55–6), which heighten the eventual resolution of the motet's ultimate return to A.

The opposition of two clearly defined sonorities a tone apart, linked to rhythmically contrasting cadences, creates a strong melodic identity for the upper voice of the *Iohanne 3* clausula that is reminiscent of monophonic troubadour or trouvère chansons, as well as of later fourteenth-century songs in the *formes fixes*, both monophonic and polyphonic. This duplum achieves a song-like profile relatively uncharacteristic of polyphonic clausulae or motets, where possibilities for such clear-cut tonal alterations can be limited by the literal quotation of a pre-existent tenor foundation. Formally also, the duplum bears a striking resemblance to another song technique. Its use of an AAB form, or *pedes cum cauda*, is once again characteristic of vernacular monophony, as well as of earlier monophonic

[18] As is typical, the concluding organal-style closing formula found in the clausula on the final pitch of the chant, D, corresponding to the syllable '-NE', is omitted in all motet versions (see also Chapter 5, pp. 153–4).

Example 7.4 *Ne sai que je die/IOHANNE*, **W2**, fol. 219av.

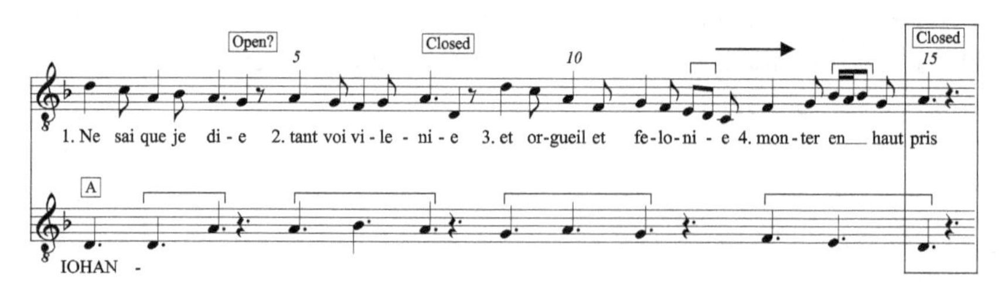

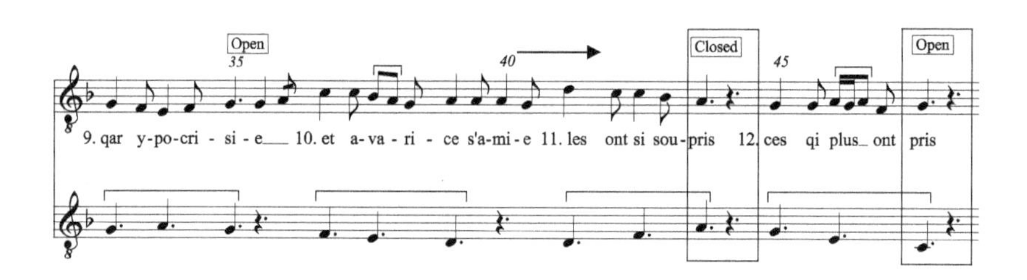

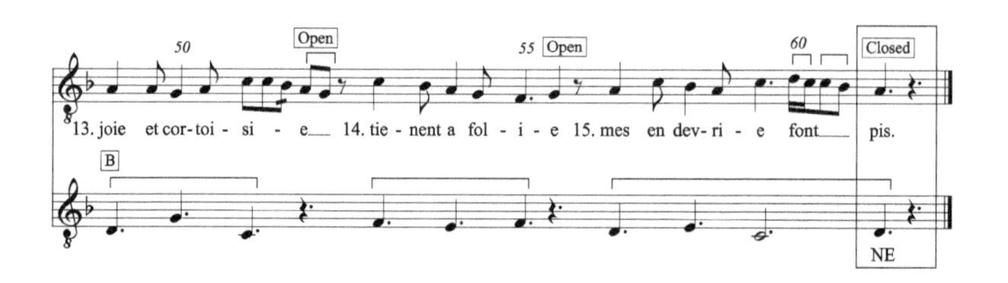

plainchant melismas such as IOHANNE itself.[19] This upper-voice structure is marked in Example 7.5, which presents the IOHANNE material in the form of the motet *Clamans in deserto/IOHAN[NE]*, and in which each A section corresponds to a single system.[20]

[19] On *pedes cum cauda* form in motets, see Gaël Saint-Cricq, 'A New Link between the Motet and Trouvère Chanson: The *pedes cum cauda* motet', *Early Music History*, 32 (2013), 179–223.

[20] In *Clamans in deserto*, the tenor is correctly designated IOHAN, since the final pitch of the melisma that corresponds to the syllable '-NE' is omitted in the motet tenor. This precision

Example 7.5 *Clamans in deserto/IOHAN[NE]*, **F**, fol. 409v.

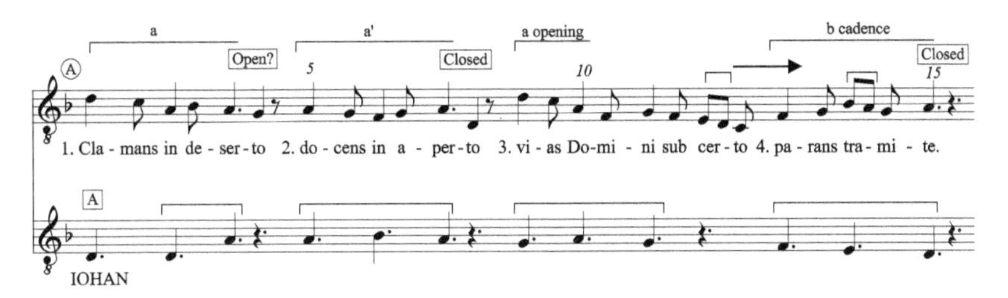

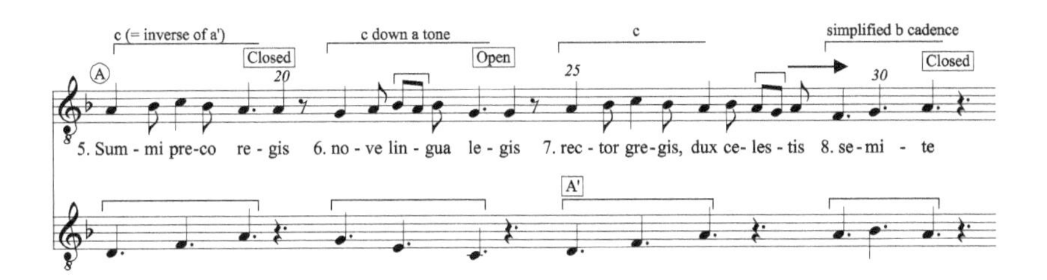

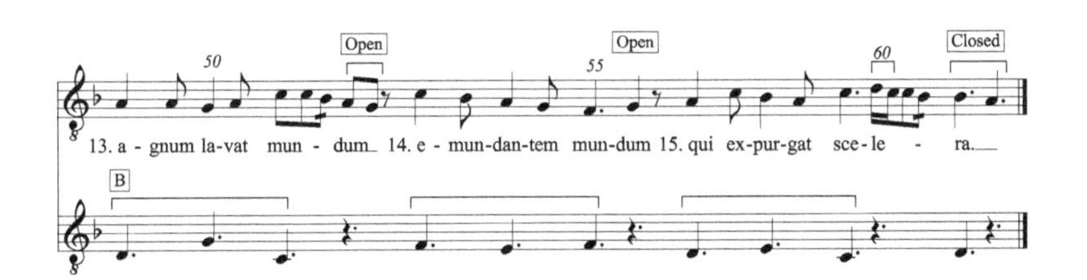

The sense of an AAB form in the upper voice is wholly independent from that of its underlying tenor chant. The two upper-voice *pedes* (perfections 1–16 and 17–32) are not identical, but they are nevertheless an indisputable pair, related chiefly by their shared phrase structure, which is abandoned in the following B section. Both *pedes* also have

with regard to the texting of plainchant quotations is characteristic of the liturgically ordered motets in **F**.

rhyming cadences (tonally and rhythmically, the second a simplified version of the first) and they behave motivically in the same way (marked in Example 7.5). Each *pes* states an opening motive (labelled a in perfection 1, and c in perfection 17), proceeds to manipulate it, and then returns to and extends the opening motive to lead towards a shared stressed and closed cadence (labelled b).

The carefully wrought and song-like design of this two-voice composition, which is achieved at the expense of literal plainchant quotation in the tenor, is much more characteristic of a vernacular motet than a clausula. As emphasised in the discussion of the *Propter veritatem* Gradual in Chapter 1, any manipulation of a chant tenor should not be equated with the denial of a liturgical function, since chant quotations were altered in organa and clausulae. Yet, as in the case of the *Propter veritatem* tenors, such manipulations usually became established as standard tenor versions (in liturgical as well as secular polyphony). That *Iohanne 3* is the *only* extant organum or clausula setting of this tenor to depart from its chant quotation, and simultaneously the only elaboration of this tenor in the *Magnus liber* to have a related motet, is significant. Whether or not this clausula in fact derives from a motet cannot be proven absolutely. In any case, the clausula's liberal and idiosyncratic treatment of its chant quotation, and the resulting formal and tonal effects achieved in its duplum, remain remarkable in this generic context. They therefore undermine the status of *Iohanne 3* as a model example of a typical clausula 'source', assumed to be part of the same tradition as other organa and substitute IOHANNE clausulae in the *Magnus liber*.

A conventional chronology for this network is complicated also by the relationship between *Iohanne 3* and its supposedly earliest incarnation as a motet, the Latin-texted *Clamans in deserto*, likewise unique to **F**. Numerous small musical variants indicate that this Latin motet was not copied or created in direct contact with the clausula preserved earlier in the same manuscript source. In fact, out of all extant two-voice motet versions, *Clamans in deserto* is probably the most distant from its related clausula: the Latin motet construes two phrases in a way that differs (though slightly) from all other versions of the clausula and its related motets (at perfections 33–6 and 45–8, marked by boxes in Example 7.5).[21] This is noteworthy in the context of a composition whose musical identity is otherwise very stable indeed. *Clamans in deserto* therefore constitutes something of

[21] The variant in this motet's final cadence is found also in the two-voice version of *Ne sai que je die* in **Mo** and in *Veritas arpie* in **Fauvel**, and is discussed in detail below.

an outlier in the written transmission of the IOHANNE clausula and the French motet *Ne sai que je die*. Furthermore, *Clamans in deserto* is extant only in **F**, enjoying a much more limited circulation than *Ne sai que je die*. It is preserved late in the **F** motet collection, within a cluster of other unica and contrafacta, at a point where the fascicle's liturgical sequence has broken down.[22] This evidence seems at odds with the idea, not only that the **F** motet represents the first texted incarnation of the clausula in the same manuscript, but also that it stands as the progenitor of a motet tradition that prompted later vernacular and Latin contrafacta.[23]

Text–Music Relationships: Chronological Clues and the Role of Text in the Motet's Identity

Regardless of their order of conception, all three motet texts associated with the IOHANNE duplum – *Clamans in deserto*, *Ne sai que je die*, and *Veritas arpie* – respond to and powerfully enhance its musical structure by essentially the same means (see Table 7.2, and Examples 7.4 and 7.5). The phrases of the IOHANNE motet are highly regular in terms of duration, strictly respecting – if occasionally eliding – the four-perfection units of the tenor ordines. As Marie Louise Göllner noted, however, the varying number and length of individual notes within each motetus phrase result in a poetic irregularity, where a tenor ordo might correspond to between three and eight syllables of text.[24] Although syllable counts and rates of musical declamation are themselves flexible within this motet, they remain identical across the three extant texts, whose rhyme schemes are likewise related. All three texts complement the *pedes cum cauda* (AAB) form of the motetus through a distinct alternation of rhymes common to both *pedes* (lines 1–4 and lines 5–8). In addition, each text consistently matches rhymes and

[22] On this group of motets, see Catherine A. Bradley, 'Ordering in the Motet Fascicles of the Florence Manuscript', *Plainsong and Medieval Music*, 22 (2013), 37–64 (pp. 55–60).

[23] Patterns of source transmission for the IOHANNE network are strikingly similar to a group of compositions on AMORIS, for which I have proposed a vernacular motet genesis, later resulting in a sacred Latin contrafactum text and clausula in **F** ('Contrafacta and Transcribed Motets', pp. 22–39). As in the case of the IOHANNE material, both the Latin troping AMORIS motet and its related clausula are unique to **F**, while the associated French motet text is much more widely transmitted. This AMORIS material also formed the basis of a three-voice double motet with a new fast-moving Franconian triplum. *Ne sai que je die/IOHANNE* and *He quant je remir/AMORIS* are the only two extant motets to appear in both the so-called 'old corpus' (fascicles 2–6) of **Mo** and an updated form in the later seventh fascicle.

[24] See Marie Louise Göllner, 'Rhythm and Pattern: The Two-Voice Motets of Codex Montpellier', *Viator*, 30 (1999), 145–63 (pp. 156–8).

Table 7.2 Comparing IOHANNE motet texts

1.	Clamans in deserto	**6a**	-erto	Ne sai que je die	**6a** -ie	Veritas arpie	**6a** -ie
2.	docens in aperto	**6a**	-erto	tant voi vilenie	**6a** -ie	fex ypocrisie	**6a** -ie
3.	vias Domini sub certo	**8a**	-erto	et orgueill et felonie	**8a** -ie	turpis lepra symonie	**8a** -ie
4.	parans tramite.	**5b**	-ite	monter en haut pris.	**5b** -is	scandunt solium.	**5b** -ium
5.	Summi preco regis	**6c**	-is	Toute cortoisie	**6a** -ie	Falsitatis vie	**6a** -ie
6.	nove lingua legis	**6c**	-is	s'en est si fouie	**6a** -ie	movent omni die	**6a** -ie
7.	rector gregis, dux celestis	**4c + 4c**	-is	qu'en tout ce siecle n'a mie	**8a** -ie	Christi veritate pie	**8a** -ie
8.	semite	**3b**	-ite	des boens dis,	**3b** -is	prelium.	**3b** -ium
9.	prodit ex effecta	**6d**	-ta	quar ypocrysie	**6a** -ie	Comites Golie	**6a** -ie
10.	partu sterilis fit leta.	**8d**	-ta	et avarice s'amie	**8a** -ie	spernunt David prophetie	**8a** -ie
11.	Culpe formite	**5b**	-ite	les ont si soupris,	**5b** -is	verba testium,	**5b** -ium
12.	proles libera	**5d'**	-era	ces qui plus ont pris	**5b** -is	perdunt premium	**5b** -ium
13.	agnum lavat mundum	**6e**	-undum	joie et cortoisie	**6a** -ie	filium Marie.	**6a** -ie
14.	emundantem mundum	**6e**	-undum	tienent a folie,	**6a** -ie	Similes Urie	**6a** -ie
15.	qui expurgat scelera.	**7d'**	-era	mes en devrie font pis.	**7b** -is	hostis tingunt gladium.	**7b** -ium

poetic stresses to the two alternative types of rhythmic musical cadence, which themselves match the tonal profile of the motetus. In the vernacular text *Ne sai que je die*, unstressed cadences are exclusively accompanied by the appropriate two-syllable feminine rhymes ('-ìe'), while stressed cadences correspond to single-syllable closing words with the rhyme '-is'. The corresponding Latinate stresses alternate in both *Clamans in deserto* and *Veritas arpie*: paroxytonic stresses ('desèrto' and 'arpìe', for instance) accompany the unstressed cadences, while stressed musical cadences receive proparoxytonic stresses ('tràmite' and 'sòlium', respectively).

Stressed and unstressed musical cadences are most starkly characterised in *Ne sai que je die* and *Veritas arpie*, both of which consistently and exclusive link rhymes and cadence types. Despite their different languages, the texts share the same feminine/paroxytonic rhyme, '-ìe'. This is a very common ending in French motets, but less so in Latin ones, and it is sustained in *Veritas arpie* principally through the use of nouns – occasionally proper nouns ('Golie', of Goliath; 'Marie', of Mary) – in the genitive case. This could indicate that *Veritas arpie* was modelled on the more widely transmitted *Ne sai que je die*, a possibility corroborated by the appearance of this Latin motet in **W2** within a group of contrafacta of widely disseminated vernacular texts.[25] A connection between the two motets is indicated also by their shared theme. *Ne sai que je die* is in the first person, mourning the growth of treachery, villainy, and hypocrisy, and the lack of joy and courtesy. These concerns are similarly expressed in *Veritas arpie*, though situated here in a more explicitly sacred context: falsehood and simony are not only destructive in themselves, but dishonour Christ.

By contrast, *Clamans in deserto* is removed from this pair of texts, thematically and structurally. This Latin text has a more intricate rhyme scheme, varying its paroxytonic rhyme between the two musical *pedes* (still linked by their shared rhyme scheme and proparoxytonic closing rhymes), and introducing three new rhymes in the motet's second half (lines 9–15). Line 7 uniquely features an internal rhyme, enhancing the musical momentum of an extended and sequential musical phrase that bridges two tenor ordines (see also perfections 25–8 in Example 7.5). Semantically, *Clamans in deserto* is a straightforward trope of its IOHANNE tenor, invoking common Johannine epithets, and emphasising the Baptist's role as Christ's precursor. The motet's suitability for liturgical use, possibly even for substitution within an organum in place of a melismatic IOHANNE clausula,

[25] On the place of *Veritas arpie* among other contrafacta in **W2**, see Anderson, *The Latin Compositions in Fascicules VII and VIII*, Part I, p. 381.

has misleadingly been equated with the necessity of its chronological priority.[26] Conversely, the alternative priority of *Ne sai que je die* has been undermined by the fact that its text is of an unusual type for a vernacular motet. It is a so-called *Rügelied* (a 'complaining text', often anti-clerical) that is much more typical of Latin motets and conducti, and particularly of texts associated with Philip the Chancellor.[27] Nevertheless, such complaints in the vernacular are not unknown. I have previously demonstrated that *Fole acoustumance/DOMINO* – a motet on the same theme as *Ne sai que je die*, and with considerable lexical overlap – probably originated as a vernacular motet that was reworked as a Latin contrafactum uniquely recorded in **F**.[28] There is, therefore, no reason why this IOHANNE material could not also have been first conceived as a French motet of this, albeit slightly atypical, cast.[29]

The basic structural similarity of the three extant IOHANNE motet texts limits chronological conclusions possible on purely musico-textual grounds. All three of the motets neatly reflect their musical structure, complementing its *pedes cum cauda* form and cadence types. *Ne sai que je die* and *Veritas arpie* are just as likely to be later and simplified responses to the more varied rhyme scheme of *Clamans in deserto*, as is this motet itself to be an elaboration of an earlier poetic model. None of the motets shows any of the kind of variants that might suggest a text accommodated to pre-existing material, such as additional notes or anacruses for additional syllables, or unconventional word stress in a Latin motetus. This consistency across these extant IOHANNE texts is, in itself, revealing. More often than not, small details of syllable count and rhyme differ between contrafactum motet texts, which frequently introduce unobtrusive extra

[26] Rebecca A. Baltzer, for instance, includes *Clamans in deserto* within her list of motets suitable for liturgical use. See 'Performance Practice: The Notre-Dame Calendar and the Earliest Latin Liturgical Motets' (unpublished paper presented at Das Ereignis Notre Dame, Wolfenbüttel, 1985), p. 42, available online at *Archivum de musica medii aevi*, www.univ-nancy2.fr/MOYENAGE/UREEF/MUSICOLOGIE/AdMMAe/AdMMAe_index.htm (accessed 1 March 2018).

[27] See, for instance, Thomas B. Payne's discussion of the date and context for 'complaining' texts by Philip the Chancellor, in 'Chancellor *versus* Bishop: The Conflict between Philip the Chancellor and Guillaume d'Auvergne in Poetry and Music', in Gilbert Dahan and Ann-Zoé Rillon-Marne (eds.), *Philippe le Chancelier: Prédicateur, théologien, et poète parisien du début du XIIIe siècle*, Bibliothèque d'histoire culturelle du Moyen Age 19 (Turnhout, 2017), pp. 265–306. I thank Professor Payne for sharing this material in advance of publication.

[28] See my 'Contrafacta and Transcribed Motets', pp. 8–22.

[29] Susan Stakel noted the rarity of vernacular 'complaining' texts, of which there are only eight in **Mo**. See Joel C. Relihan and Susan Stakel (eds.), *The Montpellier Codex, Part IV: Texts and Translations*, RRMMA 8 (Madison, 1985), p. xix.

pitches or anacruses.[30] Stressed and unstressed cadences – easily altered by the simple addition or removal of a single pitch – are likewise typically unstable between clausulae and motets, and also occasionally between contrafacta.[31] The consistency of music and texts associated with this IOHANNE material makes chronologising difficult, but it is revealing in another respect. Such unusual consistency seems to be testament to the memorability and coherence of this piece of music, a piece that 'works' so well that it simply cannot be misremembered or altered, particularly not if one knows one of its accompanying motet texts, in which notes, syllables, rhymes, and cadences are so closely interwoven.

A Memorable Motet of 'Classic' Status?

What exactly, then, might make these IOHANNE motets 'work' so well? It seems to be the combination of multiple and complementary aspects of their design noted above: the opposition of clearly defined tonalities and of rhythmic cadences, matched to text stresses and rhymes in the motetus; the regularity of phrase units in combination with variety in the individual rates of text declamation and syllable counts; and the large-scale repetitive structure of the *pedes cum cauda* form, again enhanced by the structure of the motet texts. Poetically, the short line-lengths of these texts – never exceeding eight syllables – might make them easier to remember. And the fact that text rhymes are principally grouped and reiterated in succession, rather than in a cross-rhyme structure, has a comparable effect (especially in *Ne sai que je die* and *Veritas arpie*, which confine themselves to just two rhymes throughout). In terms of musical motives, the motet's palette is likewise tightly controlled. Similarities in motivic treatment between the two motetus *pedes* were emphasised above, but the musical character of these motives themselves, and of the motet's opening in particular, is also very distinctive.

[30] See, for instance, the discussion of Latin contrafacta in which syllable count and rhyme schemes vary, in Catherine A. Bradley, 'Re-workings and Chronological Dynamics in a Thirteenth-Century Latin Motet Family', *Journal of Musicology*, 32 (2015), 153–97 (pp. 161–3).

[31] Stressed and unstressed cadences vary between the LATUS clausula and its related motets analysed in ibid. For an example of a motet family in which the use of stressed and unstressed cadences varies between contrafactum motet texts, see the discussion of the VIRGO motets *Crescens incredulitas* and *Por conforter mon corage*, in Catherine A. Bradley, 'The Earliest Motets: Musical Borrowing and Re-Use', Ph.D. diss. (University of Cambridge, 2011), pp. 168–79.

As a musical beginning, the first eight perfections of the IOHANNE material are both aurally striking and remarkably efficient in setting the compositional parameters of the whole piece (see Example 7.5). The motetus immediately delineates its modal range and character in a pair of phrases, falling (in perfections 1–4) from the upper D down to A, and then (in perfections 5–8) from A down to the lower D. In perfection 3, A seems to be a stable tonal goal, only to be immediately unsettled by the motetus G in perfection 4, effectively setting up a dichotomy between closed and open pitches in the very first ordo. This unstressed cadence is answered in perfections 7–8, when the motetus A descends, not a tone to G, but – in stark contrast to its hitherto step-wise movement – by the interval of a fifth to D, another closed sonority, and the final of the chant tenor as well as the motetus's opening pitch. The function of this pair of phrases is confirmed and clarified by the following eight-perfection phrase, which concludes the first *pes*, where perfections 9–16 re-enact the descent from upper D to lower D, rising to culminate in a strongly articulated stressed cadence on A.

That the IOHANNE material was indeed memorable is confirmed, not only by the evidence that it itself was well travelled, but also by its influence, perceptible in the repertoire at large. As emphasised above, the version of the IOHANNE tenor particular to *Ne sai que je die* and its related clausula and motets unconventionally begins D–D–A, unlike any other extant version of the IOHANNE plainchant melisma or polyphonic tenor. On one occasion in **Mo** (fol. 93v), the scribe of fascicle 4 encountered this D–D–A opening in the context of the tenor chant *Ave maris stella*. He mislabelled the tenor of the motet *Ave beatissima/Ave Maria gratia plena/AVE MARIS STELLA* as IOHANNE, evidently familiar with the particular version of the chant employed in the *Ne sai que je die* motet family and thereby associating its D–D–A opening with the IOHANNE tenor.[32] Motivations for a musical variant at the opening of the IOHANNE melisma in the motet *Sans orgueil/IOHANNE* as recorded in **W2** are similarly revealing.[33] The only other extant version of *Sans orgueil* in **Mo** begins (conventionally) D–A, with the tenor in ternary longs, according to its rhythmic pattern. The copy of *Sans orgueil/IOHANNE* in **W2**, however, features an extra initial tenor

[32] See Friedrich Ludwig's discussion of this motet (Mt603a–b) in his *Repertorium organorum recentioris et motetorum vetustissimi stili*, ed. Luther A. Dittmer, 2 vols. in 3 (New York, 1964–78 [1910]), Vol. I/2, pp. 393–4.

[33] The motetus opening in this two-voice motet is reminiscent of *Ne sai que je die*, beginning with the pitches D–C–A in the same rhythm. See the edition of *Sans orgueil/IOHANNE* in Hans Tischler, *The Earliest Motets (to circa 1270): A Complete Comparative Edition* (New Haven, 1982), Vol. II, no. 197, pp. 1134–5.

D, which is both unnecessary and rhythmically disruptive in this context. Once again, this appears to betray the influence of the *Ne sai que je die* motets, whose initial manipulation of the IOHANNE tenor opening seemingly became widely known, such that the scribes of motets considered it typical, adopting or identifying it (admittedly incorrectly) in independent contexts.[34]

It was surely this classic status that ensured, later in the thirteenth century, the reworking of *Ne sai que je die* with a fast-moving so-called Franconian triplum in the double motet *Quant vient en mai/Ne sai que je die/IOHANNE* (see Example 7.6). It was highly unusual for an older two-voice work to form the basis of a new one in this way, and only a single other motet in the repertoire – the similarly widely attested *He quant je remir/AMORIS*, from which a sacred Latin motet and clausula recorded uniquely in **F** apparently derived – received comparable treatment.[35] In both cases, the musical impact of the added triplum on the older two-voice motet is considerable. In order to accommodate a third voice in which – according to a new theoretical system attributed to Franco – breves can be subdivided into as many as three semibreves, the length of time allotted to a breve in performance must increase.[36] That is, the pulse of the pre-existing motet must be slowed down substantially to facilitate many extra fast notes in the added triplum. This compromises or at least obscures the musical character of *Ne sai que je die/IOHANNE*: what was once a jaunty, melodic motetus becomes part of a rather more staid musical foundation, its melody drawn out rhythmically in the middle of a three-voice texture.[37]

[34] Of the seven IOHANNE motets, only three include the opening D–A of the tenor melisma: *Ne sai que je die* (with an added D), *Sans orgeuil*, and *Ioanne Yelisabet* (recorded uniquely in **Ma**). The four remaining vernacular motets on this tenor begin instead on the melisma's third pitch, opening A–B–A. See also the summary of these different types of IOHANNE motet tenors in Thomas, 'The *Iohanne* Melisma', p. 11. The elimination of the melisma's opening pitches in vernacular motet tenors may have been the result of confusion about the 'correct' version of the IOHANNE opening, prompted by *Ne sai que je die* and its related motets. Additionally or alternatively, it may reflect a cross-fertilisation with the AMORIS tenor, which also begins A–B–A. This kinship between IOHANNE and AMORIS explains – as demonstrated by Fred Büttner (*Das Klauselrepertoire der Handschrift Saint-Victor*, p. 151) – why the tenor of *Quant vient/Ne sai que je die* in **Ba** is mislabelled AMORIS, even though the motet tenor here actually includes the IOHANNE tenor's opening D–A.

[35] On a vernacular motet origin for this AMORIS material see my 'Contrafacta and Transcribed Motets', pp. 22–39. See also the discussion of its remarkable similarities in transmission with the IOHANNE network in n. 23 above.

[36] On the erroneous tenor designation AMORIS in **Ba** see n. 34 above.

[37] On theoretical evidence for the slowing down of tempo occasioned by semibreves, see Margaret Bent, *Magister Jacobus de Ispania, Author of the 'Speculum musicae'*, Royal Musical Association Monographs 28 (Ashgate, 2015), pp. 39–42.

Example 7.6 Opening of *Quant vient en mai/Ne sai que je die/AMORIS* (*sic*), **Ba**, fols. 44r–45r.

In a sense, this is analogous, more generally, to the treatment of pre-existing plainchant melodies in motet tenors. The fluency with which plainchant melismas would presumably have been sung monophonically is curtailed in polyphony by their arrangement, note by note, in a typically strict and slow-moving rhythmic pattern.

Arguably, the memorability of *Ne sai que je die* led to its appearance as the basis for a Franconian triplum, but in this transformation, the character of its own musical material was ultimately compromised, overshadowed, and to some extent disregarded. This is corroborated by certain textual and musical features of the added triplum, which is thematically distinct from *Ne sai que je die* and its Latin counterparts, since it is neither a tropic nor a 'complaining' text. *Quant vient en mai* is instead a highly conventional *pastourelle*: out on a spring-time ride, a knight encounters a shepherdess who confides that her lover, Robin, has been unfaithful and that she seeks to win him back. Although Michael Alan Anderson has suggested that certain mid-summer themes in this text (the shepherdess's search for a mate, or her references to flowers and dancing) may resonate with the IOHANNE tenor, the stark generic contrast of this *pastourelle* text and the complete independence of its rhymes and poetic structure are nonetheless marked.[38]

The triplum is musically more consonant with its lower voices.[39] It frequently produces the sonority characteristic of three-part writing, in which a fifth is framed within an octave. At the motet's opening, for instance, the triplum supplies the pitch A, within the motetus and tenor's D–D octave. Similarly, at perfection 15, the arrival on the first stressed cadence at the end of the opening A section in the motetus, the triplum provides the D an octave above the tenor, framing the motetus A. Initially, then, the added voice largely preserves the tonal character, and indeed the phrase structure, of its underlying motetus. But this is short lived: a shared upper-voice phrase structure breaks down at perfection 15, from which point on the triplum cuts across the regular motetus phrases, operating independently of its stressed and unstressed, closed and open, cadences. The sense of binary opposition of the cadences on A and G in the motetus is undermined in the double motet, by the fact that the triplum sounds the D above in combination with both closed and open sonorities. In addition, the triplum alternatively pairs motetus As with the E a fifth above (as at perfection 19), thereby diluting the identity of this cadence. I do not argue that the triplum is unsympathetic to its musical foundation, nor do I question its quality, but seek instead to emphasise its fundamentally different compositional approach to this material. Surely a result of the memorability, simplicity, and regularity of *Ne sai que je die*, the two-voice motet became a vehicle for musical experimentation in a declamatory and highly florid vocal style. It was an excellent basis upon which to build a triplum that was principally preoccupied with the exploration of new technological possibilities in rhythmic notation, which consequently dictated a slower tempo for its two-voice foundation, and surely dominated the aural impression of the motet in performance.

The Reception of Thirteenth-Century Motets in the *Roman de Fauvel*

The final appearance of the IOHANNE material in the fourteenth-century *Roman de Fauvel* is not in this most up-to-date double motet version, but in its earlier two-voice form with the Latin text *Veritas arpie*, also recorded

[38] See Anderson, 'Fire, Foliage, and Fury', pp. 30–3.

[39] The triplum lacks the B flat signature of motetus and tenor in both **Ba** and **Mo**.

in **W2**. This motet is a perfect fit for the programme of the **Fauvel** manuscript, where it appears at the point in the narrative when the eponymous protagonist is at the height of his powers, ruler of all religious orders. Fauvel is about to cement his position in society further by attempting to marry Fortune. In preparation for this marriage in which Fortune is ultimately substituted for Vaine Gloire, the motet *Veritas arpie* is presented in the context of a long list of Fauvel's courtiers, all of whom are similarly allegorical figures of various vices. The Latin motet opens with a comparable list of sins (simony, hypocrisy, falsity), which resonate with the corruption of the Fauvel narrative, since they have likewise been used to achieve power. And as Anderson has emphasised, the motet text closes with allusions to biblical figures (Goliath, Uriah the Hittite) whose downfall was – like Fauvel's own – imminent.[40] The vernacular motet text *Ne sai que je die* would have served equally well to paint this moral. Yet the majority of musical interpolations in fr. 146 are in Latin rather than the vernacular, and all of the compositions (prosae, conducti, and motets) that are either attested in thirteenth-century manuscripts or are in a so-called *Ars vetus* or *Ars antiqua* style are Latin-texted.[41] The choice of *Veritas arpie*, a lesser-known Latin text and without any obfuscating Franconian triplum, is in keeping with the style of thirteenth-century interpolations in this manuscript more generally, arguably enhancing their status as recognisably 'old', possibly with attendant connotations of textual authority.[42]

Although *Veritas arpie* seems almost tailor-made for the satirical *Roman de Fauvel* the circumstances of its selection by the compilers of fr. 146 remain elusive. How or why did they know a musical composition that had been conceived nearly a century ago, and how exactly did they access it? Edward H. Roesner, François Avril, and Nancy Freeman Regalado have emphasised that the interpolated *Roman* was an idiosyncratic compilation of various texts and music, placed alongside one another for the first time in this source rather than simply reproducing a single already-existing exemplar. Underlining the importance of written records in this compilation project they observed:

> That most of what appears in the manuscript was indeed copied from already existing material is obvious, both on its face and from the large number of scribal

[40] See Anderson, 'Fire, Foliage, and Fury', pp. 41–3.

[41] For a complete list of *Ars vetus*-style compositions in **Fauvel**, see Maria Vedder Fowler, 'Musical Interpolations in Thirteenth- and Fourteenth-Century French Narratives', Ph.D. diss., 2 vols. (Yale University, 1979), Vol. I, Table 19, pp. 125–6.

[42] The use of noticeably 'older' musical interpolations in vernacular texts is, for instance, evident also, and perhaps similar in purpose, in Gautier de Coinci's *Miracles de nostre dame*.

errors ... these materials ... must have been of various sorts and included several different kinds of manuscripts ... finished books, less formal *libelli* or loose fascicles, single sheets ... several different books of music.[43]

In his survey of thirteenth-century conducti in **Fauvel**, Lorenz Welker corroborated the view that the fourteenth-century scribe engaged with this older music in its written form. Welker identified, for example, an instance in which the text scribe in **Fauvel** was evidently referring to a manuscript that resembled extant thirteenth-century music books. The text scribe left space for a lengthy melisma recorded in these earlier sources but that was later expunged in the accompanying music as copied in **Fauvel**.[44] In addition, certain voices of polyphonic conducti were apparently excerpted in **Fauvel**, and some quite heavily reworked, in ways that reveal a dependence principally on written sources, rather than any oral memory of the pieces in question.[45] Welker suggested that the conducti in **Fauvel** were probably drawn from a single thirteenth-century book, and one that must have closely resembled **F**, since all but one of the twenty-three conducti in **Fauvel** are also recorded in **F**.

In the case of the motet *Veritas arpie*/*IOHANNE*, none of the extant *Ars antiqua* manuscripts offers a neat match as a source for the **Fauvel** version, but a written transmission of this piece is highly probable. That the scribe worked from a mid-thirteenth-century book like **W2**, the only earlier extant manuscript to record the text *Veritas arpie*, seems most likely. This fits with Joseph Morin's hypothesis that *Veritas arpie* was copied into **Fauvel** from an exemplar that was in pre-mensural notation.[46] The **Fauvel** scribe confuses his breve and long rests in this motet, indicating that he probably worked from a source (like **F** or **W2**, but unlike **Mo**, **LoC**, or **Ba**) in which the length of rests was not prescribed. Musically and textually, however, the **Fauvel** copy of *Veritas arpie* diverges in various slight ways from that in **W2**. Most notable is the different choice of musical ending

[43] See Edward H. Roesner, François Avril, and Nancy Freeman Regalado (eds.), *'Le Roman de Fauvel' in the Edition of Mesier Chaillou de Pesstain: A Reproduction in Facsimile of the Complete Manuscript Bibliothèque nationale de France, Fonds Français 146* (New York, 1990), p. 29.

[44] Lorenz Welker, 'Polyphonic Reworkings of Notre-Dame Conductûs in BN f. 146: *Mundus a mundicia* and *Quare fremuerunt*', in Margaret Bent and Andrew Wathey (eds.), *Fauvel Studies: Allegory, Chronicle, Music, and Image in Paris Bibliothèque nationale de France, MS Français 146* (Oxford, 1998), pp. 615–36 (p. 618).

[45] Ibid., pp. 631–5. See also Joseph Charles Morin, 'The Genesis of Manuscript Paris Bibliothèque nationale, fonds français 146, with Particular Emphasis on the "Roman de Fauvel"', Ph.D. diss. (New York University, 1992), pp. 325–44.

[46] See Morin, 'The Genesis of fr. 146', p. 271 n. 54.

for the two versions of this Latin motet. The version in **Fauvel** concludes with an appoggiatura-like cadence, in which B flat sounds above the ultimate tenor D before falling to resolve on the final pitch A.[47] This closing cadence is found also in *Clamans in deserto* in **F** (see Example 7.5), and in *Ne sai que je die* in **Mo**, but crucially in neither version of the material recorded in **W2**.

Textually, the key discrepancy between the two sources of *Veritas arpie* concerns its first word. In **Fauvel**, this is unambiguously 'Veritas', but the **W2** motet opens 'Oecitas'. The painted initial 'O' here is erroneous, since the intended word must have been 'Cecitas', the sin of blindness, and an appropriate start to the motet's list of comparable evils.[48] 'Cecitas arpie' – meaning the blindness of the harpy, or the person consumed by greed – makes better sense than 'Veritas arpie', which ascribes to rapacity the virtue of truth.[49] A change from 'Cecitas' (in **W2**) to 'Veritas' (in **Fauvel**) does not seem to indicate a Fauvelian adaptation: in fact, quite the reverse. Had the **Fauvel** scribe known the 'Cecitas' opening, then he would surely have employed it: it fittingly leads with a vice, rather than a virtue, mimicking the catalogue of vices in the prosa *Carnalitas luxuria* on the preceding folio (12r-v), which includes 'cecitas' in its list.[50] The erroneous initial in **W2** seems testament to some confusion about the motet's incipit in the thirteenth century.[51] And the adoption of the 'veritas' opening in fr. 146, seems further confirmation that the compilers of this manuscript were not working from an exemplar related directly to **W2**, in which 'cecitas' is the most obvious solution and the most attractive choice for the Fauvel narrative.

The copy of *Veritas arpie* in **Fauvel**, therefore, is evidence of a lost written record, further confirming the status of this IOHANNE motet, for which

[47] The final cadence in **Fauvel** recalls similar appoggiatura-like cadence figures in perfections 3–4 and 55–6. Anderson ('Fire, Foliage, and Fury', p. 44) has underlined the 'threatening quality' of this ending, which 'deepens the emotion' of the satirical texts *Veritas arpie* and *Ne sai que je die*. This argument is, however, undermined by the fact that the 'threatening' ending also features in the Latin tropic motet *Clamans in deserto*.

[48] The sixteenth-century Lutheran reformer Matthias Flacius Illyricus established the incipit as *Cecitas* in his transcription of motet texts in **W2**.

[49] I thank Andrews Hicks for his assistance in translating these Latin texts. Anderson interprets 'Veritas arpie' as 'Truthfulness to the sword' ('Fire, Foliage, and Fury', p. 41), but the Latin word *(h)arpe* (sword) cannot be declined *arpie*.

[50] See the discussion of 'cecitas' in **Fauvel** in Elizabeth A. R. Brown, 'Rex ioians, ionnes, iolis: Louis X, Philip V, and the Livers de Fauvel', in Bent and Wathey, *Fauvel Studies*, pp. 54–72 (p. 68).

[51] Curiously, [C]*ecitas arpie* appears in **W2** as the penultimate piece in an alphabetically ordered series (preceding *O viri Israhelite*/*OMNES*), a position that would be more appropriate if the motet began 'Veritas'.

extant sources, though ample, are evidently only a partial reflection of its fame. The case of *Veritas arpie* also indicates that the state of *Ars antiqua* motet exemplars in **Fauvel** stands in complex relation to surviving manuscripts. No previous study has focused in detail on the eight compositions in **Fauvel** with concordances (full or partial) in the thirteenth-century motet repertoire. In identifying and scrutinising this corpus some significant patterns emerge (see Table 7.3). The eight 'old' motets adopted in **Fauvel** are fairly widely transmitted by thirteenth-century standards: all are extant in at least two sources, with the majority of the pieces in at least four different manuscripts, and two are cited in theoretical treatises. The only exception is the **Fauvel** motet *Ade costa dormientis/Tenor*, whose thirteenth-century concordance is known only through the appearance of its text in a surviving index (**LoHa**) for a now lost English motet book, dated to the 1290s.[52] The paucity of manuscript witnesses for this motet is surprising, as is its only known appearance in an insular source, which suggests that the range of materials at the disposal of the **Fauvel** scribes was wide indeed.[53]

Interestingly, all eight of the old motets in **Fauvel** existed in thirteenth-century sources as three-voice pieces – either monotextual or 'conductus' motets and/or double motets – of which six circulated additionally in two-voice forms. Three of the motets are found also as clausulae in **F**, and a fourth is transcribed as a clausula in the St Victor manuscript. Half of the motets have contrafacta texts in both French and Latin. Such dissemination in a variety of sources and versions seems to confirm the overall status of these thirteenth-century pieces as relatively well known. This was musical material that was adapted to various forms and – with two exceptions – spanned mid- and late-thirteenth-century written records.[54] No single

[52] For more information on **LoHa**, the so-called Harley index, see Peter M. Lefferts, 'Sources of Thirteenth-Century English Polyphony: Catalogue with Descriptions', *University of Nebraska Lincoln Faculty Publications: School of Music*, Paper 45 (2012), http://digitalcommons.unl.edu/musicfacpub/45/ (accessed 14 March 2018).

[53] On English pieces in **Fauvel**, see Morin, 'The Genesis of fr. 146', p. 23 n. 44. Only one other piece in **Fauvel** – also a motet – has been identified as English; see Ernest H. Sanders, 'Peripheral Polyphony of the 13th Century', *Journal of the American Musicological Society*, 17 (1964), 261–87 (p. 285 n. 121). Sanders asserts the English origin of *Zelus familie/Iehsu tu dator/*[*Tenor*] (**Fauvel**, fol. 44r), purely on stylistic grounds. This hypothesis may, however, be undermined by a concordance – of which Sanders was apparently unaware – for the motetus text (but not its music) in two fourteenth-century Italian manuscripts: **ArsC**, fol. 177r (text only: *Ihesue tu dator venie ... penetentie* follows within a text that begins *Ave Gesu Christe*), and Florence, Biblioteca nazionale II. I. 122, fols. 84r–85r (where the text in **ArsC** is found as the motetus of a two-voice motet, *Ave Jesu Christe verbum patris/Tenor*, with music that differs from **Fauvel**). On these concordances, see Ludwig, *Repertorium*, Vol. I/2, pp. 707, 709.

[54] The exceptions are *Et exaltavi* (recorded only in **F** and **W2**) and *Ade costa dormientis* (only in **LoHa**).

Table 7.3 Fauvel interpolations with concordances in the thirteenth-century motet repertoire

Fauvel interpolation and description in relation to thirteenth-century model	Thirteenth-century motet concordances
Fauvellandi vicium/Tenor, fol. 1r (two-voice motet) Motetus, with new Latin text, based on triplum of Latin monotextual motet; newly composed tenor	Three-voice French double motet *Bien me doi Cum li plus desperes/IN CORDE*: **W2** (fols. 202v–203r); **Mo** (fols. 185v–188r) Three-voice Latin monotextual or 'conductus' motet *De gravi seminio/De gravi seminio*: **Ma** (fols. 2v–3r, lacking tenor) Two-voice Latin motet *De gravi seminio/IN CORDE*: **W2** (fols. 157v–158r)
In marie miserie/Tenor, fol. 2v (two-voice motet) Triplum and tenor, with added (dissonant) Fauvelising coda	Three-voice French double motet *De la vile/A la vile/MANERE*: **W2** (fol. 212r–v); **R** (fol. 207r–v); **N** (fols. 186v–187r); **StV** (fol. 288r, clausula transcription a fifth higher with marginal motet incipit) Three-voice Latin double motet *In marie miserie/Gemma pudicicie/MANERE*: **Mo** (fols. 99v–100v)
Ad solitum vomitum/Tenor, fol. 2v (two-voice motet) Motetus and tenor, with added Fauvelising coda (for which the tenor is too short)	Two-voice clausula *Regnat 13*, **F**, fol. 167r–3 Three-voice Latin monotextual or 'conductus' motet: *Ad solitum vomitum/Ad solitum vomitum /REGNAT*: **F** (fol. 394v); **W2** (fols. 128v–129r) Two-voice Latin motet *Ad solitum vomitum/REGNAT*: **W2** (fols. 155v–156r); **Ma** (fol. 127v, lacking tenor) Three-voice Latin double motet *Despositum creditum/Ad solitum vomitum /REGNAT*: **Ba** (fol. 4v–5r)
Et exaltavi plebis humilem, fol. 9r (monophonic prosa) Motetus voice only, unaltered	Three-voice clausula **F**, fol. 46r Three-voice Latin 'conductus' or monotextual motet: *Et exaltavi plebis humilem/Et exaltavi plebis humilem/ET EXALTAVI*: **F** (fols. 395r–396r); **W2** (fols. 124r–125r) Two-voice Latin motet *Et exaltavi plebis humilem/ET EXALTAVI*: **W2** (fols. 159v–160r)
Condicio/O natio nephandi/MANE PRIMA SABBATI, fol. 11v (three-voice double motet)	Three-voice Latin double motet *Condicio/O natio nephandi/MANE*: **Mo** (fols. 87v–89r); **Ba** (fols. 49v–50v); **Da** (fol. 7r–v); **Bes** (no. 5 in index of text incipits, no extant music)

Triplum, motetus, and tenor, unaltered	Two-voice Latin motet *O natio nephandi/MANE*: **LoD** (fol. 52v) Two-voice Latin motet *Condicio/MANE*: **Worc** (fragment 35, fol. 5v) Cited in *Discantus positio vulgaris* and by anonymous St Emmeram
Veritas arpie/Tenor IOHANNE, fol. 13v (two-voice motet) Motetus and tenor, unaltered	Two-voice clausula *Iohanne 3*: **F** (fol. 164v–1) Two-voice Latin motets *Clamans in deserto/IOHANNE*: **F** (fol. 409v) *Oecitas arpie/IOHANNE* (*sic*): **W2** (fols. 191v–192r) Two-voice French motet *Ne sai que je die/IOHANNE*: **W2** (fol. 219ar); **Mo** (fols. 234v–235r); **LoC** (fol. 3r); **Bes** (no. 26 in index of text incipits, no extant music) Three-voice French double motet *Quant vient en mai/Ne sai que je die/IOHANNE*: **Mo** (fols. 305v–306v); **Ba** (fols. 44r–45r) Franco cites incipit *Arida frondescit/IOHANNE*
Ade costa dormentitis/Tenor, fol. 13v (two-voice motet) Motetus and tenor, with added Fauvelising coda (for which the tenor is too short)	Three-voice double motet [*Triplum*]/*De costa dormientis*/[*Tenor*]: **LoHa** (fol. 161r, no. 19 in an index of double motets, for an English codex dated to the 1290s). Only motetus texts are recorded, under the heading 'item [moteti] cum duplici littera'
Celi domina/Maria, virgo virginum/PORCHIER, fol. 42v (three-voice double motet) No musical concordance Latin triplum text is employed in full with Fauvelised ending Latin motetus incipit is adapted and the text continues independently Tenor is **Fauvel** *rondeau, Porchier miex ester ameroie* (fol. 10r)[a]	Three-voice French double motet *None sans amor/Moine qui a cuer jolif/ET SUPER*: **W2** (fol. 207r–v); **Mo** (fols. 152v–154r); **Cl** (fol. 374r) Three-voice Latin double motet *Celi domina/Ave, virgo virginum/ET SUPER*: **Ba** (fol 3r–v); **Da** (fol. 3v, incomplete); **Hu** (fol. 115r) Two-voice Latin motet *Ave, virgo virginum/ET SUPER*: **ArsB** (fol. 2v) Two-voice French motet *Nouvelement m'a soupris/ET SUPER*: **N** (fol. 181v, probably also copied in **R**, but now missing)

[a] For an edition of this **Fauvel** motet, a summary of previous scholarly observations, and discussion of its relationship to the **Fauvel** *rondeau, Porchier*, see Yolanda Plumley, *The Art of Grafted Song: Citation and Allusion in the Age of Machaut* (Oxford, 2013), pp. 96–9.

thirteenth-century source contains all eight of the pieces, although **W2** preserves six of them, while **Mo** has five. Yet just two of the **W2** motets could offer any direct match with versions in **Fauvel**.[55] Similarly, only two of the five **Mo** motets are found in the same form as in fr. 146.[56] Unlike the larger repertoire of thirteenth-century conductus in **Fauvel**, which overlaps significantly with the contents of **F**, no such convincing conclusion can be drawn about a single possible prototype exemplar for this small group of motets. Perhaps there was once such a thirteenth-century book containing all of these motets. But more probably, the compilers of **Fauvel** mined a rich and diverse array of documents, some of which were the same as, or very like, those that survive today.

Regardless of their thirteenth-century motet exemplar(s), certain selection criteria seem to have remained consistent in **Fauvel**. With two exceptions, **Fauvel** eschews three-voice versions of these pieces, possibly because of concerns of space and presentation.[57] Vernacular texts seem also to have been avoided, and in two instances otherwise unique Latin texts were adopted instead of better-known French ones.[58] The majority of these old motets were subjected to reworking in their fourteenth-century incarnations. Three of the pieces had their endings 'Fauvelised';[59] in two cases motet voices were excerpted and presented in new reduced contexts;[60] in the Fauvel motet *Fauvellandi vicium*, a thirteenth-century triplum was radically recomposed and given a new tenor;[61] and the motet *Celi domina/*

55 The versions of *Et exaltavi* and *Ad solitum* in **Fauvel** correspond to those in **W2**. I have argued that the versions of *Veritas arpie* in **Fauvel** and **W2** stem from different sources; *In Marie miserie* and *Celi domina/Maria, virgo virginum* are found only in French contrafactum versions in **W2**. In the case of *Fauvellandi vicium*, Morin proposes that the reworked triplum is closest musically to French motets in **W2** and **Mo** ('The Genesis of fr. 146', p. 339). Yet Edward H. Roesner has recently emphasised that the interpretation of *Fauvellandi vicium* depends on the Latin motet version, *De gravi/De gravi/IN CORDE*. See Edward H. Roesner, 'Labouring in the Midst of Wolves: Reading a Group of Fauvel Motets', *Early Music History*, 22 (2003), 169–245 (pp. 185–91). This Latin motet in **W2** lacks the relevant triplum.

56 *In marie miserie* and *Condicio/O natio nephandi/MANE* appear in the same form in **Fauvel** and **Mo**. *Veritas arpie* and *Celi domina/Maria, virgo virginum* appear in **Mo** with vernacular texts, while the Latin triplum reworked in *Fauvellandi vicium* (see n. 55) is extant only in the context of a vernacular contrafactum in **Mo**.

57 The exceptions are the double motets *Condicio/O natio nephandi/MANE PRIMA SABBATI*, and *Celi domina/Maria, virgo virginum/PORCHIER*, whose music was newly created in **Fauvel**.

58 In *Veritas arpie* and *In marie miserie*.

59 *Ad solitum vomitum*, *In marie miserie*, and *Ade costa dormentitis*.

60 In *Exaltavi plebis humiles* (presented as a monophonic *prosa* in Fauvel) and *In marie miserie* (where the thirteenth-century triplum and tenor appear only in **Fauvel** without the motetus).

61 Morin ('The Genesis of fr. 146', pp. 325–44) demonstrated the adaptation of this triplum from a written exemplar that is no longer extant, presented in **Fauvel** in new polyphonic combination with a tenor melody loosely modelled on the existing IN CORDE chant. On *Fauvellandi*

Maria, virgo virginum/PORCHIER bears no musical relationship at all to its thirteenth-century textual counterpart.[62] These adaptions occasionally compromised musical sense: the tenors of *Ad solium vomitum* and *Ade costa dormientis* are too short to accompany the Fauvel-specific material at the end of their upper voices, while the removal of the thirteenth-century motetus *Gemma pudicicie* in **Fauvel**'s *In marie miserie* showed little concern for the harmonic interdependence of the upper voices of the earlier double motet.[63]

In this context, it is remarkable that *Veritas arpie* appears in **Fauvel** relatively untouched. Admittedly, the motet text itself was already very pertinent, but the compilers nevertheless retained its standard two-voice musical form, without any alteration, excerption, or the addition of a Fauvellian coda. Only the exceptional double motet *Condicio/O natio nephandi/ MANE PRIMA SABBATI* was preserved so faithfully and *in toto*, perhaps because it was a late addition to the manuscript, as Morin has suggested, or alternatively owing to greater challenges faced in altering or adding to a three-voice composition.[64] It is tempting to ascribe the unusual stability of *Veritas arpie* to the character and status of the IOHANNE material: the **Fauvel** compilers did not wish to tamper with such a well-known piece, which in itself was so coherent as to discourage alteration.

A predominantly written engagement with *Ars antiqua* motets in **Fauvel** – copied from books and *libelli* that may have been seventy years old – does not exclude the possibility that at least some of these pieces were still part of a living oral tradition. It is self-evident that the compilers of fr. 146 are most likely to have had to hand copies of pieces that had been widely disseminated, and in multiple incarnations (with voices added or removed, and contrafactum texts), in the thirteenth century. Nevertheless, if they had simply been leafing through old books to find suitable pieces, then there is a high chance that they would have stumbled upon more unica. The **Fauvel** compliers, therefore, evidently had some sense of what constituted a well-known *Ars antiqua* motet. This may have been because they themselves had heard or sung these pieces, whose dissemination must be at least some indication of frequency

vicium see also Welker, 'Polyphonic Reworkings of Notre-Dame Conductûs', pp. 631–5. On the importance of the Latin motet *De gravi* as fundamental to the interpretation of *Fauvellandi vicium*, see Roesner, 'Labouring in the Midst of Wolves', pp. 185–91.

[62] Roesner, Avril, and Freeman Regalado have proposed that the thirteenth-century material was accessed in a text-only source. See their *Le Roman de Fauvel*, p. 25.

[63] The triplum text *In marie miserie* – a prayer directly addressing the Virgin – here depicts Fauvel's own Marian petition in the *Roman*. The more generic motetus text in praise of the Virgin, *Gemma pudicie*, was evidently considered unnecessary in **Fauvel**.

[64] Morin, 'The Genesis of fr. 146', pp. 118–20.

in performance. Significantly, four of the eight motets found in **Fauvel** were seemingly reworked in 'late' double motet versions preserved in **Ba**. *Veritas arpie* belongs in this category, and so it is possible that this motet would have retained in the context of the Fauvel narrative some of the familiarity that it presumably had in the thirteenth century. The appearance of *Veritas arpie* in **Fauvel** could, therefore, additionally have conjured a memory of the vernacular text on which it seems to have been modelled, and which was generally better known: *Ne sai que je die*.

Conclusions

Through engagement with the musical details of *Ne sai que je die/IOHANNE* in its various incarnations and contexts, I have questioned the conventional narratives of motet development previously exemplified by this clausula–motet network. These IOHANNE motets, arguably, do not necessarily descend, as hitherto presumed, from a clausula source; nor does the liturgically appropriate *Clamans in deserto* represent the earliest motet version. Such interrelationships within the IOHANNE network challenge the straightforward progressions from clausula to motet, from Latin to vernacular, and from sacred to secular, inscribed in catalogues and historical narratives of thirteenth-century polyphony. Yet the significance of this challenge does not reside simply in overturning orthodoxy, or replacing one linear narrative with another that proceeds in the opposite direction. More importantly, this case study – previously championed as a general model – underlines the problems inherent in applying such paradigms to this repertoire, and in approaching it with chronological preconceptions. The IOHANNE network demonstrates a fundamental fluidity in thirteenth-century genres, their functions, and notational systems: motets may turn into clausulae, or vice versa, and their musical material may be variously rendered in mensural notation, in undifferentiated *cum littera*, or in the ligature patterns of *sine littera* modal clausulae.

These IOHANNE compositions seem to encapsulate the advance in specificity of available notational systems for motets across the thirteenth century. It is, therefore, paradoxical that there was apparently little if any need to prescribe notationally the rhythm of this two-voice polyphony, whose regular modal profile is entirely unambiguous. At a distance of more than half a century, for instance, the compilers of **Fauvel** were well able to interpret the rhythms of *Veritas arpie* from what was most probably a copy of the motet in undifferentiated *cum littera*. Present-day editors may have the greater luxury of a variety of available notated sources, several mensuralised, but they would surely have achieved the same transcriptions on the basis of *cum littera* manuscripts alone. It is worth noting also that, although the double motet *Quant vient en mai/Ne sai que je die/IOHANNE* depends on and seems designed to exploit the notational possibilities of the new diamond-shaped semibreve, motet composers had been able to achieve similar effects in practice long before the codification of Franco's system. Even in the earliest extant motet source, **F**, there exist motets that divide the breve (principally through the use of melisma) as well as rhythmically stratified double motets (created by combining voices in the fifth, first, and sixth modes). At the same time as showcasing available notational technologies, therefore, the IOHANNE motets serve also as a useful reminder that the prescription of rhythmic information in writing might understandably assume greater significance in the present – in historical narratives, and given the loss of contextual information and musical memory with the passing of time – than it did in the past.

Preoccupation with a chronological progression of genres and notations has previously overshadowed the compositional characteristics of these IOHANNE pieces. Their treatment of a pre-existing tenor melody is once again revealing: the plainchant quotation is not an 'immutable guiding foundation', but it is subtly and uniquely manipulated here in ways that do not compromise the identity or conventions of its monophonic melody, and that have significant polyphonic consequences.[65] It seems that the creators of this two-voice polyphony went to some trouble to craft a tenor whose ordines underlined melodic symmetries in the IOHANNE melisma, while maximising the chant's potential as a tonal foundation through the careful placement of pitches at the beginning and end of ordines. This potential was fully exploited in the accompanying motetus, whose phrase structure and motivic material were also tightly controlled. Both tenor and motetus, therefore, exhibit a high degree of musical planning and design, which is complemented by their associated texts.

Such concern for compositional craft places these IOHANNE motets within the kind of creative and intellectual milieu that has long been associated with thirteenth-century motets: the products of a highly educated clerical and university culture, whose members were deeply familiar with liturgical plainchant, as well as with the organa and clausulae associated with Notre Dame and with vernacular song, both monophonic and polyphonic. Such a

[65] Dolores Pesce, 'Beyond Glossing: The Old Made New in *Mout me fu grief/Robin m'aime/PORTARE*', in Dolores Pesce (ed.), *Hearing the Motet: Essays on the Motet of the Middle Ages and Renaissance* (New York, 1997), pp. 28–51 (p. 28). This is Pesce's characterisation of the way in which tenor chants are typically understood, and which she seeks to challenge.

context, in which one imagines a spirit of compositional competition as well as collaboration, would naturally encourage multiple reworkings, additions, and recompositions. It accounts for Latin texts that explore and amplify the liturgical and biblical contexts of their tenors, as well as an enduring interest in texts that seek to expose and complain about the society from which they emanate, the authors bemoaning the corruption of their peers, presumably at the risk of incurring the charge of hypocrisy against themselves. It seems realistic to imagine that a member of this elite group of clerical composers and singers might have known several different texts associated with the same music, and that the interpretative and allusive potential of various musical and textual components, together and in isolation, was considerable.

These clerics must have known how to read and to notate such music. Engagement with written materials seems fundamental, for instance, to the construction of plainchant tenor foundations: the careful groupings of the IOHANNE tenor discussed here; examples of retrograde chant tenors; and the kinds of complex tenor patterns that, as Susan Rankin has suggested, involve a basic 'disengagement of pitch and rhythm', which – even if actually undertaken in the imagination – is motivated or encouraged by a primarily textual bias.[66] The transcription of motets as clausulae might reflect a similar preoccupation, perhaps carried out as an intellectual exercise in notational translation, in deriving one written musical incarnation from another. As is most clearly the case in the fourteenth-century interpolated *Roman de Fauvel*, the transmission and reworking of thirteenth-century music relied on engagement with earlier manuscript sources. Inevitably, there is a lack of such concrete evidence to demonstrate that these old pieces were also sung and/or remembered, but they surely were – especially a motet such as *Ne sai que je die*, whose singable and stubbornly memorable qualities I have sought to unpick here, and whose exceptional lack of alteration in **Fauvel** seems testament to the durability of its oral identity. This composition highlights the alchemy that can occur between music and text in a motet: the poetry, with its irregular line-lengths, has no coherent structure of its own, but it derives regularity from its musical setting, and in turn enhances this music, its rhymes and syllables helping to fix musical declamation and cadences in the mind. In *Ne sai que je die*, accessibility and memorability are the products of a sophisticated and intricate musico-textual design, which achieves a powerfully distinctive identity in sound, as sung, heard, or remembered.

[66] Susan Rankin, 'The Study of Medieval Music: Some Thoughts on Past, Present, and Future', in David Greer (ed.), *Musicology and Sister Disciplines: Past, Present, Future. Proceedings of the 16th International Congress of the International Musicological Society, London, 1997* (Oxford, 2000), pp. 154–68 (p. 160).

8 Conclusions

This book has explored various arts of using plainchant in thirteenth-century polyphony, the motivations for doing so, and attendant compositional consequences and challenges. The contrasting case studies presented here demonstrate a diverse range of analytical approaches to thirteenth-century organa, clausulae, and motets. Chapter 1 showed how the transmission of plainchant melodies can profitably be compared across polyphonic genres and in relation to monophonic chant books, thereby identifying groups of compositions that share the same versions of plainchant tenors, and possible motivations for tenor alterations at the point that plainchant is polyphonised. A comparison of chant melodies was applied also in the corpus-wide study of mini clausulae in Chapter 2, and contextualised here within an examination of patterns of ordering and concordances across this body of works that, in turn, raised bigger questions about its provenance and function. Upper-voice variants were the focus of Chapter 3, which scrutinised clausulae and their related Latin motets with the aim of identifying differences induced by the addition of texts to pre-existing music. Chapter 4 investigated the opposite generic relationship, establishing key notational and musical features that identify clausulae as motet transcriptions, while Chapter 5 explored and tested the status of refrains as quotations in motets, showing how they might generate internal melodic content. Chapter 6 revealed the hermeneutic possibilities of engaging closely with motets that share the same tenor melody. Finally, Chapter 7 re-evaluated a text-book motet 'family', eschewing the traditional tendency to assume or establish a definitive chronology between various versions of the same musical material. It focused instead on questions of memorability, to offer ways of thinking about why certain types of musical material proved such an enduring basis for creative reworking into the fourteenth century.

Close engagement with the compositional processes of these polyphonic creations, all based on liturgical chant melodies, has revealed multi-faceted attitudes to the sacred heritage of their pre-existing monophonic material, as well as the degree to which it can be musically manipulated. Narratives of musical developments across the thirteenth century tend to trace a broad progression from sacred to secular genres – organum, clausula, Latin motet, French motet – and to envision a gradual decline in polyphony with a liturgical or sacred function, matched by an increasingly liberal attitude to the quotation and manipulation of plainchant tenors, which eventually culminated in the appearance of French song tenors in late-thirteenth-century vernacular motets. This book presents a much more complicated picture, through case studies that undercut presumed sacred and secular behaviours, as well as expected generic relationships and characteristics. Expectations for liturgical or broadly sacred genres are confounded by the *Propter veritatem* organa that knowingly open with the 'wrong' chant incipit, the clausulae in **F** that represent transcriptions of French motets, and the Latin REGNAT motets that are indifferent to the liturgical implications of their Assumption tenor. On the apparently secular side of the presumed divide, the vernacular motets in Chapter 5, whose upper voices depend heavily on refrain quotations, nonetheless insist on the strict quotation of their plainchant tenors and show awareness of other motets based on the same chant melismas, while close investigation of a French love-song text reveals its deep and multi-layered engagement with the hagiography of St Elizabeth of Hungary.

In complicating and unsettling conventional developmental narratives, this book rethinks and repositions relationships between the motet – which became the thirteenth century's most significant and enduring generic innovation – and the earlier repertoire of the so-called Notre Dame School, with its 'Great Book of Organum', which occupies such a central position in music history. Organa, clausulae, and motets undeniably belong within the same creative milieu, sharing many compositional techniques and conventions. The chronological priority and historiographical authority of the Notre Dame repertoire has encouraged a view of the motet as a necessarily Latinate and sacred genre in origin, initially created through the addition of syllabic texts to pre-existing clausulae. In fact, the number of motets created in this way – almost all of them indeed Latin-texted – is marginal in the wider thirteenth-century corpus. And the foregoing chapters have underlined instead the evidence in favour of the motet's possible origins as a vernacular genre, one heavily dependent, from the outset, on refrain quotation.

It may seem contradictory to continue to stress connections among motets, clausulae, and organa on the one hand, while simultaneously asserting a vernacular origin for motets on the other. These apparently conflicting strands are reconciled within a culture of intense and quotation-fuelled compositional play – interests in reworking musical material in different forms, exploring multiple possibilities presented by a plainchant foundation, and in self-imposed compositional challenges – that this book has illuminated in sacred and secular, liturgical and non-liturgical genres alike. There is, perhaps, a latent or implicit sense in modern scholarship that a straightforwardly liturgical function is somehow antithetical to compositional virtuosity. This is in tune with concerns about the explicitly musical or performative nature of works for use in the liturgy that have surfaced throughout the history of the Christian Church. Yet the very expression of such concerns by medieval commentators is itself confirmation that liturgical music was frequently virtuosic. The Cistercian order, for instance, saw fit to attempt a ban on polyphony in the mid-thirteenth century. This substantiates the status of polyphony in this period as something unusual and special, highlighting the almost dangerously gratuitous extravagance of elaborating sections of plainchant with organum in a thirteenth-century context. A sense of musical opulence surely applied to the mini clausulae explored in Chapter 2, which seem to be remnants of an organum cycle that was relatively prosaic in comparison to that of the *Magnus liber*. And this throws into relief the extraordinary compositional self-consciousness of the *Magnus liber* repertoire itself; its manifest preoccupation with its own musical craft; and with its preservation, museum-like, in presentation manuscripts.

This spirit of compositional play, and a profound interest in quotation, are consonant with the beginnings of the motet as a vernacular genre that delights in the combination of apparently contradictory materials: the plainchant foundations that were also the basis of organa and clausulae, and vernacular-texted upper voices and refrains characteristic of courtly song. These motets powerfully exemplify the twelfth- and thirteenth-century interest in 'crossover', as theorised by Barbara Newman: the taste for *coincidentia oppositorum* that produced works of an 'edgy, experimental quality'.[1] Motets are often subversive, not only in their challenging juxtaposition of vernacular and liturgical elements, but also in those vernacular texts that seem deliberately to thwart the conventions of the *pastourelle*, as well as in both French and Latin satirical texts that criticise the clergy.[2]

[1] Barbara Newman, *Medieval Crossover: Reading the Secular against the Sacred* (Notre Dame, 2013), p. 4.

[2] On the subversion and cutting-short of *pastourelle* narratives in motets, see the example discussed by Christopher Page in *Discarding Images: Reflections on Music and Culture in Medieval France* (Oxford, 1993), pp. 48–9. See the overview of satirical Latin texts by Philip the Chancellor, in Thomas B. Payne (ed.), *Philip the Chancellor: Motets and Prosulas*, RRMMA 41 (Middleton, 2011), pp. xviii–xix.

The poetic irregularity of motet texts has traditionally been attributed to their origins as prosulae – Latin texts created for the music of pre-existing clausulae, and thus necessarily unable to maintain conventional or regular poetic forms. Yet it is plausible that irregularity – driven by refrains, as generically and formally disruptive agents, as well as by primarily musical games of quotation and repetition common also to clausulae – was instead cultivated as part of an aesthetic of compositional play and crossover. This aesthetic arguably reached its summation in the proliferation of three- and four-voice polytextual motets, which present unparalleled opportunities to explore multi-layered semantic, allegorical, and/or parodic interactions between texts, as well as intricate and overlapping relationships between melodic lines.

The playful mix of liturgical and vernacular song elements in motets reflects the broad musical interests of their creators – educated clerics with a deep knowledge of liturgical plainchant as well as of the idioms of courtly songs and vernacular refrains.[3] A clerical compositional context is confirmed by the intimate familiarity with plainchant melodies and practices that underpins all of the compositional scenarios explored in this book. The creators of *Propter veritatem* organa discussed in Chapter 1, for instance, exploit the formulaic nature of fifth-mode Graduals, while the mini clausulae treated in Chapter 2 reveal a keen awareness of minute differences between related responsory melodies. Clausula and motet creators show a similarly detailed knowledge of polyphonic conventions and possibilities for particular tenor melodies. And scribes too frequently reveal themselves to be discerning about chant conventions: scribal error or confusion often occurs at moments where tenors deviate from established chant melodies, and some scribes even go so far as to 'correct' tenors that have been musically manipulated.[4]

The sheer level of compositional game-playing revealed by analyses in this book is evidence that composers, singers, listeners, readers, and scribes of this repertoire had shared expectations, an intimate familiarity with musical and poetic materials, and with generic conventions. Those listening to, singing, or reading polyphony were presumably highly alert to repetitions and recastings of its plainchant foundations, as well as subversions of an original chant quotation or of its typical treatment in organa, clausulae,

[3] On clerical and monastic contexts for vernacular refrains, see Jennifer Saltzstein, *The Refrain and the Rise of the Vernacular in Medieval French Music and Poetry* (Cambridge, 2013), pp. 35–79.

[4] See, for instance, the discussion in Chapter 7 of confusions and corrections resulting from the IOHANNE tenor's altered opening.

and motets. They surely realised when the melodic integrity of a plainchant tenor was respected absolutely, often conspicuously, at considerable compositional exertion. Similarly, they would have grasped the conceit of a piece such as the patchwork cento motet *Ja pour longue demouree*/*DIES*, where the creator has sought out an obscure and melodically very simple chant segment in order to accommodate refrain quotation in the upper voice, thereby retaining (against the odds) the status of a motet tenor as a genuine plainchant quotation. The quotational game of vernacular motets depends on a similar familiarity with refrain materials and the conventions of courtly chansons. This familiarity enables the subversion of narrative or lyric norms to be appreciated, and it facilitates the identification of refrains as quotations, conjuring the poetic and musical qualities of their broader host contexts: other motets (perhaps on the same tenor), or monophonic chansons and the identities of their trouvère creators. In consequence, listeners, singers, and readers can perceive the combinatorial virtuosity of the cento motet – which not only strings together a series of refrains in its upper voice, but presents this patchwork melody at the same time as a rigorously literal quotation of a plainchant tenor – or of a polytextual motet in which several refrain quotations are stacked on top of one another, once again above a tenor quotation. The astute may equally spot those refrains that are not, in fact, true quotations, but that carefully employ conventional vocabulary and melodic formulae to give the appearance of such.

The idea of an 'audience' – in the modern sense of a group of people, distinct from composers and performers, who appreciate music – seems anachronistic for thirteenth-century polyphony. Especially in the genres of motet and clausula, it is tempting to posit that polyphony was principally created by and for a relatively small community: probably a coterie of clerical musicians in which the roles of composer, listener, singer, reader, and perhaps even scribe, heavily overlapped.[5] Of course, these circumstances would not confine musical activity to Paris – as the northern French DECANTATUR motets discussed in Chapter 6 confirm – although it is probable that many composers received their education there (as in the case of Adam de la Halle, who was a native of Arras).[6] Nor do they deny the existence of a broader and/or lay context for the appreciation

[5] Christopher Page traces a community of singers of polyphony whose professional employment was limited and precarious, suggesting that motets originated within this milieu. See his *The Owl and the Nightingale: Musical Life and Ideas in France 1100–1300* (London, 1989), pp. 134–54.

[6] On Adam's Parisian education, and that of other Arrageois trouvères and polyphonists, see Saltzstein, *The Refrain and the Rise of the Vernacular*, pp. 119–23.

of polyphonic compositions, in which their subtleties could be grasped to varying degrees. Nevertheless, the nature of this repertoire – its preoccupation with reworking a defined group of plainchant tenors – creates a strong sense that this is primarily music for musicians and the musically literate.[7]

The importance of musical notation for thirteenth-century polyphony supports the hypothesis that those creating and appreciating this music were also conversant with its notational systems, and may even have been its scribes. John Haines has proposed that the late-thirteenth-century theorist dubbed Anonymous IV, from whom we learn the names of Léonin and Pérotin, could himself have been a music copyist,[8] and I have demonstrated that the scribe of **F** undertakes tasks that show a high degree of musical and notational understanding, and in some cases effectively amount to composition.[9] The new method of modal notation and the musical idioms of discant, clausulae, and motets are mutually dependent: the notation was determined by musical practice, just as practice was in turn shaped and influenced by notational possibilities. Notation encourages and facilitates the patterned rhythmic arrangement of what were once fluid plainchant melodies: for example, the retrograde presentation of the DOMINUS tenor in the clausula on NUSMIDO, the appreciation of which seems to depend in large part on engagement with its written form.[10] And the act of notating music can at times seem to be a game in itself, as in the transcription of French motets as clausulae in **F**, perhaps, or in those clausulae that seem to be deliberately testing, even parodying, the limitations of modal rhythm by insisting on multiple reiterations of the same pitch that prevent the use of ligatures necessary to convey rhythmic information.[11]

The status and function of a manuscript such as **F** underlines how a written record can be deeply intertwined with musical and compositional practice, and serve both public and private purposes. **F** was by no means a working musician's book.[12] It was undeniably a prestige object

[7] It is notable that tenors outside this defined and conventional group – such as the unusual DECANTATUR tenor discussed in Chapter 6, which is wrongly labelled PRO PATRIBUS in **Mo** – were subject to misidentification by scribes.

[8] John Haines, 'Anonymous IV as Informant on the Craft of Music Writing', *Journal of Musicology*, 23 (2006), 375–425.

[9] See Catherine A. Bradley, 'Re-workings and Chronological Dynamics in a Thirteenth-Century Latin Motet Family', *Journal of Musicology*, 32 (2015), 153–97 (pp. 164–84). See also Edward H. Roesner's exploration of 'compositional' aspects of copying and writing music down in his 'Who "Made" the *Magnus liber*?', *Early Music History*, 20 (2001), 227–66.

[10] The *Nusmido* clausula is **F**, clausula no. 34, on fol. 150v–2.

[11] Perhaps the most extreme, and strikingly visible, example of a clausula containing multiple repeated notes is [*Captivi*]*ta*[*tem*] 6, **F**, no. 120, fol. 160v–2.

[12] On **F** as a treasury item, see Edward H. Roesner (ed.), *'Antiphonarium, seu, Magnus liber de gradali et antiphonario': Color Microfiche Edition of the Manuscript Firenze, Biblioteca Medicea*

commissioned by a patron and/or institution of considerable importance; Barbara Haggh-Huglo and Michel Huglo propose that the manuscript was presented to King Louis IX at the consecration of the Sainte-Chapelle in 1248.[13] 'The prime example of Parisian book production' according to Edward H. Roesner, **F** surely cost a considerable sum.[14] It stands as a monumental testament to the sophistication of music-making in twelfth- and thirteenth-century Paris, sponsored by a patron who evidently wished publicly to associate himself with, recognise, and conserve this refined repertoire of compositions. Nevertheless, it is difficult to imagine that much of the contents of **F** (the mini clausulae are a case in point) would have been of real practical use or relevance, or even intelligible, to such a patron or to any single institution. In many respects, **F** represents what seems to be a largely private and introspective compositional ethos, at times apparently depending entirely on the personal skills and interests of the manuscript's lone scribe. This musical culture had developed its own notational technologies, ensuring its preservation for posterity in books whose owners were probably not fully conversant with details of the book's contents, but esteemed their symbolic value and aesthetic importance.

To give prominence to the personal compositional games of thirteenth-century composers and scribes, appreciated chiefly by an in-crowd of fellow musicians, might seem unfortunate in a current-day climate increasingly preoccupied by populism. But the study of medieval music and poetry is necessarily that of an elite, in the sense that only institutions and individuals with sufficient wealth and education could ensure the documentation and perpetuation of their art. Scholarly debates have raged about the educational and social status of the audience for thirteenth-century motets, à propos Johannes de Grocheio's famous recommendation (in the 1270s) that such pieces should not be set before the 'vulgaribus', but instead before the 'litterati', who would appreciate their 'subtilitas'.[15] 'Litterati', in particular, has invited a range of translations and interpretations: from 'men of letters' or 'an intellectual elite', to Christopher Page's rendering as 'clergy'.[16] Obviously,

Laurenziana Pluteus 29.1. Introduction to the 'Notre-Dame Manuscript' F, Codices illuminati medii aevi 45 (Munich, 1996), esp. p. 23.

13 See Barbara Haggh and Michel Huglo, '*Magnus liber – Maius munus*: Origine et destineé du manuscrit F', *Revue de musicologie*, 90 (2004), 193–230.

14 Roesner, *Antiphonarium*, p. 14.

15 For the most recent edition and translation of Grocheio's treatise, see Constant J. Mews, John N. Crossley, Catherine Jeffreys, Leigh McKinnon, and Carol J. Williams (eds. and trans.), *Johannes de Grocheio: 'Ars musice'* (Kalamazoo, 2011). The relevant passage is at pp. 84–5. On the dating of the treatise, see pp. 11–12.

16 See Page's presentation of these various translations in *Discarding Images*, p. 43. For his own retranslation and discussion of Grocheio, see pp. 71–84.

clergy still constitute a learned minority in medieval society because they could read and write, but Page helpfully disassociates them from notions of class or social elitism conjured in modern minds by the term 'litterati'. Unlike Page, I have continued to argue for manifold and intricate subtleties in thirteenth-century compositions, but my emphasis on compositional playfulness owes much to his less rarefied and very human conceptualisation of music-making by a community of medieval clerics.

It may be this compositional introspection, depending on and perpetuating a closed and ludic creative culture, that most sharply distinguishes thirteenth-century motets from their fourteenth-century counterparts.[17] Fourteenth-century motets use a much wider and more diverse range of plainchant tenors, and do not tend to rework the same chant melodies multiple times. *Ars nova* motets are, on the whole, much longer and grander in scale, and their poetry is more conventionally regular and more obviously ambitious: the thirteenth-century *pastourelle* topos is abandoned in favour of texts that cite Classical authors and maxims.[18] The increasing regularity of fourteenth-century motet texts is matched by an increase in 'isoperodicity', a move away from the irregular overlapping phrase structures that characterise thirteenth-century motets.[19] While thirteenth-century motets may have delighted in the new possibilities of rhythmic notation precisely to record and conceive of such irregularities, fourteenth-century pieces avail themselves instead of a more recently available breadth of rhythmic

[17] I employ the categories of the 'thirteenth-' and fourteenth-century' motet to refer to the traditions generally associated with these centuries. Mark Everist offers a productive critique of the idea of 1300 as a hard-and-fast boundary, since older thirteenth-century motets were still copied in the early decades of the fourteenth century. See his 'Machaut's Musical Heritage', in Deborah McGrady and Jennifer Bain (eds.), *A Companion to Guillaume de Machaut*, Brill's Companions to the Christian Tradition (Leiden, 2012), pp. 143–58, esp. p. 144.

[18] On the importance of Classical citations in fourteenth-century motets, see, for example, Margaret Bent's discussion of Ovidian references in 'Polyphony of Texts and Music in the Fourteenth-Century Motet: *Tribum que non abhorruit/Quoniam secta latronum/Merito hec partimur* and Its "Quotations"', in Dolores Pesce (ed.), *Hearing the Motet: Essays on the Motet of the Middle Ages and Renaissance* (New York, 1997), pp. 82–103. See also the citation of Horace in Vitry's *In virtute/decens* discussed by Anna Zayaruznaya in *The Monstrous New Art: Divided Forms in the Late Medieval Motet*, Music in Context (Cambridge, 2015), pp. 70–105. References to Classical and scholastic authorities are rare in the thirteenth century, but are most common in conducti, especially among lyrics attributed to Philip the Chancellor; see Payne, *Philip the Chancellor: Motets and Prosulas*, p. xvi. On an exceptional group of thirteenth-century motets that allude to a vernacular translation of Ovid's *Ars amatoria*, see Jennifer Saltzstein, 'Ovid and the Thirteenth-Century Motet: Quotation, Reinterpretation, and Vernacular Hermeneutics', *Musica disciplina*, 58 (2013), 351–72.

[19] On changing attitudes to isoperiodicity in thirteenth- and fourteenth-century motets, see Lawrence Earp, 'Isorhythm', in Jared C. Hartt (ed.), *A Critical Companion to Medieval Motets* (Woodbridge, 2018), pp. 77–101.

durations. The results are clearly stratified compositions, in which tenor melodies move at a significantly slower rate than their upper voices. This development goes hand in hand with so-called isorhythmic structures and isomelic recurrences in fourteenth-century motets, a characteristic also at odds with earlier tendencies to obscure the repetitions of a tenor melody, and to recast them rhythmically and harmonically. All this seems to represent a shift away from an irregular and playful thirteenth-century aesthetic, and a broadening and loosening of the conventions delineating its quotational remit.

Admittedly, an interest in vernacular refrain traditions persists in the fourteenth century, where poets such as Guillaume de Machaut clearly situate themselves within a trouvère heritage.[20] Yet it is striking that older refrain quotations in fourteenth-century motets are often purely textual, lacking associated musical material, even though notated chansonniers were probably available and certainly continued to be copied in the fourteenth century.[21] A poetic emphasis is characteristic of the *Ars nova* more generally, whose principal proponents – Philippe de Vitry and Machaut – also, or even chiefly, had reputations as poets as well as composers. It is unsurprising, therefore, that polytextuality was the thirteenth-century motet's enduring poetic legacy, the generic characteristic that was most in tune with the textual aspirations of the fourteenth-century genre. That a declining interest in the musical quotation, and especially in the polyphonic combination of short vernacular refrains, was balanced by an increase in allusions to other polyphonic works, and in internal structural or formal symbolism, reflects the loftier musical and poetic aesthetics of fourteenth-century motets.[22]

I have proposed a contained thirteenth-century environment of compositional play, the preserve principally of a small coterie of clerical musicians. This by no means implies that fourteenth-century composers

[20] See, for example, Jacques Boogaart, 'Encompassing Past and Present: Quotations and Their Functions in Machaut's Motets', *Early Music History*, 20 (2001), 1–86, esp. pp. 13–33.

[21] On thirteenth-century refrain citation (predominantly text-only) in Machaut's oeuvre, see Saltzstein, *The Refrain and the Rise of the Vernacular*, pp. 149–64. On the continued production of trouvère chansonniers in the fourteenth century, see Yolanda Plumley, *The Art of Grafted Song: Citation and Allusion in the Age of Machaut* (Oxford, 2013), p. 415.

[22] The declining fourteenth-century interest in the polyphonic combination of refrains is surely linked to the stratification of rhythmic values: a slower rate of tenor motion (and an increase in tenor rests) makes it significantly easier to combine plainchant and refrain quotations polyphonically, thus negating the thirteenth-century compositional game. For examples of citation of polyphonic works, see Plumley, *The Art of Grafted Song*, pp. 231–49. On formal and structural symbolism, see Zayaruznaya, *The Monstrous New Art*, esp. pp. 106–41.

did not also have erudite (and musical) quotational games of their own, for they undeniably did, as most recently illuminated by Yolanda Plumley.[23] Significantly, however, these *Ars nova* quotations typically have an authorial dimension – both the citations and the cited material itself are linked to a creative identity – that is conspicuously lacking in thirteenth-century polyphony. It is not that authorship was of no consequence in this earlier period: attributions to Philip the Chancellor exist for Latin conducti, and sources of vernacular song from the twelfth century onwards almost invariably record the identity of their troubadour and trouvère poet-composers. Notably, motet voices that exist also as monophonic songs are often attributed in these chanson contexts.[24] Is authorship, therefore, privileged for poets, for genres whose texts are generally more substantial, more formally conventional, and less musically dependent than motets?

Given this book's emphasis on the compositional subtleties and sophistication of thirteenth-century polyphony, its attempts to reconstruct authorial moves and mindsets, it may seem paradoxical that barely any organum, clausula, or motet composers are known to us by name.[25] This could indicate a collaborative compositional culture: different people, perhaps known to each other, may add text, create contrafacta, and fashion additional voices for existing musical materials, to the point where the work of different authors becomes indistinguishable. Anonymous IV's much-quoted description of the activities of Léonin and Pérotin suggests precisely this kind of collaboration: Pérotin adding to and/or reworking Léonin's older *Magnus liber*.[26] At the same time, collaboration does not necessarily negate a spirit of competition, which is evident when Anonymous IV goes on to report that Pérotin was 'better' at discant than Léonin had been. Some thirteenth-century reworkings may be attempts to display personal

[23] Plumley, *The Art of Grafted Song*.

[24] For a list of motet voices also transmitted as songs, see Matthew P. Thomson, 'Interaction between Polyphonic Motets and Monophonic Songs in the Thirteenth Century', D.Phil. diss. (University of Oxford, 2016), pp. 345–61. It must be acknowledged that the quotation of refrains is more persistent in fourteenth-century song forms, especially the ballade. In their interest in refrains, fourteenth-century vernacular *formes fixes* are perhaps closer to the thirteenth-century motet than its fourteenth-century namesake, a relationship that may reflect the close vernacular ties, and possible origins, of the motet genre.

[25] Léonin and Pérotin are the only known named composers of organa and clausulae. Motets explicitly attributed to the trouvère Adam de la Halle in the late thirteenth century are a notable exception. In the earlier part of the century, certain Latin motet texts are attributed to Philip the Chancellor, but he is never identified as a composer of music. See Payne, *Philip the Chancellor: Motets and Prosulas*, p. xxii.

[26] See Edward H. Roesner's translations of this passage from Anonymous IV in 'Who "Made" the *Magnus liber*?', pp. 227–8.

compositional skill, to improve or modernise older works. In these cases, it is conceivable that those on the inside of this musical community knew precisely which earlier versions and later reworkings of a certain composition were the work of whom. This kind of multi-layered authorship would presumably be difficult, if not impossible, to inscribe in manuscript sources. Moreover, the attribution would probably be unintelligible to any broader audience and superfluous to those within the circle of performers, creators, and scribes.

This book about compositional process, in which there is an absence of known composers, proffers ways of thinking about musical creativity that are independent of well-worn concepts of originality and authorship.[27] It has sought to elucidate the rich compositional and hermeneutic possibilities that arise within a circumscribed environment of musical and textual reworking and quotation, in which participants are acutely aware of conventions in Latin and vernacular, sacred and secular spheres. Reimagining this culture through the close analysis of particular works is not simply a way of counteracting the lack of historical or theoretical documents to explain exactly how and when this music was produced, and who produced it. Rather, it is an attempt to get inside the mentalities of unnamed composers, to uncover and probe the wider contexts against which they fashioned certain pieces, and to engage with thirteenth-century music on primarily musical terms, a priority that is sympathetic to the priorities of its creators. As a productive means of circumventing and unsettling traditional historiographical narratives, the analysis of individual organa, clausulae, and motets and their interactions itself presents opportunities to participate in and perpetuate thirteenth-century cultures of creativity and play.

[27] Only one of the pieces discussed in this book is linked in any way to a known composer: Barbara Haggh has proposed that the motet *Un chant renvoisie/DECANTATUR* may have been the work of Peter, Canon Saint-Aubert of Cambrai. See Barbara Haggh (ed.), *Two Offices for Saint Elizabeth of Hungary: 'Gaudeat Hungaria' and 'Letare Germania'* (Ottawa, 1995), p. xvi, discussed in Chapter 6, n. 19.

Bibliography

Facsimile Reproductions

Aubry, Pierre (ed.), *Cent motets du XIIIe siècle publiés d'après le manuscrit Ed.4.6 de Bamberg*, Vol. I (Paris, 1908). [**Ba**]

Beck, Jean and Louise Beck (eds.), *Le Manuscrit du Roi, fonds français no. 844 de la Bibliothèque nationale: Reproduction phototypique publié avec une introduction*, Corpus cantilenarum medii aevi 1: Les chansonniers des troubadours et des trouvères 2, 2 parts (London, 1938). [**R**]

Bell, Nicolas (ed.), *El Códice musical de las Huelgas Reales de Burgos*, Colección scriptorium 7, 2 vols. (Madrid, 1997–2003). [**Hu**]

Dittmer, Luther (ed.), *Eine zentrale Quelle der Notre-Dame Musik: Faksimile, Wiederherstellung, Catalogue raisonné, Besprechung und Transcriptionen*, PMMM 3 (Brooklyn, 1959). [**MüA**]

(ed.), *Faksimile-Ausgabe der Handschrift Madrid 20486*, PMMM 1 (Brooklyn, 1957). [**Ma**]

(ed.), *Faksimile-Ausgabe der Handschrift Wolfenbüttel 1099*, PMMM 2 (Brooklyn, 1960). [**W2**]

(ed.), *Paris 13521 & 11411: Faksimile, Einleitung, Register und Transcriptionen aus den Handschriften Paris Bibl. nat. nouv. acq. Fr. 13521 (La Clayette) und Lat. 11411*, PMMM 4 (Brooklyn, 1959). [**Cl**]

Roesner, Edward H. (ed.), *'Antiphonarium, seu, Magnus liber de gradali et antiphonario': Color Microfiche Edition of the Manuscript Firenze, Biblioteca Medicea Laurenziana Pluteus 29.1. Introduction to the 'Notre-Dame Manuscript' F*, Codices illuminati medii aevi 45 (Munich, 1996). [**F**]

Roesner, Edward H., François Avril, and Nancy Freeman Regalado (eds.), *'Le Roman de Fauvel' in the Edition of Mesire Chaillou de Pesstain: A Reproduction in Facsimile of the Complete Manuscript Bibliothèque nationale de France, Fonds Français 146* (New York, 1990). [**Fauvel**]

Rokseth, Yvonne (ed.), *Polyphonies du XIIIe siècle: Le manuscrit H196 de la faculté de médecine de Montpellier*, 4 vols. (Paris, 1935–9). [**Mo**]

Staehelin, Martin (ed.), *Die mittelalterliche Musikhandschrift, W1: Vollständige Reproduktion des Notre Dame-Manuskripts der Herzog August Bibliothek Wolfenbüttel Cod. Guelf. 628 Helmst.*, Wolfenbütteler Mittelalter-Studien 9 (Wiesbaden, 1995). [**W1**]

(ed.), *Kleinüberlieferung mehrstimmiger Musik vor 1550 in deutschem Sprachgebiet I: Die Notre-Dame-Fragmente aus dem Besitz von Johannes Wolf*, Nachrichten der Akademie der Wissenschaften in Göttingen, 1. Philologisch-historische Klasse, Jg. 1999, no.6 (Göttingen, 1999), pp. 1–35. [**MüA**]

Music and Text Editions

Anderson, Gordon A. (ed.), *Compositions of the Bamberg Manuscript*, Corpus mensurabilis musicae 75 (Neuhausen-Stuttgart, 1977).

(ed.), *The Latin Compositions in Fascicules VII and VIII of the Notre Dame Manuscript Wolfenbüttel Helmstadt 1099 (1206)*, Musicological Studies 24, 2 parts (New York, 1968–76).

(ed.), *Motets of the Manuscript La Clayette: Paris Bibliothèque nationale, nouv. acq. f. fr. 13521*, Corpus mensurabilis musicae 68 (Dallas, 1975).

Anglès, Higini (ed.), *El còdex musical de Las Huelgas*, Publicacions del Departament de Música 6, Vol. III (Barcelona, 1931).

Asensio Palacios, Juan Carlos, *El Códice de Madrid: Biblioteca nacional, Mss. 20486. Polifonías del siglo XIII: Introducción, índices y transcripción musical, Juan Carlos Asensio Palacios; edición y traducción de los textos, Julián Paz Hidalgo* (Madrid, 1997).

Baltzer, Rebecca A. (ed.), *Le 'Magnus liber organi' de Notre-Dame de Paris V: Les clausules à deux voix du manuscrit de Florence, Biblioteca Medicea-Laurenziana, Pluteus 29.1, fascicule V* (Monaco, 1995).

Buffum, Douglas Labree (ed.), *Gerbert de Montreuil: Le Roman de la violette ou de Gerart de Nevers*, Société des anciens textes français (Paris, 1928).

Doss-Quinby, Eglal, Joan Tasker Grimbert, Wendy Pfeffer, and Elizabeth Aubrey (eds.), *Songs of the Woman Trouvères* (New Haven, 2001).

Everist, Mark (ed.), *Le 'Magnus liber organi' de Notre-Dame de Paris II: Les organa à deux voix pour l'office du manuscrit de Florence, Biblioteca Medicea-Laurenziana, Plut. 29.1* (Monaco, 2003).

(ed.), *Le 'Magnus liber organi' de Notre-Dame de Paris III: Les organa à deux voix pour la messe (de Noël à la fête de Saint-Pierre et Saint-Paul) du manuscrit de Florence, Biblioteca Medicea-Laurenziana, Plut. 29.1* (Monaco, 2001).

(ed.), *Le 'Magnus liber organi' de Notre-Dame de Paris IV: Les organa à deux voix pour la messe (de l'Assomption au Commun des saints) du manuscrit de Florence, Biblioteca Medicea-Laurenziana, Plut. 29.1* (Monaco, 2002).

Faral, Edmond and Julia Bastin (eds.), *Œuvres complètes de Rutebeuf*, 2 vols. (Paris, 1960).

Gilles, André and Gilbert Reaney (eds.), *Franco de colonia: Ars cantus mensurabilis musicae*, CSM 18 (Rome, 1974).

Granger Ryan, William (trans.), *Jacobus de Voragine, 'The Golden Legend': Readings on the Saints* (Princeton, 1993).

Hammond, Frederick H., *Walteri Odington: 'Summa de speculatione musicae'*, CSM 14 (Rome, 1970).

Haub, Rita (ed.), *Die Motetten in der Notre-Dame-Handschrift MüA (Bayer. Staatsbibl., Cod. gall.42)*, Münchner Editionen zur Musikgeschichte 8 (Tutzing, 1986).

Huff, Jay A., *Walter Odington: 'De speculatio musicae' Part VI*, Musicological Studies and Documents 31 (Rome, 1973).

Mews, Constant J., John N. Crossley, Catherine Jeffreys, Leigh McKinnon, and Carol J. Williams (eds. and trans.), *Johannes de Grocheio: 'Ars musice'* (Kalamazoo, 2011).

Payne, Thomas B. (ed.), *Le 'Magnus liber organi' de Notre-Dame de Paris VIA-B: Les organa à deux voix du manuscrit de Wolfenbüttel, Herzog August Bibliothek, Cod. Guelf. 1099 Helmst.* (Monaco, 1996).

(ed.), *Philip the Chancellor: Motets and Prosulas*, RRMMA 41 (Middleton, 2011).

Reimer, Erich, *Johannes de Garlandia: 'De mensurabili musica'*, 2 vols., Beihefte zum Archiv für Musikwissenschaft 10–11 (Wiesbaden, 1972).

Relihan, Joel C. and Susan Stakel (eds.), *The Montpellier Codex, Part IV: Texts and Translations*, RRMMA 8 (Madison, 1985).

Roesner, Edward H. (ed.), *Le 'Magnus liber organi' de Notre-Dame de Paris I: Les quadrupla et tripla de Paris* (Monaco, 1993).

(ed.), *Le 'Magnus liber organi' de Notre-Dame de Paris VII: Les organa et les clausules à deux voix du manuscrit de Wolfenbüttel, Herzog August Bibliothek, Cod. Guelf. 628 Helmst* (Monaco, 2009).

Saint-Cricq, Gaël, Eglal Doss-Quinby, and Samuel N. Rosenberg (eds.), *Motets from the Chansonnier de Noailles* (Middleton, 2017).

Schrade, Leo (ed.), *The Roman de Fauvel; The Works of Philippe de Vitry; The French Cycles of the Ordinarium Missae, Polyphonic Music of the Fourteenth Century 1* (Monaco, 1974 [1956]).

Tischler, Hans (ed.), *The Earliest Motets (to circa 1270): A Complete Comparative Edition*, 3 vols. (New Haven, 1982).

(ed.), *The Montpellier Codex: I–III*, 3 vols., RRMMA 2–7 (Madison, 1978–85).

Wilmart, André (ed.), *Gérard de Liège: Quinque incitamenta ad Deum amandum ardenter*, Analecta reginensia, Studi e testi 59 (Vatican City, 1933).

Secondary Literature

Anderson, Gordon A., 'Clausulae or Transcribed Motets in the Florence Manuscript?', *Acta musicologica*, 42 (1970), 109–28.

'A Small Collection of Notre Dame Motets *ca.* 1215–1235', *Journal of the American Musicological Society*, 22 (1969), 157–96.

Anderson, Michael Alan, 'Fire, Foliage, and Fury: Vestiges of Midsummer Ritual in Motets for John the Baptist', *Early Music History*, 30 (2011), 1–54.

Apel, Wili, *Gregorian Chant* (Bloomington, 1958).

Arlt, Wulf, 'Zur frühen Geschichte der Motette: Funktionen – historische Schichten – Musik und Text – Kriterien der Interpretation' (unpublished paper presented at Das Ereignis Notre Dame, Wolfenbüttel, 1985).

Arlt, Wulf and Max Hass, 'Pariser Modale Mehrstimmigkeit in einem Fragment der Basler Universitätsbibliothek', *Formum musicologicum*, 1 (1975), 223–72.

Baltzer, Rebecca A., 'Notation, Rhythm, and Style in the Two-Voice Notre Dame Clausula', Ph.D. diss., 2 vols. (Boston University, 1974).

'Performance Practice: The Notre-Dame Calendar and the Earliest Latin Liturgical Motets' (unpublished paper presented at Das Ereignis Notre Dame, Wolfenbüttel, 1985), available online at *Archivum de musica medii aevi*, www.univ-nancy2.fr/MOYENAGE/UREEF/MUSICOLOGIE/AdMMAe/AdMMAe_index.htm.

'The Polyphonic Progeny of an *Et gaudebit*: Assessing Family Relations in a Thirteenth-Century Motet', in Dolores Pesce (ed.), *Hearing the Motet: Essays on the Motet of the Middle Ages and Renaissance* (New York, 1997), pp. 17–27.

'Review of Jutta Pumpe, *Die Motetten der Madrider Notre-Dame-Handschrift* (Tutzing, 1991)', *Notes*, 51 (1994), 579.

'The Thirteenth-Century Motet', in Mark Everist and Thomas Forrest Kelly (eds.), *The Cambridge History of Medieval Music* (Cambridge, 2018), pp. 1004–29.

Bernhard, Michael (ed.), *Lexicon musicum latinum medii aevi*, available online at www.lml.badw.de/lmlonline/index.htm.

Black, Nancy B., *Medieval Narratives of Accused Queens* (Gainesville, 2003).

Blume, Clemens and Guido M. Dreves (eds.), *Historiae rhythmicae: Liturgische Reimofficien des Mittelalters, fünfte Folge*, Analecta hymnica 25 (Leipzig, 1897).

Boogaart, Jacques, 'Encompassing Past and Present: Quotations and Their Functions in Machaut's Motets', *Early Music History*, 20 (2001), 1–86.

Bradley, Catherine A., 'Comparing Compositional Process in Two Thirteenth-Century Motets: *Deus omnium/REGNAT* and *Ne m'oubliez mie/DOMINO*', *Music Analysis*, 33 (2014), 263–90.

'Contrafacta and Transcribed Motets: Vernacular Influences on Latin Motets and Clausulae in the Florence Manuscript', *Early Music History*, 32 (2013), 1–70.

'The Earliest Motets: Musical Borrowing and Re-Use', Ph.D. diss. (University of Cambridge, 2011).

'New Texts for Old Music: Three Early Latin Motets', *Music and Letters*, 93 (2012), 149–69.

'Ordering in the Motet Fascicles of the Florence Manuscript', *Plainsong and Medieval Music*, 22 (2013), 37–64.

'Origins and Interactions: Clausula, Motet, Conductus', in Jared C. Hartt (ed.), *A Critical Companion to Medieval Motets* (Woodbridge, 2018), pp. 43–60.

'Re-workings and Chronological Dynamics in a Thirteenth-Century Latin Motet Family', *Journal of Musicology*, 32 (2015), 153–97.

'Seeking the Sense of Sound', *Journal of the Royal Musical Association*, 139 (2014), 405–20.

'Song and Quotation in Two-Voice Motets for Saint Elizabeth of Hungary', *Speculum*, 92 (2017), 661–91.

Brown, Elizabeth A. R., 'Rex ioians, ionnes, iolis: Louis X, Philip V, and the Livers de Fauvel', in Margaret Bent and Andrew Wathey (eds.), *Fauvel Studies: Allegory, Chronicle, Music, and Image in Paris Bibliothèque nationale de France, MS Français 146* (Oxford, 1998), pp. 54–72.

Beiche, Michael, 'Motet/motetus/mottetto/Motette', in Hans Heinrich Eggebrecht (ed.), *Handwörterbuch der musikalischen Terminologie*, Vol. XXXVI (Stuttgart, 2003/4), pp. 1–23.

Bent, Margaret, *Magister Jacobus de Ispania, Author of the 'Speculum musicae'*, Royal Musical Association Monographs 28 (Ashgate, 2015).

'Polyphony of Texts and Music in the Fourteenth-Century Motet: *Tribum que non abhorruit/Quoniam secta latronum/Merito hec partimur* and Its "Quotations"', in Dolores Pesce (ed.), *Hearing the Motet: Essays on the Motet of the Middle Ages and Renaissance* (New York, 1997), pp. 82–103.

Bertelsmeier-Kierst, Christa (ed.), *Elisabeth von Thüringen und die neue Frömmigkeit in Europa* (Frankfurt, 2008).

Blume, Dieter and Mathias Werner (eds.), *Elisabeth von Thüringen: Eine europäische Heilige. Aufsätze* (St Petersburg, 2007).

Busse Berger, Anna Maria, *Medieval Music and the Art of Memory* (Berkeley, 2005).

Butterfield, Ardis, '"Enté": A Survey and Reassessment of the Term in Thirteenth- and Fourteenth-Century Music and Poetry', *Early Music History*, 22 (2003), 67–101.

'Repetition and Variation in the Thirteenth-Century Refrain', *Journal of the Royal Musical Association*, 116 (1991), 1–23.

Büttner, Fred, *Das Klauselrepertoire der Handschrift Saint-Victor (Paris, BN, lat. 15139): Eine Studie zur mehrstimmigen Komposition im 13. Jahrhundert* (Lecce, 2011).

'Weltliche Einflüsse in der Notre-Dame-Musik? Überlegungen zu einer Klausel im Codex F', *Anuario musical*, 57 (2002), 19–37.

Bynum, Caroline Walker, *Holy Feast and Holy Fast: The Religious Significance of Food to Medieval Women* (Berkeley, 1987).

Caldwell, Mary Channen, 'Singing, Dancing, and Rejoicing in the Round: Latin Sacred Songs with Refrains, *circa* 1000–1582', Ph.D. diss. (University of Chicago, 2013).

Catalunya, David, *Music, Space and Ritual in Medieval Castille, 1221–1350*, Ph.D. diss. (Universität Würzburg, 2016).

Cazelles, Brigitte, *The Lady as Saint: A Collection of French Hagiographic Romances of the Thirteenth Century* (Philadelphia, 1991).

Clark, Suzannah, '"S'en dirai chançonete": Hearing Text and Music in a Medieval Motet', *Plainsong and Medieval Music*, 16 (2007), 31–59.

Coakley, John W., *Women, Men, and Spiritual Power: Female Saints and Their Male Collaborators* (New York, 2006).

Crocker, Richard, 'French Polyphony of the Thirteenth Century', in Richard Crocker and David Hiley (eds.), *The Early Middle Ages to 1300*, NOHM 2 (Oxford, 1990), pp. 636–78.

Curran, Sean Paul, 'Feeling the Polemic of an Early Motet', in Almut Suerbaum, George Southcombe, and Benjamin Thompson (eds.), *Polemic: Language as Violence in Medieval and Early Modern Discourse* (Farnham, 2015), pp. 65–94.

'Vernacular Book Production, Vernacular Polyphony, and the Motets of the "La Clayette" Manuscript (Paris, Bibliothèque nationale de France, nouvelles acquisitions françaises, 13521)', Ph.D. diss. (University of California, Berkeley, 2013).

Curry, Robert Michael, 'Fragments of *Ars antiqua* Music at Stary Sącz and the Evolution of the Clarist Order in Central Europe in the Thirteenth Century', Ph.D. diss. (Monash University, 2003).

Dalomi, Davide, 'Notre Dame's New Clothes', *TRANS – Revista transcultural de música/Transcultural Music Review*, 18 (2014), 2–26.

Dillon, Emma, *The Sense of Sound: Musical Meaning in France 1260–1330*, New Cultural History of Music Series (New York, 2012).

Earp, Lawrence, 'Isorhythm', in Jared C. Hartt (ed.), *A Critical Companion to Medieval Motets* (Woodbridge, 2018), pp. 77–101.

Everist, Mark, *French Motets in the Thirteenth Century: Music, Poetry, and Genre* (Cambridge, 1994).

'Machaut's Musical Heritage', in Deborah McGrady and Jennifer Bain (eds.), *A Companion to Guillaume de Machaut*, Brill's Companions to the Christian Tradition (Leiden, 2012), pp. 143–58.

Polyphonic Music in Thirteenth-Century France: Aspects of Sources and Distribution (New York, 1989).

'The Refrain Cento: Myth or Motet?', *Journal of the Royal Musical Association*, 114 (1989), 164–88.

'The Rondeau Motet: Paris and Artois in the Thirteenth Century', *Music and Letters*, 69 (1988), 1–22.

'The Thirteenth Century', in Mark Everist (ed.), *The Cambridge Companion to Medieval Music* (Cambridge, 2011), pp. 67–86.

Everist, Mark, and Anne Ibos-Augé, *REFRAIN: Musique, poésie, citation. Le refrain au moyen âge/Music, Poetry, Citation: The Medieval Refrain*, at http://medmus.soton.ac.uk/view.html.

Flotzinger, Rudolf, *Der Discantussatz im 'Magnus liber' und seiner Nachfolge*, WMB 8 (Vienna, 1969).

Frobenius, Wolf, 'Zum genetischen Verhältnis zwischen Notre-Dame-Klauseln und ihren Motetten', *Archiv für Musikwissenschaft*, 44 (1987), 1–39.

Gennrich, Friedrich, *Bibliographie der ältesten französischen und lateinischen Motetten*, SMMA 2 (Frankfurt, 1957).

Bibliographisches Verzeichnis der französischen Refrains des 12. und 13. Jahrhunderts, SMMA 14 (Frankfurt, 1964).

Rondeaux, Virelais und Balladen aus dem Ende des XII., dem XIII., und dem ersten Drittel des XIV. Jahrhunderts mit dem überlieferten Melodien 2, Gesellschaft für romanische Literatur 47 (Göttingen, 1927).

Göllner, Marie Louise, 'Rhythm and Pattern: The Two-Voice Motets of Codex Montpellier', *Viator, 30* (1999), 145–63.

Goudsenne, Jean François, 'L'office de S. Winoc de Bergues (Flandres, XIe siècle) est-il à l'origine d'une teneur dans les motets du XIIIe siècle?', in Bruno Bouckaert and Eugeen Schreurs (eds.), *The Di Martinelli Music Collection (KULeuven, University Archives): Musical Life in Collegiate Churches in the Low Countries and Europe; Chant and Polyphony*, Yearbook of the Alamire Foundation 4 (Leuven, 2000), pp. 283–96.

Grau, Anna Kathryn, 'Representation and Resistance: Female Vocality in Thirteenth-Century France', Ph.D. diss. (University of Pennsylvania, 2010).

Grochowska, Katarzyna, 'Tenor Circles and Motet Cycles: A Study of the Stary Sącz Manuscript [PL-SS MUZ 9] and Its Implications for Modes of Repertory Organization in Thirteenth-Century Polyphonic Collections', Ph.D. diss. (University of Chicago, 2013).

Gross, Guillaume, 'Organum at Notre-Dame in the Twelfth and Thirteenth Centuries: Rhetoric in Words and Music', *Plainsong and Medieval Music*, 15 (2006), 87–108.

Haggh, Barbara, 'The Beguines of Bruges and the Procession of the Holy Blood', in M. Jennifer Bloxham, Gioia Filocamo, and Leofranc Holford-Strevens (eds.), *Uno gentile et subtile ingenio: Essays in Honour of Bonnie J. Blackburn* (Turnhout, 2009), pp. 75–85.

(ed.), *Two Offices for Saint Elizabeth of Hungary: 'Gaudeat Hungaria' and 'Letare Germania'* (Ottawa, 1995).

Haggh, Barbara and Michel Huglo, Michel, '*Magnus liber – Maius munus*: Origine et destineé du manuscrit F', *Revue de musicologie*, 90 (2004), 193–230.

Haines, John, 'Anonymous IV as Informant on the Craft of Music Writing', *Journal of Musicology*, 23 (2006), 375–425.

Hamilton, Elina Grace, 'Walter of Evesham Abbey and the Intellectual Milieu of Fourteenth-Century English Music Theory', Ph.D. diss. (Prifysgol Bangor University, 2014).

Hoekstra, Gerald R., 'The French Motet as Trope: Multiple Levels of Meaning in *Quant florist la violete/El mois de mai/Et gaudebit*', *Speculum*, 73 (1998), 32–57.

Hofmann, Klaus, *Untersuchungen zur Kompositionstechnik der Motette im 13. Jahrhundert durchgeführt an den Motetten mit dem Tenor 'In seculum'*, Tübinger Beiträge zur Musikwissenschaft 2 (Neuhausen-Stuttgart, 1972).

'Zur Entstehungs- und Frühgeschichte des Terminus Motette', *Acta musicologica*, 42 (1970), 138–50.

Holford-Strevens, Leofranc, 'Latin Poetry and Music', in Mark Everist (ed.), *The Cambridge Companion to Medieval Music* (Cambridge, 2011), pp. 225–40.

Hucke, Helmut, 'Zu einigen Cantus Firmi der Notre-Dame Organa', in Michel Huglo, Christian Meyer, and Marcel Pérès (eds.), *Aspects de la musique liturgique au moyen âge*, Actes des colloques de Royaumont de 1986, 1987, et 1988 (Paris, 1991), pp. 159–75.

Huot, Sylvia, *Allegorical Play in the Old French Motet: The Sacred and the Profane in Thirteenth-Century Polyphony* (Stanford, 1997).

Husmann, Heinrich, 'The Enlargement of the "Magnus liber organi" and the Paris Churches St Germain l'Auxerrois and Ste Geneviève-du-Mont', trans. Andres P. Briner, *Journal of the American Musicological Society*, 2 (1963), 176–203.

'The Origin and Destination of the "Magnus liber organi"', trans. Gilbert Reaney, *Musical Quarterly*, 49 (1963), 311–30.

Immel, Steven C., 'The Vatican Organum Treatise Reexamined', *Early Music History*, 20 (2001), 121–72.

Jauss, Hans Robert, *Toward an Aesthetic of Reception*, trans. Timothy Bahti (Minneapolis, 1982).

Jeanroy, Alfred, *Chansons, jeux partis et refrains inédits du XIIIe siècle* (Toulouse, 1902).

Kidwell, Susan A., 'The Selection of Clausula Sources for Thirteenth-Century Motets: Some Practical Considerations and Aesthetic Implications', *Current Musicology*, 64 (1998), 73–103.

Körndle, Franz, 'Von der Klausel zur Motette und zurück? Überlegungen zum Repertoire der Handschrift *Saint-Victor*', *Musiktheorie*, 25 (2010), 117–28.

Lefferts, Peter M., 'Sources of Thirteenth-Century English Polyphony: Catalogue with Descriptions', *University of Nebraska Lincoln Faculty Publications: School of Music*, Paper 45 (2012), http://digitalcommons.unl.edu/musicfacpub/45/.

Lefferts, Peter M. and Ernest H. Sanders, 'Motet §I: Middle Ages. 1. France, Ars antiqua', in Stanley Sadie and John Tyrrel (eds.), *The New Grove Dictionary of Music and Musicians*, 2nd edn, 29 vols. (Oxford, 2001), Vol. XVII, pp. 190–5.

Ludwig, Friedrich, *Repertorium organorum recentioris et motetorum vetustissimi stili*, ed. Luther A. Dittmer, 2 vols. in 3 (New York, 1964–78 [1910]).

Maw, David, '"Je le temoin en mon chant": The Art of Diminution in the Petronian Triplum', in Catherine A. Bradley and Karen Desmond (eds.), *The Montpellier Codex: The Final Fascicle. Contexts, Contents, Chronologies* (Woodbridge, 2018), pp. 161–83.

Meyer, Wilhelm, 'Der Ursprung des Motett's: Vorläufige Bemerkungen', in *Nachrichten von der königlichen Gesellschaft der Wissenschaften zu Göttingen: Philologisch-historische Klasse, 1898* (Göttingen, 1898), Vol. II, pp. 113–45; repr. in *Gesammelte Abhandlungen zur mittellateinischen Rhythmik* (Berlin, 1905), Vol. II, pp. 303–41.

Morin, Joseph Charles, 'The Genesis of Manuscript Paris Bibliothèque nationale, fonds français 146, with Particular Emphasis on the "Roman de Fauvel"', Ph.D. diss. (New York University, 1992).

Nathan, Hans, 'The Function of Text in French 13th-Century Motets', *Musical Quarterly*, 28 (1942), 445–62.

Newman, Barbara, *Medieval Crossover: Reading the Secular against the Sacred* (Notre Dame, 2013).

Pacha, Danielle, 'The *VERITATEM* Family: Manipulation, Modeling and Meaning in the Thirteenth-Century Motet', Ph.D. diss. (Washington University, 2002).

Page, Christopher, 'Around the Performance of a Thirteenth-Century Motet', *Early Music*, 28 (2000), 343–57.

Discarding Images: Reflections on Music and Culture in Medieval France (Oxford, 1993).

The Owl and the Nightingale: Musical Life and Ideas in France 1100–1300 (London, 1989).

Payne, Thomas B., 'Chancellor *versus* Bishop: The Conflict between Philip the Chancellor and Guillaume d'Auvergne in Poetry and Music', in Gilbert Dahan and Ann-Zoé Rillon-Marne (eds.), *Philippe le Chancelier: Prédicateur, théologien, et poète parisien du début du XIII*[e] *siècle*, Bibliothèque d'histoire culturelle du Moyen Age 19 (Turnhout, 2017), pp. 265–306.

Peraino, Judith A., *Giving Voice to Love: Song and Self-Expression from the Troubadours to Guillaume de Machaut* (Oxford, 2011).

Pesce, Dolores, 'Beyond Glossing: The Old Made New in *Mout me fu grief/Robin aime/PORTARE*', in Dolores Pesce (ed.), *Hearing the Motet: Essays on the Motet of the Middle Ages and Renaissance* (New York, 1997), pp. 28–51.

'A Case for Coherent Pitch Organization in the Thirteenth-Century Double Motet', *Music Analysis*, 9 (1980), 287–31.

Pfeffer, Wendy, 'Complaints of Women and Complaints by Women: Can One Tell Them Apart?', in Barbara K. Altmann and Carlton W. Carroll (eds.), *The Court Reconvenes: International Courtly Literary Society 1998* (Cambridge, 2003), pp. 125–32.

Planchart, Alejandro Enrique, 'The Flower's Children', *Journal of Musicological Research*, 22 (2003), 303–48.

Plumley, Yolanda, *The Art of Grafted Song: Citation and Allusion in the Age of Machaut* (Oxford, 2013).

Rankin, Susan, 'The Study of Medieval Music: Some Thoughts on Past, Present, and Future', in David Greer (ed.), *Musicology and Sister Disciplines: Past, Present, Future. Proceedings of the 16th International Congress of the International Musicological Society, London, 1997* (Oxford, 2000), pp. 154–68.

'Thirteenth-Century Notations of Music and Arts of Performance', in Andreas Haug and Andreas Dorschel (eds.), *Vom Preis des Fortschritts: Gewinn und Verlust in der Musikgeschichte*, Studien zur Wertungsforschung 49 (Vienna, 2008), pp. 110–41.

Roesner, Edward H., 'Labouring in the Midst of Wolves: Reading a Group of Fauvel Motets', *Early Music History*, 22 (2003), 169–245.

'The Problem of Chronology in the Transmission of Organum Duplum', in Iain Fenlon (ed.), *Music in Medieval and Early Modern Europe: Patronage, Sources, and Texts* (Cambridge, 1981), pp. 365–99.

'Review of *The Earliest Motets (to circa 1270): A Complete Comparative Edition* by Hans Tischler', *Early Music History*, 4 (1984), 362–75.

'*Subtilitas* and *Delectatio*: *Ne m'a pas oublié*', in Jane E. Burns, Eglal Doss-Quinby, and Roberta L. Krueger (eds.), *Cultural Performances in Medieval France: Essays in Honor of Nancy Freeman Regalado* (Cambridge, 2007), pp. 112–32.

'Who "Made" the *Magnus liber*?', *Early Music History*, 20 (2001), 227–66.

Rothenberg, David J., *The Flower of Paradise: Marian Devotion and Secular Song in Medieval and Renaissance Music* (New York, 2011).

Saint-Cricq, Gaël, 'Formes types dans le motet du XIIIe siècle: Etude d'un processus répétitif', 2 vols., Ph.D. diss. (University of Southampton, 2009).

'A New Link between the Motet and Trouvère Chanson: The *pedes cum cauda* Motet', *Early Music History*, 32 (2013), 179–223.

Saltzstein, Jennifer, 'Ovid and the Thirteenth-Century Motet: Quotation, Reinterpretation, and Vernacular Hermeneutics', *Musica disciplina*, 58 (2013), 351–72.

The Refrain and the Rise of the Vernacular in Medieval French Music and Poetry (Cambridge, 2013).

'Relocating the Thirteenth-Century Refrain: Intertextuality, Authority and Origins', *Journal of the Royal Musical Association*, 135 (2010), 245–79.

Sanders, Ernest H. 'The Medieval Motet', in Wulf Arlt, Ernst Lichtenhahn, and Hans Oesch (eds.), *Gattungen der Musik in Einzeldarstellungen: Gedenkschrift Leo Schrade* (Bern, 1973), pp. 497–573.

'Peripheral Polyphony of the 13th Century', *Journal of the American Musicological Society*, 17 (1964), 261–87.

Smith, Norman E., 'The Clausulae of the Notre Dame School: A Repertorial Study', Ph.D. diss., 3 vols. (Yale University, 1964).

'The Earliest Motets: Music and Words', *Journal of the Royal Musicological Association*, 114 (1989), 141–63.

'An Early Thirteenth-Century Motet', in Mark Everist (ed.), *Models of Musical Analysis: Music before 1600* (Oxford, 1992), pp. 20–40.

'From Clausula to Motet: Material for Further Studies in the Origin and Early History of the Motet', *Musica disciplina*, 34 (1980), 29–65.

'Some Exceptional Clausulae of the Florence Manuscript', *Music and Letters*, 59 (1973), 405–14.

'Tenor Repetition in the Notre Dame Organa', *Journal of the American Musicological Society*, 19 (1966), 329–51.

Smith, Robyn E., 'Gennrich's *Bibliographisches Verzeichnis der französischen Refrains*: Tiger or Fat Cat?', *Parergon*, 8 (1990), 73–101.

Spanke, Hans G., *Raynaud's Bibliographie des altfranzösischen Liedes neu bearbeitet und ergänzt* (Leiden, 1955).

Stenzl, Jürg, *Die vierzig Clausulae der Handschrift Paris, Bibliothèque nationale, latin 15139 (Saint Victor-Clausulae)*, Publikationen der schweizerischen musikforschenden Gesellschaft, series 2:22 (Bern, 1970).

Stones, Alison, Appendix IV, 'Illustrated Miracles de Nostre Dame Manuscripts Listed by Stylistic Attribution and Attributable Manuscripts whose *MND* Section is Unillustrated', in Kathy M. Krause and Alison Stones (eds.), *Gautier de Coinci: Miracles, Music and Manuscripts* (Turnhout, 2006), pp. 373–96.

'Notes on the Artistic Context of Some Gautier de Coinci Manuscripts', in Kathy M. Krause and Alison Stones (eds.), *Gautier de Coinci: Miracles, Music and Manuscripts* (Turnhout, 2006), pp. 65–98.

Symes, Carol, *A Common Stage: Theater and Public Life in Medieval Arras* (Ithaca, 2007).

Thomas, Wyndham, 'The *Iohanne* Melisma: Some Aspects of Tenor Organization in Thirteenth-Century Motets', *The Music Review*, 54 (1993), 1–13.

Thomson, Matthew P., 'Interaction between Polyphonic Motets and Monophonic Songs in the Thirteenth Century', D.Phil. diss. (University of Oxford, 2016).

Tischler, Hans, 'The Evolution of Harmonic Style in the Notre-Dame Motet', *Acta musicologica*, 28 (1956), 87–95.

The Style and Evolution of the Earliest Motets (to circa 1270), 4 vols., Musicological Studies 40 (Ottawa, 1985).

Treitler, Leo, 'The Marriage of Poetry and Music in Medieval Song', in *With Voice and Pen: Coming to Know Medieval Song and How It Was Made* (Oxford, 2007 [1995]), pp. 457–81.

Van den Boogaard, Nico, *Rondeaux et refrains du XIIe siècle au début du XIVe*, Bibliothèque française et romane, Série D: Initiation, textes et documents 3 (Paris, 1969).

Van der Werf, Hendrik, *Hidden Beauty in Motets of the Early Thirteenth Century: XXV Vignettes* (Tuscon, 1999).

Integrated Directory of Organa, Clausulae, and Motets of the Thirteenth Century (Rochester, 1989).

Vedder Fowler, Maria, 'Musical Interpolations in Thirteenth- and Fourteenth-Century French Narratives', Ph.D. diss., 2 vols. (Yale University, 1979).

Waite, William G., 'The Abbreviation of the "Magnus liber"', *Journal of the American Musicological Society*, 14 (1961), 147–58.

The Rhythm of Twelfth-Century Polyphony: Its Theory and Practice, Yale Studies in the History of Music 2 (New Haven, 1954).

Walker, Thomas, 'Sui *Tenor* Francesi nei motetti del "200"', *Schede medievali: Rassegna dell' officina di studi medievali*, 3 (1982), 309–36.

Welker, Lorenz, 'Polyphonic Reworkings of Notre-Dame Conductûs in BN f. 146: *Mundus a mundicia* and *Quare fremuerunt*', in Margaret Bent and Andrew Wathey (eds.), *Fauvel Studies: Allegory, Chronicle, Music, and Image in Paris Bibliothèque nationale de France, MS Français 146* (Oxford, 1998), pp. 615–36.

Wogan-Browne, Jocelyn and Marie-Elisabeth Henneau, 'Liège, the "Medieval Woman Question", and the Question of Medieval Women', in Juliette Dor,

Lesley Johnson, and Jocelyn Wogan-Browne (eds.), *New Trends in Feminine Spirituality* (Turnhout, 1999), pp. 1–32.

Wolf, Kenneth Baxter, *The Life and Afterlife of Saint Elizabeth of Hungary: A Testimony from her Canonization Hearings* (Oxford, 2010).

Wolinski, Mary E., 'Drinking Motets in Medieval Artois and Flanders', *Yearbook of the Alamire Foundation*, 6 (2008), 9–20.

Wright, Craig, *Music and Ceremony at Notre Dame of Paris, 500–1550* (Cambridge, 1989).

Zayaruznaya, Anna, *The Monstrous New Art: Divided Forms in the Late Medieval Motet*, Music in Context (Cambridge, 2015).

Index of Compositions

General Index

CPSIA information can be obtained
at www.ICGtesting.com
Printed in the USA
LVHW062029270120
644936LV00011B/205